1/95

Representing the French ~~Revolution~~

*

REPRESENTING THE FRENCH REVOLUTION

*

Literature, Historiography, and Art

Edited by James A. W. Heffernan

DARTMOUTH COLLEGE

Published by University Press of New England / Hanover and London

DARTMOUTH COLLEGE
Published by University Press of New England, Hanover, NH 03755
© 1992 by the Trustees of Dartmouth College
All rights reserved
Printed in the United States of America   5 4 3 2 1
CIP data appear at the end of the book

Contents

III. Crossing the Border: The French Revolution in the German Imagination

IV. Crossing the Ocean: The French Revolution in the Caribbean Imagination

Illustration sections follow pages 78 and 210.

Preface

On 14 July 1989, the two-hundredth anniversary of the storming of the Bastille was celebrated in Paris by an international parade of eight thousand performers making their way from the Arc de Triomphe to the place de la Concorde. Convoked and mobilized by an impresario named Jean-Paul Goude, they included Senegalese drummers sitting on a rolling staircase and beating accompaniment to native chants sung by a women's choir, a flag-bearing skater from the Soviet Union carving figures in the ice on a rink borne by French soldiers through a steady downfall of artificial snow, the British Royal Tattoo horns and drums playing in fake fog under a cloud dripping fake rain, the Florida A & M Marching Band break-dancing backward down the Champs-Elysees, two elephants carrying disk jockeys, two zebras pulling a six-sided glass pyramid bearing two hundred African dancers and drummers, and—bringing up the rear—Jessye Norman singing the *Marseillaise*.

If we ask how much of what Goude wrought actually represents the French Revolution, the answer could be: nothing or everything. Had Louis XIV and his unfortunate grandson been watching, they might have been disturbed by the words of the *Marseillaise* and bewildered by the break-dancers, but the sheer extravagance and artificiality of this spectacle would have reassured and delighted them. Yet it is precisely *as* spectacle that Goude's parade evoked the Revolution at its outset. In August 1789 Edmund Burke wrote, "As to us here our thoughts of everything at home are suspended, by our astonishment at the wonderful Spectacle which is exhibited in a Neighbouring and rival Country—what Spectators, and what Actors! England gazing with astonishment at a French struggle for Liberty and not knowing whether to blame or applaud!"[1] Serious students of the French Revolution today face a similar problem. Though Burke himself soon found nothing in the Revolution to applaud, and though in 1989 the American Committee on the French Revolution proclaimed 1789 "that rapturous year," anyone who seriously examines the Revolution today must experience something between these extremes of revulsion and euphoria, must reckon and wrestle with contradiction.

A sense of contradiction arises whenever we try to say just what the Revolution was or what the bicentennial of the Revolution commemorated. Did 14 July 1989 mark the two-hundredth birthday of liberty in France? Or was it simply the two-hundredth anniversary of the day on which a fourteenth-century fortress already proposed for official demolition was attacked by a crowd of some nine hundred Parisians who succeeded in liberating from the prison within it four legally convicted forgers, two lunatics, and one lecherous count?[2] The contradictions inherent in these two ways of representing a single day multiply when we try to say what followed it. Should we trace the impact and implications of the Declaration of the Rights of Man, which some students of the Revolution regard as its most important product? Should we recall the Festival of the Federation on the first anniversary of the storming of the Bastille, when delegates from all parts of France came to Paris for what many historians have seen as a dazzling and spontaneous display of national unanimity?[3] Or should we follow the trail of blood that begins with a spurt from the neck of Bernard-René de Launay, governor of the Bastille, who—without notable regard for the rights of man—was decapitated with a pocketknife on 14 July 1789? Should we follow the bloody trail that leads from de Launey's severed head to the slaughter of at least fourteen hundred prisoners in Paris in September 1792, to the beheading of the king and queen in 1793, to the 35,000 slain by the guillotine, and finally to the hundreds of thousands—perhaps as many as a quarter of a million—men, women, and children living in the Vendée and the Loire who were systematically exterminated by soldiers of the French republic in the winter of 1794?

There are no ready answers to these questions. Nonetheless, they clearly suggest one thing: to understand the French Revolution adequately, we must be willing to contemplate the radical contradictions embedded in the history of the way it has been remembered, commemorated, and represented for the past two hundred years.

The premise of this volume is that the study of history inevitably leads to study of representation. In 1834 Leopold von Ranke declared that history should record each event "wie es eigentlich gewesen war"—as it actually happened. Ever since, history has been commonly regarded as a science that labors dispassionately to retrieve and assemble facts about the past. Yet recent studies of historiography by theorists such as Linda Orr, Lionel Gossman, and Hayden White have shown that historical narratives are never simply objective records of fact; often rhetorical, literary, and even "fictive" in the strict sense of that word, they are not so much transparent windows on the past as *representations* of it. There is no better illustration of this point than the record of attempts to write the history of the French Revolution. To study the histories written by men such as Michelet, Jaures, and Taine is not only to confront the conflicting interpretations formulated by French historians of the right and left. It is also to see that because we have no direct access to it, the Revolution is for us an inescapably *mediated* event or series of events: something we can scarcely confront at all without scrutinizing and comparing the various media—literature, historiography, and art—that have been used to represent it.

The history of the attempts to represent the Revolution, I submit, is entwined with the history of the rivalry between images and words.[4] Consider the image of the Bastille and the text of the Declaration of the Rights of Man and Citizen. Which of the two more truly represents the French Revolution? According to Professor Thomas Bishop, who teaches French at New York University and who organized a highly conspicuous series of bicentennial events there, "Nothing has emerged from the French Revolution that was more important than" the Declaration.[5] It is not hard to see why an American professor should make such a statement, nor to see why the American Committee on the French Revolution (of which Professor Bishop was a member) would all have *wanted* to believe in the primacy of the Declaration. It was not only proclaimed by the National Assembly in the same year as the American constitution first took effect; it was first proposed in Paris by the thirty-two-year old Marquis de Lafayette after he had served in the American Revolution, after he had absorbed the paternal wisdom of George Washington, and while he was continually being advised by the American ambassador to France, Thomas Jefferson, who read all of Lafayette's drafts for the Declaration and added his own suggestions (Schama, 442–43). The Declaration of the Rights of Man and Citizen was very nearly ghost-written for the new republic by the founding fathers of the United States. So the Declaration was the perfect thing with which France could officially represent its great Revolution *in* the United States. When François Mitterand declared at New York University in September 1988 that "the message of 1789 has not faded,"[6] he was clearly referring to the words of the Declaration, which begins (after its preamble), "Men are born and remain free and equal in their rights."

Deferring the question of just how brilliantly these unfading words about the rights of man speak to twentieth-century women, we may usefully ask just how potently the Declaration speaks for the Revolution. During the years of the Revolution itself, its potency seems to have depended on its iconization, on its conversion into an image. For the festival of Châteauvieux in April 1792, a contemporary journalist reported that the Declaration was "written on two stone tablets as the Decalogue of the Hebrews is represented to us, though it is no match for our declaration." In a grand procession through Paris from the site of the Bastille to the champ de Mars, we are told, "four citizens carried this venerable burden on their shoulders."[7] We may wonder if any of the four grasped the full burden of the iconography they bore, or realized that to associate the Declaration with the ten commandments was plainly to signify the potentiality for coercion and prohibition that lurked within its ostensibly liberating words.[8] In any case, the ambiguity of this new revolutionary decalogue was exemplified by the centerpiece of the procession. Enthroned in a triumphal chariot was a colossal statue of liberty, mother of the lady who stands in New York Harbor and grandmother of the lady who bravely—though briefly—stood in Beijing's Tiananmen Square in the spring of 1989. But unlike her American and Chinese descendants, this particular statue was seated in a chariot with a prow made of six daggers, and instead of holding up a torch, her hand rested on a bludgeon. The significance of that was certainly not lost on the journalist who reported it. "We must never forget," he editorialized, "that the sceptre of liberty is a bludgeon" (quoted Ozouf 68).

Just as important as the bludgeon in the hand of liberty is the place where the statue of liberty was inaugurated—so to speak—at the start of the procession: the site of the Bastille. Whatever may be claimed for the Declaration of the Rights of Man, nothing has ever overpowered the storming of the Bastille as an image of the Revolution at its originating moment. On 14 July 1790, the Festival of the Federation was held on the champ de Mars and, according to Mona Ozouf, "images and reminiscences of the Bastille played a very small part in it" (33). But how could any festival held on the first anniversary of the storming of the Bastille suppress the memory of an event that had already provoked a succession of plays reenacting it and a mass of prints, engravings, poems, and songs? The fédérés who journeyed to Paris for the Festival of the Federation came to see the place where the Bastille once stood, to dance on its ruins at a vast ball given by Pierre-François Palloy, who supervised its demolition, and to carry home a piece of its stone along with one of the miniature Bastilles manufactured and distributed by the extraordinarily enterprising Monsieur Palloy (Schama, 412, 416).

With or without Palloy and his souvenir business, the storming of the Bastille has become—in the annals of historiography as in the popular imagination—the one event that signifies the beginning of the French

Revolution. In 1989, as in every year since 1789, the date commemorated above all others in France was not 26 August, when the Declaration was proclaimed, but rather 14 July, Bastille Day. That date preempts all others. What Charles Peguy wrote nearly sixty years ago about the storming of the Bastille still exemplifies the prevailing view of its primordial importance. "The taking of the Bastille, says History, was the first celebration, the first commemoration, and already so to speak the first anniversary of the storming of the Bastille; or at least the zero anniversary. . . . It was not the Festival of the Federation that was the first commemoration, the first anniversary of the storming of the Bastille. It was the storming of the Bastille that was the first Festival of the Federation, a Federation *avant de lettre*" (quoted in Ozouf, 289).

Why should the storming of the Bastille thus usurp—in historiographical tradition—the Festival of the Federation, which had its own separate agenda? Why should we customarily date the French Revolution from the storming of the Bastille rather than from the opening of the Estates General on 5 May, the swearing of the Tennis Court Oath on 20 June, or the Declaration of 26 August? A good part of the answer to this question comes to us from Jean-Jacques Rousseau, who died eleven years before the storming of the Bastille and yet who uncannily foresaw what the Bastille could be made to signify for the revolutionary imagination. In Part I, Book IV of the *Confessions* he writes:

It is a very strange thing that my imagination never works more delightfully than when my situation is the reverse of delightful, and that, on the other hand, it is never less cheerful than when all is cheerful around me. . . . If I want to describe spring it must be in winter; if I want to describe a fine landscape I must be within doors; *and I have said a hundred times that if ever I were confined in the Bastille, there I would draw the picture of liberty [et j'ai dit cent fois que si jamais j'étois mis à la Bastille, j'y ferois le tableau de la liberté].*[9]

By a transforming act of imagination, the Bastille becomes the sign of liberty, which is precisely what happened to it in the iconography of the Revolution. To grasp this simple fact is to see why, in the annals of historiographical representation, the words of the Declaration could never overcome the image of the Bastille. The words of the Declaration are rhetorically elevating, but they offer no drama, no story, no violence. All three are embodied and embedded in the image of the Bastille, which signifies a story of liberation, which dramatizes the conflict between the oppressive power of the old regime and the explosive energy of the new republic, and which above all evokes the violent overthrow of the old order: liberty with a bludgeon in her hand.

In his recent history of the French Revolution, Simon Schama argues that violence was not just a product of the Terror but an essential part of the Revolution from the very beginning. "It was," he writes, "what made the Revolution revolutionary" (p. 447). This is not surprising, since nearly all revolutions—including our own—have required violence. But as we Americans salute our fellow revolutionaries across the Atlantic, we should also be willing to recognize what separates our bicentennial and theirs. The American bicentennial commemorated the signing of a declaration; the French bicentennial commemorated the invasion of a fortress. There is surely something to be learned from contemplating the difference between these two ways of representing a revolution.

Since we can likewise learn much by seeing how revolution in one country is viewed by another, this volume begins with a series of essays on English responses to the French one. Scrutinizing the dark mirror of Edmund Burke's *Reflections* as well as several of his other works, Steven Blakemore argues that Burke represents the Revolution as a terroristic attack on linguistic order, specifically on the meanings of the words traditionally used to constitute the world. By contrast, William Keach finds in Blake's visionary prophecies a mirror that turns revolutionary terror into sublime Christian apocalypse, and thus provokes disturbing questions about just where the worship of energy leads. In my essay on the autobiographical mirror of Wordsworth's *Prelude*, which locates a history of the Revolution within a history of the poet's life, I argue that Wordsworth tells an unfinished story of how the power of the Revolution passed from Robespierre to himself. Finally, Mark Cumming concludes part I by showing how Carlyle's explicitly epic history of the Revolution at once reflects and reviews the symbol-making of the revolutionaries themselves.

In the first two essays of part II, which considers how the French envisioned their own Revolution, Lionel Gossman reveals the mythic and evangelical features of Michelet's *Histoire* as well as its kinship with Romantic autobiography, and Ann Rigney shows how the "representative" figure of Robespierre was variously constituted by Michelet and three other French historians of the mid-nineteenth century. The rest of the essays in part II treat representations of the French Revolution that are also *manifestations* of it: verbal and graphic phenomena generated from within the Revolution itself. Like the Burke of Steven Blakemore's essay, Carol Blum argues that revolutionary discourse was terroristic, cutting certain groups from the body politic with words before they were destroyed in the flesh. Marie Hélène-Huet explains how Robespierre's quest for a political sublimity that would transcend all representation paradoxically led to a succession of morbid spectacles culminating in the impromptu festival surrounding his own death. Exploring a similar paradox, Madelyn Gutwirth argues that the feminist aspirations released by the Revolution were stifled by the rigidly allegorical forms in which women were made to represent—both verbally and graphically—the all-too-traditional abstractions needed by revolutionary men.

To complement this analysis of revolutionary iconography, Donna Hunter and James Cuno successively scrutinize the high and generally neglected low art of Jacques-Louis David. Hunter argues that in David's lost painting of the dying Le Peletier, the multiple meanings of the sword undermine Jacobin ideology even as the picture sanctions regicide and signifies the Jacobins' determination to crush the Girondins for their reluctance to endorse it. Likewise, Cuno finds a two-edged sword in David's low art. He shows how David uses the scatalogical techniques of contemporary French caricature to represent the desperation of counterrevolutionary England and—at the risk of ideological ambiguity—the unbridled license of revolutionary France.

The authors of parts III and IV consider how the French Revolution was represented in Germany and reenacted—as well as represented— in the new world of the Carribean and Latin America. Linking these two worlds of representation, Susanne Zantop demonstrates that German writers etched the Revolution in terms of female transgression, New World savagery, and Haitian slave rebellions, which the doomed protagonist of Kleist's *Betrothal in Santo Domingo* finds just as vicious and incomprehensible as the Reign of Terror in France. It is precisely the task of comprehending the Haitian Revolution that VèVè Clark confronts. Scrutinizing six of the many plays that represent and misrepresent this tragic reenactment of the French Revolution, she finds its radical contradictions most fully dramatized in Aimé Cesaire's portrayal of "revolutionary" Haiti as a theater state that preserves rank and hierarchy even in the face of death. Finally, in *El siglo de las luces*, a modern Cuban novel set in the period of the French Revolution, Beatriz Pastor finds Alejo Carpentier using Goya to help him reveal the consequences of an Enlightenment in which "pure reason" is symbolized by the guillotine, and also to undermine the notion that Latin American revolutions were modeled on the French one.

Like any other volume of essays, this one can be read selectively, in any order the reader may choose. But it is designed to be read as a kind of history: a history of attempts to represent a Revolution that no one mode of representation—verbal, graphic, literary, dramatic, or historiographical— can adequately reflect. Collectively, these essays aim to generate new ways of thinking about the Revolution, about the problems of representing it, and about the problematic nature of representation itself.

A few words of acknowledgement. This volume grows out of a conference on the French Revolution that was held at Dartmouth College in July of 1989 with the aid of a grant from the National Endowment for the Humanities. I am extremely grateful to Dartmouth and the NEH for their support, and for special help I am also happy to thank a number of Dartmouth colleagues: Vivian Kogan-Benn, William Spengemann, Margaret Darrow, Virginia Swain, Michael Ermarth, Ulrike Rainer, William Cook, Leo Spitzer, and Errol Hill.

Some of the essays in this book include material previously published by the contributors. Harvard University Press has kindly allowed Lionel Gossman to use portions of an essay appearing in his recent book, *Between History and Literature* (1990); the University of Pennsylvania Press has generously permitted Mark Cumming to use portions of *A Disimprison'd Epic: Form and Vision in Carlyle's French Revolution* (1988); and the University Press of New England has kindly allowed Steven Blakemore to use material from *Burke and the Fall of Language: The French Revolution as Linguistic Event* (1988). Carol Blum has used material from two of her previous publications: *Rousseau and the Republic of Virtue: the Language of Politics in the French Revolution*, by kind permission of Cornell University Press, and "Rousseau and the Democratization of Language in the French Revolution," *Studies in Eighteenth-Century Culture* 17 (1987): 309–317, by kind permission of the editor.

Hanover, New Hampshire, June 1991   J.A.W.H.

NOTES

1. *The Correspondence of Edmund Burke*, vol. 6, ed. Alfred Cobban and Robert A. Smith (Cambridge: Cambridge University Press, 1967) 10. For extended discussion of the Revolution as theater, see Marie Hélène-Huet, "Performing Arts: Theatricality and the Terror," in this volume.

2. For the historical facts mentioned in this paragraph see Simon Schama, *Citizens: A Chronicle of the French Revolution* (New York: Knopf, 1989), 398–405, 631, 789–92. Hereafter cited as Schama.

3. See Mona Ozouf, *Festivals and the French Revolution*, trans. Alan Sheridan (Cambridge, Mass.: Harvard University Press, 1988), 35. Hereafter cited as Ozouf.

4. For an incisive account of this rivalry, see W. J. T. Mitchell, *Iconology: Image, Text, Ideology* (Chicago: University of Chicago Press, 1986).

5. *New York Times*, 29 September 1988.

6. *New York Times*, 29 September 1988.

7. Quoted in Ozouf, 67.

8. A few months after the festival, William Blake celebrated the French republican victory over the allied monarchies at Valmy by writing a "Song of Liberty"

in which Revolution becomes an apocalyptic "son of fire" that "stamps the stony law to dust" (*Marriage of Heaven and Hell*, plate 27, verses 19–20). Blake had not yet realized that the Revolution was already writing its own laws in stone.

9. *The Confessions of Jean-Jacques Rousseau*, trans. J. M. Cohen (Baltimore: Penguin Books, 1954) 166; *Les Confessions de J.-J. Rousseau* (Paris: Garniers Frères, 1877) 151; emphasis added.

Representing the French Revolution

PART ONE

The View from England

*

Revolution in Language: Burke's Representation of Linguistic Terror

STEVEN BLAKEMORE

When Edmund Burke responded to the ongoing French Revolution two centuries ago, both the Revolution and Burke seemed immediately to become polar opposites and Manichaean antagonists—two forces that dialectically defined and delineated each other and practically everything else involved in the tumultuous events of the French Revolution. In a sense, Burke was subsumed by the Revolution; its contradictory, controversial "meaning" has become so much a part of his political philosophy that today he is principally remembered for his antirevolutionary oeuvre. Likewise, the Revolution and what it does or does not represent is often posited against Burke, for admirers of the Revolution have, in many ways, been responding to Burke for two centuries.

In 1789, when the great iconoclastic power of the Revolution erupted into European consciousness, Burke believed that the inherited, traditional European world—a world he contended had evolved over 2000 years— was forever changed. He believed that this world had psychologically ceased to exist once the Revolution had changed man's sense of a continuous, correspondent past. By articulating his vision of the old European world, Burke intended to show what was lost and the attendant consequences of this loss. From this followed his analysis of the Revolution's genesis and its constituent parts—an analysis culminating in his argument that the Revolution was the greatest assault on reality in the world's history.

Reality for Burke, of course, included precisely those traditional values embodied in the inherited institutions that the Revolution threatened to destroy. For Burke, such concepts as prescription, primogeniture, religion, and hierarchy were incarnated in institutions inherited from time out of mind. Consequently the Revolution's attack on what he felt to be the "natural" order of reality constituted, for him, an unprecedented distortion of this reality. In other words, Burke believed that traditional institutions and their values were being changed or destroyed by a prior transformation of the traditional semantic vocabulary—a vocabulary through which the very meaning of culture and civilization had been expressed.

This explains, in part, his furious denunciations of the new class of intellectuals—the journalists, the *philosophes,* and the self-described "enlightened" men and women whom he felt were transforming the entailed "sense" of the world by altering the inherited social vocabulary of a linguistically unified Europe. He realized that language was intimately bound with the very things the Revolution was attacking—institutions, history, tradition, and law—and hence he believed that the fate of Europe and the world was inextricably intertwined with the fate of language. In this sense, the war between Burke and his revolutionary opponents was, inter alia, a war over language and meaning. It was a war over whose representation of reality would prevail.

Because both Burke and the revolutionary writers were formulating oppositional representations of both the Revolution and each other, the language in which they crystallized their representations became a pivotal issue. Since the revolutionaries questioned and challenged the traditional European world, the debate over revolution and counterrevolution often involved the very meaning of that world and the language that sustained it. Revolutionary and counterrevolutionary writers realized or intuited this to varying degrees. They knew that the linguistic, ideological war was an extension of the military war; they sensed that language and ideology were intimately intertwined and that whoever controlled language controlled not only the terms of war but the terms of "reality" itself. It is this special linguistic self-consciousness that shapes their vision of the Revolution as, among other things, an astonishing linguistic event.

In the voluminous textual war waged by Burke and the revolutionaries against each other—as in Burke's opening volley against Price's sermon in the *Reflections* and the counterattacks by Wollstonecraft and Paine—each side insisted that a higher and truer representation of the Revolution required a "purer" language. Hence each side tacitly argued that only "its" language accurately reflected "reality." In this context, I will briefly consider how the revolutionaries represented language before focusing on Burke's seminal contribution.

I

As the French Revolution accelerated, its supporters proceeded to attack the culture and languages of the past—specifically the classical languages of Latin and Greek. In his *Report on Education* (1792), Condorcet, for example, encouraged the study of the natural sciences as "a remedy for prejudices and narrow-mindedness" because the natural sciences were articulated in French—a language suited to promote progress and to eradicate superstition and error. In contrast, he argued that the study of dead languages inculcates the values and errors of the past; hence "a prolonged and assiduous study of the languages of ancient peoples . . . might be more harmful than useful."[1] Implicit in Condorcet's philosophy of education is a philosophy of language depicting Latin and other dead languages as contagious tongues infecting modern minds with old, pernicious values.

But just as the revolutionaries wanted to break from the language of the past, the counterrevolutionaries envisioned this "language" preserving values that are passed down to posterity. They envisioned hereditary "classical" language embodying tradition and continuity, enabling the dead to speak to the living.

In terms of contemporary language, France had not been linguistically unified for most of its history. In the eighteenth century, the different French provinces had their own dialects and patois. In the Revolution's impetus toward nationalization, the revolutionaries argued that these dialects fragmented the country, preventing the people from uniting with "la patrie" and, more dangerously, perpetuating the counterrevolution by keeping the people confused. Speaking for the Committee of Public Instruction (4 June 1794), the Abbé Grégoire expressed the Revolution's increasing linguistic xenophobia. Noting that French was the language of the common people in only fifteen out of more than eighty departments, he insisted that French be universalized and the patois extinguished.[2] Moreover, foreign languages had to be suppressed: they were "a medium in which disaffected priests, aristocrats, royalists, foreign spies, and other enemies of the revolutionary government could easily operate."[3] In short, the Revolution generated a linguistic paranoia and was preoccupied with the exclusive expression of its own message.

But since French was to be the revolutionary language of France, the revolutionaries distinguished between two kinds of French—prerevolutionary and revolutionary. In a report by the Committee of Public Safety (27 June 1794), Barére and his associates refer to the former as a class language spoken and written by the *ancien régime*'s elite—a language that "one had to spew out . . . in a special way to appear well bred."[4] Likewise, Condorcet maintained that "correct" French had separated the people into two classes.[5]

Thus, according to the revolutionaries, since the old language was based on elitist class lines, created artificial distinctions, and transmitted its erroneous values by confusing and mystifying the people, and since it served as the medium through which, as Robespierre complained, the counter-revolution still perpetuated itself,[6] the Revolution had to destroy the old linguistic order. Indeed, the Revolution concentrated on "revealing" the covert, oppressive meaning of the old order through the names and language that perpetuated it. Hence anything linguistically reminiscent of this order became fraught with danger. Certain words and names were suddenly taboo. *Citoyen* replaced the civil title *monsieur,* and *le peuple* became the new code word for a unified French nation. In short, there was an onomastic revolution; everything from the French calendar to place names was changed to reflect the new revolutionary reality.

Implicit in the onomastic and linguistic revolution is a theory of language, a theory that indicts the "old" contaminated vocabulary of the past. The effort to change words and names was an effort to rename and re-word "reality"—in a sense to "relanguage" the traditional world. Because the revolutionaries intuitively knew that language is intertwined with our perception of reality, they attempted to purge traditional language of its contaminated past. They believed that revolutionary Adams could begin naming a new world into being.

Since both revolutionaries and counterrevolutionaries saw the French Revolution as a revolution in language, they each held the other's language accountable for the world's radical defects. Just as the revolutionaries insisted that a linguistic revolution was necessary to purge corrupt ideas and values transmitted through the contaminated language of the past, the counterrevolutionaries claimed that this revolution threatened to destroy the "real" meaning of European world order. In response, the revolutionaries sought to attack the counterrevolutionary language of Burke—to expose his "normative" values as a language disguising feudal power behind rhetorical "veils" and "drapery."

In this textual war of words, revolutionary language was, for the most part, triumphant. Until recently, Burke and the Revolution have both been seen largely through windows constructed by revolutionary words—especially in Marxist French historiography. But this is not to suggest that Burke's window on the Revolution is any more transparent—any truer or better. Though he is often cogently compelling, Burke, like the revolutionaries, is often reductive, so that "reality" becomes what he says it is. In addition, he sometimes gets entangled in his own contradictions and discrepancies, as can be shown by three brief examples from *Reflections on the Revolution in France.*

Burke's deconstruction of Richard Price's eulogy for the French people's "triumph" over their king on 6 October is triumphantly devastating, yet here he employs the same rhetorical practices for which he castigates Price. For instance, he accuses Price of committing sacrilegious blasphemy by appropriating the words of the *Nunc Dimittis,* in which Simeon's pious prayer on seeing the child Jesus at the Temple (Luke 2:29–32) is inappropriately applied to the French people's "triumph." But Burke himself invests the king (and the royal family) with the mantle of Christ by creating what Peter Hughes calls a "sacred parody" of the *Via Dolorosa:* the king's painful journey from Versailles to Paris is allusively compared to Christ's dolorous journey from Pilate's judgment hall to Golgotha.[7] Burke's appropriation of Scripture here is hardly less sacrilegious than Price's.

In a famous correspondent scene, Burke describes a revolutionary mob invading the Queen's bedchamber: a vulnerable Marie-Antoinette barely escapes violence as the mob pierces her bed "with an hundred strokes of bayonets and poniards . . . from whence the persecuted woman had but just time to fly almost naked."[8] Despite Burke's indignant lament for the Queen's potential degradation, it is Burke himself who linguistically "exposes" her to both revolutionary rage and rape in a chivalric text that supposedly defends her honor. In the latently sexual language of his text, where revolutionary rage is consummated by (or transferred to) the phallic thrusts that pierce the Queen's bed, Burke unwittingly exploits the Queen's sexual "reputation," for she had been repeatedly described as a monstrous woman with dark, insatiable desires gratified in multitudinous affairs and orgies. Hence Burke inadvertently raises the specter of the Queen's sexuality, even though his chivalric code is expressed in terms of protection, repression, and restraint.[9]

On another linguistic level, Burke continually uses his language to taint his opposition. At the beginning of the *Reflections,* for instance, he describes those who had heard Price's sermon as "reeking" from its effects (*Works* 3:16). He uses this word only once again—when the revolutionary mob that invades the Queen's bedchamber first murders her sentinel and then enters "reeking with his blood" (*Works* 3:93). The word reverberates in the reader's mind as Burke subtly connects linguistic violence to the revolutionary violence that it excites and inspires and that, he suggests, is murdering France and threatening England. As Burke uses his language to represent a traditional world of grace and light, he also uses it to indict the revolutionary world with accumulated images of madness, murder, and death.

Thus while Burke's language, like the revolutionary language he criticizes, bristles with contradictions and discrepancies, his argument that inherited meanings were being transformed by a revolution in language constitutes a crucial constituent of the Revolution's still-evolving meaning.

In this context, Burke's representation of the revolution in language is as much about the lost meaning of traditional words and a traditional world as it is about the revolutionary language that would sweep these words and world away.

II

Readers of Burke are familiar with the sense of desperation and despair that emerges from his writings on the French Revolution, which he characterizes as a "total revolution," a "great revolution in all human affairs"— "the most astonishing that has hitherto happened in the world" (*Regicide Peace, Works* 5:79, *Remarks* 4:104, *Reflections* 3:28). The French Revolution threatens Burke's precarious eighteenth-century world not only with social and political upheaval but also with a new linguistic terror in which old words are torn from their historical context, emptied of their historical meaning, and then "filled" with the "new" revolutionary meaning. In Burke's eyes, those who ransack the accumulated cultural treasures of the European world also vandalize the very language that had brought and held that world in "presence." In his *Preface to the Address of M. Brissot to his Constituents,* Burke specifically connects the revolution in language with the revolution in France (see *Works* 4:217), and in his *Appeal from the New to the Old Whigs,* he links the new linguistic revolution with the revolution that has abolished the French monarchy and threatened the principles of the English Revolution of 1688. He contrasts the "danger" of the "new theoretic language" with the "form of sound words" the English Parliament "religiously adheres to"—the "principles upon which the English Revolution was justified" (*Works* 3:375). Burke believed in a kind of Gresham's law of language in which "bad" meaning drove out "good" meaning, drastically altering people's psychic and social lives.

In *A Philosophical Enquiry,* written long before the Revolution began, he had discussed the power of words to move the "passions" (*Works* 1:203–206), and in his *Letter to Richard Burke, Esq.* (1793), he warned that "a very great part of the mischiefs that vex the world arises from words" (*Works* 5:312). Burke believed that words could create a linguistic world of illusion and fantasy, and he often alluded to the error of confusing word with thing, and language with reality. But in his thinking about the French Revolution, his concept of language became more Manichaean. For instance, while he warns about the dangerous powers of the "new" language, he also insists that the traditional vocabulary of Europe, the semantic vocabulary shared by the European community despite the differences in respective "languages," profoundly expresses the permanent values and truths of European civilization. He contrasts this traditional vocabulary with the new cant and "gipsy jargon" of the Revolution (Letter 1, *Regicide Peace, Works* 4:350). Burke felt that the French Revolution violently fragmented the coherent linguistic community of Europe. Consequently, there was no shared language; there was no way to "talk" to the new government of France (Letter 3, *Regicide Peace, Works* 4:501).

In this context, Burke's reflections on language constitute a new battle of words and books in which documents of what Burke considers the ontological order of civilization—documents ranging from biblical quotations and other "classical" sources to extracts from various legal charters and laws—are thematically positioned against quotations from various modern pamphlets and books that Burke regards with apprehension and alarm. The result is a battle of "texts" in which Burke's own words and works are reflexively at war with oppositional texts (for instance, Price's sermon in the *Reflections*). In this new Battle of the Books, there is a linguistic battle over "meaning" in which Burke speaks for the "ancients" in his defense of tradition and classical sources, while the supporters of the Revolution speak for the "moderns" in their celebration of the new revolutionary literature issuing from England and France. Burke sees these modern books and pamphlets in terms of a radical new language, a language of corruption and subversion. His controlling metaphor for this sinister new language is that of Babel, and Babel becomes the symbol and metaphor for all the insane chaos and confusion that threaten to darken and destroy the established "written" monuments of civilization. Burke considers the propagation of this new Babel an assault on the very fabric and structure of civilization. Since civilization, in his view, is ordered by the language that expresses and supports it, he believes that language can be used to assault civilization while altering the perceived meaning and "facts" of human reality. In short, Burke sees the French Revolution as a radical linguistic event; he sees it as a new Babel, as a new fall of language, and he presents a theory of language that explains both the old world and the Revolution that causes it to fall.

III

In the *Reflections*, Burke aims to distinguish the French Revolution of 1789 from the event that its English supporters took as a precedent for it—the Glorious Revolution of 1688 in England. Burke felt that if the French Revolution could be justified by reference to the English Revolution, then the very legitimacy, the very principles of the English Revolution could be called into question. To Burke, the principles of the English Revolution were sacredly spelled out in a series of unalterable documents ranging from the Magna Charta to the *ratio scripta* of English legal tradition. Therefore, Burke suggests that the English Revolution was "natural": it embodied the organic rhythms of English history and its fundamental principles had been incarnated and written into various documents, documents that constitute a mystical and corporate contract of the English people. He meticulously traces these fundamental principles from the Magna Charta to the Declaration of Rights, accepted by William and Mary in 1689, both of which he sees as organic expressions of the English constitution. There was and is, of course, no single English document corresponding to the Constitution of the United States, for the English constitution comprises a series of historical documents and legal precedents. But Burke often refers to it as if it were a single, coherent document because he sees and feels a whole tradition of language that expresses the coherent order of the English world he wishes to defend.

In the *Reflections*, Burke insists that his English adversaries have fallen from the language of the constitution, the language through which Burke sees the past and present world. Moreover, Burke sees history and tradition embodied in and passed through the inherited language of the constitution, and he locates the real meaning of England in the language of its documents. In his discussion of the Declaration of Rights, he stresses its "traditionary language" and traces "as from a rubric the language of the preceding acts of Elizabeth and James . . . the orderly Succession [on] which the 'unity, peace, and tranquility of this nation doth, under God, wholly depend' " (*Works* 3:37). Burke locates this orderly process of circumscribed change *in* the "traditionary language" that crystallizes and orders the English polity. Alluding to Jeremiah 31:33, he declares that the clarity of this language "engraved in our ordinances, and in our hearts, the words and spirit of that immortal law" (*Works* 3:38). As Burke reviews what to him is the natural order, the natural succession of English principles expressed in various historical documents, he envisions a coherent and consistent order of English history, incarnated and expressed in the language of these documents. Burke attempts to repossess English history through them; he seeks to recover the palpable presence of the English mind through a series of inviolable "contracts" between the past, present, and future; between the dead, the living, and the unborn.

Burke's great insight was that history, tradition, and reality are essentially linguistic and that the recovery of their presence resides in the recovery of their meaning through the inherited documents of the "written past" recreated and reaffirmed in present and future documents. From this follows his effort to crystallize and conserve the "real" authority and meaning of words.

Burke insists that these documents compose a concrete link with the real and, hence, lived experience of the English people. He contrasts these "human" documents with various proclamations and statements issued by the French assembly, proclamations that have no inherent link with the historical and lived experience of the French people. In this sense, Burke's *Reflections* is a sustained attack on the abstraction of language; it attacks a language that no longer expresses human reality. Burke exposes the radical split between word and thing, a split in which language no longer brings the real world into presence. Burke sees the new, written "world" as a falsification of man's experience in time, a falsification that constitutes a kind of radical antihistory. But even as he reveals a semantic split between the new written word and the thing it expresses, Burke acknowledges the power of the written word, the power of human language to change and affect human lives. For instance, the French revolutionaries dismiss ecclesiastics as "fictitious persons," as abstract creatures of the state who may be concretely robbed and destroyed (*Works* 3:130); this culminates in the "intolerance of the tongue and pen" that strikes "at property, liberty, and life" (*Works* 3:136). In Burke's eyes, the revolutionaries reduce concrete people to what Orwell would later call "nonpersons" by falsely treating them as mere linguistic abstractions—fictitious creations of the old European language. In his *Appeal from the New to the Old Whigs*, Burke specifically rejects these new linguistic fictions of revolutionaries who speak a "jargon" that is "unintelligible," and he vehemently denies that they can rob people of their land and money by merely proclaiming that it is theirs (*Works* 3:423).

Burke also notes that the removal of men's liberty and property is connected to the removal of their "real" names. Thus the "old aristocratic landlords" are unrecognizably "displumed, degraded, and metamorphosed," and the sign of their transmogrification is the onomastic robbery of their identities:

we no longer know them. They are strangers to us. They do not even go by the names of our ancient lords. Physically they may be the same men; though we are not quite sure of that, on your new philosophic doctrine of personal identity. (*Reflections, Works* 3:257)

In addition, just as Burke no longer recognizes the old aristocratic landlords, so he no longer recognizes old familiar words suddenly changed by subversive meanings acquired from "new dictionaries."[10] Later, in the first letter on a *Regicide Peace*, Burke exclaims:

God forbid, that if you were expelled from your house by ruffians and assassins, that I should call the material walls, doors and windows of ———, the ancient and honorable family of ———. Am I to transfer to the intruders, who, not content to turn you out naked to the world, would rob you of your very name, all the esteem and respect I owe to you? (*Works* 4:405)

Burke sees that the power of the human name also gives material walls, doors, and windows their corresponding "identity," and he refuses to countenance a corresponding onomastic robbery that would reduce the concrete person to an abstract blank: the violence of the dash empties and crosses out the name that brings the house and the person into presence. It denies the frustrated genitive its identity. There is a thematic parallel between the expropriation of property and the absence of the name. Burke repeatedly sees the Revolution as a new form of linguistic terror; he sees the language that embodies it as a radical new violence that tears man from his word and world.

In fact, the murderous powers of the new language become a kind of linguistic alchemy, a Black Mass where the "ink" of language is turned into blood, where the spilling of ink on pamphlets and proclamations causes real blood to be spilled and shed. For instance, Burke notes that the victims of the Revolution were "delivered over to lawyers; who wrote in their blood the statutes of the land, as harshly, and in the same kind of ink, as they and their teachers had written the rights of man" (*Appeal, Works* 3:431). Likewise the revolutionaries (with "malice" in "their tongues and hearts") tore the "reputation of the clergy to pieces by their infuriated declamations and invectives, before they lacerated their bodies by their massacres" (Letter 3, *Regicide Peace, Works* 4:435).

This connection between linguistic and revolutionary violence is emphasized again when Burke describes the Revolution as a process of leveling "all conditions of men" and fragmenting the inherited social order with a plan that would abolish all "hereditary name and office" (*Thoughts on French Affairs, Works* 4:13). When the inherited language of society is altered, Burke suggests, the order and "meaning" of that society is also altered. He implies that the old names and titles express the social and psychic identities of concrete men. Indeed, he implies that the old names and words are ontologically connected to the persons, places, and things they bring into presence. Therefore, for Burke, the attempt to abolish and erase human names and peoples, the attempt to write away or erase kings, queens, and states, is the result of a subversive linguistic ideology. To Burke, the revolutionaries' attitude toward language is expressed in their attitude toward concrete societies and peoples. Their belief that human language is arbitrary and transient is reflected in their belief that kings, queens, societies, and laws are arbitrary and transient. Thus their effort to destroy old meanings and old societies by creating new meanings and new societies involved a language theory masking an ideology that justified both radical change and the categorical destruction of the existing political and linguistic order (see, for instance, Burke's quotation, in the *Reflections*, of Jean-Paul Rabaut Saint-Etienne, *Works* 3:196).

IV

This connection between people and names leads to one of Burke's more provocative thematic equations—the equation of regicide with logocide. In the *Reflections*, Burke's famous lament for the death of chivalry is as much about the death of the old language as it is about the degradation and death of kings and queens. When the "decent drapery of life" (the language and ideas of chivalry) is "rudely torn off," a king is reduced to "but a man; a queen is but a woman; a woman is but an animal, and an animal not of the highest order" (*Works* 3:99). Burke connects the degrading physical reduction to the corresponding semantic reduction of kings and queens. This reduction is traced to a linguistic violence that tears the palpable idea of kings and queens from their bodies, stripping them of connotative titles—the linguistic drapery that had covered and surrounded them. This violent removal of the "wardrobe of . . . moral imagination" is a second Fall in which man is also left exposed, like Adam and Eve, with no "covering" for the "defects of our naked shivering nature" (*Works* 3:99). Burke's subsequent lament that "all homage paid to the [female] sex in general is forgotten" then conjures up the "plight" of the French queen in terms of the physical and linguistic violation he has just suggested: the reader remembers his description of Marie-Antoinette fleeing *en déshabillé* from her frenzied pursuers (see *Works* 3:93). The implied stripping of the queen symbolizes the stripping of language, the removal of the linguistic wardrobe with which she had been draped in the hearts and minds of the people. The linguistic violence that reduces the queen to an animal leads to the sexual violation that Burke imagines the queen to have nearly suffered.[11] Without the "drapery" of a royal title," the queen is monstrously exposed to the lewd eyes of the new masses—exposed to a degrading linguistic rape.

Moreover, Burke connects the murder of kings and queens to a perverted vocabulary that glosses over "regicide . . . parricide . . . and sacrilege" as "fictions of superstition," and that treats "The murder of a king, or a queen, or a bishop, or a father, [as] only common homicide" (*Works* 3:99). When he refers to "the French King, or king of the French," he

sarcastically adds, "or by whatever name he is known in the new vocabulary of your constitution" (*Works* 3:105–6). In *A Letter to a Member of
the National Assembly,* the link between regicide and logocide becomes
even clearer. Burke predicts that the revolutionaries will look for any pretext to "throw off the very name of a king," as they now use it solely
to "catch those Frenchmen to whom the name of king is still venerable"
(*Works* 3:300–301). When these sentiments are "expiring," they will "not
trouble themselves with excuses for extinguishing the name, as they have
the thing"; when the connotations of the name expire in the minds of
men, the king will be killed (*Works* 3:301). As the imprisoned king has
already been reduced to a "thing," the revolutionaries use the name "as a
sort of navel-string to nourish their unnatural offspring from the bowels
of royalty itself" (*Works* 3:301). The allusion to *Paradise Lost* (2:648–59)
connects the revolutionaries with Satan, Sin, and Death as their "unnatural" children (read their "incestuous" followers) linguistically devour the
monarchy. The anticipated murder of the king means that "his name will
no longer be necessary to their designs" (*Works* 3:301). In *Appeal from
the New to the Old Whigs,* Burke traces this method of killing the king to
the two contending revolutionary parties: "the one contending to preserve
for awhile his name and his person, the more easily to destroy the royal
authority—the other clamoring to cut off the name, the person, and the
monarchy together, by one sacrilegious execution" (*Works* 3:456).

In his war against a logocide peace, Burke believed that to tamper with
language was to tamper with all human endeavor. He insisted that language severed from the facts of human existence, language used to arti-
ficially rewrite human nature and reality, inevitably leads with a kind of
insane logic to assassinations and death by fiat. In analyzing the peculiar
human mentality that dislocates language from its human context, Burke
also found its correspondent expression in the economic destruction of
France, in which reams of worthless *assignats* were issued by a bankrupt
government.

In fact, the economic bankruptcy of France is a microcosm of the moral,
spiritual, and intellectual bankruptcy that Burke finds in the Revolution. In
Burke's opinion, France's new economists speak the language of *assignats*
"as no other language would be understood" (*Reflections, Works* 3:268).
If the old *assignats* are depreciated, these economists merely issue more of
the same, like the doctor in Molière's *Le Malade Imaginaire:*

*Mais si maladia, opiniatria, non vult se garire, quid illi facere? assignare—postea
assignare; ensuita assignare.* The word is a trifle altered. The Latin of your present
doctors may be better than that of your old comedy; their wisdom, and the variety
of their resources, are the same. (*Works* 3:268)

In Molière's satire of pompous doctors and pompous Latin, the doctors are examining a medical candidate. They ask him what he would do to the patient if the "stubborn sickness will not be cured?" The unqualified candidate answers as he does every question, "Give him a clyster, then bleed, then purge." [12] Burke changes the "word" to the "remedy" of the new quackery: issue more *assignats*. The allusion to Molière's play connects medical quackery with economical quackery, and it provides a moral context in which the economic placebo is judged no better than the pointless degradation of gratuitous enemas and purgings.

Moreover, I suggest that the allusion to the Latin in the old comedy is an insider's joke. It depends on an audience who would recognize the allusion and understand the Latin; thus Burke's ironic reference to the "better" Latin of the new "doctors" actually exposes them as bogus doctors who would neither understand the Latin nor the allusion, albeit their "wisdom" is the same. Burke identified the French Revolution as a bourgeois revolution, a revolution, as he saw it, of parvenus who lacked the culture and language of the past. In the past, Latin had been used to separate men from women. For example, Walter Ong has shown that Latin (A.D. 500–700) briefly became "a sex-linked language, a kind of badge of masculine identity," used to exclude women from the "difficult" linguistic terrain of the masculine world.[13] Similarly, Burke and his ideological allies used Latin and its "classical" associations to separate the "gentlemen" from the new middle class.[14] Burke, of course, used Latin throughout his life; it was the natural linguistic environment in which he moved and lived. But with the threatening revolution of the new middle class, Latin became a class-linked language that set off and separated the "gentlemen" from the parvenus. Burke was writing for an audience that shared his education and his antirevolutionary values, so when he ironically alludes to the nonexistent Latin of the bourgeois "doctors," he skewers them with the literature and language of the past, writing in a language they cannot understand or "enter." Thus, even as Burke finds all order and distinctions arbitrarily abolished or removed by the revolutionary middle class, he reestablishes linguistic and hence social boundaries through the language of his classical sources. Consciously or unconsciously, he attempts to reestablish in his linguistic "world," at least, that sense of circumscribed order that he sees either threatened or destroyed in the external world.

V

Burke sees his world threatened, however, on two linguistic fronts. He traces the "revolution in sentiments, manners and moral opinions" (*Reflec-*

tions, Works 3 : 102) not only to the words of the parvenus and the mediocre writers of England and France, but also to the writings of established men of literature. Prominent writers, Burke notes, assisted and defended the Revolution; they even planted in the French mind the subversive seeds from which it grew. The very intellectuals who had traditionally sustained and defended the organic order of civilization have—in Burke's view— betrayed and corrupted it. Indeed, he believes the linguistic power of this new class has subverted both the Christian religion and the legal forms of civil government, erasing all distinctions and "rewriting" the majestic communal contracts that have traditionally given man his expressed sense of place. More precisely, Burke's world is threatened by old words with new meanings. What Burke documents is the transvaluation of specific words that were torn from their historical context and then emptied of their accumulated cultural meaning by a linguistic violence that then imposed its revolutionary meaning on what Burke sees as the violated corpus of the traditional linguistic order. Thus such words as *nature, liberty, freedom, property, the People, natural law,* and *natural rights* were "changed" in a semantic revolution that aided and abetted the political one.

Burke scholars have elucidated Burke's own understanding of these words.[15] With notable exceptions, there is a general consensus that Burke was reacting against the semantic pillage of rich, traditional words that were emptied of old meanings and then filled with antithetical new ones. Various critics maintain that this revolution in meaning actually started with Hobbes and then Locke, who used the traditional vocabulary of "natural law," for instance, but emptied it of its old meaning. Consequently, there was a semantic shift from the traditional emphasis on man's "duty" to man's "rights." This semantic shift radically altered the "meaning" of the European world. In this context, it is crucial to observe that Burke's lament for the *ancien régime* is a lament, among other things, for the fall of what he imagines as a coherent European linguistic community once united in its celebration of what words and world meant. Burke does not fear French or English words per se, but he is alarmed about the new pseudomeanings that separate people from their history, their society, and themselves. He fears the subversive semantics of words that distort and hide the "real" semantic relationship between people and the world that is created and sustained through their language.

For even when Burke does not refer specifically to the French Revolution, the corrupt state of language corresponds to the corruptness of the revolutionary period. For instance, in his *Letter to Richard Burke, Esq.,* he associates his son's efforts in behalf of the "oppressed people" of Ireland with his own on behalf of the oppressed people of France (*Works* 5 : 304).

He notes that the old word *ascendancy,* meaning "an influence obtained over the mind of some other person by love and reverence, or by superior management and dexterity," has been perverted into a new meaning—"*honestum nomen imponitur vitio*" (*Works* 5:307). An honorable name is placed over vice; the old word is used to gloss over the vicious new meaning. "New ascendancy is the old mastership. . . . In plain old English it signifies *pride* and *dominion* on . . . one part . . . and on the other *subserviency* and *contempt*—and it signifies nothing else" (*Works* 5:308–9). This semantic transformation leads to his warning about the "untuning" of old words:

The poor word *ascendancy,* so soft and melodious in its sound, so lenitive and emollient in its first usage, is now employed to cover to the world the most rigid, and perhaps not the most wise, of all plans of policy. . . . The old words are as fit to be set to music as the new; but use has long since affixed to them their true signification, and they sound as the other will, harshly and odiously to the moral and intelligent ears of mankind. (*Works* 5:308–9)

The allusion to the music of the spheres suggests that words once set in an orderly orbit now clash with discordant sounds, and as they fall out of their semantic orbit, the "sound" sense of the old words clashes with the new imposed sense, violating and breaking the semantic harmony of the linguistic universe.

Likewise, Burke observes that the word *protestant* has ceased to have an essentially religious meaning. Since it is unnaturally yoked to the new meaning of *ascendancy* and the "policy which is engrafted on it, the name protestant becomes nothing more or better than the name of a persecuting faction" (*Works* 5:309). Indeed, this word is "the charm that locks up in the dungeon of servitude three millions of your people" (5:312). It is a "spell of potency," an "abracadabra that is hung about the necks of the unhappy, not to heal, but to communicate disease" (5:312). Burke suggests that to tamper with the established meaning of words is to simultaneously tamper with the social and psychic meaning of society, unleashing oppressive new powers in *old* forms: the word *protestant* is changed into its semantic opposite; it becomes a new kind of persecuting superstition, a new kind of contagious disease. Burke's own language evokes the semantic and hence, in his terms, the moral corruption of the word's meaning, associating it with a new kind of old witchcraft, superstition, and black magic—a new dungeon of meaning that locks up an already enslaved people, wounding and contaminating them with the authority of its dark power. To Burke, a radical breach of language constitutes a radical breach of world order, and a language that is diseased and contaminated reflects a society that is diseased and contaminated. In this sense, the new semantic disease he saw contaminating the world was also a semantic Black Mass—an inversion of all established meaning, a violation of word and world.

Burke's war against this new semantic disease, his war against a logocide peace, was an effort to prevent a perversion of meaning that would keep man from a "true" understanding of his "real" history, society, and self. His lament for the passing of chivalry and for the fall of kings and queens is simultaneously a lament for the fall of language—for the fall of a linguistic community and the semantic vocabulary that had ordered and sustained it. The new words flaming through England and France suddenly threaten all that Burke holds dear: tradition, place, property, and religion—in short, the civil and transcendent order of eighteenth-century man. But Burke simultaneously tries to repossess and see again his world through language, especially the written language of the traditional and classical works of religion, government, and literature—all of which give him a palpable sense of human time that is immediate, concrete, and meaningful. At several points, Burke strongly implies that this body of literature constitutes a mystical contract binding all generations (past, present, and future) in a communal understanding of each person's place in that "civilization." Concurrently, he intimates that any tampering with these "contracts" virtually breaks the Great Chain of Being. Similarly, Burke's quotations from the Bible, political tracts, and literature serve as links in a Great Chain of Words that are meant to remind eighteenth-century man of his history and place within the timeless space of his "tradition." As Burke moves the reader back into "history" through the language of these documents, they form a semantic chain. The reader is thus taken from the past to the present through an inherited language Burke believes is consistent and unchanging. His analysis of the documents provides a linguistic perspective in which past, present, and future are crystallized in a common language that expresses the cosmic ordering of the eighteenth-century world. In a profound sense, the words of this language reflect and mime, for Burke, the cosmic ordering of the Logos.

In Burke's writings, then, he pits the established and traditional language of his "world" against the new and disturbing vocabulary of English hacks and French *philosophes*. This war of words turns into a battle of books and pamphlets. In his text and footnotes, Burke quotes and exposes the absurdity and madness of revolutionary texts, which he contrasts to the lucidity and integrity of traditional texts: texts in which words are tied to the ontological "facts" of human reality. Indeed, Burke delights in exposing a kind of Cartesian split between the words and "facts" of his enemies, conjuring up a chaotic world of falsification and fantasy in which France becomes a library for the insane. This new insanity is part of the new and pernicious power of the written word to pervert human nature: "These writings and sermons have filled the populace with a black and savage atrocity of mind, which supersedes in them the common feelings of nature, as well as all sentiments of morality and religion" (*Reflections, Works* 3:181).

VI

The central metaphor Burke uses for this new corrupting power of language is Babel. In the *Reflections,* for instance, Babel is the metaphor and symbol for all that Burke feels is radically wrong with a world in which language deforms and distorts the essential facts of human reality. For instance, Burke contrasts those who speak a kind of prelapsarian language with the fallen French and English men who speak the new language of Babel: "We, on our parts, have learned to speak only the primitive language of the law, and not the confused jargon of their Babylonian pulpits" (*Works* 3:48). Likewise the French constitution, unlike the English one, is written in a "new vocabulary" (*Works* 3:105). In the British constitution, Burke tells us, "you will find other ideas and another language" (*Works* 3:50). Burke seriously maintains, both figuratively and literally, that the language of the Revolution is part of a new fallen world—an "antagonistic world of madness, discord, vice, confusion, and unavailing sorrow." In contrast, those who have kept the original purity of their laws, their contracts, and their language remain in the "world of reason, and order, and peace, and virtue, and fruitful penitence" (*Works* 3:121).

The new Fall is a fall into a world of madness where men "are obliged to adopt all the crude and desperate measures suggested by clubs composed of a monstrous medley of all conditions, tongues, and nations" (*Works* 3:89). Babel remains the controlling metaphor for all this chaos and confusion. Indeed, as Burke sees the lights going out all over Europe, the combination of jargon, cant, new dictionaries, and new meanings becomes in his eyes an objective correlative for the new Babel, the new linguistic disorder of Europe. But despite his dark pessimism, he reaffirms the capacity of the "prelapsarian" English people to recognize the deceptive language spoken by "fallen" English Jacobins. The unfallen English, Burke writes, know the language of lies and babel when they hear it: "They hear these men [the Jacobins] speak broad. Their tongue betrays them. Their language is in the *patois* of fraud; in the cant and gibberish of hypocrisy" (*Works* 3:128).

Fallen Englishmen "speak broad" in various senses: their words miss the mark, and Burke's pun suggests that they are appropriately addressing to a revolutionary audience "abroad." In addition, the word *broad* linguistically suggests diction that is vulgar, unrefined, and low; the word is always pejorative, as in the language of a speaker whose accent or pronunciation is vulgar (*OED*, meaning 3), who is "plain-spoken, outspoken (often in a bad sense); unseasoned, not mincing matters" (*OED*, 6A) or "Loose, gross, indecent" (*OED*, 6C). In light of this meaning, Burke may be suggesting that English Jacobins are illicitly making love to the revolutionary government "abroad." Dr. Johnson reaffirms what Burke implies when he defines "broad" as "Gross, coarse" (*Dictionary* meaning #4) and "Obscene; fulsome, tending to obscenity" (5). Moreover, the word *patois* suggestively makes the English users of this gibberish the speakers of an alien dialect (again reflecting the corrupting "French" influence) and reinforces their provincial narrowness, their illiteracy—in short, their *lowness.*

Against this new Babel, Burke wields the language of old-world Latin. In his declining age, he refuses "to squall in [the revolutionaries'] new accents, or to stammer, in my second cradle, the elemental sounds of their barbarous metaphysics. *Si isti mihi largiantur ut repueriscam, et in eorum cunis vagian, valde recusem!*" (*Works* 3:249). The quotation is from Cicero's essay on old age (*Cato Maior De Senectute* 23.83), and it illustrates how Burke uses the established language of the old world to banish his opponents. Cicero himself ascribes these words to Cato the Elder, the conservative censor who expressed the traditional values of the Roman Republic. Thus, Burke metaphorically becomes Cato of England, the eloquent defender of traditional values and language. In Cicero's version, which Burke has modified, Cato exclaims: "But if some god should allow me to return to infancy from my old age, to weep again in my cradle, I should vehemently protest." Burke changes "some god" to the (in this context) pejorative pronoun *isti* (similar to "those guys") and "my cradle" to "their cradle": "But if those guys should allow me to return to infancy from my old age, to weep once more in their cradle, I should vehemently protest." The two changes emphasize the encroaching presumption that is checked by the language and the authority of Burke's classical source. By proclaiming his vigorous refusal in Cicero's Latin, Burke exorcises the revolutionary squall of the new babel—eloquently underscoring his defiance in the old language of classical world order.

VII

In retrospect, we can see that Burke's reflections on language are important for many reasons. He is one of the first to recognize that language alters and shapes our perception of reality. He was among the first to see how language makes or deconstructs our "world" and how it shapes our perception of what our world "is"; he realizes that any perspective or "talk" about great human interests is bounded by the very language that expresses it. His hostility to the French Revolution can be traced, in part, to his feeling that the new semantic vocabulary dealing with the rights of man was, in effect, a new and dangerous language that tore man from his history and his heritage, both of which were linguistic in nature. He cannily saw how history is often not what happened but what is written; he saw how written history is part of the linguistic horizon of the writer, and he offered what can be characterized as one of the first modern critiques of totalitarian language. He documented the emergence of ideology as a national force that would chain history and language to its procrustean bed.

The additional relevance of totalitarian distortions of language in the twentieth century provides another context for Burke's concerns, for he decried the radical transvaluation of language by which "the most meaningful of words (*the people, reason, liberty, philosophy, humanity,* etc.) are debased into omnibus abstractions and used to justify crimes." [16] Burke showed how language is used to hide and distort "reality," how words are perverted into their semantic opposites:

[how] the whole compass of language is tried to find synonymes and circumlocutions for massacre and murder. Things are never called by their common names. Massacre is sometimes *agitation*, sometimes *effervescence*, sometimes *excess;* sometimes too continued an exercise of a *revolutionary power. (Preface to M. Brissot, Works* 4:208)

He recognized that language shapes our perception of world and reality, and he anticipated the beginning of a nightmare world of language in which words, as he saw them, deracinated from certain existential and moral facts, would become an awesome force of distortion and oppression.

As he writes about the death of words and kings, as he laments the linguistic and physical assaults on families, societies, and Christianity, Burke depicts the French Revolution as a second Fall, a second Babel, a second Golgotha in which the cosmic ordering of the Logos, the sanctity and authority of the Word is also assaulted. In the dark interstices of Burke's texts, the new murder of language, the new experiment in logocide, swells into a vicious and presumptuous parody of the old logocide. Burke was convinced that the health and sanity of a society are intimately intertwined with its language, and he used his own crusading words to battle against homocide, regicide, and logocide, to war against the murder of men, kings, fathers, and "mother" tongues. In his references to the old meanings of words, he focuses on their new meanings and insists that the violent removal of their historical contexts and circumstances "robs" them of their special meaning and life: the very thing that was happening to people in France was happening to language. We see now that his probing semantic analysis was a linguistic strategy to reestablish the context, the circumstances, the history, and the meaning of the old world. It was a linguistic effort to reestablish the semantic links between the old world and its language. For as Burke attempts to focus on the meaning of words and world, he attempts to recover that world through the language which made it flesh.

To read Burke, then, is to read about a battle, a logomachy of good and evil in which the real presence of the human word reflected through the Logos struggles against the dark chaos of the new pseudoword, or what Pope, at the end of *The Dunciad*, called the "uncreating word." In this battle, Burke dialectically sets off documents, books, and pamphlets in a war of words, a battle of books and languages in which the dominant biblical and classical quotations eventually establish a semantic space where Burke's world and vision are brought into presence. But the enduring presence of Burke's own language semantically sustains this linguistic world of order and grace, banishing briefly the conflicting chaos and confusion of the antagonistic revolutionary world. The potent presence of Burke's language brings this world into our presence and "presents" his reflections on the French Revolution as the last great flowering expression of the old European order.

NOTES

    1. John Hall Stewart, ed. and trans., *A Documentary History of the French Revolution* (Toronto: Macmillan, 1951), 353–54.
    2. R. R. Palmer, *The Improvement of Humanity: Education and the French Revolution* (Princeton: Princeton University Press, 1985), 187–188.
    3. Palmer, 186.
    4. Palmer, 186.
    5. Patrice Higonnet, "The Politics of Linguistic Terrorism and Grammatical Hegemony during the French Revolution," *Social History* 5 (January 1980): 58.
    6. Philip Dawson, ed., *The French Revolution* (Englewood Cliffs, N.J.: Prentice-Hall, 1967): 136.
    7. Tom Furniss, "Stripping the Queen: Edmund Burke's Magic Lantern Show," in *Burke and the French Revolution: Bicentennial Essays*, ed. Steven Blakemore (Athens, Georgia: University of Georgia Press, 1992), p. 76. Peter Hughes, "Originality and Allusion in the Writing of Edmund Burke," *Centrum* 4 (1976): 39.
    8. *The Works of Edmund Burke*, 9 vols. (Boston: Charles C. Little and James Brown, 1899), 3:93.

9. For the numerous pornographic caricatures of Marie-Antoinette, see Simon Schama, *Citizens: A Chronicle of the French Revolution* (New York: Alfred A. Knopf, 1989), 203–207. Despite the Queen's reputation for promiscuously bestowing her sexual favors, Burke was historically correct in contending that she had in fact been defamed through gossip, innuendo, and distortion, as well as in suggesting a connection between the violent textual attacks on the Queen's honor and her actual degradation. In addition, although his own text ironically jeopardizes her "honor," his primary meaning and intention is to suggest that it is the Revolution that degrades and "dirties" the Queen, and hence he inverts the terms of the revolutionary caricature—the sexually voracious Queen is turned into the potential victim of revolutionary violence and rape, becoming the proverbial "damsel in distress." See also Furniss, "Stripping the Queen," p. 83.

10. See, for instance, *Works* 3:22. Burke attacked linguistic radicalism not only in France but in England, where he found it in the writings of Priestley, Tooke, Spence, Piggot, and all the pamphleteers in the London corresponding society who were producing new dictionaries in the 1790s.

11. See Isaac Kramnick's psychobiography *The Rage of Edmund Burke: Portrait of an Ambivalent Conservative* (New York: Basic Books, 1977), 152–54, for a discussion of Burke's preoccupation with the "violation" of the queen.

12. See Molière, *Le Malade Imaginaire*, Troisième Intermède, II, 9–15.

13. Walter J. Ong, *The Presence of the Word: Some Prolegomena for Cultural and Religious History* (New Haven, Yale University Press, 1967), 250. See also Ong's "Latin and the Social Fabric," in *The Barbarian Within* (New York: Macmillan, 1962), 206–19, and "Latin Language Study as a Renaissance Puberty Rite," *Studies in Philology* 56 (1959): 103–24.

14. It never occurred to Burke whether or not the revolutionaries and their supporters were actually competently learned in Latin and the classics. Burke assumes they are not, just as he assumes they have middle- and lower-class origins. See James T. Boulton on how Burke's "learned" language was made an issue by his opponents: *The Language of Politics in the Age of Wilkes and Burke* (London: Routledge and Kegan Paul, 1963), 139 ff.

15. For a discussion of what these specific words meant for Burke and the revolutionaries, see the following works, passim: Jeffrey Hart, "Burke and Radical Freedom," *Review of Politics* 29 (April 1967): 221–38; Burleigh Taylor Wilkins, *The Problem of Burke's Political Philosophy* (Oxford: Clarendon, 1967); Peter J. Stanlis, *Edmund Burke and the Natural Law* (Ann Arbor: University of Michigan Press, 1958); Gerald W. Chapman, *Edmund Burke* (Cambridge, Mass.: Harvard University Press, 1967); Boulton, *The Language of Politics*.

16. Chapman, *Edmund Burke*, 233.

Blake, Violence, and Visionary Politics

WILLIAM KEACH

"William Blake is the rebel *par excellence* of English poetry": this is how Alicia Ostriker opens her introduction to the Penguin edition of the *Poems.*[1] I begin with her words because they confirm a view that is rarely challenged and yet at the same time they energize a borrowed French phrase through its casual historical pertinence. Blake is accepted, even celebrated, as a revolutionary poet by readers who themselves have no serious commitment to revolution—Puritan, American, French, Bolshevik, Sandinista, or otherwise. He has become institutionalized as "the rebel *par excellence* of English poetry" to such a degree that it is hard to find anyone asking difficult questions about the integrity and efficacy of his revolutionary art. I don't deny Blake's preeminence as the English revolutionary poet; he has a stronger claim than Milton, certainly than Shelley. But the *excellence* of what is revolutionary about him is not beyond question; the visionary terms in which he represents revolutionary history and himself as revolutionary prophet can be coercive and objectionable as well as liberating and truthful.

My particular focus is revolutionary violence in the works Blake produced between 1789 and 1794—between Bastille and Thermidor. In concentrating on Blake's work from *Songs of Innocence* through *Europe: A Prophecy,* I must anticipate the argument that Blake doesn't fully articulate his attitude toward revolution until the later "major prophecies," and that our understanding of Orc, Blake's dominant mythic embodiment of revolutionary energy and defiance, must reckon with changes in Blake's treatment of this figure in *The Four Zoas* and *Milton.* But my concern is with Blake's immediate response to events in France at the height of the Revolution, when those events colored his perception of English society. Blake's view of revolution may well have shifted in ways that are politically and artistically important, but we should not allow mythic syntheses or resolutions in *The Four Zoas* (ca. 1796–1807?) to dominate readings of *America* (1793) or *Europe* (1794). To the extent that Blake's later syntheses and resolutions indicate a retreat from the immediacy of political struggle or a subordination of historical actuality to the demands of an increasingly visionary "system," they don't show us Blake at his most forcefully revolutionary. For this Blake, we have to look at the work he created during the crucial years of the Revolution.

There is another kind of view that insists on softening and qualifying, rather than emphasizing, the force of the overtly revolutionary Blake. John Beer wrote in 1968: "Blake's basic sympathies lay with the revolutionaries," but "the strength of his revolutionary fervour can easily be overestimated. . . . he was attracted more by the idea and promise of liberty than by the physical force which was used to achieve it. Terrors and bloodshed could give him no pleasure."[2] The assumption that real revolutionaries take pleasure in violence ought to be resisted. But I particularly question Beer's denial that Blake was attracted to physical force. Ronald Paulson offers a version of this view: "For Blake paradox seems to be the characteristic feature of revolution itself, as well as the interpretation of it. . . . The Revolution, like his art, inhabits . . . the mythic area of ambiguity and doubleness where contraries can coexist."[3] My argument is directed against positions like these, as well as the belief that Blake's later mythopoeic visions put his earlier rebellious assertions in proper perspective. Blake *was* attracted to the force unleashed in the struggle for liberty; liberty without such force would have seemed to him not just impossible but undesirable. And while I don't wish to argue that bloodshed gave him pleasure, I do think that "Terrors"—some kinds of "Terrors"—did. Blake's response to the violence of the Revolution as historical event and as representable subject cannot be so conveniently accommodated within "a mythic area of ambiguity and doubleness" as Paulson—and some other very good readers of Blake—claim. Though Blake saw and represented the terrible sacrifices and uncertainties of armed rebellion, his art does not transcend them. It is powerfully and problematically caught up in the convulsions of his historical subject.

In focusing on the problem of violence in Blake's revolutionary work, I may seem to follow the reigning fashion in bicentennial reassessment of the French Revolution. Simon Schama's *Citizens* is the most highly publicized and brilliantly entertaining of a whole wave of recent revisionist history, much of it driven by a broad and barely disguised antirevolutionary or counterrevolutionary agenda that aims to characterize the Revolution as primarily an event of unprecedented savagery and regressive destruction.[4] To the extent that this revisionist preoccupation has exposed mindless celebrations of, or defensive aversions from, the facts of revolutionary violence, its effect has been good. But in their own one-sided and self-interested emphasis on revolutionary violence, the revisionists have virtually ignored the systemic violence of the old regime and the reactionary brutality of counter-revolutionary "White Terror." A critical look at Blake's representations of revolutionary violence can help us see what is wrong with the bicentennial backlash by throwing into relief problems swept aside in the flood of books, essays, talks, and television programs about the Revolution, and by giving us clearer reasons for valuing what is truly strong in Blake's revolutionary art: his depictions of the grinding, deceptive cruelty endemic to prerevolutionary society in France and especially in his own country.[5]

Three problems complicate Blake's verbal and visual representations of revolution. The first is the difficulty of representing collective, collaborative activity and struggle in an artistic mode dominated by individual symbolic figures with superhuman powers. The second is that Blake's revolutionary vision is contorted by a phallocentric myth of liberating erotic potency and feminine dependency. The third springs from Blake's idiosyncratic, personalized appropriation of Christian apocalypse and millenarian fantasy. Given these problems, I aim to set what seems to me artistically and politically objectionable in Blake against alternatives suggested in the writing of his contemporaries, and against aspects of his own work that triumph over its limitations. This latter effort commits me to an old-fashioned but still popular preference for the lyrics over the prophetic books, and in this case I believe the popular preference to be good, politically as well as poetically.

Two preliminary considerations bear upon the questions I've just raised about Blake's most important revolutionary work. First, there is his involvement in the Gordon Riots of June 1780, an upheaval that began with the Protestant Association leading a tolerably organized demonstration in London against the Catholic Relief Act, but that ended, after several days of fighting, with more than eight hundred dead and with twenty-one rioters executed. Alexander Gilchrist, our only source for Blake's actual involvement, says that Blake later recalled his "involuntary participation" in the Riots:

On the third day, Tuesday, 6th of June . . . the artist happened to be walking in a route chosen by one of the mobs at large. . . . Suddenly, he encountered the advancing wave of triumphant Blackguardism, and was forced (for from such a great surging mob there is no disentanglement) to go along in the very front rank, and witness the storm and burning of the fortress-like prison, and release of its three hundred inmates.[6]

Many Blakeans have rewritten this moment, rightly convinced that the Gordon Riots were not just "triumphant Blackguardism" but expressed an array of genuine if confused social grievances. David Erdman is sure "that Blake shared the sentiments of Gilchrist's 'triumphant Blackguardism' insofar as 'the mob' believed that freeing their fellows from Newgate was a step toward freeing Albion from an oppressive [American] war." [7] Likewise, Jack Lindsay construes the event as preparing Blake to identify with the crowd that stormed the Bastille nine years later. [8] What motivates these Blakeans is more than a conjectural conviction that Blake's joining the Gordon rioters couldn't have been "involuntary"; one of Blake's most famous designs, alternatively titled "Glad Day" and "Albion Rose," was sketched in 1780 and subsequently given that date when it was engraved in the 1790s to commemorate the Gordon Riots and the turning of the tide in the American colonies' fight against England. [9] Blake knew from direct experience what it meant to participate in mass violence, and he associated that experience with the image of what Paulson calls "a naked male youth at the center of a sunburst, breaking the Vitruvian circle that circumscribes him, [with] his center of gravity [at] his loins." [10]

But Blake was also engaged at this time in producing quite different images of political violence. The *Poetical Sketches* of 1783 contains, in addition to the familiar pastoral lyrics, "Gwin, King of Norway," which tells in ballad stanzas of a time when with "cruel sceptre" Gwin ruled "Over the nations of the North" and "The Nobles of the land did feed / Upon the hungry Poor." [11] A giant named Gordred rouses himself "From sleeping in his cave" and leads the oppressed in bloody battle against the king:

> "Pull down the tyrant to the dust,
>   Let Gwin be humbled,"
> They cry; "and let ten thousand lives
>   Pay for the tyrant's head."   (29–32)

The poem's language is ambiguously aroused in the scenes of carnage it appears to condemn:

> The god of war is drunk with blood,
>   The earth doth faint and fail;
> The stench of blood makes sick the heav'ns;
>   Ghosts glut the throat of hell!   (93–96)

Erdman, who stresses the importance of this poem as an anticipation of *America: A Prophecy*, says that it is "Blake's earliest and plainest account of a revolution and . . . evidence of how far he entered imaginatively into the drama of civil conflict" (p. 19). So how are we to respond to the climactic moment when Gordred—"a kind of George Washington and Tom Paine in one," says Erdman (p. 20)—meets King Gwin in single combat?

> Down from the brow unto the breast
> Gordred his head divides!   (107–108)

Erdman's comment on this is, "The revolutionary act of justice . . . is relatively surgical." "Relatively surgical" is a bit like "relatively dead." And while there may be some sort of egalitarian precision in Gordred's blow, Blake's image makes decapitation by guillotine seem humane indeed. At one level the political allegory may be clear, but the implications of Blake's imaginative investment in such representations of violence are not.

Related questions arise from Blake's unfinished history play published in *Poetical Sketches*, "King Edward the Third." The relevance of this early project to *America* and to the other revolutionary prophecies of the 1790s has been established by Erdman in careful detail. The play is filled with bloodthirsty praise of war by the king's followers: "Grim war shall laugh and shout, decked in tears, / And blood shall flow like streams across the meadows" (scene 5, 53–4). Erdman hastens to remark, "These are plausible imitations. They are not the real thing," though he has to acknowledge that "the impulse to *expose* the sentiments of his dramatis personae interferes with the imperfect effort to give them verisimilitude. . . . Our problem in reading *Edward* is not simply to account for the characters' expression of delight in bloodshed but to account for the fact that much of the hidden irony which underlies that expression remains hidden" (p. 66). The convolutions in Erdman's otherwise illuminating historical analysis, such as the "hidden irony" that "remains hidden," point to difficulties that don't disappear in Blake's mature revolutionary art.

Already in "Gwin, King of Norway" the question of representing revolutionary conflict as a collective social phenomenon comes into view. We begin the poem with "the num'rous sons of blood; / Like lions' whelps" in combat; by the end, the conflict contracts to the typical (in this instance Spenserian and Ossianic) epic encounter between two individual leaders. Blake's prophecies of the 1790s recurrently stage revolutionary conflict as a contest between colossal individuals: historical figures in what we have of the incomplete and unpublished *French Revolution* (1791), historically informed symbolic figures in the other Lambeth prophecies. From the point of view of Blake's pictorial art, this concentration on individual figures makes sense: crowd scenes rarely interested him. The result, nevertheless, is that very little of Blake's energy goes into representing the complication, the precarious confused power, of mass action. The images of this kind that Blake does offer are often negative, as in *The French Revolution*, where ironically the Archbishop of Paris conveys the power of mass action through the counterrevolutionary fear it provokes in him:

> . . . a curse is heard hoarse thro' the land, from a godless race
> Descending to beasts; they look downward and labour and forget my
>   holy law; . . .
> For the bars of Chaos are burst; her millions prepare their fiery way
> Thro' the orbed abode of the holy dead, to root up and pull down
>   and remove . . .   (138–42)

In *Visions of the Daughters of Albion*, where politics and history are most radically contracted to the sadomasochistic entanglement of a trio of symbolic individuals, collective social reality intrudes fleetingly as the voice of those subject to institutionalized violence:

> Bound back to back in Bromions caves terror & meekness dwell
> At entrance Theotormon sits wearing the threshold hard
> With secret tears; beneath him sound like waves on a desart shore
> The voice of slaves beneath the sun, and children bought with money.
>   (2:5–8)

Even here, though, the plural simile "like waves on a desart shore" immediately gives way in its historical tenor to a singular "voice of slaves . . . and children." Oothoon later pleads eloquently on behalf of difference and the multifariousness of instincts, but Blake's own instinct in the prophecies is to condense difference and multifariousness into the singular colossal instance.

There is a related example in *America*, when Albion's Angel sends a plague to blight the rebellious colonies:

> Fury! rage! madness! in a wind swept through America
> And the red flames of Orc that folded roaring fierce around
> The angry shores, and the fierce rushing of th'inhabitants together:
> The citizens of New York close their books & lock their chests;
> The mariners of Boston drop their anchors and unlade;
> The scribe of Pensylvania casts his pen upon the earth;
> The builder of Virginia throws his hammer down in fear.   (14:10–16)

From the mass "rushing of th'inhabitants together," to the plural citizens and mariners, to the singular scribe and builder: the passage moves to a point where Franklin and Jefferson are made to personify an entire population's momentary faltering under British attack. There is little place for internal dissension or the diverse historical interplay of competing interests, reactions, and tactics.

It may of course be argued that Blake aims precisely to show, as he says
in his 1810 Notebook entry on the Last Judgment, that "Multitudes of Men
in Harmony" may appear "as One Man"; Erdman notes that handbills distributed during the Gordon Riots appealed to this familiar political ideal
(p. 9, n. 16). But representations of revolution dominated by this visionary principle may nonetheless simplify the dynamics of converging masses.
There is nothing in Blake like Wollstonecraft's intensely uneasy description
of the "multitude of women by some impulse . . . collected together" who
marched on Versailles in early October 1789,[12] or like Wordsworth's sur-
viving memory of early and unexpected revolutionary solidarity in Book 6
of *The Prelude*:[13]

> it was our lot
> To land at Calais on the very eve
> Of that great federal day; and there we saw,
> In a mean city and among a few,
> How bright a face is worn when joy of one
> Is joy of tens of millions.   (355–60)

Shelley's depictions of revolutionary resistance in *The Revolt of Islam*,
though at times subordinated to his own quite different fantasies of elitist
heroism, provide unreductive responses to the questions posed about the
French Revolution—plurally and singularly, with a sharp sense of irony—
in the preface: "Could they listen to the plea of reason who had groaned
under the calamities of a social state according to the provisions of which
one man riots in luxury while another famishes for want of bread? Can
he who the day before was a trampled slave suddenly become liberal-
minded, forbearing, and independent"?[14] The poem answers "no" more
convincingly than "yes"—and doesn't flinch from confronting the uncertain political consequences. Even Shelley's idealizing appeal to aggressively
passive resistance in the face of official brutality at the end of *The Mask of
Anarchy* suggests what's missing in Blake:

> Rise like Lions after slumber
> In unvanquishable number—
>
> .   .   .   .
> Ye are many—they are few.

One figure standing in front of an advancing company of soldiers—or
squadron of tanks—can make a myth but not a revolution. If enough
people stand there, in the strength of their collective resistance, they can
make both.

What Blake by and large fails to do in the early prophetic books, he
powerfully succeeds in doing in some of the lyrics, where he is more

engaged in representing the actual suffering and struggle of what he would call "fallen" existence. In the lyrics, too, he usually prefers the representative individual to the diversity of a group. But these representative individuals are socially alive and responsive, like "The Chimney Sweeper" in *Songs of Innocence*:

> Theres little Tom Dacre, who cried when his head
> That curl'd like a lambs back, was shav'd, so I said.
> Hush Tom never mind it, for when your head's bare,
> You know that the soot cannot spoil your white hair.   (5–8)

The irony of representing this kind of socially sanctioned violence as something one of its innocent victims can accept and recommend to another depends on the tension among diverse perspectives: Tom's, the speaker's, the uninnocent reader's. In the *Songs* Blake's "doctrine of contraries" produces visions of collective suffering, and of potential collective struggle, that aren't reductively subordinated to the representational demands of a gigantistic symbolism.

The politically telling effects come through viscerally concrete acts of generalizing. Though Sir Joshua Reynolds irritated Blake into protesting that "To generalize is to be an Idiot," in the lyrics Blake practices a fiercely specifying art of generalization. The speaker in "London" wanders through "*each* charter'd street," "marks . . . Marks of weakness, marks of woe" "in *every* face" he meets (my emphasis). Yet as John Brenkman has recently argued, "The poem does not . . . articulate a single situation or a fixed relation between Blake and the city's populace; rather, the poem moves . . . through a series of such relations." [15] The motile visual force of "every" in the first stanza accumulates an even greater aural force in the five "everys" of the second—an aural force that is performed alliteratively in "The mind-forg'd manacles I hear." "Man" is caught inside the word "manacles," and yet, as Brenkman says, these sounding shackles start a process in which "manifestations of suffering" take on "the active power to condemn and protest." [16] The "chimney sweeper's cry" "appalls"—shocks and also blanches—the church whose hypocrisy blackens him and itself; "the hapless Soldiers sigh" runs "down Palace walls" "in blood" that may soon be his commanders' and not just his own; "the youthful Harlot's curse" converts her own and her child's disease into a plague on her respectable exploiters. Each figure is every member of an oppressed class; the violence of collective suffering generates a comprehensible violence of collective retaliation.

At the end of "London" Blake sees the "youthful Harlot" almost hero-

ically, as an avenging angel. Elsewhere the subversive valuing of pros-
titution sounds a more sinister note—in a three-line fragment from his
Notebook, for example:

> In a wife I would desire
> What in whores is always found
> The lineaments of Gratified desire   (*Complete Poetry and Prose*, 474)

In *Visions of the Daughters of Albion*, engraved in 1793, Oothoon is
branded a harlot as soon as she is raped by Bromion. The political allegory is clear: she is at once oppressed woman, brutalized African slave,
and possessed natural landscape ("thy soft American plains are mine, and
mine thy north & south"). But the more immediate sexual politics of the
poem are murky. David Bindman comments on the pictorial design at
the bottom of plate 1 (fig. 1): "Bromion and Oothoon are stretched upon
the rocks in post-coital abandon." [17] That an art historian could say this
about a scene of rape testifies to the ambiguity of Blake's design, to the
way it elicits a conventional eroticized response disturbingly at odds—or
disturbingly in keeping—with the violence of the text.

What's murky in Blake's representation of counterrevolutionary rape in
Visions becomes more densely overcast in the revolutionary rape at the
beginning of *America: A Prophecy* (also engraved in 1793). Most recent
commentators acknowledge that what the youthful Orc does to the "nameless" "shadowy female" in plate 2 of the Preludium is rape, though Paulson
isn't quite sure—"[Orc] . . . rapes her (or rather she allows him)" [18]—and
Bloom isn't at all bothered: "The silence of the shadowy female identifies
her with nature, barren when not possessed by man. Orc's rape is intended
to give her a voice, and succeeds." [19] Here are the crucial lines from the
Preludium of *America*:

> Silent as despairing love, and strong as jealousy,
> The hairy shoulders rend the links, free are the wrists of fire;
> Round the terrific loins he siez'd the panting struggling womb;
> It joy'd: she put aside her clouds & smiled her first-born smile;
> As when a black cloud shews its light'nings to the silent deep.   (2:1–5)

In Orc's embrace the "shadowy female" is first reduced to a "panting
struggling womb," which here, as in Oothoon's speeches in *Visions*, is
identified with the genitals, the locus of erotic arousal. As the "womb"
itself is personified ("panting struggling"), the woman is depersonalized.
The reduction is carried further in "It joy'd," another instance of deper-
sonalizing personification. The "shadowy female" is deprived of subjec-
tivity altogether, even of gender, under the pressure of Orc's revolutionary

energy. That she is then made to speak and claim an identity for herself is no extenuation of the sexual, and poetic, violence. The entire scene is complicit with the worst kind of masculine fantasy, with the belief that what women need in order to be freed sexually is to be forced.[20]

As for Blake's political symbolism in the Preludium to *America*, grounding the unleashing of revolutionary force in such a phallocentric scenario contorts and limits his prophetic recasting of history. To image the desire, pain, and sacrifice of revolutionary struggle in these terms is historically aberrant—at least with respect to the role played by women in the early years of the French Revolution—as well as politically repellent. Blake might actually have approved of the late shift in official revolutionary iconography analyzed by Lynn Hunt, when previous feminine allegories of "Liberty marching bare-breasted and fierce of visage" were replaced, after November 1793, by depictions of the giant Hercules with his club as emblem of the Republic.[21] If Blake's range of historical reference in *America* does extend, as Paulson argues, to the revolt of the slaves in Santo Domingo that began in 1791,[22] then Orc's rape of Urthona's daughter reinforces the white myth of black male potency. As in *Visions*, but more positively and directly, phallic aggression is seen eventually to lead to the erotic liberation of women:

> The doors of marriage are open, and the Priests in rustling scales
> Rush into reptile coverts, hiding from the fires of Orc,
> That play around the golden roofs in wreaths of fierce desire,
> Leaving the females naked and glowing with the lusts of youth
>
> (15:19–22)

Blake's hairy youth leaves the women glowing. It's a male-dominated vision of revolutionary release, motivated by assumptions such as those that appear in Blake's annotations to Lavater's *Aphorisms of Man* of 1788: "let the men do their duty & the women will be such wonders, the female life . . . lives from the light of the male. See a mans female dependants you know the man" (*Complete Poetry and Prose*, p. 596).

Blake's vision of revolutionary energy as phallic uprising pervades his political appropriations of Christian millenarian apocalypse. In plate 5 of *America* (fig. 2), the text represents Albion's Angel watching in fear as "the terror" Orc approaches "like a comet, or more like the planet" Mars:

> The Spectre glowd his horrid length staining the temple long
> With beams of blood. . . .
>
> (5:6–7)

The extraordinary design surrounding the text on this page depicts, in Erdman's account, "a revolutionary tribunal of three naked youths up in the heavens . . . with fiery sword and scales of justice. . . . At the top the King, bound, is tried and found wanting . . . then sent hurtling to the bottom, where his possibly decapitated body is encircled by a blood-red serpent with human face but forked tongue."[23] The forked tongue and other details of both design and text suggest Blake's critical reservations about such a reign of terror. Gilchrist reports that when Blake heard about the 1792 September massacres, "he tore off his white cockade, and assuredly never wore the red cap again" (Blake had worn the prorevolutionary *bonnet rouge* openly in the streets of London).[24] Whatever the accuracy of Gilchrist's recollection, Blake's imaginative investment in violent apocalyptic revolution is inescapable in plate 5 of *America* and in the plate that follows, which shows a naked young man sitting with his legs spread on top of a grave-mound as he looks up in hope (fig. 3):

> The morning comes, the night decays, the watchmen leave their stations;
> The grave is burst, the spices shed, the linen wrapped up;
> The bones of death, the cov'ring clay, the sinews shrunk & dry'd.
> Reviving shake, inspiring move, breathing! awakening!   (6:1–4)

The movement from apocalyptic violence to the dawning of a new age had been implicit in the more peaceful and reformist vision of *The French Revolution*[25]—in the transition from the horrifying "dens" of the Bastille to the convening of the Commons: "like spirits of fire in the beautiful / Porches of the Sun, to plant beauty in the desart craving abyss, they gleam" (52–55). A more overtly revolutionary anticipation of plates 5 and 6 from *America* is the juxtaposition of verbal images near the end of "A Song of Liberty," which concludes *The Marriage of Heaven and Hell* and which Blake probably composed in the autumn of 1792 as a response to the victory of the French Republican army over the invading Austrian forces at Valmy:

> 19. Where the son of fire in his eastern cloud, while the morning plumes her golden breast,
> 20. Spurning the clouds written with curses, stamps the stony law to dust, loosing the eternal horses from the dens of night, crying
>   Empire is no more! and now the lion & wolf shall cease.

In *America*, the terrible energy of the lion and the wolf are intrinsic to the Revolution's way toward rebirth. The innocent-looking youth who awakens to the dawning of a new age in figure 3 is a transfiguration of the revolutionary angel flying through the night of Orc's terror in figure 2 (upper right), his huge sword flaming between his legs. If the figure hurled into the coils of the red serpent at the bottom of figure 2 is "The Guardian Prince of Albion" without his head, then the flying youth holds onto—

appears to be soaring aloft on—the weapon of execution. Louis XVI had been guillotined in January of the year *America: A Prophecy* was published. Blake's imagining of an apocalyptic future for Albion that will derive its impetus from what has happened in England's American colonies and in France fuses phallic mystique with the mysteries of a Christian millennium.

The fundamental historical importance of dissenting Christian millenarianism to the English tradition of radical protest has been decisively demonstrated by E. P. Thompson, Christopher Hill, and others. Blake figures prominently in Thompson's *Making of The English Working Class*, and Thompson usefully reminds us that "Against the background of London Dissent, with its fringe of deists and earnest mystics . . . Blake seems no longer the cranky untutored genius that he must seem to those who know only the genteel culture of the time. On the contrary, he is the original yet authentic voice of a long popular tradition."[26] Blake's authenticity need not be further debated, but I do wish to consider one aspect of his undeniable originality—his idiosyncratic artistic relation to apocalyptic Christian politics. In the famous credo set out in plate 3 of *The Marriage of Heaven and Hell*, Blake announces his critique of Swedenborg's Church of the New Jerusalem by implicitly claiming a personal role in the unfolding of biblical prophecies that are distinctly violent, and distinctly masculine:

As a new heaven is begun, and it is now thirty-three years since its advent: the Eternal Hell revives. And lo! Swedenborg is the Angel sitting at the tomb; his writings are the linen clothes folded up. Now is the dominion of Edom, & the return of Adam into Paradise; see Isaiah xxxiv & XXXV Chap:

When Blake wrote this in 1790, the year in which the fall of the Bastille was celebrated, he had himself reached the Messianic age of thirty-three. No account of the ironic and satirical impulses in *The Marriage of Heaven and Hell* can gainsay the prophetic position Blake claims for himself, or the implications of his references to the Old Testament book of Isaiah. In Isaiah 34 we hear that "the indignation of the Lord is upon all nations":

. . . he hath delivered them to the slaughter.
     Their slain also shall be cast out, and their stink shall come up out of their carcases, and the mountains shall be melted with their blood.
     The sword of the Lord is filled with blood . . .
For it is the day of the Lord's vengeance . . .
They shall call the nobles thereof to the kingdom, but none *shall be* there, and all her princes shall be nothing.   (34:1–12)

The "dominion of Edom" to which Blake refers is from Isaiah 63, where the man with garments dyed red appears in Judea and says: "I will tread [the people] in mine anger, and trample them in my fury; and their blood shall be sprinkled upon my garments, and I will stain all my raiment" (63:3). The land of Edom takes its name from Esau, the "cunning hunter" of Genesis 25 whose very name means "covered with hair." The figure of the hairy youthful Orc in *America* is already implicit in the personalized Old Testament apocalypse evoked in *The Marriage*.

Most readers of Blake know all this; students who bother to read the notes in the *Norton Anthology* know it. But why is there so little discussion of the kind of violent revolutionary vision Blake's art communicates in these moments? I said earlier that Blake took artistic pleasure in terror; to see how and where, consider the language of "terror," the "terrible," and the "terrific" in the early prophecies. In *The French Revolution*, the language of terror is applied to the nobility and the old regime: the Bastille's towers are "terrible" (19); Sieyès deplores the way an enslaved populace has been "kept in awe with the whips, / To worship terrors" (214–15). But in *America: A Prophecy* such language assumes a different status. Orc in the Preludium is "the terrible boy" who seizes the nameless female's "terrific loins" (2:6, 3). Albion's Prince interrupts Washington's defiant speech with "a terrible blast" (3:13), only to be confronted by the figure of Orc rising redundantly over the Atlantic:

> his terrible limbs were fire
> With myriads of cloudy terrors . . .   (4:9–10)

I've already glanced at the textual representation of "terror" in plate 5; many more instances from *America* might be cited. Such language is superfluously significant in Blake's version of the revolutionary—which is also for him the apocalyptic millenarian—sublime.

Paulson suggests, far too sketchily in my view, that Blake's vision of revolutionary terror is a direct response to the contradiction between Edmund Burke's enthusiastic theorizing of aestheticized terror as a primary source of the sublime in his early *Philosophical Enquiry into the Origin of our Ideas of the Sublime and Beautiful*, and his later denunciations of actual terror in *Reflections on the Revolution in France* and subsequent writings.[27] Burke was instrumental in introducing the words "terrorist" and "terrorism" into English, and it is to Blake's credit that he resisted these formations: already in the 1790s the words were corrupted, as they are now, by being exploitatively applied only to some and not to all acts of ruthlessly intimidating and indiscriminant violence.[28] But it is *not* to Blake's credit that he represents revolutionary terror in the sublime terms of Christian apocalypse—in terms, that is, that are bound to subordinate individual and collective human responsibility for political violence to the worship of energy as a divinely retributive, ultimately self-validating absolute.

As a concluding example of what's politically and artistically troubling about Blake's apocalypse, consider the final plate of *Europe: A Prophecy* (fig. 4). *Europe* represents the history of the Christian era as "the night of Enitharmon's joy," as an eighteen-hundred-year "female dream" in which woman has exerted a repressive, secretive dominion. Enitharmon calls upon Orc, her first-born son, who in this poem is closely associated with Christ, to arise and take his place under her reign of sexual secrecy and institutionalized religious mystery. Instead he rises up in all his flaming energy, and at the end of the poem

> terrible Orc, when he beheld the morning in the east,
>
> Shot from the heights of Enitharmon;
> And in the vineyards of red France appear'd the light of his fury.
> The sun glow'd fiery red!
> The furious terrors flew around!
> On golden chariots raging, with red wheels dropping with blood;
> The Lions lash their wrathful tails!
> The Tigers couch upon the prey & such the ruddy tide:
> And Enitharmon groans & cries in anguish and dismay.   (14:37–15:8)

At this moment Los, the prophet-poet in Blake's mythic system, makes his first decisive move in the work of the 1790s:

> Then Los arose his head he reard in snaky thunders clad:
> And with a cry that shook all nature to the utmost pole,
> Call'd all his sons to the strife of blood.   (15:9–11)

For Erdman, Los appears here determined "to frame into prophetic symmetry the 'furious terrors' of armies of lions and preying tigers."[29] Whatever its applicability to the design of plate 15, this is surely an idealization of what happens in the text: Los arises in language that recalls Orc's own violent appearance and calls "all his sons to the strife of blood." In the visual design, if the naked frontal figure striding up stone steps away from the flames is Los, then Erdman might seem to be right in suggesting a benevolent pictorial alternative to the textual terror. Los, he says, is rescuing "his children (the daughters here . . .)." But in a work that has envisioned all of prerevolutionary Christian history as a delusive and corrupting dominion of the female will, this image of a powerful male removing one inert and one walking female—both faceless—from a field of revolutionary battle to be occupied by Los and his sons confirms the phallocentrism (this design is quite literally phallocentric) that determines so much in

Blake's politics. Erdman rightly reads the entire plate as "apocalyptic": it is visually indebted to depictions of the Last Judgment and of Christ's Harrowing of Hell. But the terms of Blake's apocalypse preserve forms of domination and mystify forms of violence. The vine that shoots out after the word "blood" at the end of the text is less a sign of hope or optimism than a gesture of prophetic self-assertion.

Is Los in the final plate of *Europe* a mythic self-portrait of the artist? If he is, then a critical reading of that plate needs to recognize that the violence represented in Blake's revolutionary prophecies is personal and artistic as well as public and historical. The degree to which Blake's personal artistic violence represents the impulses of an entire class of dissident English artists and artisans in the 1790s is a very difficult, still unresolved matter. More than forty years ago, Mark Schorer wondered about the personal origins of the aggression in Blake's anti-authoritarian art and asked, "When did the violence begin?"[30] Since then such questions have usually been avoided. It is my position that Blake's revolutionary violence expresses resentment and revenge and a will to prophetic power that shapes, and sometimes distorts, his response to what was happening in France, in America, and in his own country. The executioner angel with the flaming phallic sword flying at the top of plate 5 of *America* (fig. 2) is also Blake with his pen, his brush, his engraving implement. The politics of such self-imaginings need to be contested. The power of Blake's art to arouse celebratory assent is evident in nearly everything that has been written about him; its power to provoke fruitful and clarifying resistance may be its least adequately celebrated virtue. "Opposition is true Friendship." Blake's friends, particularly those who, like him, believe in the possibility of a just revolution, need to take that proverb of his more commitedly to heart.

NOTES

1. *William Blake: The Complete Poems* (Harmondsworth, U.K.: Penguin, 1977), 7.

2. *Blake's Humanism* (Manchester, U.K.: Manchester University Press, 1968), 95.

3. Ronald Paulson, *Representations of Revolution* (New Haven, Conn.: Yale University Press, 1983), 110.

4. Simon Schama, *Citizens: A Chronicle of the French Revolution* (New York: Knopf, 1989). Colin Jones's review of Schama's book and of William Doyle's *The Oxford History of the French Revolution* in the *TLS* (21–27 July 1989), 791–92,

focuses sharply on many of the key difficulties and relates them to the work of Francois Furet and other revisionist historians.

5. Jerome McGann's recent reflections on "our heritage of violence" as it relates to Blake in "The Third World of Criticism," *Rethinking Historicism: Critical Readings in Romantic History* (Oxford: Basil Blackwell, 1989), 85–107, are pertinent to, though quite different in emphasis from, my argument here.

6. G. E. Bentley, Jr., *Blake Records* (Oxford: Clarendon Press, 1969), 18.

7. David Erdman, *Blake: Prophet Against Empire. A Poet's Interpretation of the History of His Own Times* (Princeton: Princeton University Press, 1954), 8. Subsequent references to this work are cited parenthetically in the text.

8. Jack Lindsay, *William Blake: His Life and Work* (New York: George Braziller, 1978), 14–15.

9. See Paulson, *Representations of Revolution*, 89 and Erdman, *Prophet Against Empire*, 9.

10. *Representations of Revolution*, 89.

11. All quotations of Blake's writings are from *The Complete Poetry & Prose of William Blake*, ed. David V. Erdman, commentary by Harold Bloom, rev. ed. (Garden City, NY: Anchor/Doubleday, 1982). Numbers in parentheses refer to lines; numbers followed by a colon are plate numbers.

12. *An Historical and Moral View of the Origin and Progress of the French Revolution and the Effect It Has Produced in Europe* (London: J. Johnson, 1795; Delmar, N.Y.: Scholars' Facsimiles and Reprints, 1975), 426.

13. *"The Prelude" 1799, 1805, 1850*, ed. Jonathan Wordsworth, M. H. Abrams, and Stephen Gill (New York: Norton, 1979).

14. All quotations are from *Shelley: Poetical Works*, ed. Thomas Hutchinson, corrected by G. M. Matthews (Oxford: Oxford University Press, 1970).

15. John Brenkman, *Culture and Domination* (Ithaca, N.Y.: Cornell University Press, 1987), 125.

16. *Culture and Domination*, 126.

17. David Blindman, *Blake as an Artist* (Oxford: Phaidon, 1977), 74. For readings that call attention to the representational confusions I refer to here, see Susan Fox, "The Female as Metaphor in William Blake's Poetry," *Critical Inquiry* (1977); Anne K. Mellor, "Blake's Portrayal of Women," *Blake: An Illustrated Quarterly* 63 (1982–83); and Brenda S. Webster, *Blake's Prophetic Psychology* (Athens: University of Georgia Press, 1981), 91–109.

18. *Representations of Revolution*, 88.

19. *Complete Poetry and Prose*, 902.

20. The mysterious four-line passage erased from all but three copies of *America* ("The stern Bard ceas'd, asham'd of his own song . . .") might be read as a self-critical retraction of the rape scene in the Preludium. But the rest of the poem will not, in my view, support such a reading.

21. Lynn Hunt, *Politics, Culture, and Class in the French Revolution* (Berkeley: University of California Press, 1984), 93–4. Also see fig. 20.

22. *Representations of Revolution*, 93.

23. David Erdman, *The Illuminated Blake: All of William Blake's Illuminated Works with a Plate-by-Plate Commentary* (Garden City, N.Y.: Anchor, 1974), 143.

24. Bentley, *Blake Records*, 40–1. Gilchrist's remark about the white cockade is puzzling; Erdman, *Prophet Against Empire*, (141), points out that "the white cockade happens to have been a royalist symbol, not a republican."

25. See Jean Starobinski, *1789: The Emblems of Reason*, trans. Barbara Bray (1973; Cambridge, Mass.: MIT Press, 1988), 43–6.

26. E. P. Thompson, *The Making of the English Working Class* (New York: Vintage, 1963), 52.

27. *Representations of Revolution*, 59–73.

28. See Edward S. Herman, *The Real Terror Network: Terrorism in Fact and Propaganda* (Boston: South End Press, 1982).

29. *Illuminated Blake*, 173.

30. *William Blake: The Politics of Vision* (New York: Vintage, 1946), 138.

History and Autobiography: The French Revolution in Wordsworth's *Prelude*

JAMES A. W. HEFFERNAN

In 1856, Alexis de Tocqueville published what Francois Furet has recently designated "the most important book of the entire historiography" of the revolutionary period—namely, *The Old Regime and the Revolution*.[1] Having analyzed the origins of the Revolution in this remarkable book, Tocqueville then set out to write a history that would represent the minds of those who lived through it: "Not what is said about them or what they said about themselves later, but what they themselves said at the time, and, so far as possible, what they really thought."[2] But Tocqueville brought to this daunting task a constitution ravaged by sickness, and sickness spawned the metaphors with which he represented the Revolution to himself. It was, he wrote,

a *virus* of a new and unknown kind. There have been violent revolutions in the world, but the character of these Revolutionaries is so immoderate, violent, radical, desperate, audacious, almost insane yet powerful and effective as to have no precedents, it seems to me, in the great social agitations of the past. . . . Beyond everything that can be explained in the French Revolution there remains something unexplained in its spirit and its acts. I sense where this unknown object is, but try as I may, I cannot lift the veil that covers it. I grope as if across a foreign body that prevents me from quite touching it or seeing it. (Palmer, 242)

In its metaphors of disease, its string of epithets ("immoderate, violent, radical"), and its characterization of the Revolution as a veiled exotic body, this passage shows signs of the "male hysteria" that Neil Hertz finds in the writings of nineteenth-century French reactionaries—including Tocqueville himself.[3] For Hertz, in fact, Tocqueville is a cocksure reactionary who knows exactly how to categorize the rebellious "other," how to diagnose a political disease on the spot. But Tocqueville's view of the French Revolution is not at all categorical. Unlike the "incurable malady" of the old regime, which he lucidly classifies in his book, the virus of the French Revolution is for Tocqueville *inexplicable*—"something peculiar that I sense without being able to describe it well or analyze its causes" (Palmer, 242).

Tocqueville's second metaphor for the Revolution reinforces this point. A veiled foreign body is exotic, covertly female, and decidedly "other," but it cannot be easily attached to the menacingly serpentine head of the Medusa, the sign with which—according to Hertz—reactionaries catego-rized the revolutionary threat to patriarchy and familial order. The veiled foreign body eludes classification. It signifies a Revolution wrapped in lan-guage—a language hardly translucent, let alone transparent, a language that keeps Tocqueville from "quite touching . . . or seeing" his subject. In his struggle to grasp the foreign body of the Revolution through the veil of language left by its participants—by their private correspondence even more than the official record of their debates (Palmer, 242)—Tocqueville reminds us that all historians, whether of a public past or a private one, must reckon with the problem of mediation: with everything that falls between the historian and the period he tries to represent.

As the historian of his own revolutionary self in *The Prelude*, Words-worth struggles to see it through a veil of intervening inhibitions. Scholar-ship alone has unveiled what his seemingly exhaustive autobiography con-ceals about his year in France: his affair with Annette Vallon, the foreign body who gave birth to their daughter in December 1792, shortly after his return to England. But no historian can directly touch the foreign body of his subject, and if there is an appreciable gap—as Tocqueville implies—between what the contemporaries of the Revolution said at the time and "what they said about themselves later," we must wonder whether anyone who lived through the Revolution can fully recover even his own experi-ence of it. Like Tocqueville, Wordsworth saw the Revolution as a "fever," and one of the things he remembers thinking at the time of the Revolu-tion was that it would make "a mockery" of historical representation: "O laughter for the page that would reflect / To future times the face of what now is!"[4]

Yet this is precisely what Wordsworth tries to do in his own history of the Revolution—a history that he locates within his autobiography, which he calls "the history of a poet's mind" (*Prelude*, 13.408). At one and the same time, he seeks to tell his own story and to retrace the course of the Revolution, or more precisely to convert the bewildering mass of events that we now collectively call the French Revolution into an intelligible and meaningful shape: a shape that could take its place in what he conceived as the providential design of a life destined to make him a poet. To fully understand Wordsworth's way of representing the Revolution, therefore, we must reckon with four different elements. There is first the viewpoint of the generative "I" who remembers and writes. Second, the viewpoint ascribed to the "I" of his remembered self. Third, the external record of what the remembered self thought and experienced during the Revolution—the extant record of what was written by, about, and to him at that time. Finally, there is the public record of the Revolution, the independent evidence for such events as the storming of the Bastille and the execution of Louis XVI.

These four elements variously cooperate and conflict in Wordsworth's poem. While the viewpoints of the generative "I" and the remembered "I" sometimes converge, they diverge radically at times, as when Wordsworth records the "painful" truth that he once rejoiced at British losses to revolutionary France (10.259). And some painful truths go unrecorded. When the letters that Annette Vallon wrote to Wordsworth and his sister in March 1793 were discovered 150 years later, they raised a question that must be faced by anyone seriously studying Wordsworth's version of the Revolution: why does he suppress the story of an affair that lasted through nearly all of his year in France? Comparable questions arise when we set the poem beside the public record of the events it re-creates. Why, for instance, does Wordsworth place the invasion of Chartres in the summer of 1790, two years before the public record says it occurred? Why does he tell us that Michel Beaupuy—the would-be hero of the Revolution according to Wordsworth—died in the Vendée rising of 1793 rather than in the battle of Elz three years later, where the public record says he died? To raise and pursue these questions is to enter the mind of an autobiographer struggling to make coherent sense out of memories profoundly disordered by guilt, loss, bewilderment, and pain.

I

The struggle begins with the task of defining his own relation to the revolutionary events he is representing. At times he presents himself as a mere bystander to these events, which seem to thrust him from the center of his own autobiographical stage. Describing the political climate of France in early 1792, he apologizes for turning to himself: "I fear / Now in connection with so great a theme / To speak, as I must be compelled to do, / Of one so unimportant" (9.111–114). With such a statement Wordsworth momentarily abandons the basic assumption underlying his whole autobiographical enterprise, which is that he himself is precisely its most important theme. Revolutionary events—and especially revolutionary figures—made him alternately self-assertive and self-deprecating. Of the events surrounding Louvet's denunciation of Robespierre, he writes:

"These are things / Of which I speak only as they were storm / Or sunshine to my individual mind, / No further" (10.103–06). Yet just a few lines later, he regrets that he himself could do nothing to check Robespierre's lust for power because he was "an insignificant stranger and obscure, / . . . and little graced with powers / Of eloquence even in my native speech, / And all unfit for tumult and intrigue" (10.130–33). Unlike Winston Churchill, Wordsworth could not make himself the hero of a public history because he had done nothing publically heroic. On the contrary, while fervently believing that "the virtue of one paramount mind" (10.179) would "have quelled outrage and bloody power" (10.179–81), Wordsworth himself withdrew from political combat by returning to England. There—as Kenneth Johnston has argued—he could do psychic battle with Robespierre for control of the Revolution and could rejoice at the bloodthirsty Jacobin's fall as if he himself had wrought it.[5] More important, he could "return / To my own history" (10.657–58): to the story of his own development as a poet, to the "heroic argument" (3.182) of a history in which he was unequivocally the hero.

The return to his own history is in many ways the return to a prerevolutionary self. In the final book of the poem, Wordsworth tells us that he experienced a revelation one night upon reaching the moonlit summit of Mount Snowdon in Wales.[6] But the revelation occurred in June 1791, several months *before* he left for his yearlong sojourn in France. And this return to a prerevolutionary moment at the end of his poem prompts us to ask whether Wordsworth simply aimed to cut the Revolution out of his memory, or parenthesize it within the main line of his autobiographical argument. Viewed from the vantage point of what he saw as its ghastly conclusion, Wordsworth's account of the Revolution in *The Prelude* seems in fact a valley of shadow and fear stretching from one elevation to another: from his unconscious crossing of the Alps in book 6 to his sublimely self-conscious conquest of Snowdon in the final book, where he symbolically emerges from darkness into light. By returning at the end of his poem to a moment of revelation that occurred just *before* his major experience of the Revolution, he situates the revelation on the far side of the revolutionary nightmare—as a beacon guiding him out of it. In this light, the bewildering process by which ascent becomes descent in the crossing of the Alps prefigures the ecstatic rise and vertiginous fall of Wordsworth's enthusiasm for the Revolution, and his apocalyptic vision of a height that transcends any measurable summit—the soul's sublime consciousness of "something evermore about to be" in book 6 (6.542)—looks beyond the finite destiny of the Revolution to the mountaintop revelation of the final book, where the moving spectacle of moonlit mist symbolizes the infinite capacity of "a mind sustained by recognitions of transcendent power" (1850 14.74–75). Indeed, Geoffrey Hartman contends that long before the crowning of Napoleon, Britain's declaration of war against France (in February 1793) left Wordsworth "with a hope deprived of the possibility of earthly realization," so that it was bound to become apocalyptic.[7]

Apocalyptic hope surely energized Wordsworth's imagination in the early 1790s. Yet to see such a hope as Wordsworth's solution to the catastrophe of the French Revolution is to overlook a crucial point: throughout the books devoted to his experience of the Revolution, Wordsworth repeatedly invokes the myth of apocalyptic renewal in contexts that undermine its authority. The most striking example is the passage expressing his reaction to the "tidings" of Robespierre's death, which he heard from a traveler as he was crossing the sands of an estuary on the coast of Westmoreland at low tide, with "the great sea . . . / at safe distance, far retired" (10.537,528–29). Like a historian of the Revolution, Wordsworth quotes his own speech—or rather, like Thucycdides, he retrospectively constructs a speech that expresses what he felt at the time:

> Great was my glee of spirit, great my joy
> In vengeance, and eternal justice, thus
> Made manifest. 'Come now, ye golden times,'
> Said I, forth-breathing on those open sands
> A hymn of triumph, 'as the morning comes
> Out of the bosom of the night, come ye.
> Thus far our trust is verified: behold,
> They who with clumsy desperation brought
> Rivers of blood, and preached that nothing else
> Could cleanse the Augean stable, by the might
> Of their own helper have been swept away.
> Their madness is declared and visible;
> Elsewhere will safety now be sought, and earth
> March firmly towards righteousness and peace.'   (10.539–552)

The irony of this ecstatic hymn to apocalyptic renewal becomes partly clear some two hundred lines later, when Wordsworth recalls that Robespierre's death did nothing to stop French armies from marching firmly toward aggression and war all over Europe, "chang[ing] a war of self-defence / For one of conquest" (10.791–92). But the real irony of this passage, which concludes book 10 in the final version of the poem, emerges only when we compare it to an earlier passage. When Wordsworth quotes his triumphant proclamation that bloodshed and terror have "now"—in 1794—given way to righteousness and peace, he tacitly reminds us that book 10 begins by describing an equally millenarian reaction to the massacres of early September 1792, when the Prussian capture of Verdun

provoked the slaughter of more than one thousand prisoners in Paris. Recalling his return to Paris in late October, little more than one month after
the massacres, Wordsworth writes:

> Lamentable crimes,
> 'Tis true, had gone before this hour—the work
> Of massacre, in which the senseless sword
> Was prayed to as a judge—but these were past,
> Earth free from them for ever (as was thought),
> Ephemeral monsters, to be seen but once,
> Things that could only shew themselves and die.   (10.31–37)

Here Wordsworth distances himself from the millenarianism he describes by using the passive voice about the recent crimes: "Earth free from
them for ever (as was thought)." He did not share this thought. Though he
had eagerly read "the master pamphlets of the day" (9.97), he drew little
hope from such undecipherable sights as the "black and empty" place de
Carousel, where the bodies of those killed in the August 10 storming of
the Tuileries had been heaped up and burned by the hundreds. He studied
these sights, he says, like a man with an impenetrable book—a volume
"written in a tongue he cannot read" (9.52). "Reading at intervals" in his
high-perched room at night, he "kept watch" over a city that defied both
comprehension and confidence:

> The fear gone by
> Pressed on me almost like a fear to come.
> I thought of those September massacres,
> Divided from me by a little month.
> . . . .
> 'The horse is taught his manage, and the wind
> Of heaven wheels round and treads in his own steps;
> Year follows year, the tide returns again,
> Day follows day, all things have second birth;
> The earthquake is not satisfied at once'—
> And in such way I wrought upon myself,
> Until I seemed to hear a voice that cried
> To the whole city, 'Sleep no more!' . . .
> . . . .
> . . . at the best it seemed a place of fear
> Unfit for the repose of night,
> Defenceless as a wood where tigers roam.   (10.62–82)

The editors of the Norton edition of *The Prelude* call these lines "apocalyptic" (p. 362n). But they actually express a radical critique of apocalyptic
expectations—of the belief that murderous violence can suddenly beget
an era of irreversible peace. Wordsworth's tropes cumulatively stress the

inevitability of repetition. When he writes that "the horse is taught his man-age," he alludes to the fact that the National Assembly regularly met in the *salle de Manège* or Riding Hall of Paris, where horses were taught to move in circles, wheeling round like "the wind / Of heaven" and "tread[ing] in [their] own steps."[8] In Wordsworth's eyes, the Revolution was not so much like a tamed or managed horse as a perpetually driven one: driven to return on itself like wind, tide, and earthquake; driven to reenact Mac-beth's regicide—the crime that would let him "sleep no more" (*Macbeth* 2.2.35)—by shortly executing Louis XVI. Apocalyptic expectations did nothing to end violence; they aggravated it. The Terror itself, Wordsworth goes on to say, exploited "the hopes of those / Who were content to barter short-lived pangs / For a paradise of ages" (10.319–21).

In thus demolishing the apocalyptic hope misbegotten by the Septem-ber massacres, Wordsworth prepares us to recognize the profound irony of his ecstatically millenarian response to death of Robespierre. When he rejoices at the "tidings" of this death, which reached him as he crossed an estuary at low tide, with the "great sea . . . / . . . at safe distance, far retired" (10.528–29) he subtly reminds us of what he has said about the massacres: "the tide returns again."[9] The very image with which he repre-sents the prospect of radical renewal after Robespierre's death actually drags a bloody past behind it. When Wordsworth proclaims the dawn of a new era of righteousness and peace, coming like "the morning . . . / Out of the bosom of the night," he is using a figure embedded in the history of the Revolution and its violence. As Jean Starobinski has shown, advocates of the Revolution typically represented it as "la lumière victorieuse des ténèbres"—light conquering darkness, the dawning of a new day—and in February 1974, Robespierre himself introduced the worst excesses of the Terror by saying, "Let us, in sealing our work with our blood, see at least the early dawn of universal bliss."[10] The fact that revolutionary rhetoric had thus perverted the image of the dawn is clearly implied by Words-worth's final comment on what the revolution became. With the crowning of Napoleon in 1804, he says, "the sun / That rose in splendor" turned into a piece of theatrical machinery and "[set] like an opera phantom" (10.935–40).

II

In thus deconstructing the revolutionary language of apocalyptic expec-tation, Wordsworth's history of his own response to the Revolution points the way toward a critical history of the Revolution itself. Francois Furet has written that "any conceptualization of the history of the Revolution must begin with a critique of the idea of revolution as experienced and perceived by its actors, and transmitted by their heirs, namely, the idea that it was a radical change and the origin of a new era" (Furet 14). In *The Prelude*, Wordsworth represents his younger self as the very embodiment of this idea—as a firm believer in the revolutionary myth of an absolute break with the past. "Dare I avow," he writes,

> that wish was mine to see
> And hope that future times *would* surely see
> The man to come, parted, as by a gulph
> From him who had been. . . .   (1850, 12.57–60)

In this startling passage, Wordsworth remembers hoping *for* precisely what his autobiography as a whole aims to prevent—obliteration of the past. This initially seductive prospect eventually threatened to destroy him. To support the revolution, he had to oppose his own country's war against it; and to accept the revolutionary ideal of Reason as supreme arbiter of right and wrong, he had to stifle his customary feelings, "to cut off [his] heart / From all the sources of her former strength" (11.77–78). He could resolve this war within himself only by returning, psychically as well as physically, to his own country. In other words, he had to recapture the very past that his enthusiasm for an apocalyptic revolution had threatened to destroy. This is why *The Prelude* assumes such a radically recursive form: why Wordsworth's account of his experience with the French Revolution is followed by two "spots of time" summoned up from memories of his childhood (11.257–384) and then by the story of the Snowdon ascent, which antedates his year in France. Within the totality of *The Prelude*, then, Wordsworth's history of his response to the French Revolution can be read as a valley of shadow between two peaks, as I have already suggested, or a phase of division in which the bond of unity formed with nature in childhood is violated, so that the final phase is a return to nature and to the self that nature has helped to form.[11]

Ideologically, this return seems overdetermined. Wordsworth returned in order to survive, to become a poet, and to write the autobiographical poem that signs itself an epic by the very act of ending with the story of his return. But this Odyssean repossession of self, nature, and native land closes the poem so firmly that we may hardly know how to open books 9 through 11 without a formula. The usual formula is that these books tell the story of a simple change, of an ideological shift from the remembered revolutionary self to the self that Wordsworth has become— or has recovered—by the time he writes the poem. Within *The Prelude*, the young radical who rejoiced at British losses in the war against France clearly troubles the middle-aged conservative who finds that fact "painful to record" (10.259). Outside *The Prelude*, Wordsworth's letters and writings of 1793–94 also show that while he at first condoned regicide and violence in unmistakeably Robespierrian terms, the Terror made him "a determined enemy to every species of violence" and in particular to the "execrable measures pursued in France." [12] Given such internal and external evidence of ideological change, we may readily conclude that Wordsworth's chief aim is to narrate this change: to offer us a two-stage story of enthusiastic support for the Revolution followed by disillusionment with it, or a three-stage story in which euphoric enchantment with revolutionary ideals gives way first to resolute acceptance of the violent measures taken to achieve them, and then to repudiation of those measures. [13]

But Wordsworth's narrative does not follow either of these chronologies. Using instead the recursive structure already established in the poem, he puts *after* his account of the Terror the well-known passage describing the Revolution "as it appeared to enthusiasts at its commencement," [14] and in this passage he dares to use even the auroral figure that revolutionary rhetoric had debased:

> Bliss was it in that dawn to be alive,
> But to be young was very heaven! O times,
> In which the meagre, stale, forbidding ways
> Of custom, law, and statute took at once
> The attraction of a country in romance—
> When Reason seemed the most to assert her rights
> When most intent on making of herself
> A prime enchanter to assist the work
> Which then was going forwards in her name.
> Not favored spots alone, but the whole earth,
> The beauty wore of promise, that which sets
> (To take an image which was felt, no doubt,
> Among the bowers of Paradise itself)
> The budding rose above the rose full-blown.   (10.692–705)

What makes this passage remarkable is not just that it represents an ecstasy of expectation but that it *follows* Wordsworth's account of the Terror. "History," writes C. V. Wedgewood, "is lived forwards but it is written in retrospect. We know the end before we consider the beginning and we can never wholly recapture what it was to know the beginning only." [15] Hence the notes of premonition in this song of anticipatory rapture. In a remarkably close reading of these lines, James Chandler argues that they subtly merge two contradictory points of view: that Wordsworth sympathetically describes the feelings of young English Jacobins at the outset of the revolution even while echoing Edmund Burke, who denounced the fatuity of believing that traditional "ways / Of custom, law, and statute" were "stale" and expendable, and who—more important—warned against the dangerous enchantments of a rationalism that claimed to be free of all passion.[16]

Burke's influence on Wordsworth's interpretation of the Revolution in *The Prelude* must certainly be recognized. Yet Burke's ideology cannot explain why Wordsworth invokes the myth of paradise to describe the way the world appeared to him and his fellow enthusiasts at the outbreak of the Revolution. To understand Wordsworth's language, we must recall that the whole purpose of *The Recluse*—the philosophic epic for which *The Prelude* would be merely a prelude—was to demonstrate that "Paradise, and groves / Elysian" could be discovered in our own universe by those who looked upon it "with love and holy passion" (*PW* 5:4). The very opening lines of *The Prelude* anticipate this discovery as the wandering Wordsworth, freshly liberated from city walls, wonders where he will alight: "What dwelling shall receive me [?]" he asks. "The earth is all before me" (1.11,15). Echoing thus the very last lines of *Paradise Lost*, where Adam and Eve are expelled from Paradise into a world that spreads out "all before them" (12.646), Wordsworth begins the quest for a paradise of his own. And the question about where he will settle has at least two answers. In the recursive unwinding of the poem, home is at first the "known vale" of Grasmere, a vale remembered from his childhood in the Lake District, a personal paradise which he reenters in order to write *The Prelude* itself. In the later books of the poem, however, home becomes a remembered vision of "the whole earth" re-created as paradise at the beginning of the Revolution. "Why should I not confess," he asks,

> that earth was then
> To me what an inheritance new fallen
> Seems, when the first time visited, to one
> Who thither comes to find in it his home?   (10.728–32)

"Why should I not confess?" he asks—as if this enchanting memory were somehow shadowed with guilt. In fact, what is wrong with this memory is that it perpetuates a radically dehistoricized moment: a moment detached from the history that came before it, which assumes the remoteness of a "country in romance," and the history that followed it, which is momentarily erased just after being recorded in book 9 and the first part of book 10.[17] The paradisiacal "home" created by revolutionary promise was placeless and timeless; it existed only for the imagination and survives only in memory. Once it entered space and time, once it entered the history of France during the Revolution, the paradisiacal home had to be lost before it could in any way be regained. For this Wordsworth needed at once the diachronic structure of narrative and the synchronic structure of prophecy. He found both in the ultimately redemptive myth of Milton's *Paradise Lost*, the paradigmatic synthesis of history and prophetic vision. But Wordsworth makes Milton reenter history. He radically rehistoricizes Milton's myth even as he uses it to write a providential history of the Revolution.

III

This ultimately prophetic purpose—this desire to reveal the meaning of what he has personally experienced even as he relives it—makes Wordsworth's history of the Revolution look forward and backward at the same time. Though he scarcely claims to have foreseen at its outset what the Revolution would become, he subtly intimates the course of the revolution even before he begins the narrative of his year's residence in France. In book 6, which tells of his European walking tour in the summer of 1790, he speaks of the joy and benevolence he met everywhere in France during its "golden hours." [18] But his description of the travelers he met on the Rhône—chiefly delegates returning from the Fête de la Fédération—defines a mood of giddiness hovering on the very edge of violence. "Like bees they swarmed," he writes,

> gaudy and gay as bees;
> Some vapoured in the unruliness of joy,
> And flourished with their swords as if to fight
> The saucy air. (6.398–401)

Beyond alluding to Milton's description of Satan and his followers as bees swarming in Hell (*Paradise Lost* 1.768–776), Wordsworth represents the newly emancipated France as a precarious paradise: a garden of violence where swordsmen flourish in the saucy air. He thus anticipates the feverish mood of Blois in the early part of 1792, when the daily news from Paris would make one of the royalist officers there reach for his sword "continually" and "the soil of common life was . . . / Too hot to tread upon." (*Prelude* 9.163, 169–70). To show that this potentiality for violence was planted in the soil of the Revolution from the outset, Wordsworth sometimes manipulates chronology. In book 6, describing the convent of the Chartreuse as it appeared to him in the summer of 1790, he claims to have seen at that time something he could not actually have seen for another two years: "Arms flashing, and a military glare / Of riotous men commissioned to expel / The blameless inmates" (1850, 6.424–426). By conflating the memory of his 1790 visit to the Chartreuse with what he knew about an invasion that took place later, Wordsworth deliberately darkens the remembered light of France's "golden hours."

This proleptic account of the invasion of a monastery in book 6 clearly looks forward to the passage in book 9 that describes what Wordsworth actually saw in the Loire valley during his sojourn at Blois in the summer of 1792: a freshly desecrated convent—"a roofless pile, / And not by reverential touch of time / Dismantled, but by violence abrupt" (9.470–72). Together with news of what French troops were even then doing to the monks of the Chartreuse, here was one more example of the havoc wrought by the suppression of religious orders that had begun more than two years before. But if Wordsworth can remember signs of revolutionary violence from the summer of 1792, he can also remember his friendship in that period with Michel Beaupuy, the army captain who inspired Wordsworth to love the Revolution. Wordsworth's Beaupuy is a walking anachronism. In 1790, the mob attack on the king and queen at Versailles had led Edmund Burke to proclaim, "the age of chivalry is gone" (p. 89). But in Beaupuy as Wordsworth represents him, the age of chivalry was come again—by means of the Revolution itself. Benevolently aristocratic, Beaupuy saw the Revolution as an "old romance" come true (9.307), as a new summons to knightly duty, as a call to serve the poor with the gallantry "Which he, a soldier, in his idler day / Had payed to woman" (9.318–20).

The explicitly chivalric nature of Beaupuy's revolutionary zeal helps to explain why Wordsworth remembers that during their "earnest dialogues" on the banks of the Loire his mind would sometimes slip to thoughts of literary ladies in distress—romance heroines such as Ariosto's Angelica (9.445–456). He also says he was enchanted by the legend that Francis I used torches to send signals from Chambord to the castle of his mistress (9.485–93). But if in fact this story made the young poet look upon those spots with "chivalrous delight" (9.503), he was implicitly accepting in the summer of 1792 the very maxim he would scornfully reject in the winter of 1793: Burke's claim that under chivalry "vice itself lost half its evil, by losing all its grossness."[19] Whatever Wordsworth actually thought about this point in 1792, he represents himself as so enraptured by romantic nostalgia in a Loire valley "innocent yet / Of civil slaughter" (439–440) that he failed to grasp the true nature of Beaupuy's chivalry, which lost half its virtue by losing all its effectiveness.

Most critics treat Beaupuy as a hero, the perfect embodiment of chivalric courtesy and revolutionary idealism. But Beaupuy's pretensions to chivalry produce nothing tangibly heroic. In the impressionable eyes of

Wordsworth's remembered self, Beaupuy's finest act is his response to the sight of a "a hunger-bitten girl" creeping along a lane with a heifer tied to her arm (9.512–515). Seeing this modern-day lady in distress, Beaupuy says passionately: "'Tis against that / Which we are fighting" (9.519–20) These words instantly lead the young Wordsworth to believe that political salvation is at hand. But they have no practical effect on the starving girl, who gets absolutely nothing—not even a word of sympathy—from the benevolent Beaupuy. Flourishing the sword of his rhetoric against invisible enemies, he resembles only too well the *fédérés* of 1790 slashing away at the "saucy air." The hunger-bitten girl is not a human being but an impersonal *that* (actually italicized in 1850, 9.517)—a revolutionary signifier. Instead of asking for help, much less getting any, she simply *denotes* all of the abstract misery that has provoked and justified the Revolution, including the worst of its violence. To end her suffering would be counterrevolutionary. It would end the justification for the fighting to come, and specifically for the "civil slaughter" (9.439) that would soon ravage the Loire valley when the Vendée rising began in March 1793.

Equally ironic is Wordsworth's claim that Beaupuy died in the effort to suppress this reactionary outbreak, that "he perished fighting, in supreme command, / . . . / For liberty, against deluded men, his fellow countrymen" (9.431–34). Since Beaupuy actually died fighting Austrians on the Rhine in 1796, Wordsworth may have simply decided that *his* Beaupuy would die in defense of the Republic, not in what Wordsworth later calls a war of conquest (10.793).[20] But in any case, we know from other sources that Wordsworth's "deluded men" of the Vendée were fighting partly to protest the suppression of religious orders, the very thing that made Wordsworth grieve when it led to the desecration of a convent.[21] Since Beaupuy himself has sworn to serve the poor as if he were taking the vows of "a religious order" (9.312–13), the way he dies in Wordsworth's poem is scarcely more glorious or heroic than the way he died in fact. Either way, we do not learn what Beaupuy's death gained for the hunger-bitten girl.

Wordsworth idealizes Beaupuy because his history of the Revolution needs singular epic heroes—figures like Abdiel and Christ in *Paradise Lost*. Knowing "how much the destiny of man had still / Hung upon single persons" (10.137–38), he hides the fact that Beaupuy's whole regiment was prorevolutionary and represents him as the only "patriot" among a band of royalists (9.296), a single spirit fired by heaven (9.376), "one" called to action by the times (9.407–09).[22] But Beaupuy scarcely acts at all, and to fit him into his history, Wordsworth must temporarily convert it from epic to romance. Essentially, he represents Beaupuy as an ineffectual idealist: a chivalric hero who wanders through the revolution "as through . . . an old romance" (9.307), who does nothing at all for the only lady in distress he meets, and who is doomed just as soon as his forest of romance—the valley of royal châteaux and love-torches—becomes a place of "civil slaughter."

In the latter half of book 9, the fate of the chivalric romance that Wordsworth tries to construct around the figure of Beaupuy is repeated in the story of Vaudracour and Julia, the passionate young nobleman and the low-born lady in distress who must bear his child out of wedlock because his father will not let him marry beneath his station. Told at length in the early version of *The Prelude* and much abridged in the later one, this story is usually read as a disguised version of Wordsworth's affair with Annette Vallon—something he is often chastised for suppressing. Yet ideologically, Wordsworth's history of his love affair with the Revolution could hardly accommodate the story of his love affair with an active royalist, which is what Annette had become by 1793 if not sooner.[23] So the untold story of Wordsworth's affair with Annette is displaced by the erotic "bliss" of his first enthusiasm for the Revolution (10.689–691) and—more important—by a political parable: a story about two young people doomed to misery by the social code that forbade them to marry. But the real point of the story is that Vaudracour—like Beaupuy—is a feckless reformer. Just as Beaupuy thought he could ride the Revolution with the reins of the chivalric code, Vaudracour thinks he can follow his heart and marry beneath him without renouncing his filial obligations, without violently rebelling against his rigidly aristocratic father. As Kenneth Johnston observes, "Vaudracour is a gradualist; he believes his father's heart will soften at the sight of a grandson. . . . [But he] is driven mad by his failure to resist parental power, even when 'the voice of Freedom' resounding through France could have roused him" (*Prelude* 9.931–934; Johnston 180).

To see Vaudracour's fecklessness as a parody of Beaupuy's ineffectual idealism is to understand why Wordsworth's remembered self undergoes—as we move from book 9 to book 10—a change that mirrors the shift of political power within the Revolution itself: the shift from Girondist idealism to Jacobin terror. This shift also takes Wordsworth's history out of chivalric romance and back to epic, for book 10 has a hero of Miltonic stature: Robespierre. But since Robespierre is also the villain of book 10, he radically intensifies the ambivalence that Wordsworth remembers feeling toward the Revolution. The Wordsworth of book 9 was enraptured by the idealistic aims of the Revolution and alarmed by its potentiality for violence; the Wordsworth of book 10 is at once drawn and repelled by the power of violence itself, by its seeming capacity to work sudden and dramatic change. Hence his barely suppressed admiration for Robespierre, who confounds his enemies by sheer force of terror and daring. Recalling Louvet's denunciation of him on 29 October 1792, when Wordsworth himself was in Paris, he writes that Robespierre "dared" the man who had obliquely accused him

> To bring his charge in openness. Whereat,
> When a dead pause ensued and no one stirred,
> In silence of all present, from his seat
> Louvet walked singly through the avenue
> And took his station in the Tribune, saying
> 'I, Robespierre, accuse thee!' 'Tis well known
> What was the issue of that charge, and how
> Louvet was left alone without support
> Of his irresolute friends.   (10.95–103)

The Louvet of this passage evokes no less than three Miltonic figures. Rising alone from the "silence of all present" at a meeting of the National Convention, he resembles at once Milton's Christ and Milton's Satan, each of whom rose to speak at a council in response to a challenge that left all others "mute" (*Paradise Lost* 2.420; 3.215). Furthermore, in solitarily charging Robespierre with a lust for *supreme pouvoir*—the accusation to which Wordsworth alludes—Louvet resembles Milton's Abdiel, who all alone denounced Satan for claiming a power equal to God's (6.833–40). Unlike Christ and Abdiel, however, Louvet is "left alone without support / Of his irresolute friends"; and unlike Satan, he fades before the power of his adversary, who not only "dared" him to make an open accusation but also—as was "well known"—answered the accusation shortly afterward and went on to attain supreme power nine months later, in July of 1793 (10.103n.).

Like Milton's Satan, Robespierre is also the supreme tempter, the man whose merciless enforcement of political "virtue" nearly seduces Wordsworth himself. On one hand, Wordsworth repeatedly casts him as the devil incarnate. On the other hand, Wordsworth represents himself as having wished for something very close to the kind of leadership Robespierre provided. On leaving France at the end of 1792, he did not doubt that "the virtue of one paramount mind / Would have . . . quelled / Outrage and bloody power" and thus would "have cleared a passage for just government" (10.179–85). Even as he denounces "bloody power," he is asking for radically effective "virtue," for someone like Robespierre, who spoke as the apostle of virtue and declared that terror was "nothing but prompt, severe, inflexible justice" (Robespierre, 38). Though Richard Onorato sees Wordsworth's Robespierre as "the extreme of what Wordsworth repressed and denied in himself,"[24] Wordsworth *ex*presses his wishes at a level re-

markably close to the surface. Two things, he says, upheld his spirits during
the Terror. One was the recollection of ancient prophets who called down
divine retribution on wicked places (10.401–408); the other was the fact
that he "felt a kind of sympathy with power" (10.416)—a point made even
more emphatically in the 1850 version of *The Prelude*:

> amid the awe
> Of unintelligible chastisement,
> Not only acquiescences of faith
> Survived, but daring sympathies with power,
> Motions not treacherous or profane, else why
> Within the folds of no ungentle breast
> Their dread vibration to this hour prolonged?   (1850, 10. 454–460)

Even as he writes, Wordsworth feels again a vibrating sense of kinship
with power, with radical action, with the spirit of vengeance that drove
the Terror itself. In fact, not long after hearing of the "vengeance" cruelly
taken by Robespierre upon his native town of Arras (10.460), Wordsworth
rejoices "in vengeance" at the news of Robespierre's execution (10.540).
Thus the joy of Wordsworth's triumphant hymn is undercut not only by
the irony of its millenarianism, as we have seen, but also by its vicarious
reenactment of Robespierrian vindictiveness.

Further darkening this would-be moment of renewal in the poem is the
striking conjunction of memories that just precede it. First he tells us that
the Terror seemed to him an overflowing reservoir of guilt that "burst and
spread in deluge through the land" (10.436–39). Then he writes that in the
very midst of the Terror, he felt impelled to recall the glad summer of 1790
when he walked through France, and above all to remember

> That day when through an arch that spanned the street,
> A rainbow made of garish ornaments
> (Triumphal pomp for Liberty confirmed)
> We walked, a pair of weary travellers,
> Along the town of Arras.   (10.450–55)

Coming as it does just after the figure of the deluge, the image of the rainbow obviously evokes the archetypal moment of renewal in Genesis. But
the biblical pattern here is yet again radically revised. Though it once signified Liberty, the remembered rainbow "made of garish ornaments" now
prefigures what the crowning of Napoleon did to the sun of revolutionary
France, which thereby turned into "a gewgaw, a machine" that set "like an
opera phantom" (10.939–40). Just as painfully, the memory of the ornamental rainbow at Arras is inseparably linked to the cruelties perpetrated

by its native son. To walk through its arch in memory is to enter once more the world of the Terror.

Characteristically, however, Wordsworth will not allow the later memory to obliterate the meaning of the earlier one. Seen through the intervening veil of the Terror, the memory of passing through Arras in the "glad time" (10.449) of 1790 now mocks him with a "strange reverse" of associations. But it nonetheless remains a "blameless spectacle" in recollection, and he recognizes its innocence even as its aftermath "almost" leads him to quarrel with it (10.464–66). Thus the strange reverse works both ways. The memory of Terror refracts the earlier memory of joy, but the memory of joy resists annihilation by Terror.

In the later books of *The Prelude*, Wordsworth struggles to find a form that will allow him to repossess his entire experience of the Revolution: the erotic bliss and the shattering despair, the premonition of violence and the indestructible memory of joy, the entrancement with Beaupuy's idealism and the daring sympathies with Robespierre's power. The struggle to write a history of all these experiences led Wordsworth to see that traditional structures of representation—whether literary or historical—could not contain them. Chronological narrative could show how joyous expectation was shattered, but not how the memory of joy survived. Crucial moments in the history of the Revolution could be made to recall the plot of *Paradise Lost*, but the providential design of Milton's epic could not explain how the Revolution undermined the myth of apocalyptic renewal itself. Finally, an apologia for the Revolution—or for his own part in it—could not express the disintegration of Reason, could not speak for Wordsworth's memory of nightmares in which he

> pleaded
> Before unjust tribunals, with a voice
> Labouring, a brain confounded, and a sense
> Of treachery and desertion in the place,
> The holiest that I knew of—my own soul. (10.376–80)

As the hopeless process of defending himself before a revolutionary tribunal becomes a nightmarish metaphor for the process of defending the Revolution itself, Wordsworth reveals the impossibility of rationally justifying his commitment to it. He could re-create his experience of the Revolution only by means of the structure he had adopted for *The Prelude* as a whole: the structure of recursive narration. Repeatedly recalling the origins of his enthusiasm for the Revolution, Wordsworth identifies with his remembered self even as he enables us to see what that self did not foresee. He does not simply show how his past self gradually discovered what his present self knows; he reveals a present self profoundly shaped by the past, a self that keeps alive the "dread vibration" of sympathies with power that he felt at the most violent stage of the Revolution.

The Revolution fired Wordsworth with a love of power that survived the very worst abuses of it. For Wordsworth, revolutionary France briefly embodied the power to change the world radically, to make it universally just, free, and happy. In re-creating his experience of this power, Wordsworth foreshadows its violence and brutality from the beginning, but nowhere does he repudiate power itself. Instead, by embedding the history of the French Revolution within a history of his own life, he sought to show why the power released by the Revolution had to pass from the world of politics, where he "both was and must be of small worth" (10.192), to the world of poetry, where he could demonstrate his spiritually redemptive force.

What he could or might have done, however, is not the same as what he actually did. For all its length and scope, *The Prelude* is a prefatory poem, and Wordsworth never completed the philosophic epic that it was designed to introduce. Instead he struggled to recover something like the mood with which his own experience of the Revolution had begun. When Napoleon was crowned in 1804, Wordsworth believed that the Revolution had come full circle, returning to monarchy like a "dog / Returning to its vomit" (11.362–63). *The Prelude* enacts a quite different return. In its concluding lines, the poem that so poignantly evokes the blissful dawn of the French Revolution returns to a mood of expectation, with a promise that Wordsworth and Coleridge will together show the way to mankind's "redemption, surely yet to come" (13.441). But the revolutionary expectation of imminent apocalyptic change now gives way to the essentially conservative hope of eventual transcendence. Having entered history in search of a heroic redeemer and failed to find one, Wordsworth now looks beyond history—to a vision of the "mind of man" raised "above this frame of things / (Which, 'mid all revolutions in the hopes / And fears of men, doth still remain unchanged)" (13.449–50). For the power to act within history—the power that filled him with admiration and dread—Wordsworth can only substitute the potentially redemptive power of imagination—the hope of something "evermore about to be."

NOTES

1. Francois Furet, *Interpreting the French Revolution*, trans. Elborg Forster (Cambridge: Cambridge University Press, 1978), 16.

2. R. R. Palmer, ed. and trans., *The Two Tocquevilles: Father and Son* (Princeton: Princeton University Press, 1987), 242.

3. Neil Hertz, "Medusa's Head: Male Hysteria under Political Pressure" in *The End of the Line: Essays on Psychoanalysis and the Sublime* (New York: Columbia University Press, 1985) 173–74.

4. *Prelude* 9.158, 171–72, and 176–77, in William Wordsworth, *The Prelude 1799, 1805, 1850*, ed. Jonathan Wordsworth, M. H. Abrams, and Stephen Gill (New York: Norton, 1979)—henceforth cited as *Prelude*. Unless otherwise indicated, I quote the version of 1805.

5. Kenneth Johnston, *Wordsworth and The Recluse* (New Haven, Conn.: Yale University Press, 1984), 181.

6. Wordsworth seems to have created this revelation in retrospect. While we have independent evidence that he climbed Snowdon, we have good reason to doubt that he experienced a revelation there. See Jonathan Wordsworth, "The Climbing of Snowdon" in *Bicentennial Wordsworth Studies*, ed. Jonathan Wordsworth (Ithaca, N.Y.: Cornell University Press, 1970), 8, and Stephen Gill, *William Wordsworth: A Life* (Oxford: Clarendon Press, 1989), 8–9.

7. Geoffrey Hartman, *Wordsworth's Poetry 1787–1814*. (New Haven, Conn.: Yale University Press, 1971), 245. Jerome McGann has observed to me that Hartman's "apocalyptic" means "psychologically displaced" rather than radically utopian. But Hartman makes it clear that Wordsworth's apocalyptic hope is founded on abandonment of "the past and its institutions" (p. 245), on faith in "abstract individual man" (p. 246), and on the wish such a man should "spread abroad the wings of Liberty" (1850 *Prelude* 11.253). In forswearing the authority of institutions and custom for the theoretically liberating power of the individual man's reason, Wordsworth—says Hartman—becomes "an apocalyptic revolutionary" (p. 246).

8. Ernest de Selincourt, ed., *The Prelude*, 2nd ed. rev. by Helen Darbishire. (Oxford: Clarendon Press, 1959), 586.

9. Though Wordsworth repeatedly uses the figure of the river to symbolize the movement of his mind in *The Prelude* as a whole (as in 2.214), the sea— and sometimes water itself—signifies destruction and violence in the books on the Revolution. Book 9 begins by comparing the poet's mind to a river that turns back on itself rather than flowing straight to the "devouring sea" (9.4), and in book 10 Wordsworth develops the apocalyptic figure bequeathed to the Revolution by Louis XIV. The Terror, he writes, resulted from

a reservoir of guilt
And ignorance, filled up from age to age,
That could no longer hold its loathsome charge
But burst and spread in deluge through the land.   (10.436–39)

Wordsworth echoes this passage in the lines on Robespierre's death, where he celebrates the overthrow of those "who with clumsy desperation brought / Rivers of blood."

10. Jean Starobinski, *1789: Les Emblemes de la Raison* (Paris: 1973), 7, 31; Maximilien Robespierre, "On the Principles of Moral Policy that ought to Guide the National Convention" (speech of 5 February 1794) in *The Ninth of Thermi-*

dor: The Fall of Robespierre, ed. Richard Bienvenu (New York: Oxford University Press, 1968), 34.

11. "In three movements of turn, counterturn, and turn again," says Carl Woodring, *The Prelude* "shows how one poet's imagination was formed in childhood; how this imagination was progressively impaired in Cambridge, France, and London; and how it was restored by Nature through the threefold mediation of Dorothy, Coleridge, and the visible universe." *Politics in English Romantic Poetry* (Cambridge, Mass.: Harvard University Press, 1970), 102.

12. *Letters of William and Dorothy Wordsworth*, ed. Ernest de Selincourt, vol. 1, *The Early Years 1787–1805*, 2nd ed. rev. Chester L. Shaver. (Oxford: Clarendon Press, 1967), 124, 128. In the unpublished *Letter to the Bishop of Llandaff* that he probably wrote in February or March 1793, shortly after the execution of Louis XVI, Wordsworth declares: "A time of revolution is not the season of true Liberty. . . . She is too often obliged to borrow the very arms of despotism to overthrow him, and in order to reign in peace must establish herself by violence. She deplores such stern necessity, but the safety of the people, her supreme law, is her consolation." *The Prose Works of William Wordsworth*, ed. W. J. B. Owen and Jane Worthington Smyser, 3 vols. (Oxford: Clarendon Press, 1974), 1:20, 33–34. In his speech on "Moral Policy" delivered a year later, Robespierre justified the Terror in precisely these terms, arguing that "the government of revolution is the despotism of liberty against tyranny" (Robespierre, 39). What Wordsworth calls "the safety of the people" was in fact overseen by the Committee of Public Safety (*Comité de Salut Public*), which was established in March 1793 to enforce the policy of revolutionary violence and which Robespierre soon came to dominate; see J. M. Roberts, *The French Revolution* (Oxford: Oxford University Press, 1978), 64, 170. He also delivered "Moral Policy" on its behalf (Robespierre, 32n). For these and other parallels between Wordsworth and Robespierre, see Brooke Hopkins, "Representing Robespierre," in *Romantic History and Myth*, ed. Stephen Behrendt (Detroit: Wayne State University Press, 1988).

13. The full story actually includes a prerevolutionary stage of indifference to the Revolution. Writing to William Mathews on the eve of his departure for France in late November 1791 (*Letters* 1:61–63), Wordsworth makes no mention of the Revolution, and even after passing through Paris he could write to his brother Richard from Orleans on December 19, "We are all perfectly quiet here [   ] likely to continue so" (*Letters* 1:70).

14. The passage first appeared (without a title) in Coleridge's *The Friend* on 26 October 1809. I have lower-cased the title Wordsworth used when he published the passage as a poem in 1815. See *Poetical Works*, ed. Ernest de Selincourt and Helen Darbishire, 5 vols. (Oxford: Clarendon Press, 1940–49), Vol 2 rev. by Helen Darbishire (1952), 264. Henceforth I cite Wordsworth's *Poetical Works* as PW.

15. C. V. Wedgewood, *William the Silent, William of Nassau, Prince of Orange, 1533–1584* (1944; New York: Norton, 1968), 35.

16. James Chandler, *Wordsworth's Second Nature* (Chicago: University of Chicago Press, 1984), 47–48. This summary of Chandler's argument includes a slight revision of it. Chandler argues that young English radicals would have seen the ways of custom as "unjustifiable, unjust, favoritist . . . and so on" but never "meagre, stale, and forbidding." Yet a boundlessly optimistic faith in the politically redemptive *power* of Reason—which is what Wordsworth here recalls—would have led young enthusiasts to see the ways of custom precisely as "meagre," obsolete

("stale"), and hence feeble in their "forbidding": no more resistant to the inexorable progress of Reason than a "country in romance" would be. This seductive or "enchant[ing]" view of custom that a mature Wordsworth plausibly ascribes to the young English Jacobins is very close to the view that Burke ascribed to the early advocates of revolution, who—he said—saw all traditional usages as "ridiculous, absurd, and antiquated" and "all homage paid to the [female] sex in general . . . as romance and folly." Edmund Burke, *Reflections on the Revolution in France* (Garden City, N.Y.: Anchor, 1973), 90.

Whether or not the English Jacobins of Wordsworth's passage saw custom as enchanted, they themselves are said to have been enchanted by a bloodless rationalism: by what Wordsworth later calls "the philosophy / That promised to abstract the hopes of man / Out of his feelings" and place them in a "tempting region . . . Where passions had the privilege to work, / And never hear the sound of their own names" (10.806–813). As often noted, "the philosophy" here described is that of William Godwin's highly influential *Enquiry Concerning Political Justice* (1793). But as Nicholas Roe has recently observed, the coolly ironic tone with which Wordsworth defines Godwinian rationalism obscures the power of its influence upon him in the 1790s. *Wordsworth and Coleridge: The Radical Years* (Oxford: Clarendon Press, 1988), 7.

17. Lionel Gossman finds the revolutionary moment similarly dehistoricized by Michelet. "The essence of the Revolution, as Michelet presents it to us," writes Gossman, "is something that cannot be sustained in history" (p. 91 in this volume).

18. *Prelude* 6.352–370. This is one of the few retrospective passages in *The Prelude* wholly confirmed by what Wordsworth wrote at the period being recalled. In a letter to Dorothy from Switzerland on 6 September 1790, he says that he has found the French uniformly courteous, benevolent, and cheerful—a whole country "mad with joy, in consequence of the revolution" (*Letters* 1.36).

19. Burke, 89. This claim moved Wordsworth to call Burke an "infatuated moralist" in the *Letter to Llandaff* (*Prose* 35–36).

20. He was, however, *wounded* in the Vendean uprising and his brother Pierre died in it, so Wordsworth may simply have misunderstood what he was told; see Mary Moorman, *William Wordsworth: A Biography: The Early Years, 1770–1803* (Oxford: Clarendon Press, 1957), 197.

21. The Vendée rising, says J. M. Roberts, was partly provoked "by the increasing ferocity of religious (and, in the end, anti-religious) legislation" (p. 53). When Wordsworth says that a war waged to defend such legislation was a fight "for liberty," he unwittingly reminds us of the last words reportedly spoken by Madame Roland as she went to the guillotine—words to which Wordsworth himself alludes in book 10: "Oh Liberty, what crimes are committed in thy name!" See 10.352–54 and the Norton editors' note.

The heroism Wordsworth imputes to French troops marshalling for war against Austria in April 1792 is likewise more rhetorical than real—though Wordsworth may have believed in their heroism when, as he says, "the bravest youth of France" were "posting on / To meet the war upon her frontier-bounds" (9.269–272). He represents France as threatened by her enemies and fighting for an unimpeachable cause (9.289–93), but France declared the war simply because the king of Austria—who did not want to fight—was unable or unwilling to disperse the French emigrants gathered in territories belonging to his vassals and adjacent to France (Roberts, 47). As for the heroism of French troops, Wordsworth's letter of 17 May

1792 describes what they had just done in Belgium: "An ignominious flight, the massacre of their general, a dance performed with savage joy round his burning body, the murder of six prisoners, are events which would have arrested the attention of the reader of the annals of Morocco, or of the most barbarous of savages" (*Letters* 1:77).

22. See Roe, 47n. Though Beaupuy's regiment was stationed at Blois (where Wordsworth met him), Wordsworth places him—in effect—among the group of royalist cavalry officers whom he knew at Orleans (men "bent upon undoing what was done" [9.137]). Orleans, where Wordsworth spent the first few weeks of 1791, and Blois, where he spent the spring and summer, become in *The Prelude* just one unnamed "city on the borders of the Loire" (9.39).

23. Moorman, 179. Wordsworth's suppression has been defended and interpreted on various grounds (see for instance De Selincourt, 592), but not—so far as I know—on grounds of specifically political ideology.

24. Richard Onorato, *The Character of the Poet: Wordsworth in The Prelude* (Princeton, N.J.: Princeton University Press, 1971), 351.

"Such a Figure Drew Priam's Curtains!": Carlyle's Epic History of the Revolution

MARK CUMMING

During the bicentennial year of the Revolution, it was gratifying for devotees of epic history to see Simon Schama's *Citizens: A Chronicle of the French Revolution* on the bestseller lists. With his deliberately old-fashioned form of narrative, Schama gave his readers the chance to recapture some of the excitement generated by the great epic histories written in the nineteenth century. He rejected the "pie charts and bar-graphs" of recent monographs and offered in their place the staples that once drew the British to Thomas Carlyle and the French to Jules Michelet: a story, human interest, vivid descriptions, and epic scope.[1] *Citizens* is long (the Bastille falls on page 403), and its cast of characters is large and fluctuating. But its length and scope make possible an encyclopedic reference (reminiscent of traditional epic) to constitutional squabbles and hairstyles, to art criticism and bread prices, to enlightenment views on breastfeeding, and notes on the sexual performance of Louis XVI. At the same time, in the best tradition of epic history, *Citizens* presents the French Revolution as a pageant of memorable pictures that entice the readers and shape their attitudes and dispositions: the pathetic little parade of seven prisoners leaving the newly liberated Bastille; dainty Republican demitasses illustrated with the dripping head of the executed king; patriot fathers taking a Sunday stroll in the park and buying toy guillotines for their sons; the plaster elephant that Napoleon built on the site of the Bastille to help France forget the Revolution, sinking into a bog, its face crumbling, its cavernous interior filled with rats.

The epic history's graphic power is both a glory and, some would argue, a menace, for it can command our imaginative assent to the author's artistic vision without first requiring our intellectual assent to the veracity of his propositions.[2] Indeed, in different epic histories of the French Revolution, remarkably similar techniques of imaginative persuasion are used to further quite different ideologies. Insisting that the Revolution was not inevitable, that the *ancien régime* was not irredeemably corrupt and decrepit, Schama displays a Burkean abhorrence of the Revolution's violence. By contrast, Michelet vituperates a debauched aristocracy, celebrates revolutionary liberation, and weeps for the betrayal of the Revolution by self-interest and terror. Carlyle, who echoes Burke and yet also anticipates Michelet, depicts the Revolution as a cosmic, necessary, and appalling manifestation of nature destroying artifice.

I

Like the publication of *Citizens* in 1989, the appearance of Carlyle's history in 1837 was something of a literary event. *The French Revolution* made Carlyle's reputation; in the minds of many British readers, it made the Revolution itself. In particular, Carlyle's history gave British readers a way of seeing the Revolution, providing them not only with images of its characters—the lion-maned Mirabeau, sea-green Robespierre, and squalid Marat—but also with an epic or mythic cosmos in which those characters wondrously move. Carlyle's transcendentalist world picture, in which a thin rind of consciousness covers huge abysses of elemental power, supplants the gods of Homer and Milton in this epic of modern France. This cosmology enables Carlyle to place local events on a universal stage. It enables him to recast the events of the Revolution as a myth of modern life and a grand drama of human symbol making, in which obsolete political and ecclesiastical machinery is violently discarded and a new order is cruelly born.

Carlyle's mythic treatment of history is nicely exemplified by his depiction of a mysterious visit to the Baron de Besenval, commandant of Paris, early in the morning of 14 July 1789. Besenval, faced with the thankless task of defending Paris against the insurgents and uncertain whether the foreign regiments under his command can be relied on, is waiting uncertainly at the École Militaire when a bold, resolute Parisian enters unannounced and urges him not to offer a futile military resistance to the burning of the government customs posts. Having despatched his message, the intruder leaves as abruptly as he entered; Besenval, stupefied and half-admiring, makes no move to stop him. This episode, recounted in Besenval's (perhaps spurious) memoirs, is a preenactment, in silence and in solitude, of the struggle that will take place at the Bastille later in the day:

Le 14, à cinq heures du matin, un homme entra chez moi. Cet homme (dont j'ai su le nom) avait les yeux enflammés, la parole rapide et courte, le maintien audacieux, et d'ailleurs la figure assez belle, et je ne sais quoi d'éloquent qui me frappa. "Monsieur le baron, me dit-il, il faut que vous soyez averti, pour prévenir une résistance inutile. Au-jourd'hui les barrières de Paris seront brûlées; j'en suis sûr, et j'y peux rien, ni vous non plus. N'essayez pas de l'empêcher. Vous sacrifieriez des hommes sans éteindre un flambeau."

Je ne me rappelle pas ce que je lui répondis, mais il pâlit de rage, et sortit précipitamment. J'aurais dû le faire arrêter: je n'en fis rien.

On the 14th [of July], at 5 o'clock in the morning, a man entered my lodgings [at the École Militaire]. This man (whose name I have since found out) had flashing eyes, breathless speech, a bold bearing, and besides a rather handsome appearance and a certain eloquence which struck me. "Monsieur le Baron," he said to me, "you must be warned in order to prevent a futile resistance. Today the custom posts of Paris will be burned. I am certain of it. I cannot do anything about it, nor can you. Don't try to prevent it. You would sacrifice lives without extinguishing a single torch." I do not recall how I answered him, but he paled with rage, and left in a hurry. I should have had him arrested: I did not. [3]

The episode's symbolic significance is not lost on Michelet and Carlyle, both of whom follow the memoirs closely in their own accounts. Michelet notes, in his characteristically lucid way, that "It was the *ancien régime* and the Revolution meeting face to face, and the latter left the former in astonishment." [4] For Carlyle, in his earlier version, the episode is also the meeting of the old regime and the revolution, but his expression of that fact is more elusive and mysterious:

At five o'clock this morning, as [Besenval] lay dreaming, oblivious in the *Ecole Militaire*, a "figure" stood suddenly at his bedside; "with face rather handsome; eyes inflamed, speech rapid and curt, air audacious": such a figure drew Priam's curtains! The message and monition of the figure was, that resistance would be hopeless; that if blood flowed, wo [sic] to him who shed it. Thus spoke the figure: and vanished. "Withal there was a kind of eloquence that struck one." Besenval admits that he should have arrested him, but did not. Who this figure with inflamed eyes, with speech rapid and curt, might be? Besenval knows, but mentions not. Camille Desmoulins? Pythagorean Marquis Valadi, inflamed with "violent motions all night at the Palais Royal"? Fame names him "Young M. Meillar"; then shuts her lips about him for ever. [5]

With the phrase "such a figure drew Priam's curtains!" (borrowed from *Henry the Fourth, Part II*), Carlyle evokes the world of classical epic, and Besenval facing the conflagration of Paris becomes Priam informed of a burning Troy. [6] "Thus spoke the figure: and vanished" points us more specifically to Pope's translation of the *Iliad*, to the incident in Book XXIV where Iris visits Priam at the behest of Zeus. [7] This second allusion transforms the mysterious visitor into the divine messenger of traditional epic. Our understanding of this moment retrieved from the chaos of contemporary history is mediated by classical epic as rendered by Shakespeare and Pope. The not yet completed action of Carlyle's epic—the making of the modern world—is explained by analogy to past literary tradition. By comparing Besenval's mysterious visitor to the messenger who draws Priam's curtains—and even by suggesting that his history is some kind of modern prose epic—Carlyle urges us to ask, in what way is the world of modern French history like the world of Homer? Is human nature the same? Are the possibilities of human greatness the same?[8]

Yet important as mythical allusion is in this passage, it is the mythic representation of the episode that is most significant. Carlyle does not present a plausible eighteenth-century Parisian foreground that gives way, in a leisurely epic simile, to a fictitious classical background. Rather, with "such a figure drew Priam's curtains!" he makes the world of classical mythology leap into the foreground of the picture along with contemporary history. Priam with his messenger and Besenval with his bold intruder both exist in the eternal present of mythic time. Besenval has been "dreaming, oblivious," but the rules of the dream, or of myth, prevail even after he has awoken. There is nothing in the way of furnishings or details to suggest a recognizable location in Paris. The scene is set in the indefinable enchanted ground of myth, where marvelous transformations take place, where eternity invades time. Nor does Carlyle portray human characters as they are ordinarily conceived. The almost anonymous "figure" (the word is repeated five times) becomes not a man who leaves abruptly, as in Besenval, but a divine messenger who vanishes, as in Pope's Homer.

The Besenval episode exemplifies the ways in which Carlyle both departs from and employs traditional epic. Absent are the calm, detached voice of the epicist and the treatment of a theme long removed in time from the life of the author. In their place are the urgent voice of the narrator, which incorporates scraps of Besenval (the epic messenger, ironically enough, speaks only indirectly), and a presentation of the past as contemporaneous with the present (through Carlyle's much discussed use of the present tense). While Carlyle's voice is decidedly unlike that of Homer or Virgil, his attempt to depict human history as the product of superhuman forces recalls the cosmos of traditional epics. The allusions to classical mythology are not in themselves sufficient to create a heroic world, since the juxtaposition of classical gods and heroes with polished eighteenth-century Frenchmen in Carlyle's narrative often produces a sense of incongruity that suggests mock epic or satire rather than epic. (Witness the names Carlyle concocts: Mercury de Brézé for the royal usher with an overly developed sense of etiquette, and Mars de Broglie for a marshal in the army.) It is the conception of contemporary history as heroic—the imaginative identification of Besenval as Priam, in spite of the possible incongruity—that typifies Carlyle's idiosyncratic epic. Juxtaposed with his firm prejudices against French life and French culture, Carlyle's heroic and cosmic sense of the Revolution provides a strangely mixed perspective on the Revolution's achievements: long-winded, effete, and ineffectual, Carlyle's French are incapable of producing a new order, yet they are—however unwittingly— the agents of the most important event of the modern era, the overthrow of outmoded political and religious institutions.

Carlyle's mixed response to the Revolution is encoded in his depictions of events. The afternoon of 14 July, in the violent aftermath of the taking of the Bastille, is pictured in a cosmic panorama of Paris and its surroundings. Here the universal significance of the event is lost on the unwitting courtiers, oblivious in their minuet:

O evening sun of July, how, at this hour, thy beams fall slant on reapers amid peaceful woody fields; on old women spinning in cottages; on ships far out in the silent main; on Balls at the Orangerie of Versailles, where high-rouged Dames of the Palace are even now dancing with double-jacketed Hussar-Officers;—and also on this roaring Hell-porch of a Hôtel-de-Ville! (*FR* 1:197)

The moment later in the evening when Louis XVI, returned from hunting, learns of the insurgency in Paris, is of course one of the standard anecdotes of the Revolution, here suffused by mystery and foreboding enchantment and played under the heavenly constellations.

The Versailles Ball and lemonade is done; the Orangerie is silent except for nightbirds. Over in the Salle des Menus Vice-President Lafayette, with unsnuffed lights, "with some Hundred or so of Members, stretched on tables round him," sits erect; outwatching the Bear. . . .
In the Court, all is mystery, not without whisperings of terror; though ye dream of lemonade and epaulettes, ye foolish women! His Majesty, kept in happy ignorance, perhaps dreams of double-barrels and the Woods of Meudon. Late at night, the Duke de Liancourt, having official right of entrance, gains access to the Royal Apartments; unfolds, with earnest clearness, in his constitutional way, the Job's-news. "*Mais*," said poor Louis, "*c'est une révolte*, Why, that is a revolt!"—"Sire," answered Liancourt, "it is not a revolt,—it is a revolution." (*FR* 1:199–200)[9]

The interplay between human illusions and cosmic realities in this passage is typical of Carlyle's word-pictures of the Revolution. The king and his court are caught in a kind of enchanted waking sleep, dreaming of "double-barrels and the Woods of Meudon," of "lemonade and epaulettes." Underlying their ephemeral perceptions of the world, however, is an undeniable pattern of divine providence and retribution, underscored by the brief but telling reference to the book of Job, which asserts the utter power of God in the face of all human knowledge and aspirations. The fleeting identification of Louis XVI as Job suggests, as do many of Carlyle's biblical and mythic allusions, the moral inevitability of the Revolution.

Carlyle's sense of the Revolution's inevitability is further displayed by his figurative use of times and seasons, as in his splendid panorama of the French people on the champ de Mars as they prepare for the Feast of the Federation. This feast, celebrated on the first anniversary of the taking of the Bastille, features prominently in Michelet's history as a sign of the Revolution's essential peacefulness and generosity of spirit.[10] Evoking Michelet at his most ardent, Carlyle begins with an idyllic celebration of the preparations:

Young Boarding-school Boys, College Students, shout *Vive la Nation*, and regret that they have yet 'only their sweat to give.' What say we of Boys? Beautifulest Hebes; the loveliest of Paris, in their light air-robes, with riband-girdle of tricolor, are there; shovelling and wheeling with the rest; their Hebe eyes brighter with enthusiasm, and long hair in beautiful dishevelment; broad-pressed are their small fingers; but they make the patriot barrow go, and even force it to the summit of the slope . . . then bound down with it again, and go for more; with their long locks and tricolors blown back; graceful as the rosy Hours.

If the pathetic fallacy were to obtain for this moment of revolutionary joy, the time would be dawn, when the light of liberty overcomes the darkness of tyranny. But Carlyle sets the scene in a prophetic (albeit gorgeous) sunset, which offers a gently ironic counterpoint to revolutionary aspirations:

O, as that evening Sun fell over the Champ-de Mars, and tinted with fire the thick umbrageous boscage that shelters it on this hand and on that, and struck direct on those Domes and two-and-forty Windows of the Ecole Militaire, and made them all of burnished gold,—saw he on his wide zodiac road other such sight? A living garden spotted and dotted with such flowerage; all colours of the prism; the beautifulest blent friendly with the usefulest; all growing and working brotherlike there under one warm feeling, were it but for days; once and no second time! But Night is sinking; these Nights, too, into Eternity. The hastiest traveller Versailles-ward has drawn bridle on the heights of Chaillot: and looked for moments over the River; reporting at Versailles what he saw, not without tears. (*FR* 2:59)

This passage, which appropriates the poetic fervor of revolutionary rhetoric, serves both to exalt and to question the Revolution. The entrancing mythic depiction of the Parisian girls as "rosy Hours" is undercut, though not effaced, by the foreboding sunset.

II

As this emblematic panorama shows, the transcendentalist cosmos that makes possible the mythification of history also underlies Carlyle's historical emblems, which link the particular to the universal and the transient to the eternal. According to Carlyle's transcendentalist conception of the world, every object or event is a symbolic revelation of a universal truth. Some parts of the Revolution—particularly moments of turbulence and violence—cast their meanings only confusedly, leaving the observer in the fitful nightmare world of a phantasmagoria. Other objects and events provide a more solid and comprehensible meaning, which the emblematic historian can use to represent a larger movement in history. The hot-air balloons launched by the Montgolfier brothers and other adventurers in the years before the Revolution offer examples of such clarity. Signs of the technological advances of the late eighteenth century,[11] these balloons reflect the spirit of prerevolutionary France, as Simon Schama suggests in his fine comic picture of one early unmanned launching at Versailles:

On September 19, 1783, at around one in the afternoon, to the sound of a drum roll, an enormous taffeta spheroid wobbled its way unsteadily into the sky over the royal palace at Versailles. Sixty feet high, it was painted azure blue and decorated with golden fleurs-de-lis. In a basket-cage suspended from its neck were a sheep named Montauciel (Climb-to-the-sky), a duck and a rooster. When a violent gust of wind made a tear near the top of the balloon, there were some fears for the safety of the barnyard aeronauts. All, however, survived the eight-minute flight reasonably well. Once it halted in the woods of Vaucresson a few miles beyond the chateau, the sheep was discovered nibbling imperturbably on straw while the cock and the duck cowered in a corner. (p. 123)

In Schama's account, the balloon "wobble[s] its way unsteadily into the sky," but it is unclear whether the wobbling indicates the unsteadiness of the French state or merely the unsteadiness of a new invention. It is also unclear whether the balloon with its "barnyard aeronauts" suggests a picture of France as an airship of fools. Schama's narrative is picturesque without being overtly allegorical.

Carlyle, working more clearly within the allegorical traditions of the Bible and John Bunyan, explicitly links a later manned flight to the fate of France during the Revolution. He sees a moral pattern of great aspiration followed by great destruction in a launching from the Tuileries, whence the scientist J.-A.-C. Charles and a companion rode in the balloon, with Etienne de Montgolfier attending:

Ducks and poultry have been borne skyward: but now shall men be borne. . . . Chemist Charles will himself ascend, from the Tuileries Garden; Montgolfier solemnly cutting the cord. By Heaven, this Charles does also mount, he and another! Ten times ten thousand hearts go palpitating; all tongues are mute with wonder and fear;—till a shout, like the voice of seas, rolls after him, on his wild way. He soars, he dwindles upwards; has become a mere gleaming circlet,—like some Turgotine snuffbox . . . ; like some new daylight Moon! Finally he descends; welcomed by the universe. Duchess Polignac, with a party, is in the Bois de Boulogne, waiting; though it is drizzly winter, the 1st of December 1783. The whole chivalry of France, Duke de Chartres foremost, gallops to receive him.

Beautiful invention; mounting heavenward, so beautifully,—so unguidably! Emblem of much, and of our Age of Hope itself; which shall mount, specifically-light, majestically in this same manner; and hover,—tumbling whither Fate will. Well if it do not, Pilâtre-like, explode; and demount all the more tragically!—So, riding on windbags, will men scale the Empyrean. (FR 1:51)

That the French spectators are the dupes of inflated expectations is suggested early in the passage by Carlyle's hyperbolic rhetoric and by his bathetic comparison of the rising balloon to "some Turgotine snuffbox." With the single phrase "Pilâtre-like," which refers to the death of Pilâtre de Rozier in 1785 in the explosion of his hydrogen balloon, Carlyle undercuts the much-acclaimed achievement of the balloon's inventors. At the same time, he recalls Icarus and other highfliers whose fate might serve as a warning to an overreaching France. In a transformation characteristic of Carlyle, the accidental (Pilâtre's death) becomes the inevitable (the downfall of France). The balloon emblem—and here lies one of the dangers of such a graphic mode of history—offers a single compelling image in the place of a sequential argument. The clipped, measured discourse of the dispassionate historian yields to the powerful incantation of Carlyle's visionary prose.

Later, in adopting Versailles as an emblem of the end of monarchy, Carlyle turns again to a universal moral, and once more prompts us to contrast him with Schama. Schama offers a striking picture of Versailles, abandoned after the insurrection of women in October 1789, when the royal family has been taken away to Paris and to eventual death:

the great palace of Louis XIV was being boarded up. Massive iron locks were placed on its gates to discourage looters, and a few guards stood sentry over silent courtyards. Le Brun's Apollo king still rode his chariot against the upstart Dutch on the ceiling of the empty Hall of Mirrors, but the walls of the marble staircase were pockmarked with shot. Versailles had already become a museum. (p. 470)

Carlyle takes the moral that lies as an implicit possibility in the event and makes it explicit: "the Chateau of Versailles stands ever since vacant, hushed-still; its spacious Courts grassgrown, responsive to the hoe of the weeder. Times and generations roll on, in their confused Gulf-current; and buildings, like builders, have their destiny" (FR I:284). The building becomes an emblem of the builders, and the weeder (an allegorical figure in disguise as a groundskeeper) gently but unmistakably reminds us that all flesh is grass. Literary patterns of Death the Leveler, the fall of princes, and *memento mori* spring to mind.

III

Carlyle is not always so explicit in affixing meanings to events, however, and despite the great popularity and didactic role it achieved in the nineteenth century, *The French Revolution* is not an easy book. While it often speaks of moral order and divine providence, it is rarely a simple Sunday-school apologue on the iniquities of the rich. Carlyle insists on the ability of facts to elude our preexistent notions. Because he feels that the truth of the Revolution lies beyond any partisan allegiance, he forces us to alter our perspective almost from sentence to sentence, forestalling judgment and expanding sympathy. Louis XVI, in many instances the sham king who must inevitably lose power, becomes at other times the loving husband and father, the lamented victim of the Revolution; even the squalid Marat, writes the generally unsympathetic Carlyle, "was wrapped once in swaddling-clothes" and had a sister who "lives still to this day in Paris" (*FR* 3:170). Moreover, Carlyle's oblique way of expressing facts—he suggests, rather than states, and assumes knowledge that the reader cannot reasonably be expected to have—further undermines the notion that our world can be easily known. Finally, despite his constant insistence that we should direct our attention to facts and not fictions, to realities and not words, Carlyle is intensely preoccupied with language, symbols, and the ways in which meanings are enacted through forms. He shares with other writers the sense that the Revolution unsettles the very foundations of perception and symbolic discourse. Conscious modernity of form becomes for Carlyle the textual complement to the quintessential modernity of the event described. Paradoxically, the features of Carlyle's work that would militate against its popular acceptance today—textual self-consciousness, shifting voices, and indeterminacy of genre—have contributed to the recent resurgence of scholarly interest in it.[12]

The complexity of Carlyle's text is embodied in its unstable visual surface, which lends an air of unreality to actual persons and events. While the impetus of his effort to write a factual history is (in a broad sense) "realistic," Carlyle does not provide what we ordinarily expect of realism, the illusion of a continuous world. Rather than offering a solid sense of locality, persons and places are the thinnest of curtains barely concealing the phantasmal realities and elemental powers beneath them. Henry

James quips that Carlyle, despite his constant exhortations to "look at realities and not at imitations, . . . gives us the sense that it is not at things themselves, but straight into this abysmal manner of his own that he is looking."[13] James might intend the word "abysmal" to be pejorative here, but it aptly captures the sense that in Carlyle's scene-painting, objects only thinly cover the abyss. Particularly in mob scenes and scenes of terror, the hard-edged clarity of the emblem gives way to the confused dreams of the phantasmagoria, and caricature gives way to chiaroscuro: the capture of the Bastille, Carlyle exclaims, is a "blaze of triumph on a dark ground of terror" (*FR* 1:197). Individuals become swallowed up by mobs and factions in the process that John D. Rosenberg calls the "eclipse of the self" in Carlyle's history.[14]

This eclipse is particularly evident in Carlyle's portrayal of the September massacres of 1792, when hundreds of prisoners were taken from the prisons and brutally murdered, sometimes without even the pretense of a trial. In Carlyle's treatment of this episode, which provided some of the Revolution's most brutal and sickening images, individual identities become lost in confusion; the pace of the narrative is accelerated, and the narrator himself surrenders his detachment and control:

What phantasms, squalid-horrid, shaking their dirk and muff, may dance through the brain of a Marat, in this dizzy pealing of tocsin-miserere and universal frenzy, seek not to guess, O Reader! Nor what the cruel Billaud 'in his short brown coat' was thinking; nor Sergent . . . ; Nor Panis the confidant of Danton;—nor, in a word, how gloomy Orcus does breed in her gloomy womb, and fashion her monsters and prodigies of Events, which thou seest her visibly bear! Terror is on these streets of Paris; terror and rage, tears and frenzy: tocsin-miserere pealing through the air; fierce desperation rushing to battle; mothers, with streaming eyes and wild hearts, sending forth their sons to die. . . . In such tocsin-miserere, and murky bewilderment of Frenzy, are not Murder, Até and all Furies near at hand? On slight hint—who knows on how slight?—may not Murder come; and, with *her* snaky-sparkling head, illuminate this murk! (*FR* 3:25)

Carlyle has come quite some distance from the balloon emblem, with its symmetrical rhythm of inflation and deflation, to this apocalyptic passage, with its apposition and syntactical fragmentation. In Carlyle's vision of the massacres, personality disintegrates. Identified individuals such as Marat, Sergent, and "the cruel Billaud 'in his short brown coat' " coexist not just with anonymous "mothers" and "sons" but also with the horrific personified abstractions one frequently encounters in revolutionary art: Frenzy, Strife, and Murder in the figure of Medusa.[15]

In portraying cartloads of naked corpses huddled in a grotesque embrace, Carlyle again moves far from the self-assured composure of the univalent emblem, achieving a horrific vision that recalls Goya. Obtrusive hands and feet become grim, half-articulate signs of disfigurement and indictments of the massacres' dehumanizing brutality:

Carts go along the streets; full of stript human corpses, thrown pell-mell; limbs sticking up:—seest thou that cold Hand, sticking up, through the heaped embrace of brother corpses, in its yellow paleness, in its cold rigour; the palm opened towards Heaven, as if in dumb prayer, in expostulation *de profundis*, Take pity on the Sons of Men! (*FR* 3:42)

Dante Gabriel Rossetti remarks of *Wuthering Heights* that it is "laid in Hell,—only it seems places and people have English names there." [16] We might transfer the remark to Carlyle, by noting that *The French Revolution* is frequently set in hell, only there the names are French.

Against the backdrop of anonymity and infernal confusion offered by September 1792, individuals do nevertheless appear, acting out their miniature comedies and tragedies. We have the pathetically humorous plight of a fugitive "Mrs. Le Blanc, a young woman fair to look upon [who], with her young infant, has to live in greenwood, like a beautiful Bessy Bell of Song, her bower thatched with rushes; catching premature rheumatism" (*FR* 3:20). We have the death of the fleeing Duke de la Rochefoucault, killed by a "paving-stone hurled through the coach-window," presented as a kind of impromptu pietà: "He dies lamented of Europe; his blood spattering the cheeks of his old Mother, ninety-three years old" (*FR* 3:44). And for a brief moment we leave the phantasmagoric blur of Paris street scenes to cower with Beaumarchais, the author of *The Marriage of Figaro*, as he attempts to escape arrest. Carlyle narrates the incident with the aid of phrases quoted from Beaumarchais' own account of his flight:

"At midnight . . . the servant, in his shirt," with wide-staring eyes, enters your room:—Monsieur, rise, all the people are come to seek you; they are knocking, like to break-in the door! . . . "I fling on my coat, forgetting even the waistcoat, nothing on my feet but slippers; and say to him"—And *he*, alas, answers mere negatory incoherences, panic interjections. And through the shutters and crevices, in front or rearward, the dull street-lamps disclose only streetfuls of haggard countenances; clamorous, bristling with pikes: and you rush distracted for an outlet, finding none;—and have to take refuge in the crockery-press, down stairs; and stand there, palpitating in that imperfect costume, lights dancing past your keyhole, tramp of feet overhead, and the tumult of Satan, "for four hours and more"! (*FR* 3:17)

In this passage, Carlyle adopts a limited, novelistic point of view to provide an individual perspective on the historical moment.[17] Apart from its ironic transposition of features associated with Beaumarchais' comedies (concealment and the comic servant), the passage allows us to envision what the Revolution means on a personal level, even down to the detail of the forgotten waistcoat, which seems so quaintly out of place in the context of the surrounding chaos. Carlyle abandons the detached voice, which characterized much previous epic writing, and preserves what for him are the more essential features of epic: particularity and multiplicity of experience, the presentation of facts in all their wonder.

Carlyle's perspective is constantly shifting, from the celestial vantage of heaven and universal truth to the confused outlook of the street-level observer who has trouble discerning faces, let alone meanings. Carlyle's shifting perspectives and voices reflect the diverse aims and intentions he brings to his elusive subject. Sometimes he adopts the detached stance of the Bunyanian emblematist or the Swiftian satirist, exhibiting moral patterns and showing the discrepancy between revolutionary aspiration and revolutionary achievement. At other times, he evokes a powerful, mythic view of historical experience that defies easy allegorization. In some instances, he places individuals—laudable or loathsome as they may be—squarely in the center of his pictures. In others, he depicts the Revolution as a process that transcends the agency and even the understanding of individuals. At one moment he will adopt the outlook of an individual or party, then suddenly reconsider an event in the light of an essential humanity that Louis XVI shares with Jean-Paul Marat. Underlying all the various impulses of Carlyle's artistry is a celebration—often in cosmic, impersonal images—of the most definitively human activity, the creation of symbols.

It is this activity that bonds Carlyle to the characters he describes. As a commonplace of recent scholarship has it, the revolutionaries themselves were intensely engaged in the creation and symbolic enactment of their own myth, with their feasts and observances, their oaths and Bastille narratives, their demitasses and toy guillotines. The efforts of Carlyle and other chroniclers like Michelet and Schama to make narrative sense of the Revolution is an extension of (and a commentary on) the revolutionaries' efforts to write their own stories. As a maker of revolutionary symbols, Carlyle acknowledges a distant kinship between himself and the symbol makers of French history, whether they be accomplished artists like "Painter David" or the sansculottic creators of bloody folk emblems.[18] For the French nation in 1789 and the British epicist at the distance of half a century share the problem of converting experience into artifact. By highlighting the act of his history's own creation, by making the reader consciously aware of the composition of his pictures, even by explicitly warning us that his history offers only a "faint ineffectual Emblem" (FR 2:185) of the Revolution, Carlyle suggests that his account is a representation and not the event itself. Carlyle knows that the artifact can easily become detached from the reality that engendered it. But as a leading proponent of epic history in the nineteenth century, he believes that it is only through the imaginative or "picture-making" faculty embodied in the artifact that the experience can be known.

NOTES

1. "Scientific—or at least sociological—history had arrived and with it, the demotion of chronicle to anecdotal unimportance. So, for a long time now, cloaked in the mantle of rigorous objectivity, historians have busied themselves with structure; with cause and effect; with probabilities and contingencies; with pie charts and bar-graphs; with semiotics and anthropologies; with microhistories of *départements*, districts, cantons, villages, hamlets" (Simon Schama, *Citizens: A Chronicle of the French Revolution* [New York: Alfred A. Knopf, 1989], 6).

2. As a form of historical writing common to authors as diverse as Carlyle, Michelet, and Schama, "epic history" must be rather broadly defined as the expansive and serious treatment in narrative form of a crucial episode from history. In the particular context of *The French Revolution*, "epic" further suggests a conscious attempt on Carlyle's part to engage in a kind of dialogue with literary epic— to use, modify, and even travesty its conventions, to rival its themes in importance and scope. The intriguing but thorny issues raised by Carlyle and his use of literary genres are treated at length in my book *A Disimprisoned Epic: Form and Vision in Carlyle's "French Revolution"* (Philadelphia: University of Pennsylvania Press, 1988). For the purposes of the present paper, suffice it to say that Carlyle's use of epic is characteristically experimental and idiosyncratic.

3. Pierre Victor, Baron de Besenval, *Mémoires du Baron de Besenval*, 2 vols. (Paris: 1821), 1:365; translation mine. I discuss Carlyle's treatment of this episode in *A Disimprisoned Epic*, 57–61.

4. Jules Michelet, *History of the French Revolution* (Books I to III), trans. Charles Cocks, ed. Gordon Wright (Chicago: University of Chicago Press, 1967), 166. It is intriguing to think that Michelet's attention might have been drawn to this episode by Carlyle's use of it; Michelet, however, bristled at suggestions that he was substantially influenced by Carlyle. See Alfred Cobban, "Carlyle's *French Revolution*," *History* 48 (1963): 315.

5. Thomas Carlyle, *The French Revolution: A History*, 1:187. The edition cited is volumes 2, 3, and 4 of *The Works of Thomas Carlyle*, Centenary Edition, ed. H. D. Traill, 30 vols. (London: Chapman and Hall, 1896–99). Hereafter cited as FR.

6.   Thou tremblest, and the whiteness in thy cheek
         Is apter than thy tongue to tell thy errand.
         Even such a man, so faint, so spiritless,
         So dull, so dead in look, so woe-begone,
         Drew Priam's curtain in the dead of night,
         And would have told him half his Troy was burnt . . .
The Second Part of King Henry IV, Arden edition, ed. A. R. Humphreys (London: Methuen, 1966), 1.1.68–73.

7.   Before the King *Jove*'s Messenger appears,
            And thus in Whispers greets his trembling Ears.
               Fear not, oh Father! no ill News I bear;
            From *Jove* I come, *Jove* makes thee still his Care:
            For *Hector*'s sake these Walls he bids thee leave,
            And bear what stern *Achilles* may receive.

            . . . .
            Fierce as he is, *Achilles*' self shall spare
            Thy Age, nor touch one venerable Hair.
            . . . .
               She spoke, and vanish'd.

The Iliad, trans. Alexander Pope, ed. Maynard Mack, vols. 7 and 8 of *The Poems of Alexander Pope* (London: Methuen, 1967), 24:207–12, 221–2, 225.

8. The available responses to these questions are various: that the ancient worthy Priam is grand and awe inspiring, unlike the ineffectual modern Besenval; that Priam is a pasteboard fiction while Besenval is, at least, a real person; that despite the incongruity of the comparison, Priam and Besenval are essentially the same because both are reflections of a constant human nature that underlies differences in time and appearance. Which of these responses comes into play in this episode cannot be determined by reading the passage in isolation: many readers who have followed Carlyle throughout his earlier writings and throughout *The French Revolution* will feel that he rules out none of these possible responses, but instead encodes in each analogy his richly charged ambivalences.

9. Carlyle's description of Lafayette "outwatching the Bear" alludes ironically to Milton's "Il Penseroso":
            Or let my Lamp at midnight hour,
            Be seen in some high lonely Tow'r,
            Where I may oft outwatch the *Bear*,
            With thrice great *Hermes*, or unsphere
            The spirit of *Plato* to unfold
            What Worlds, or what vast Regions hold
            The immortal mind that hath forsook
            Her mansion in this fleshly nook . . .   (ll.85–92)

10. Mona Ozouf provides a thorough discussion of this and other festivals in *Festivals and the French Revolution*, trans. Alan Sheridan (Cambridge, Mass.: Harvard University Press, 1988).

11. For a detailed discussion of French ballooning, see Charles Coulston Gillispie's handsomely illustrated volume, *The Montgolfier Brothers and the Invention of Aviation 1783–1784* (Princeton, N.J.: Princeton University Press, 1983).

12. For a fuller citation of scholarly work on *The French Revolution* than I can offer here, see *A Disimprisoned Epic*. Among the most notable literary studies from recent decades are Albert J. LaValley, *Carlyle and the Idea of the Modern: Studies in Carlyle's Prophetic Literature and its Relation to Blake, Nietzsche, Marx, and Others* (New Haven, Conn.: Yale University Press, 1968); Chris R. Vanden Bossche, "Revolution and Authority: The Metaphors of Language and Carlyle's Style," *Prose Studies* 6 (1983): 274–89; John Clubbe, "Carlyle as Epic Historian," *Victorian Literature and Society*, ed. James R. Kincaid and Albert J. Kuhn (Columbus: Ohio State University Press, 1984), 119–145; John D. Rosenberg, *Carlyle and the Burden of History* (Cambridge, Mass.: Harvard University Press, 1985); and Clyde

de L. Ryals, "Carlyle's *The French Revolution*: A 'True Fiction,'" *ELH* 54 (1987): 925–40. The historiographic context of Carlyle's text is provided by Alfred Cobban in the article cited above; Hedva Ben-Israel, *English Historians on the French Revolution* (Cambridge, Cambridge University Press, 1968); Rosemary Jann, *The Art and Science of Victorian History* (Columbus: Ohio State University Press, 1985); and Barton R. Friedman, *Fabricating History: English Writers on the French Revolution* (Princeton, N.J.: Princeton University Press, 1988), 109–144.

13. Henry James, "The Correspondence of Carlyle and Emerson," *Century* 26 (1883): 272.

14. Rosenberg, 98.

15. For a discussion of the Medusa figure and political rhetoric see Neil Hertz's paper "Medusa's Head: Male Hysteria under Political Pressure" and the responses to it by Catherine Gallagher and Joel Fineman in Neil Hertz, *The End of the Line: Essays on Psychoanalysis and the Sublime* (New York: Columbia University Press, 1985), 161–215. See also figures 17 and 18 in this volume.

16. From a letter of 19 September 1854 to William Allingham. Quoted in Miriam Allott, *The Brontës: The Critical Heritage* (London: Routledge and Kegan Paul, 1974), 300.

17. See Cynthia Cox, *The Real Figaro: The Extraordinary Career of Caron de Beaumarchais* (New York: Coward-McCann, 1963), 181–183, for a description of Beaumarchais' flight.

18. For instances of these folk emblems, see *FR* 1:206–207 and 2:260.

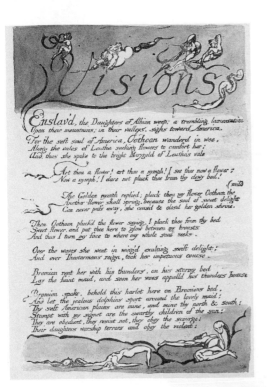

1. William Blake, *Visions of the Daughters of Albion*, plate 1. Yale Center for British Art, Paul Mellon Collection.

2. William Blake, *America: A Prophecy*, plate 5. Yale Center for British Art, Paul Mellon Collection.

3. William Blake, *America: A Prophecy*, plate 6. Yale Center for British Art, Paul Mellon Collection.

4. William Blake, *Europe: A Prophecy*, plate 15. Yale Center for British Art, Paul Mellon Collection.

5. The Sculptures of Notre-Dame, Musée de Cluny, Paris. General View.
Reproduced by permission of the Cliché des Musées Nationaux, Paris.

6. The Sculptures of Notre-Dame, Musée de Cluny, Paris. Fragment. Reproduced by permission of the Cliché des Musées Nationaux, Paris.

7. (Opposite page) Charles-Nicolas Cochin, drawing for the frontispiece of the *Encyclopédie* (1751). Photo Bibliothèque Nationale, Paris.

8. *Now She Will Enlighten All* [*Jam Illustrabit Omnia*] (ca. 1770). Medallion for the Dauphine, Marie-Antoinette. Photo Bibliothèque Nationale, Paris.

9. Jacques-Louis David, *The Lictors Returning to Brutus the Bodies of His Sons* (1788–1789). The Louvre, Paris. Photo Giraudon/Art Resource, New York.

10. *Royalty Overthrown*, or *The Aristocracy's Nightmare*. Musée Carnavalet, Paris. Photo Bulloz.

11. *Without you I was about to die.* Musée Carnavalet, Paris. Photo Bulloz.

12. *Dying Aristocracy.* Photo Bibliothèque Nationale, Paris.

13. *Liberty Handing the Scarf of Municipal Office to Péthion.* From Camille Desmoulins, *Révolution de France et de Brabant,* 10 (1791), No. 103. Photo University of North Carolina.

14. J.-B. Lucien and Paucquet. *Aristocracy and its Agents Buried under the Ruins of the Bastille*, engraving of a sculpture by Jean-Guillaume Moitte. Photo Bibliothèque Nationale, Paris.

15. *To Versailles, to Versailles: October 5, 1789.* Musée Carnavalet, Paris. Photo Bulloz.

16. (Opposite page) *Aristocratic Lady Cursing the Revolution.* Musée Carnavalet, Paris. Photo Bulloz.

Dame Aristocrate maudissant la Révolution.

Within the image:
- *Discour du Roi le 4 Fevr 1790, et sa Proclamation de 28 Mai.*
- *Protestation du Chapitre de Notre-Dame*
- *Le fanatisme armé d'un Crucifix amene la discorde en France, mais le génie de ce Royaume découvre leur manœuvres et les menace de son glaive.*

17. *Conduct of the Clergy in 1790.* Musée Carnavalet, Paris. Photo Bulloz.

18. *The Republic.* Musée
Carnavalet, Paris. Photo Bulloz.

19. *The Fountain of
Regeneration—on the
Ruins of the Bastille,
August 10, 1793.* Photo
Bibliothèque Nationale, Paris.

20. Dupré, *Hercules,
Hathor, Liberty, Equality.*
Musée Carnavalet, Paris. Photo Réunion
des Musées Nationaux.

21. *Republican France
Offering Her Breast to All
Frenchmen.* Musée Carnavalet,
Paris. Photo Bulloz.

22. (Opposite page) *Yet
Onward We Press.* Musée
Carnavalet, Paris. Photo Bulloz.

23. J. Chinard, *Apollo Crushing Superstition Underfoot*. Sculpture. Musée Carnavalet, Paris. Photo Bulloz.

24. Boizot, *Peace Led by Victory*. Biscuit de Sèvres.
Musée National de Céramique, Sèvres.
Photo Réunion des Musées Nationaux.

PART TWO

Crossing the Channel

*

Revolutionary France in

French Mirrors

Michelet and the French Revolution

LIONEL GOSSMAN

Il me faut un Dieu pour le coeur, pour l'esprit, pour la cité, le sacrifice.
—Jules Michelet, *Cours du Collège de France*, 1849.

If we attempt to force and "invent" a monumental style in art, such miserable monstrosities are produced as the many monuments of the last twenty years. If one tries intellectually to construct new religions without a new and genuine prophecy, then, in an inner sense, something similar will result, but with still worse effects.
—Max Weber, *Science as Vocation*

Like the Revolution as he recounted it, Michelet's *History of the French Revolution* was a brief interval of light in an otherwise dismal time. The preface was written in the declining years of the July Monarchy, the conclusion of the bleak aftermath of the Revolution of 1848. The book itself opens and closes on images of dereliction. The Revolution, we are told in the Preface, is embodied in no physical monument or institution; it has left nothing comparable to the cathedrals of the Middle Ages or the secular palaces of the *ancien régime*. It survives only as what it always was, according to Michelet, a pure spirit; its sole monument—fittingly— is an empty space, the champ de Mars, "that sandy piece of ground as flat as Arabia," site of the great Fête de la Fédération. But an unworthy and forgetful generation has allowed that temple of the Revolutionary spirit to be desecrated by the Revolution's enemies. English horses now "gallop insolently" across the Champ de Mars, which has been turned into a fashionable racecourse.[1]

The dismal tone of the conclusion is anticipated by a bitter anecdote, at the end of the last chapter of the last book, about a child of ten—a child of the Revolution—who, on being taken to the theater after the death of Robespierre, hears for the first time, as the audience leaves at the end of the performance, words till then completely foreign to his young ears—"Faut-il une voiture, *mon maître?*" ("Will you need a carriage, master?"). The central image of the conclusion itself is a cemetery: Monceau, the burial-place of Danton, Robespierre, Saint-Just. Again, the historian laments the desecration of a hallowed site and the betrayal of a sacred memory. A common dancing spot draws crowds where once the revolutionary heroes were laid to rest. "Gay and careless," the historian observes, "France dances on her dead" (*HR*, 2:993)

Whether we consider the book itself or the event it narrates, the *History of the Revolution* emerges from drabness and emptiness and peters out again in drabness and disillusionment. The Revolution, it seems, is always an interlude, a flash of illumination in the dreary round of indifference and routine, a momentary penetration of matter by spirit, in the terms Michelet himself liked to use. In both preface and conclusion, however, the gap between present nothingness and absent being is bridged by an ardent profession of faith.

The desecrated champ de Mars remains the dwelling place of a God ("ici réside un Dieu"), and a "mighty breath still blows across it, such as you will feel nowhere else, a soul, an all-powerful spirit." Appropriately, the historian's profession of faith is couched in the form of a biblical parallelism: "And though that plain be arid, and though that grass be withered, it will be green again one day."[2] The end of the book reiterates this message of hope and confidence in the ultimate triumph of spirit. In the pages of his history, Michelet writes, the men of the Revolution "will be resuscitated and will retain through all future time the life that history owes them in return for the life they heroically gave up" (*HR*, 2:996).

Though he was not raised as a Christian, Michelet had been deeply affected in late adolescence by the *Imitatio Christi* of Thomas à Kempis.[3] Later, as a young professor, he was drawn to philosophies of history deriving in some measure from Christianity. (His career would not have started so well if he had not had the reputation of being moderately *bien pensant*). Victor Cousin's watered-down version of Hegelianism left a considerable mark on him, and it was also through Cousin that he was led to study and translate Vico, whom he interpreted in a strongly liberal and progressivist, but still spiritualist light. In the enthusiasm of the July Revolution of 1830 ("sur les pavés brûlants de juillet"), he produced an intoxicating thirty-page *Introduction to Universal History*, in which the culmination of all human history was seen to have been reached in Paris in the year 1830. As an interpretation of history, this apparently secular work is every bit as figural as Christian exegesis traditionally had been in its interpretation of Old Testament history.

Greece, which—as Michelet puts it—translated and rationalized the native, mute wisdom of the East, and Rome, which translated and universalized what would otherwise have remained the particular possession of a hundred petty Greek city-states, appear in the *Introduction to Universal History* as figures of France, which in turn gathers up the cultures of the various European peoples—the nominalism and individualism of the English, the realism of the Italians, and the enthusiastic, totalizing, but all confusing pantheism of the Germans—relieves each of its onesidedness, and translates them all together into a world doctrine. France speaks the *logos* or *verbe* of Europe, as Greece is said to have once spoken that of the Orient.[4] "France speaks what the world thinks," we read again later in the *History of the Revolution* (*HR*, 1:70). If Greece and Rome are figures of France, France itself is a figure of Paris, which gathers up, fuses, and raises to a "higher level" the experience, wisdom, and language of all the provinces of France, from the granitic poetic symbolism of the brooding Celts of Brittany to the winy rhetoric of Burgundy and the sparkling, flinty prose of Champagne.[5] Michelet's worldview is based on universal analogy, on the "harmonies," as he put it (*HR*, 1:9), among all the fragments of a whole, whose basic patterns are inscribed in each of its parts. As one might expect from such a world view, which is both the strength and the weakness of Michelet as an historian, these processes of historical life are also said to characterize the life of natural organisms as well as the life of the individual mind. As France speaks for all of Europe and Paris for all of France, Michelet himself, as a historian and a son of Paris, claims to speak for "all those who have no history," that is to say, for all those whose voices were never heard by the writers of official history—women, the poor, the defeated and humiliated—and ultimately, in his natural histories, animals and even rocks.[6] It ought not, after all, to come as a surprise that for the future historian of the Revolution, in 1833, "Christ is still on the Cross. . . . The Passion endures and will endure for all time. The world has its Passion, as does humanity in its long historical march, and each individual heart during the brief span in which it is given to beat. To each his cross and his stigmata."[7]

The man who wrote those words cannot be assumed to have chosen the terms of his famous definition of history casually: *résurrection de la vie intégrale* (resurrection of life in its totality). History was Michelet's religion, the Revolution was its Revelation, and his own *History of the Revolution* was intended as nothing less than the gospel of a new religion of humanity, through which alienation would be overcome, the dead resurrected to eternal life, and man at last set free by the searing, liberating truth that the god he worships is himself.[8] The *History of the French Revolution* was from the beginning a *sacred* history—the story of the Passion of the Christ-people, through whose sacrifice humanity was to be redeemed—and it aimed to inspire its readers and promote an *imitatio*, an identification and dedication equivalent to those inspired by the Gospels. Michelet quotes with satisfaction a remark by the popular poet Beranger, who is supposed to have said of the *Histoire de la Révolution*: "For me it is a holy book" (*HR*, 1:15); and he invariably presents himself as the evangelist of a new faith.[9] "I am endeavouring to describe today," he wrote in the 1847 Preface, "that epoch of unanimity, that holy period, when a whole nation, free from all party distinction, as yet a comparative stranger to the opposition of classes, marched as one beneath the banner of brotherly love. Nobody can behold that marvellous unanimity, in which the self-same heart beat in the breasts of twenty millions of men, without returning thanks to God. These are the sacred days of the world" (*HR*, 1:8). If they were to come again, however, the original spirit of the Revolution had to be revived; and to achieve that was the stated purpose of Michelet's history. "May the sublime vision we had [of the new God] . . . raise us all, author and readers alike, above the moral misery of the times and restore to us a spark of the heroic fire that consumed the hearts of our fathers" (*HR*, 1:608–609).

The *sacred* character of the Revolution is a constant theme of the *History*. The unanimity, generosity, and childlike faith of those who brought it about, we are told, are signs of its *divine*, providential nature.[10] Michelet not only makes ample use of biblical language and imagery, he frequently suggests analogies to the Gospels. The hundred thousand armed peasants of the Vivarais, who set out from their homes in the midst of winter in a spontaneous gesture of fraternity at the time of the first federations, recall those who almost two millennia earlier had heard the "bonne nouvelle" of the birth of Christ. "A new breath of life was in the air, which inspired them with a glow of enthusiasm; citizens for the first time, and summoned from their remote snowy regions by the unknown name of liberty, they set forth, like the kings and shepherds of the East at the birth of Christ, seeing clearly in the middle of the night, and following unerringly, through the wintry mists, the dawn of spring, and the star of France" (*HR*, 1:328). France herself, like Christ, brings to the nations, we are told, not peace but a sword; by that sword, however, as by the message of Christ—"tellement Dieu était en la France"—they are not harmed but healed, not enslaved but liberated, reawakened to new life (*HR*, 1:1225). "La France," he had proclaimed in his lectures at the Collège de France in 1846, "La France est le sauveur" ("France is the redeemer").[11]

The words *miracle* and *miraculous, prodigy* and *prodigious* are never absent for long from Michelet's text. The taking of the Bastille—"le grand coup de la Providence"—is of course a "miracle" and is fittingly recounted in deliberately biblical language. "A voice was heard in every heart: Go forth and ye shall take the Bastille" (*HR*, 1:146, 141, 145). The use of the past historic tense—the effect of which is difficult to render into English—underlines the miraculous immediacy of thought and action. On the morning of 14 July, "one idea dawned upon Paris, . . . and all were suddenly illuminated with the same light." ("Une idée se leva sur Paris . . . et tous virent la même lumière.") Despite the practical difficulties, "All immediately had faith" in the call to attack the Bastille ("Tous crurent"), "and it was done forthwith" ("Et cela se fit"). The whole affair, in short, was "completely unreasonable. It was an act of faith." There was no preparation, no proposal, no plan. "No one proposed. But every one believed, and every one acted" (*HR*, 1:145).

Later, evoking the universal feeling of fraternity created by the federations, Michelet asks the rhetorical question, "Is it a miracle?" The answer is of course a resounding affirmative: "Yes, the grandest and the most simple" (*HR*, 1:404). In particular, the twelve months from the taking of the Bastille to the Fête de la Fédération are a "miraculous year extending from July to July" (*HR*, 1:396)—always, as we shall see, a magical month for Michelet; July 1789 announced July 1790 *and* July 1830. Obstacles disappear as if by magic, whether it be the rain which abruptly lets up, allowing a momentary illumination of the sodden Champ de Mars on that famous 14 July 1790, or the obstacles to fraternity itself: "At length the shades of night disappear, the mist is dispelled, and France beholds distinctly what she had loved and followed, without ever having been able to grasp it—the unity of the native land. . . . Every obstacle vanishes and all opposition is removed" (*HR*, 1:403). The unmediated nature of events is always the most effective marker of their miraculous and mythic character: "France," we are told, "was born and rose to her feet to the sound of the canon of the Bastille. In a single day, with no preparation" (*HR*, 1:397). Not surprisingly, the historian asserts that "it is impossible to assign a specific cause to those great spontaneous events" (*HR*, 1:326). "Those millions, who were serfs yesterday and who today are men and citizens, who have been summoned up suddenly in a single day from death to life, these newborn of the Revolution . . . what were they? A miracle. Born around April 1789, already men by the 14th July, they rose fully armed from the furrow . . ." (*HR*, 1:428).

The contrast with Tocqueville, which underlies François Furet's argument in his recent but already classic *Penser la Révolution française* (1978), is nowhere more glaring than in Michelet's insistence on the abruptness of the change signified and accomplished by the Revolution. Michelet represents the Revolution as nothing less than an irruption of a different temporality into the time of profane history. The Revolution does not belong to ordinary history; it occurs in a time out of time, the sacred time of origins. On the day of the Fête de la Fédération, we are advised, "Everything was possible. Every division had vanished. There was neither nobility nor bourgeoisie nor people. The future was present. That is to say: time was no more: a lightning flash and eternity" (*HR*, 1:430). "Time is abolished," the narrator had already pronounced several chapters earlier; "space is abolished: those two material conditions to which life is subject have ceased to be. A strange *vita nuova* is now beginning for France, an eminently spiritual one, which makes her entire Revolution into a kind of dream. That new life knows neither time nor space" (*HR*, 1:406). The Revolution, in short, is more than a political, social, or economic change for Michelet. It is a veritable rebirth, the beginning of a *vita nuova*, as he so often liked to say, an intimation of universal redemption. It is not for nothing that the revolutionary people is described as fundamentally innocent, "bonne enfant" (*HR*, I, 142, 181–82, 225–26, 276, 400), the new France as a newborn child. A miracle occurred, Michelet tells us at the Fête de la Fédération, that first celebration of 14 July, which drew thousands from all over France to the champ de Mars: "From that sublime moment, from so many pure and sincere desires, from so many mingled tears . . . a God was [about to be] born" (*HR*, 1:428)—France, the Christ child of the nations, ready to sacrifice herself on the altar of history for the redemption of mankind.[12]

The end of the *ancien régime* thus "by no means" signals "death, but on the contrary, birth, the coming renewal." "It sent a tremor through the whole world," we are told (*HR*, 1:9, 11). Kosciusko in Poland, Tom Paine in England, and Beethoven and old Klopstock in Germany wept for joy, and—a miracle in its own way—Kant in far-off Konigsberg changed the direction of his daily walk. Images of renewal had often marked the traditional *entrées solennelles* of newly crowned kings into their capitals. But the renewal Michelet expects is not to be thought of as a late, pale copy of Christ's entry into Jerusalem. The Revolution is portrayed as a radical new beginning (*HR*, 1:77, 79), a new and higher Revelation. "Did France exist before that time? It might be disputed" (*HR*, 1:200). "An entire people emerged at one blow from nonentity to existence" (*HR*, 1:77, 78). If the day the Bastille fell was a day of deliverance—"o beau jour, premier jour de la délivrance" (*HR*, 1:203)—Michelet made sure to use a term that in French also signifies the bringing forth or delivery of a child. (The accepted translation, "First day of *liberty*," misses the point.) The opening of the Estates General was a time if ever there was one, he tells us, to sing a prophetic hymn: "Thou wilt create peoples, and the face of the earth shall be renewed," for on that great day, "the first of an immense future," "a mighty thing began" (*HR*, 1:88). Like an infant pushing its way out of the womb, France emerged from the tomb of the *ancien régime* to a prodigious *vita nuova:* "The resurrection of the people which at long last breaks open its tomb" inaugurates a new era, accomplishing "the labor of ages in a single night." And that, writes Michelet is "the first miracle—the divine and authentic miracle—of the new Gospel" (*HR*, 1:217).

As in many myths, and as one might expect from the historian of universal "harmonies," the rebirth of the hero marks a new season of fertility: "In the midst of the federations, there was a proliferation of the natural federation, marriage. In that glorious year of hope, the number of marriages increased by a fifth—something unheard of before" (*HR*, 1:428). For the same reasons, no doubt, the philosopher Condorcet, at the age of forty-nine, "se retrouvait jeune . . . commençait une vie nouvelle" ("rediscovered his youthful vigor and began a new life"). The only child of his many years of marriage to the "noble et virginale" Madame Condorcet "was born nine months after the taking of the Bastille, in April 1790" (*HR*, 1:656). The miracle of nature—conception and creation through the self-transcendence of male and female—and the miracle of history—the French Revolution—are of a kind. "Rare instant in which a world can come to birth! . . . Who will undertake to explain the profound mystery of the birth of a new man, a new people, a new God. Who will explain conception! that unique, rapid and terrible instant!" (*HR*, 1:429)

As Michelet presents it, then, the French Revolution is not what it became in Tocqueville's ironical vision—a prosaic phenomenon, whose underlying causes and significance have to be understood by the detached scientific analyst and were not necessarily accessible to those who acted in it and who, in their blindness, may have promoted what they thought they were undoing. The truth of the Revolution, for Michelet, is no less hidden from view than it was for Tocqueville. But it lies precisely, as we shall see, in the consciousness of Tocqueville's ignorant actors, and it is to that consciousness that the historian, according to Michelet, must find his way back. The deepest reality of the Revolution is a "spiritual" one; it is an experience, an idea, a project, a "prodigious dream" (*HR*, 1:414)— not simply the working out of subterranean historical forces. It is not at all surprising, given their different points of view, that Tocqueville's *The Ancien Régime and the Revolution* shows at length how two centuries of the old regime gave birth to modern France and tells nothing, virtually, of the Revolution itself, whereas Michelet's *History* highlights the Revolutionary moment and largely ignores the process of gestation that preceded it. Belonging to a special time, a sacred time, a time of renewal, the Revolution—for Michelet—is fundamentally different from and impervious to the profane history that preceded and followed it. As the living spirit of France, it is, as Michelet declares in the 1847 Preface, like the Kingdom of God for the Christian, "within us" (*HR*, 1:1).

It needs to be emphasized, however, that Michelet rejected every attempt to present the Revolution as "a necessary outcome of Christian ideas," in the words of his friend Alphonse Esquiros.[13] A good deal of his polemic against Christianity, not only in his histories but in his popular writings on love, women, the Jesuits, and so on, was without doubt directed at the so-called Christian socialists of his time, to whom Christ had been the first and greatest of the *sans-culottes*. But his enemy was not, I think, religion, or a religious understanding of history or the Revolution. On the contrary, it was the attempt to deny the religion of the Revolution by absorbing it back into Christianity. As the prophet of an up-to-date, modernized religion, the religion of France and of the Revolution, Michelet was as intolerant of the earlier, rival religion as Christians had often been of the religion of the Jews. Between the old, alienated religion of Jews and Christians alike, in which man worships a transcendent God, and the new immanent religion, in which Frenchmen worship themselves in the form of France, there could be no compromise, he maintained. Both vied for the same territory. "I . . . see only two great facts, two principles, two actors, two characters on the stage: Christianity and the Revolution" (*HR*, 1:21).

The *History of the Revolution* marks Michelet's farewell to his own optimistic belief, which had reached its zenith in the enthusiasm of the July Revolution of 1830 and the *Introduction to Universal History*, that the whole history of mankind, from the civilizations of the ancient world through the Middle Ages down to the great monarchical states of the seventeenth century and the Revolution, was about to be gradually and, as it were, effortlessly, fulfilled. The ferocious suppression of workers' protest movements in Paris and Lyons in the early 1830s quickly cooled the enthusiasm with which Michelet had at first greeted the regime of Louis Philippe, and in later years he recalled with bitterness the "loss of high hopes," the "moral cholera" that—like a spiritual reality of which the medical epidemic sweeping through Paris at the time was the physical sign or figure—"followed so soon after July." [14]

By the mid-1840s Michelet's disenchantment with the bourgeois monarchy was so great that he decided to interrupt his *History of France*, which told the story of a progressive movement toward social and national union, and embark on the *History of the Revolution*, the message of which is that true union can be achieved only through a prior transgression, a sacred act of violence and rupture, such as the storming of the Bastille.

The old must be repudiated, he now argued, the old idols expelled from the temple of the new faith. Christianity and monarchy were finished (*HR,* 1:219). The Revolution was neither, as some have claimed, "the fulfillment of the Christian promise" (*HR,* 1:24) nor, as others would have it, its mere negation or reverse image. "The Revolution goes beyond Christianity and contradicts it. It is at once Christianity's heir and its adversary" (*HR,* 1:25). In other words, the religion of the Revolution was destined to supersede Christianity in the same way that Michelet and many of his contemporaries believed Christianity, as a young religion of faith and spontaneity, had once superseded its mother Judaism, allegedly grown old, sterile, and legalistic.

Echoing the opinions of contemporaries or near-contemporaries, like Constant and Feuerbach, Michelet held that Christianity was already a spent force by the end of the eighteenth century. The Jansenists, he claimed, had been the last authentic Christians. Like Nietzsche's friend Franz Overbeck some three decades later, Michelet deeply admired these obstinately faithful survivors of the old religion, who refused to compromise their faith even for the sake of its historical or worldly survival, but he had no doubt that their time had passed. "I . . . seek my faith elsewhere," he declared (*HR,* 1:384). The Revolution was the new world faith, the new Church—"la grande Eglise" (*HR,* 1:20)—at long last the true Church universal. Judaism had been the religion of a single people; Christianity, though it promised universality, in fact left many, the majority, outside— all the graceless and wretched of the earth. But "we who, by its monopoly, are deprived of temple and altar . . . we had a temple on that day [the day of the Fête de la Fédération]—such a temple as no one had ever had before" (*HR,* 1:412).[15] If Michelet completely rejected every attempt to represent the Revolution as the realization of Christianity, that was, in his own words, "because [the Revolution] was itself a Church." And one that was truly superior to all those that had preceded it. "As agape and communion, nothing in this world was ever comparable to 1790, to the spontaneous impulse of the Federations" (*HR,* 1:609; 1:12). Michelet could even claim that the difference between the Revolution and the Counterrevolution was that the latter, though posing as the champion of religion, was not a religion, whereas the Revolution was (*HR,* 1:394).

As a church, a communion, the Revolution stands for unity, not only the breaking down of all barriers to communication and exchange, but the transcendence of difference, the unanimity of wills in brotherly love: "No more classes, only Frenchmen; no more provinces, a single France" (*HR,* 1:327). In the famous "Tableau de la France" at the beginning of Book III of his *History of France,* Michelet had described the gathering

up of all the various provinces of France, beginning with the most primitive and "poetic," into a final unity to which all contributed but in which
all were "fulfilled" and relieved of their exclusiveness and particularity.
The movement—in space, in time, and in the historian's own narrative—
had the characteristic Romantic form of a spiral, the figure of progress
toward unity. For what chiefly attracted Michelet, it appears, was not
the condition of unity, not a featureless identity, but the *experience* of
union, the realization of continuity with others and with the universe as
a whole. In other words, it is the transgressive act of overcoming separation that is Michelet's ideal, the "spasmodic" moment, in Georges Poulet's
apt formulation.[16] Michelet's politics, one might say, is an erotic politics.
His unflagging criticism of the Jacobins' efforts to *impose* permanent and
absolute uniformity and of their willingness to sacrifice the living present
to an ideal condition in the future [17]—in short, his rejection of their austere
emphasis on abstract morality—is entirely consistent with his longing for
a spontaneous, creative union of wills; so, too, is his rejection of a liberal
parliamentarianism founded on the pessimistic premise that division and
disagreement are a permanent condition.

Innumerable passages from Michelet's work, nearly all of them colored
by his characteristic erotic symbolism, could be brought forward to illustrate his longing for a miraculous synthesis of the particular and the universal, the individual and the communal, the moment and eternity. "One
France, one faith, one oath," he demanded (*HR*, 1:395), and that seemed
to him to be also the aspiration of all nature. The entire universe and every
individual in it, according to Michelet, yearns to overcome division and
recover "unity," or rather, continuity. "'Ah! if I were *one*,' says the world;
'if I could at length unite my scattered members, and bring my nations
together!' 'Ah! if I were *one*,' says Man; 'if I could cease to be the complex
being that I am, rally my divided powers, and establish concord within
myself!' In that fugitive hour a nation seemed to be realizing that ever
unfulfilled desire both of the world and of the human soul, seemed to be
playing the divine comedy of concord and union which we never behold
but in our dreams" (*HR*, 1:416). The reader is reminded here of the curious comment some ten pages earlier that the Revolution was "une sorte
de rêve"—"a kind of dream" (*HR*, 1:406).

Reality, especially historical reality, seems curiously destructive of this
dream. Michelet's Julys, like all epiphanies, wither and fade in the winter
of history. "How many centuries have passed since the Federation of July?"
he exclaims (*HR*, 1:471). Time and again, he emphasizes the brevity of
the Revolution's supreme moment of union and brotherhood—always the
Fête de la Fédération, the pure and spontaneous expression of the national

spirit, uncontaminated by any partisan "political" design. "Oh! who would not be touched by the remembrance of that incomparable moment, when we started into life? It was short-lived, but it remains for us the ideal we shall ever strive toward, the hope of the future! O sublime Concord, in which the nascent liberties of the classes, subsequently in opposition, embraced so tenderly like brothers in the cradle,—shall we never more see thee return upon our earth?" The participants themselves sensed it, Michelet notes. One of them closes his account of the unforgettable day with the comment: "Thus passed away the most beautiful moment of our lives" (*HR,* 1:409).

At various points, the historian reflects whether such a fall from grace might not be inevitable, whether the perfection of that moment of time could be sustained. "That day, everything was possible . . . ," he wrote triumphantly of 14 July 1790. "Nothing, it seems, prevented the realization of the social and religious age of the Revolution, which we see presently receding constantly before us" (*HR,* 1:430). A new day might have dawned, in other words, on which the light would never go out, an eternal July, that Joachimite "troisième âge du monde" of whose advent Michelet wrote with burning desire.[18] But it did not, and the historian asks himself the obvious question: "Can such a condition endure?" (*HR,* 1:430). Is the moment of perfection not always also the moment of decline? Is there not, in other words, a radical discontinuity between sacred and profane time, between the time of origins and ends, and the time of maturation? "The time of waiting, striving, longing, during which all dreamed and labored to realize this day, is over! . . . It is here. . . . Whence these feelings of anxiety? Alas, experience teaches us the sad fact, strange to relate and yet true, that unity brings a diminution of union. In the will to unite there was already the union of hearts, perhaps the best kind of unity" (*HR,* 1:423). The essence of the Revolution, as Michelet presents it to us, turns out to be something that cannot be sustained in history. Not only could the initial unanimity of the Revolution not be sustained, the very effort to preserve it contributed to its undoing. "If it is not to will its own destruction, the Revolution cannot linger in the age of innocence" (*HR,* 1:426). Spontaneity ceases and the era of Jacobinism begins. The Revolution is destroyed, however, by the practical effort to save it. "Who slew the Republic? Its government. The form obliterated the content" (*HR,* 2:794),[19]—rather as, according to a certain tradition of Christian thought, the Church and theology destroyed Christianity.

What is at issue here is Michelet's attitude to history and the historical. Surprisingly, the Romantic historian's relation to history seems to be no less ambivalent than that of his Enlightenment predecessors. In a striking

passage, curiously reminiscent of the eighteenth century, Michelet declares
that history is mostly the description of error and evil—"the register of the
crimes, follies and misfortunes of mankind," as Gibbon had put it—except that in Michelet's more dynamic, teleological vision, "follies" become
"obstacles" and the ideal is not a community of "philosophes" or reasonable men, but a condition of brotherhood, a union of consciousnesses. Just
as the obstacles that delay the accomplishment of a quest are the condition
of narrative (without them there would be nothing to tell), the obstacles
that prevent the full realization of human brotherhood—the end of history
and the goal of the Revolution—are the condition of history for Michelet. Without them, time would collapse into a single instant and the final
Parousia would have come. As a historian, therefore, Michelet is bound
to be chiefly concerned with the obstacles that prevented the Revolution
from achieving its promise. At the same time, he constantly denounces this
ordinary history, the indispensable material of his narrative, as *néant*, a
non-thing, while its transcendence is said to be "true history":

I have related fully the resistance offered by the old principle,—the *parlements,*
the nobility, and the clergy; I am now going to introduce, in a few words, the
new principle, and to expound briefly the immense fact in which all those various
movements of resistance were absorbed and annihilated, the admirably simple . . .
fact of the spontaneous organization of France. That is history, the real, the positive, and the durable; and the rest is nothingness. It was, however, necessary to tell
at great length the story of that nothingness. Precisely because it is nothing but an
exception, an irregularity, Evil requires a minute narration of particulars in order
to be understood. The Good, in contrast, the natural, which flows forth evenly and
of its own accord, is almost known to us beforehand in virtue of . . . the eternal
image of the good which we carry within us. (*HR,* 1: 395–396)

As many readers of Michelet have remarked, from Georges Poulet to
Roland Barthes, his history—be it the history of France or the history of the
Revolution—is a long and weary road punctuated by moments of brilliant
illumination. "The narrative," Barthes observed, "is calvary; the vision is
glory."[20] Michelet himself describes the task of realizing the Revolution as
"Sisyphean" (*HR,* 2: 986).

One begins to see what it was that drew Michelet to the Jansenists—
and made him hate and scorn the Jesuits. If the Revolution is a religion,
like Christianity, if it is destined to replace Christianity as a truly universal religion, as Michelet everywhere suggests, does it then suffer from the
same fatal defect that some nineteenth-century historians and theologians
attributed to Christianity, namely the inability to subsist in time, in history, in the world, without compromising itself beyond repair? "Can such
a condition endure?" According to Nietzsche's friend, Franz Overbeck,

Christianity was a world-denying religion; its earliest adherents expected the imminent end of the world. Worldly success, historical success, had no meaning for them, since as far as they were concerned there would be no worldly future. The time of revelation did not belong to historical time, it was outside of time, a turning point opening onto eternity, "un éclair et l'éternité," in Michelet's words (*HR,* 1:430). The fact that the end of the world did not take place presented Christians with an acute problem. They could continue to live and believe as though the world was about to end, and to prepare themselves for that moment, but that meant renouncing historical and worldly existence and living on its fringes. Or they could become politicians, adroitly maneuvering among the forces of history so as to ensure their historical survival as a Church, and theologians, rationalizing their faith and adapting it to a world that continued obstinately to exist— in other words, consent to the transformation of a world-denying eschatological belief into a theology and of a simple community into an institution that was itself a considerable worldly and historical power. Overbeck admired the Jansenists because, as he understood them, they refused those compromises with the world that the Jesuits eagerly embraced; refused to give up purity of principle for the base brokerage of politics; and remained essentially indifferent to worldly success and historical survival, faithful to the original doctrine of Christ.[21]

Michelet admires the Jansenists for similar reasons. The proof that they are the true modern Christians, persecuted as they are by the Church, lies in their very refusal of modernity, their unworldliness, the way they bear witness not stridently and publicly in the manner of Molière's Alceste, whose criticism of the world only confirms his intense participation in it, but "in concealment and resignation, dying off in silence and without revolt" (*HR,* 1:384–385). Michelet is fascinated both by the Jansenists' stubborn, undeviating loyalty to what they construe as the pure and original Christian message, and by their vigorous eschatology. "I have been unable to behold without the deepest emotion those men of another age noiselessly becoming extinct," he writes, yet never wavering in their faith that "the great and last day when both men and doctrines will be judged, cannot be far off; the day when the world will begin to live and cease to die" (*HR,* 1:384–385).

As an advocate of secularism and progress, Michelet had to believe that his own religion of brotherhood and equality would ultimately be vindicated by the realization of liberty, equality, and fraternity in the world— that is, by the redemption of the original totality of nature in the world. Nevertheless, there is evidence that he was troubled more often than his reputation as the prophet of the Revolution would lead one to expect by

the thought that it might be the same with the Revolution and his entire
view of history as it was with Christianity, that they too might be a "prodigious dream" to which no mundane reality can ever correspond. There
were times of terrible doubt, when the possibility of regression and illusion—a persistent nightmare in all his writings from the 1830s down to
the natural history books of the 1850s and 1860s, but increasingly frequent
after 1848—overwhelmed his faith in the order of nature and the meaning
and direction of history; the future spiritual transcendence and fulfillment
of individuality in fraternal union sometimes appeared to him in the disturbingly similar form of what he conceived as its opposite, that is to say,
a regressive retreat from individual identity—which Michelet saw as the
painfully won, but still incomplete, achievement of history and civilization, and as essentially masculine—back to the original, material (and, in
his imagination, feminine) continuity of nature. As early as the *Tableau de
la France* (early 1830s) he had admitted to a feeling of uneasiness at the
pantheistic tendencies of the German Romantic philosophies to which he
himself was strongly attracted. "There is an all-powerful lotos flower there
that makes one forget one's fatherland." [22]

Michelet wavered all his life between confidence that a spiritual power
informs the material substance of nature, rendering it orderly and intelligible despite its sometimes cruel or chaotic appearances and guaranteeing
its progressive redemption from its own materiality, and a nightmarish
fear that the reality of nature is nothing but the endless cycle of birth and
death, and that nothing "makes sense." It is in the later natural history
writings (*The Bird, The Insect, The Sea, The Mountain*)—because they are
so patently at odds with modern scientific modes of thought and inquiry,
so transparently projections of his own imagination—that this ambivalence strikes the reader most forcibly, but it is present in all Michelet's
historical work as well, from the *Roman History* and the *Introduction to
Universal History* on.

On the one hand, he salutes the Promethean triumphs of nineteenth-
century science. By discovering the laws of the winds and the ocean cur-
rents, he announces, the heroes of modern science have tamed the tempests
and mapped the mysterious ocean depths, the home of "the man-eaters, the
monsters, the leviathan, the kraken, and the great sea-serpent." [23] (Incidentally, Michelet followed with at least equal intensity the efforts of physio-
logical research to penetrate the secrets of what was for him the most
mysterious ocean of all, the female body.) The investigations of pioneers
like Maury and Romme have demonstrated, he proclaims, that "What had
been thought of as caprice could be reduced to law." [24] On the other hand,
however, Michelet's writing is punctuated by moments when this intelli-

gible nature, seemingly obedient to law, suddenly uncovers or reverts to its dreaded, undecipherable underside—the seductive, incestuous Circe, the lawless, unredeemable female beneath the gentle, suckling mother. And as the *mère* (good, redeemable nature) turns into a *marâtre* (chaotic and cruel nature), so the patently masculine *peuple*, the hero of the Revolution, takes on the terrifying aspect of a raging, shapeless, and patently female populace—no longer men, as Michelet puts it himself, but "howling dogs, a million, hundreds of millions of relentless, . . . raging hounds. . . . Not even that. Hideous and nameless apparitions, beasts without eyes or ears, nothing but foaming jaws."[25] Everywhere, as he probes beyond the boundaries of the familiar and everyday, the investigator discovers forces that are destructive of order, thought, and sanity itself—an irrational, often orgiastic, and dangerously alluring subterranean continuity. In the virgin forest the precarious and hard-won identity of individual forms is threatened, literally, with disintegration. "If you were to yield to your weariness, a silent army of implacable anatomists would take possession of you, and with a million lancets would make of all your body tissue a fantastic piece of lace, a gauze, a vapor, a nothing."[26]

Meaninglessness and the danger of regression in nature are the mirror of meaninglessness and the danger of regression in history. In a few pages devoted to Sade and the survival of aristocratic libertinism, Michelet evokes the "terrible situation of a still fragile Republic, which in the chaos of a world in ruins, found itself surprised from below by frightful reptiles. Vipers and scorpions seethed in its foundations" (*HR*, 2:847–848). At the other end of the social spectrum, the dark face of the people is revealed in a figure like the Capuchin Chabot, "a hero of the populace, violent and licentious" (*HR*, 1:1063). Michelet's often expressed fear of the modern industrial proletariat—his concern at the displacement of the independent male artisan by the female factory worker—seems neither trivial nor incidental, for he saw the proletariat as a dangerous regression from his ideal *peuple*. For that reason, he was forced to defend his optimistic vision of the *peuple* as the subject of a progressive history by disputing what the pioneer social scientists of his time, such as Parent-Duchâtelet, Buret, and Villermé, had been reporting about the character and conditions of popular life in urban France.[27] Nevertheless, on many occasions he himself acknowledged his doubt and anxiety. Seeking a refuge in nature from the desolation of history, he writes in *L'Oiseau*, "I encountered for the first time the head of the viper." "Shattered, silenced to death" by this manifestation of "evil" in Eden, he is obliged to confess that "The great mother, nature, in whom I had sought refuge, terrified me."[28]

It is at this point, where the optimism and progressivism usually attributed to Michelet appear to falter, that we can begin to measure the importance of his presentation of the history of the Revolution as the Gospel of a new religion and, in general, of the mythical dimension of his narrative. At the high points of that narrative, the indication of times that are repeated—mythic times, such as time of day and season or month of the year—becomes at least as important as chronology.[29] July, in particular, has a significance that appears to have little to do with chronology. It always designates a moment of unity, transparency, and plenitude, the burning light of the high summer sun—in Michelet's own words: "Universal history as the struggle of liberty, its victory over the world of fatality, constantly renewed, brief as an eternal July."[30] The July of the taking of the Bastille is repeated in the July of the federations and in the July of the 1830 Revolution, and it is identified in Michelet's text with the climaxes, the moments of illumination of his own spiritual (and no doubt sexual) itinerary. "O mon Vico! ô mon juillet," he exclaimed once.

The intrusion of the time of myth into the chronological time of history in Michelet's narrative has led Frank Bowman to raise—quite properly, in my view—the question of Michelet's understanding of the Revolution as an historical event. "What is in fact the date of the Revolution?" Bowman asks. "Is it 1789, 1848, is it in the past or in the future? . . . The Revolution is at once event, goal, and continuity. Need one remark that . . . for Michelet the time of the Passion and the Imitation of Christ is the same as the time of the Revolution?"[31]

In introducing his *History of the French Revolution*, Michelet writes: "From the priest to the king, from the Inquisition to the Bastille, the road is straight, but long. Holy, holy Revolution, how slowly dost thou come!— I, who have been waiting for thee for a thousand years in the furrows of the middle ages,—what! must I wait still longer? Oh! how slowly time passes! Oh! how I have counted the hours!—Wilt thou ever arrive?"[32] When the historian thus invokes the Revolution, he does not say whether he is speaking for France or for himself, whether the temporal perspective is that of the narrative (France on the eve of the Revolution in 1789) or that of the act of narration (the eve of the Revolution of 1848). It is as though the "Revolution" belongs to a different order of things from ordinary history, into which it erupts from time to time, like an ever-renewed promise of redemption. The longing for holy Revolution, it appears, is without end, and may belong to any time.

Claiming to have discovered an affinity between Michelet and Nietzsche in their common condemnation of their own century as "lifeless" ("en quelque sorte éteint"), Roland Barthes argued that what Michelet shared with Nietzsche is the "apocalyptic" idea that "we are in the time of the End of history."[33] If Barthes's suggestion has any validity, it seems to me that it underscores the moral and political dubiousness of the idea of a post-historical time.

The religion of Revolution—with its longing for union and redemption, its expectation of a miraculous transcendence of the humdrum world of practical politics and class struggle ("n'importe où hors de ce monde"), and its rejection of the prosaic compromises that practical politics entail—can lurch unpredictably from passionate idealism to pessimism and despair. Moreover, it seems capable of attaching itself to a wide variety of policies and programs, provided these promise immediate deliverance from the world as it is, characterized by division and conflict between the classes and between the sexes. Though Michelet thought of himself as a champion of democracy (and there is no doubt, in my view, of the authenticity and intensity of his hatred of every tyranny and oppression) one is bound to ask how compatible his Gospel of Revolution and his historical writings are with the actual practice of democracy, at least the liberal democracy we are most familiar with.

In the original, pure faith of the Revolution—obscured, misunderstood, or simply forgotten in the half century since 1789 but buried deep, he claimed, in the heart of every French man and woman—Michelet hoped to find the ground of a still unrealized national union that would put an end to the bitterly divisive social and political struggles of his own time. "In moments of weakness," he declared, "when we seem to have forgotten who we are, it is there that we must seek ourselves" (*HR*, 1:2). The aim of the *History of the French Revolution* was to promote union and resolve class conflict by resurrecting the original faith. Michelet's task as historian of the Revolution was not therefore primarily critical. There is an essential connection between the way he wrote history and his conception of his subject. His aim was not to "think" the French Revolution, as François Furet would have us do, to disengage himself from its continuing legends in order to study it as a remarkable though contingent historical phenomenon. It was the opposite: to recover what people believed, the power of the founding myth. What Michelet appears to have expected from the spirit of the Revolution was something similar to what he expected from sexual relations—a reusable means of renewal or rejuvenation. ("Woman," he once said, is "the elixir of man.") In keeping with this objective, he not only presented his narrative as a founding history; he explicitly rejected critical, conceptual, and "scientific" historiography in the form most familiar to him—that of the Enlightenment—as an arbitrary projection of mental constructs onto a reality that had in the end broken over them in an immense tidal wave and swept them away. As the past is not a lifeless cadaver, he claims, the analytical or anatomical methods of Enlightenment historiography, characterized as "cutting, cutting, and cutting again" (HR, 1:301), are as inadequate and inappropriate to history as Jacobin political methods were to the body politic. The proper model for the historian is not the surgeon or the anatomist, but the physician-healer—the hermeneut— "sounding" the patient with his stethoscope. His first task is to listen to what the people whose story he proposes to write has to tell him. His history will be no more or less than that story, only so interpreted that it gives the people a clearer understanding of itself. "Our confidence in a superior education and culture, in our specialised research, in the subtle discoveries we believe we have made must not be allowed to make us despise the national tradition. We must not lightly undertake to alter that tradition, to create or impose another" (HR, 1:282).

So it was clear from the outset that Michelet's history of the Revolution was going to follow the lines that those who made the Revolution— in his view—had drawn for it and to reflect their understanding of it. He accepted what he called the revolutionary catechism—the basic understanding of the Revolution that he claimed was shared by the entire French people with the exception of a few misguided intellectuals (HR, 1:283). "Have I not lived with them, followed each one of them, like a faithful companion through his deepest thoughts and in all his changes," he wrote of the revolutionary actors. "In the end I was one of them, a denizen of that strange world. I had trained my eyes to see in that world of shadows. . . . I was thousands of miles away from thinking of the public, of literary success. I was full of love, that's all. I went here and I went there, eager and hungry; I breathed in and I wrote the tragic spirit of the past" (HR, 1:14–15).

Michelet frequently asserts that he *is* France, that he *is* the Revolution. In several passages of his *History* he presents his own life at the time of writing as a reenactment or reliving of an episode in the history he is writing, and he speaks of the heroes of the Revolution in the same terms he uses to speak of himself.[34] Not surprisingly, he held that it is not by detached scientific analysis, but by an intense effort of identification, a kind of magical transsubstantiation, or as he put it himself, a "strange alchemy" that the historian may hope to penetrate the secrets of the past.

For this method of doing history, however, the object of the historian's investigation must always be in fact a subject like himself. The historian does not start with a problem or a question—either a classic problem such as the causes of the military and political decline of states (taken up once again only recently by Paul Kennedy) or a more modern one, such as the transformations of family structure and demographic patterns in Western Europe since the Middle Ages, or the conditions favoring the rise of different varieties of fascism. He starts with an active subject, and his aim is to get inside that subject and reconstitute its experience as a story so that all its seemingly disparate parts come together to form a single "meaningful" whole. It is entirely apt that Michelet's *History of the French Revolution* is full of personalities and dramatic scenes and episodes—in stark contrast with the austere, dedramatized, heroless histories of Tocqueville (1856) or Fustel (1864) only a few years later. Romantic history, as practised by Michelet, is a close cousin of other forms of Romantic narrative, especially Romantic biography and autobiography. It is a search for—or an invention of—unity and identity. Just as Romantic autobiography defined an identity for the modern *individual* that was no longer dependent on lineage, community, or traditional models, Romantic historiography set out to invent an identity for the modern *nation* that could replace that once provided by the representative figure of the King.

On the other hand, the reader is not expected to stand back critically from the history he is reading as he was from the texts of the Enlightenment historians. Michelet's *History* does not invite discussion or debate. It is not an argument, it is a revelation. Just as the author claims to have eschewed the rules of selection and composition that had governed classical narrative and to have grasped the inner form or spirit of reality by an act of love, an all-encompassing imaginative insight into it and identification with it, the reader is expected to immerse himself in the narrative and to identify, as the author did, with its "spirit." Reading, in a word, no less than writing, is a kind of *imitatio*. Michelet's aim could not be to encourage criticism and reflection. Conversion, not inquiry, had to be the goal of his history. One might even say that his history of the Revolution is offered not as a work of historical analysis, but as a kind of Eucharist. Through the child of the historian's labor, the flesh of his flesh, the short-lived unity of the Revolution is to be restored and France is to become one, all its citizens joined together in fraternal communion. If Michelet understood revolution in general, and the French Revolution in particular, in a quasireligious light rather than as a mundane historical phenomenon occurring in certain conditions that one might wish to investigate and try to understand better, that is also how he thought of his own work.[35]

Michelet's practice as its historian thus corresponds to the value he attributed to the Revolution. Just as the *History of the Revolution* was not really a contribution to a collective and continuing critical investigation, a dialogue with other historians, but a revelation of the truth, the Revolution itself meant above all the immediate experience of revolutionary fervor, an erotic participation rather than the inauguration of a sustained and difficult ethical and political practice. The "Trois Glorieuses" of 1830 had already inspired the young professor of history and philosophy to compose an enthusiastic hymn to the French people and its aptitude for revolutionary transcendence. "No people," he wrote in the *Introduction to Universal History*, "is more electrified in battle by the feeling of community. . . . It is in the midst of danger, when a brilliant July sun illuminates the fête, when fire responds to fire, when bullets and death burst forth inexhaustibly, that stupidity becomes eloquent and cowardice courageous. At such moments the living dust of the people coheres and scintillates, stupendously beautiful. A burning poetry sparks forth from the mass."[36]

Where breaking through to such an intense experience of community is the ideal, everyday political life must finally seem second-rate, banal, diminished by compromise and self-interest. "Toute la politique est un expédient" ("All politics is expediency"), Hugo wrote disparagingly in *L'Année terrible*. But where revolution is hypostatized to the point that it far outweighs any specific objectives, one is bound to ask whether revolutionary politics does not have more to do with religion or anesthetics than with ethics, more to do with poetry than with history, for "ethics," as Constant observed, "has need of time."[37] Is it not, in fact, by transforming it into literature that Michelet hopes to suspend the fragile epiphanic moment and make it eternal, indefinitely re-presentable and renewable? And could the actual events of 1789–90, or any actual events, which must inevitably be hostage to time and fortune, ever match their representation in the *History* or realize as fully that spirit of the Revolution, which, as Michelet said, "is within us"? The best Revolution for Michelet, one feels, is the Revolution that has been remembered and represented by the historian in literature. The best of times is that "temps des cerises" of the famous song, which brings tears to the eyes of old revolutionaries and old lovers. It is well known that Michelet played almost no part in the 1848 Revolution but spent most of his time worrying that he was finding it difficult to write and occasionally lamenting the sparse attendance at the once crowded classes where, in the years leading up to 1848, he had excited the young men of France with his oratory and his poetic evocations of history.[38]

What I have emphasized here does not, of course, exhaust Michelet's immensely rich, generous, and often dazzlingly insightful *History*. But my analysis of it leads me to wonder about its effects. On the one hand, does it not prompt a vicarious participation in Revolution as a literary experience that can be comfortably enjoyed in the drawing room, a kind of political pornography that is equally compatible with political quietism and with radical negation or nihilism? And, on the other hand, does it not excite a potentially dangerous inclination to play out personal, probably erotic fantasies on the stage of politics, using other people as props?

It has even been suggested that there may be an inner link between the Romantic, anarchist revolt against the philistinism of nineteenth-century bourgeois existence—Hedda Gabler playing with General Gabler's pistols and dreaming of a beautiful and authentic act—and certain features of fascist ideology. The experience of transcending the bounds of the everyday, as we now know, may be completely indifferent to ethical considerations. Romantics glorify the *moment*—the moment of crisis or illumination, Barthes' "End of history," or that "state of exception" when "the strength of real life breaks the hardened crust of mechanical repetition," to quote Carl Schmitt, a Nazi intellectual who is back in vogue again. But this glorification of the moment—at the expense of the banal bourgeois time of cause and effect, maturation and compromise, calculation and preparation—leads easily into a political Walpurgisnacht, in which all the cows are black.

"The difference between Left and Right," an Italian scholar observed recently, "is, first and foremost, a product of temporality: of the weight and memories of the past, the open-ended conflicts of the present, the prospects and hopes of the future. . . . When a culture concentrates on the superstitious uniqueness of the moment of crisis . . . temporality will be contracted and abolished: past, present and future will all vanish, and with them all meaningful political determinations." Writing from the point of view of a chastened post-1968 Left, Franco Moretti insists that revolution "should be seen neither as a value in itself, nor as a mechanism to generate values: but [only] as the possible consequence of a given set of values in given circumstances." The Left, in other words, must rid itself of "the most equivocal of contemporary political phenomena, left-wing terrorism." For an answer to those who would charge that the sobriety he recommends is at best an unprincipled pragmatism, at worst a capitulation to compromise and intrigue, Moretti looks, as I too am often inclined to do, to Max Weber, and quotes from a speech of Weber's from which, as he says, "there is still a lot to learn," and on which I shall end these reflections on the writing of Revolution.

From a human point of view I don't find anything inspiring in [those who feel unconcerned about the consequences of their actions and are simply intoxicated by their romantic sensations]. What does move me deeply, on the other hand, is . . . a mature person—whether young or old in years—who, feeling truly and wholly his personal responsibility for consequences, and acting according to the ethic of responsibility, still of a sudden says: "I cannot do otherwise. I will not retreat from here." That is behaviour that is truly moving and truly human; and such a situation must be possible at any moment for all of us who have not yet lost our inner life.[39]

NOTES

1. Jules Michelet, *Histoire de la Révolution française*, ed. G. Walter (Paris, 1952), 2 vols. Hereafter cited as *HR*. Passages quoted in English are from the 1847 Charles Cocks translation of Books I–III, reedited by Gordon Wright as *History of the French Revolution* (Chicago: University of Chicago Press, 1967), with occasional modifications. Translations of passages from Book IV onward are my own.

2. *HR*, 1:2. See an entry in Michelet's journal for 2 April 1854: "Ma montagne est chauve, mais elle refleurira" (*Journal*, ed. P. Viallaneix and C. Digeon [Paris, 1959–76], 4 vols., 2:242).

3. Jules Michelet, *Le Peuple*, ed. Lucien Refort (Paris, Société des textes français modernes, 1946), 17.

4. Jules Michelet, *Introduction à l'histoire universelle. Tableau de la France. Préface à l'histoire de France*, ed. Charles Morazé (Paris, 1962), 75–76.

5. This is discussed in *Tableau de la France* (cited previous note).

6. "Nous voulons faire l'histoire de cette pauvre créature muette, dont personne ne s'est soucié, l'histoire de ceux qui n'ont pas d'histoire, de ceux qui ont souffert, travaillé, langui, fini sans pouvoir dire leur souffrance. C'est l'histoire des castes laborieuses et méprisées utiles et foulées: grand peuple innombrable." Cours du Collège de France, 1841, quoted in Oscar Haac, "La Révolution comme Religion: Jules Michelet," *Romantisme* 50 (1985): 75–86.

7. Jules Michelet, *Histoire de France*, Book 5, ch. 8, "Eclaircissements," *Oeuvres complètes*, ed. P. Viallaneix. 14 vols. to date (Paris, 1971–), 4:593.

8. "My God, my fatherland, my fellow-citizens had become myself," an enthusiastic nobleman declared at the opening of the Estates General (*HR*, 1:89).

9. See, for instance, a journal entry for 13 April 1854: "Dans l'*Histoire de la Révolution française* la Révolution a été une création, quoi qu'en dise Saint-Simon, une religion du droit opposé à la religion de la grâce, un banquet pour tous, non pour les élus" (Jules Michelet, *Journal*, 2:242.

10. *HR*, 1:11.

11. Quoted by Haac, 79.

12. "La France est l'enfant sur l'autel" (*HR*, 1:414–415).

13. Alphonse Esquiros, *Histoire des Montagnards* (Paris: 1847), 1:4–5. Like Michelet, Esquiros probably had in mind P.-J.-B. Buchez and P.-C. Roux, who claimed in their immensely popular *Histoire parlementaire de la Révolution française* (Paris, 1834) that "La révolution française est la conséquence dernière et la plus avancée de la civilisation moderne, et la civilisation moderne est sortie tout entière de l'Evangile. C'est un fait incontestable, si l'on examine et si l'on compare à la doctrine de Jésus, tous les principes que la révolution inscrivit sur ses drapeaux

et dans ses Codes; ces mots d'égalité et de fraternité qu'elle mit en tête de tous ses actes" (1:1).

14. *Histoire de France*, "Preface de 1869," in *Oeuvres complètes*, 4:15.

15. On the Revolution as the religion of all, see *Journal*, 13 April 1854, 2:242.

16. Georges Poulet, *Mesure de l'Instant* (Paris, 1968), 272. Cf. Frank Bowman, "Michelet et les métamorphoses du Christ," *Revue d'histoire littéraire de la France* 74 (1974): 824–844: "Attiré par la grâce, Michelet refuse néanmoins la figure du Christ quand elle se métamorphose en figure de la grâce, refuse les joies de l'union; ne sont valables que la Passion, et l'imitation de cette Passion dans l'espoir de créer la Révolution" (p. 844).

17. *HR*, 1:466 (criticism of Jacobin model of the "cité antique" or the "petite cité monastique du moyen âge, qu'on appelle couvent, abbaye"); 2:914 ("Les comités guillotinés, la Convention épurée, Robespierre allait fonder une république de Berquin ou de Florian, commencer ici l'âge d'or, inaugurer le paradis, où tout ne serait que douceur, tolérance et philosophie, où les loups, désapprenant leurs appétits sanquinaires, paîtraient l'herbe avec les moutons"); 2:203 (the impossibility of imposing unity by fiat from above: "Dans leur foi naive à la toute-puissance de la loi . . . ils croyaient que l'unité, pourvu qu'elle fût décrétée, à coup sûr existerait; ils ne semblaient pas se rendre bien compte des moyens indispensables qui doivent la préparer. L'unité, pendant que la loi la decrète en haut, doit fleurir d'en bas, du fond des volontés humaines; elle est la fleur et le fruit des croyances nationales").

18. *Histoire de France*. 17 vols. (Paris: Hachette, 1833–67), 7:ix.

19. "La Révolution, entrant dans le jacobinisme . . . y trouvait une force, mais elle y trouvait une ruine, comme ces malheureux sauvages qui n'ont, pour remplir leur estomac, que des substances vénéeuses; ils trompent un moment la faim, ils mangent, mais ils mangent la mort" (*HR*, 2:173).

20. Roland Barthes, *Michelet par lui-même* (Paris, 1954), 21.

21. See Franz Overbeck, *Christentum und Kultur*, ed. C.A. Bernoulli (Basel, 1919).

22. *Tableau de la France*, in *Introduction à l'Histoire universelle*, 130.

23. Jules Michelet, *La Mer* (1861; Paris, 1900), 5. On Romme, Reid, etc., see 289–302.

24. *La Mer*, 291.

25. *La Mer*, 85–86.

26. Jules Michelet, *L'Oiseau* (Paris, 1858), 143.

27. *Le Peuple*, ed. Refort, 134–135.

28. *L'Oiseau*, 163–164.

29. On this feature of Michelet's historical writing, see Paul Viallaneix's introduction to his edition of *Jeanne d'Arc et autres textes* (Paris, 1974) and his contribution to the special Michelet number of *Clio 6* (1977): 196–198.

30. *Histoire de France*, "Préface de 1869," in *Oeuvres complètes*, 4:15.

31. Bowman, 843–844.

32. "Du prêtre au roi, de l'Inquisition à la Bastille, le chemin est direct, mais long. Sainte, sainte Révolution, que vous tardez à venir! . . . Moi qui vous attendais depuis mille ans, sur le sillon du moyen âge, quoi! je vous attends encore! . . . Oh que le temps va lentement! oh! que j'en compte les heures! . . . Arriverez-vous jamais?" (*HR*, 1:75.)

33. Roland Barthes, "Modernité de Michelet," *Revue d'histoire litteraire de la France* 74 (1974):804–805.

34. He knows the sense of rupture felt by the participants in the Revolution, he says, because he himself experienced it: "While I was happily engaged in recovering the true tradition of France, my own link with the past was broken for good. I lost the being who would so often tell me the story of the Revolution . . . my father with whom I have spent my entire life—forty-eight years. When that blow struck me, I was looking elsewhere; I was elsewhere, as I busily wrote this work which I had been dreaming of for so long. I was at the foot of the Bastille, I was about to take the fortress, to plant our immortal flag on its towers. . . . That blow hit me unforeseen, like a shot from the Bastille" (Preface of 1847, *HR*, 1:8). Later, when it came time to recount the falling away from the great days of the Revolution during the Terror, he too was living in wretched exile in Nantes, "in a leaky house that let in the great rains, in January 1853." It was there, and then, that he wrote "about the corresponding month of the terror. . . . I plunge with my subject into darkness and winter. The relentless storm winds that have been battering my windows on those hills of Nantes for two months are the constant accompaniment, sometimes heavy, sometimes piercing, of my Dies Irae of '93" (Preface de 1868, *HR*, 1:9). Sometimes the historian's identification with his subject is less explicit. "Et si cette plaine est aride, et si cette herbe est sèche, elle reverdira un jour," Michelet wrote of the Champ de Mars, the locus of the great Fête de la Fédération (*HR*, 1:2). "Ma montagne est chauve, mais elle reverdira," he wrote in his Journal on 2 April 1854, from his exile in Italy, referring both to the dashing of his political hopes and to his own feelings of physical, moral, and intellectual exhaustion and impotence (*Journal*, 2:242). Even when he promised the revolutionary actors that in the pages of his book they would be resurrected to eternal life in exchange for the earthly life they had sacrificed for the sake of the Revolution, he was offering exactly what he hoped he himself would obtain from his work. As he often noted, he had not really lived, but had sacrificed living to the supreme law of his existence: writing. "I have to live and die as a book, not as a man," he used to say (*Journal*, 1:330 [23 June 1840]; also 1:385, 1:502, 1:677, 2:544).

35. Though I am arguing that Michelet's way of writing history leaves little room for the discussion and debate we usually associate with science, scholarship, and democratic processes, but aims rather to promote the unity formed around myth, there is no doubt of his deep-seated hatred of tyranny and oppression. Unity, in his own mind, almost certainly stood for a condition in which no class of Frenchmen could or would oppress any other. He was acutely conscious of class divisions in the revolutionary parties themselves. The leaders of the Jacobins as well as the Girondists, he insisted, were bourgeois who never doubted their superiority to the common people, the "dumb cattle" they were called upon to "save," in spite of themselves if necessary (*HR*, I:301). "Voilà une bien terrible aristocratie, dans ces démocrates," he noted. Any fanatical elite that is cut off from the mass of the people and so obsessed with its theories and visions of the future that it loses sight of the present is likely to end in cruelty and tyranny (*HR* II:855, 995). Again and again Michelet warned, as Trotsky was to do later, that Jacobinism prepares the way for military dictatorship (*HR*, II:1004). The Revolution's need to defend itself against internal and external enemies, which led to the emergence of outstanding leaders like Robespierre and Napoleon, has had a disastrous consequence, he asserted: it has produced in the French people a "grave and deep-seated

evil, which will be hard to eradicate"—the worship of strong men, "l'adoration de la force" (*HR*, I:2). Michelet's own position concerning this cult of power was clear: Anacharsis Clootz's admonition, "France, guéris des individus" ["France, cure yourself of faith in individuals"], was placed at both the beginning and the end of the special section of the *History of the Revolution* devoted to the Terror.

36. *Introduction à l'histoire universelle*, 72.

37. Benjamin Constant, *De l'Esprit de conguête et de l'usurpation*, I, v, in *Oeuvres*, ed. Alfred Roulin (Paris, 1957), 999.

38. Though the authorities worried that Michelet's audiences of eight hundred to a thousand students at the Collège de France would "become a center of revolt and revolution . . . the historian never called on them to rise. He resisted the messianic fervor of Mickiewicz. . . ." (Oscar Haac, "The Nationalism of a Humanist," *Gradiva* 5 [1987]: 36).

39. Franco Moretti, "The Moment of Truth," *New Left Review* 159 (September–October, 1986): 39–48. Also see a debate in the journal *Telos* in the form of a series of articles by Ferenc Fehér, Joel Whitebrook, Richard Wolin, and others, on the propriety and usefulness of the so-called politics of redemption that has marked a good deal of left-wing thinking since the early nineteenth century (*Telos* 63 [1985], 147–168; 65 [1985], 152–170; 69 [1986], 46–57).

Icon and Symbol: The Historical Figure Called Maximilien Robespierre

ANN RIGNEY

Il est un temps où Robespierre et démocratie étaient synonymes. Ce jour reviendra.
—Albert Mathiez, "Robespierre orateur" (1912)

I

In a recent article in the *Times Literary Supplement,* Jacques Le Goff sets out a program for writing a new sort of biography, "the life as history." By situating the individual within the social configuration in which he or she belongs, this new biography would complement the *Annales* school's studies of social structures, collective behavior, and long-term trends: "Now that history has been so profoundly renewed, can the historian not return, better equipped both scientifically and mentally, to those inevitable subjects of history—to the 'event,' to politics and to the individual, including the 'great man'"?[1]

Politics, events, individuals, and "great men," of course, are among the recognized trademarks, if not the "inevitable subjects," of nineteenth-century historiography. And it is to a number of nineteenth-century works that I wish to return here. The current revival of interest in "the life as history" makes it opportune to reflect back on the biographical dimension in nineteenth-century historical narratives and consider the ways in which the symbolic articulation of the individual life through the collective history was already effected there.

In light of this concern, I wish to consider the representation of the "great men" in a number of nineteenth-century histories of the French Revolution. In particular, I shall focus on the four histories that appeared, either as a whole or in part, in 1847, and that can be seen as the ideological breeding grounds for the Revolution of 1848: Lamartine's best-selling *Histoire des Girondins* (1847), Esquiros's *Histoire des Montagnards* (1847), Michelet's *Historie de la Révolution française* (1847–53), and Louis Blanc's *Histoire de la Révolution française* (1847–62).[2]

In a sense, articulating the lives of outstanding individuals with collective events may be seen as the heart of these historians' enterprise.[3] For their histories are premised on the democratic belief—itself a part of the revolutionary heritage—that the nation or *peuple* is the true, the only legitimate subject of historical representation; that "history" is synonymous with "the history of the *peuple*." Within the framework of such a belief, the historian resembles a (self-appointed) national deputy or public servant: claiming to speak for the nation as a whole, he represents the national past to the latter-day nation through the medium of a narrative.[4] But through what figure(s) is the history of the nation to be represented in the historian's narrative of events? Recognizing the nation as the legitimate subject of historiography is one thing; it is quite another to decide which individual or collective figures represented the nation at any given moment in the past.

A historian wishing to represent the political history of the period from 1789 to 1794, for example, must deal with mass actions as well as with events in which individual figures are known to have played decisive roles. While the *journées révolutionnaires* of the early years of the Revolution are characterized by the direct intervention of crowds, the narrative of its final years is traditionally dominated by leaders. If the principal actor in the later phases of the Revolution was indeed the *peuple,* then it seems that the *peuple* can only have acted indirectly, through the agency of particular individuals. One of the key questions for the historian thus inevitably becomes: which, if any, of the leaders represented the will of the *peuple* in the final stages of the Revolution? A related but somewhat different question was put by Lamartine: can any of these well-known men be allowed to go down in history as the model or "type" for democracy (*le type de la démocratie*)?[5] These questions suggest that the narrative representation of the Revolution will involve not simply selecting, articulating and describing those incidents that the historian considers exemplary of the events of 1789 to 1794. Narrating the Revolution also means establishing the representative status of the different "men of the Revolution." What and whom did they stand for? Or, what comes down to the same thing in practice, what and whom are they to "stand for" or represent for the historian's latter-day public?

In a letter to *Le Temps* in 1865, Louis Blanc attempted to justify the attention he had paid in his history to the individual figure of Robespierre. Robespierre, he wrote, was a "great man" and, what for Blanc is synonymous with that, a "representative man" (*un homme représentatif*):

It is only possible to play a great role in history if one is, what I would like to call, a representative man. Individuals draw only a fraction of their strength from themselves. . . . Their life is simply a concentration of the collective life in which they are immersed. . . . it is precisely for that reason that a true judgment of their individuality is so important. In attacking or defending them, one is in fact attacking or defending the idea which was incarnated in them, the ensemble of aspirations which they represented. . . . In blessing or cursing their influence, one blesses or curses the general influence . . . of which theirs was the energetic manifestation, the living summary.[6]

Blanc's definition of a "representative man" illustrates his self-consciousness about the very problem of historical representation. But the plethora of terms that he uses in his definition also indicates the sheer variety of the symbolic relations that in practice may be designated by the common term, "representation." According to Blanc (and we shall see other examples from his fellow historians) the lives of representative men are "living summaries," "distillations," "energetic manifestations," or "incarnations"; as such, they represent such different if related objects as a collective life, collective influence, aspirations, and ideas. Whatever the nature of the relationship between the representative and what he represents (embodiment, spokesmanship, agency, typification, manifestation, symbolisation), and whatever the nature of the represented object (a collective will, a particular group, an idea, an event, a situation), it is clear that the life of the unique individual, the "great man," is retrospectively regarded by the historian as having "stood for," or as being a sign of, something else. Thus, in a complex interaction of literary and political modes of representation, the historian represents discursively a collective situation characterized by a variety of representational relations.[7]

II

When Blanc defined "the representative man," he was of course writing with a particular man in mind: Robespierre. And it is the figure of Robespierre—that is to say, the retrospective representations of his life—that I wish to examine in particular here. The name "Robespierre," as we all know, designates a certain individual who was born in Arras on 6 May 1758 and died under the guillotine in Paris on 28 July 1794. The very fact that "we all know" who Robespierre was shows that his name does not merely have a designative function, but also serves to invoke a reputation. Since the *Incorruptible's* death, and even during his lifetime, the famous name "Robespierre" has become a cultural unit with a significance prior to any particular representation of the individual's life.[8] To be sure, the significance of "Robespierre" may be changed by new accounts of his life, based on alternative information or on different interpretations of the accepted facts. But if a new account is to acquire authority as a legitimate representation of historical reality, it will have to recognize, even if it is only then to refute, the commonplace association between the name "Robespierre" and the final stages of the Revolution. It will have to recognize the cultural fact that since Thermidor, "Robespierre" has come to mean (among other things) *Terreur*. Yet precisely because the name "Robespierre" is thus inextricably bound up with the last phases of the Revolution, any change in his image or reputation will also involve a change in the public's perception of "1793–94."

Transforming the public's perception of "1793–94" was of particular urgency for the historians of 1847. Implicit in their enterprise was their common opposition to the tottering constitutional monarchy headed by Louis Philippe, which Thiers's often reprinted *Historie de la Révolution française* (1823–27) had helped legitimize. Thus, although they may have differed in their interpretation of the Revolution and in their hopes for future change, the Christian-democrat Lamartine, the Christian-socialist Esquiros, the nationalist-republican Michelet, and the socialist Blanc were all commonly concerned with "going beyond" the constitutional monarchy. In historiographical practice, this meant they were concerned with rehabilitating the later, republican phases of the Revolution and, as one of their critics complained, with "rehabilitating the exterminating types of the 1793 democracy"[9]—including Robespierre. For if the figure of the historical individual Robespierre is no longer seen as representing extermination in general and the extermination of 1793 in particular, then *terreur* may no longer be considered a necessary or defining feature of democracy in general and of the democracy of 1793 in particular. Alternatively, Michelet explores a somewhat different possibility: If the figure of Robespierre represents neither extermination nor democracy, then the reign of the *peuple* may have been represented (should be represented) by some other figure.

The fact that "Robespierre" had become a cultural unit is revealed in the regularity and the lack of self-consciousness with which the historians refer to the figure of Robespierre *as* a sign or *as* a word. Esquiros, for example, writes in his account of Robespierre's speech on the death of Mirabeau that "one was the first word, the other the last word of the Revolution" (1:296). In similar terms, Lamartine points out to his readers that the unremarkable and unnoticed presence of Robespierre at the opening of the *Etats généraux* can retrospectively be seen as indicating the future course of the Revolution: "he was the last word of the Revolution, but nobody could read him" (1:56). Lamartine's narrative goes on to end, almost two thousand pages later, with a survey of the different tombstones of the dead men of the Revolution "upon each one of which is written a word which characterises the man": here "eloquence," there "philosophy," and, what is implied in the case of Robespierre, the word "virtue"—"But on all tombstones it is written: Died for the future and Worker for humanity" (2:923). Such comments point not only to the semiotic status of the "men of the Revolution" within the historical culture, but also to the historians' concern with making manifest what each figure represents. And indeed, a closer look at the histories reveals the extent to which the retrospective narrators openly intervene as *interpreters* of the events, actions, speech acts, or persons they describe: this is how things were and this is what they signified. Or, what comes down to the same thing, this is what they are henceforth to represent for the public as a *lieu de mémoire.*

Hermeneutic interventions may take the form of a straightforward translation of a figure into the timeless moral qualities he represented or embodied, as in Lamartine's reference to Robespierre as "the type of truth and virtue" (1:795), or in Esquiros's allegorical description of a confrontation between Robespierre and Brissot in terms of "anxious probity facing cynicism masked by adroit pride" (2:32–33). More often, however, hermeneutic interventions involve establishing a figure as the spokesman or representative for a particular idea or program of action that was "in the air," which is to say a driving spiritual force at that particular historical moment. (While it is generally implied that these ideas were also adhered to by the public at large, this is not always specified.) Esquiros, for example, explains that the Revolution collapsed with the death of Robespierre because the latter "contained" the religious idea which was its driving force.[10] Likewise, Blanc explains the animosity of Duport toward Robespierre by the fact that Robespierre "had come forth to represent" (*venait représenter*) the ideal of universal political equality: "an idea which wanted, which was striving to find its rightful place within the Revolution" (1:674). Lamartine, having praised the Convention for its ideals but criticised it for its ultimately bloody failure to see how these could be realised, concludes with the statement that "Robespierre, more than any of his colleagues, personified these tendencies" (2:287). Similarly, Michelet concludes his account of the rousing, patriotic speeches that Danton made in September 1792 by identifying Danton as spokesman for the collective will at that moment in time: "the very voice of the Revolution and of France" (1:1025).

If the hermeneutic interventions are thus used to establish the individual figure as the spokesman or representative of a collective program, on other occasions they are used to constitute a particular biographical event as the sign or "personification" of a collective change. Thus Michelet presents Danton's death as the death of the true Revolution, suggesting paradoxically that Danton had incarnated the Republic: "He had been . . . the life of the Revolution, the heart of the Republic, and she died with him" *(en lui).*[11] In an analogous way, Blanc presents the fall of Robespierre as the death of the Republic: "gendarmes appeared and, in the person of the prisoners, led away the Republic" (3:73). Readers may go on to try to rationalise these personifications of the Republic in terms of the political role played by the individuals in question (e.g., "their deaths 'announced' the beginning of the end"). In any case, it is clear that Michelet and Blanc instruct them to see the deaths of Danton and Robespierre respectively *as* the death of the Republic.

Such directives to see a particular figure "as" or as "standing for" something else have by themselves no force—although they may gain some force by being repeated on different occasions in the narrative. As statements within a historiographical discourse, they are theoretically based on—i.e., they draw their authority from—the historical reality to which they refer. Such hermeneutic directives must be considered, therefore, in the light of that historical reality as represented within each narrative: when Robespierre dies in Blanc's account or in Michelet's, he does so with a particular reputation constructed by the narrative on the basis of his prior reputation and whatever new facts the historian has at his disposal. This reputation is made up of what the figure is seen to have actually done in words and deeds, what he wanted to do, what sort of a man he was, and who his associates were. A more detailed study would show how, through a variety of discursive strategies, Robespierre's name is associated with or dissociated from, on the one hand, the propagation of the *Terreur* and, on the other hand, the institutional and social reforms of 1793–1794. A more detailed study would also show how, through the editorial mediation of the narrator, Robespierre's speeches are selected, quoted, or paraphrased in such a way that certain aspects of his program are emphasized rather than others (from the few passages quoted above, it can already be seen that Blanc foregrounds his political ideas and Esquiros his religious ones). In what follows here, I have opted to focus my attention on a particular aspect of the figure of Robespierre: the representations of his person and his private life, the portraits of "the man himself." In other words, I shall focus on those features that define him as an individual, features that, at first sight, might seem most irrelevant to a narrative of collective events but that Blanc suggests may nevertheless be of vital importance in the recognition and judgment of "great men." And what more inalienable aspect of the individual called Robespierre than his own body, his face and his physique?

III

In the four midnineteenth-century narratives considered here, retrospective exegesis works together in complicated ways with the dramatic, "unmediated" representation of unique moments. In other words, the historians implicitly (and sometimes explicitly) invite their readers to see and to hear what was going on from 1789 to 1794; to become, as it were, an eyewitness to events as they were taking place in the past.[12] This emphasis on the dramatic "making present" of historical moments and actors reflects the influence of the Romantic poetics of figurative history, which assumes that to *see* is to *know* the past as it essentially was.[13] As I shall show, however, this "seeing" is inseparable from "seeing as."

The historians of this study stress visualization by giving extensive portraits of the "men of the Revolution" and even more so by repeatedly evoking different aspects of their subject's physique in particular narrative contexts. In studying the function of such portraits, then, one must consider not only *what* is seen, but also *when* or in what context it is seen. Blanc, for example, introduces his first extensive portrait of Robespierre, that spokesman for "political equality," immediately before he treats of Robespierre's speech in the Assembly criticizing the proposed distinction between active and passive citizens (1:667). Similarly, Michelet's account of Danton's speaking "with the very voice of France" is accompanied by a lengthy evocation of the physical presence of the speaker himself. In each case, the portrait is directly or indirectly juxtaposed with a particular speech-act in which expression is given to a political program identified as "that of France" (Michelet) or "as an idea whose time had come" (Blanc). But *what* is it that the public saw when in the presence of these speakers or—what comes down to the same thing—what are latter-day readers given to see?

The different descriptions of Robespierre and Danton are based on a certain consensus regarding their physical identities.[14] A protypical figure, as it were, remains recognizable throughout, composed of a particular set of features and the particular qualities which make them noteworthy. Whereas Danton is known by his large physique, his thundering voice, and his leonine head, Robespierre is known above all by his small and thin physique, his pale complexion, and the fact that he generally wears the same, neat, *ancien régime*-style clothes.[15] A number of other characteristics of Robespierre's person (his rhetorical style, the quality of his voice, his nervous tics, his stiff posture, the look in his eye, an association with the color green) are also frequently remarked upon, but without being essential or defining properties of his image in the same way as his pallor and his size (the figure of a "Robespierre" might be recognizable without his nervous tic, but not if he were large, sanguine, and jolly). "The Third Estate already carried the Convention in its obscure depths," writes Michelet of the opening of the Estates General, "But who could have seen it? Who spotted among that crowd of lawyers the stiff body, the pale face [*la pâle figure*] of a certain lawyer from Arras?" (1:90). If the other deputies did not notice him in 1789, it is clear that Michelet's reader is expected to retrospectively see, to recognize, and to put a name to this *pâle figure* from Arras.

Yet if the prototypical figure of Robespierre remains recognizable across the different representations, he is nevertheless portrayed in each case in a significantly different way. Take the matter of his size. While he may never become large and corpulent like Danton without ceasing to be "Robespierre," his noncorpulence may be variously designated. Whereas Mercier had referred to him as "that dwarf called Robespierre"[16] and Michelet refers to his "meager sad figure" (*sa maigre et triste figure*, 1:476), Blanc refers to his "thin face" (*mince visage*, 1:340), Lamartine to his "small" size (he was *"petit de taille,"* 1:56), Esquiros to his "mediocre stature" (*taille médiocre*, 1:195), and Mathiez to his "neat, slim waistline" (*taille mince et bien prise*).[17] In actually describing Robespierre's physique, then, the different historians choose a different property from within the semantic field of "noncorpulence," along an evaluative scale running from meager to slim.[18] The choice of descriptive term clearly has the effect of investing the not particularly well-endowed figure of Robespierre with more (or less) aesthetic value or, literally, with more (or less) *grandeur*. Blanc can be seen attempting to compensate for Robespierre's lack of physical stature in a somewhat different way when, in describing Robespierre's rise to power, he relates how the Jacobins in 1790 suddenly noticed the "magnified figure" (*figure grandie*) of Robespierre "looming up" out of its obscurity (1:618): Robespierre's political ascendancy is thus presented figuratively, but in terms which in turn suggest an impressive physical presence.

Now the significance or value associated with Robespierre's physical features is not merely a product of the particular terms chosen to describe them, but of the way in which they are contextualised. By this I mean the way in which they are brought into significant relation with each other and with other aspects of his person and his biography. Take another of Robespierre's trademarks: his pallor. In relating Robespierre's speech on religious renewal, Esquiros refers to the "ardent pallor" (*pâleur ardente*) of the speaker (2:57); the distinguishing feature of paleness is thus invoked at the same time as it is transformed—indeed, almost negated—by the ardor of his conviction. Blanc also invokes Robespierre's pallor in relating the latter's attack on the proposal that the Assembly should condemn the popular agitation in the summer of 1789:

Le geste absolu de Robespierre, le feu couvert qui brillait dans ses yeux, le mouvement convulsif de ses lèvres minces, son visage d'une pâleur formidable . . . tout cela fit sur l'Assemblée une impression profonde sans doute, car tout à coup la scène changea d'aspect. (1:313)

[Robespierre's absolute gesture, the smouldering fire of his eyes, the convulsive movement of his thin lips, the formidable pallor of his face . . . together must have made a deep impression on the Assembly because, all of a sudden, the scene changed.]

In this narrative context, Robespierre's pallor becomes the physical manifestation of the strength of his conviction as defender of the people's rights. And not only that: the narrator implies that it is the strength of the speaker's conviction, as this is manifested in his external appearance, that ensured the force of his statements and the Assembly's adoption of his position.

Within the broader context of Blanc's narrative, moreover, the characteristic features of Robespierre's image are constituted as an index to, i.e., as the result of, his willingness to sacrifice himself to the cause of the people and the Revolution. In the extensive exegesis that accompanies his first lengthy portrait of Robespierre, Blanc suggests that the man's present appearance does not reflect his original nature. When younger and living in Arras, Robespierre enjoyed life, love, laughter, and writing poetry; if he has now become this rather unattractive, rigid figure "with the pale face," this is because, retaining only a "vague sweetness," he has sacrificed himself entirely to the Revolution, who has fashioned him as her own instrument (1:666–67). Robespierre's habit of wearing the same clothes is similarly interpreted: his dress reflects his poverty, and so provides further visible proof that he lacks the worldly ambition of his opponents (1:666–67). Blanc also suggests that Robespierre's old-fashioned clothes support his refusal to indulge in mere rhetoric and his rejection of the *bonnet rouge* favored by the eloquent Girondins. His attitude to dress, like his attitude to speech, reflects his consistent preference for substance over mere appearances, for the realities of democracy over its superficial trappings (2:85). By referring to them in specific narrative contexts and by his own mediating exegesis, Blanc connects the characteristic features of Robespierre's image in such a way that they become the physical manifestation of an ethical consistency: the visible and public proof that his pale appearance is to be trusted.

In Michelet's representation, the same traits are mentioned but are related to different aspects of Robespierre's biography and person. While the *pâle figure* of the deputy from Arras remains recognizable, it is invested with a very different significance. Not only does Michelet make Robespierre's "paleness" salient by repetition (1:622, 865); he also uses related terms in describing other features of Robespierre's person and personality. Thus, if his face is pale, his eyes too are pale in the manner of steel: "Gleaming like pale steel, and with a more and more anxious look, his eyes shifted about, expressing the effort of a shortsighted man trying to see" (2:61). Robespierre is also a man of "colorless talent" (2:1005) whose "colorless" speeches (1:483) nevertheless have a chilling effect (1:868). This lack of color in intellectual matters is linked not only to his pallor, but also to the general *monotony* of his physical image. For Michelet, the predictability of Robespierre's clothing reinforces the "monotony" of his speeches, the rigidity of his posture, the lack of creativity in his thinking and writing (1: 870, 868; 2:56). This regular foregrounding and combining of such properties as "paleness," "monotony," "rigidity," and "coldness" results in the formation of an underlying isotopy around the notion of "sterility." Where Blanc's Robespierre was consistently honest, Michelet's Robespierre is consistently "noncreative," even deathlike. Far from being a world-historical individual capable of responding to, initiating, or personifying collective changes, he signifies a sort of "death in life." This nonvitality is made manifest in the portrait given of him at the *Fête de l'Etre suprême* when, with the color now completely drained from his cheeks, the *Incorruptible* finally smiles:

Ce sourire fait mal. La passion, qui visiblement a bu tout son sang et séché ses os, laisse subsister la vie nerveuse, comme d'un chat noyé jadis et ressuscité par le galvanisme, ou peut-être d'un reptile qui se raidit et se dresse, avec un regard indicible, effroyablement gracieux. (2:870)

[His smile is painful. His passion, which has visibly drunk up his blood and dried out his bones, has left only his nervous system, like that of a drowned cat resuscitated by galvanism or of an erect reptile as it reaches up with an indescribable, frighteningly gracious look.]

In Blanc's account of the same festive occasion, Robespierre's happiness is presented in quite different terms as a momentary release from his revolutionary cares and, as such, a return to his own pre-1789 nature. But like Michelet, Blanc invites his reader to visualize the figure of Robespierre:

transfigured as he faced the flower-bearing men, women, and children, Robespierre "lifted up his pale face and smooth brow which shone with a ray of tenderness" (2:742).[19]

These brief *aperçus* of Robespierre's face indicate not only how much the historians emphasized his physical presence as a supplement to their narrative of events, but also how much in representing his physical presence, they seek to give it a particular significance through both exegesis and description (i.e., through the highlighting of common features in different aspects of his person or personal life). Inviting the reader to "see" the man himself, his icon, is thus bound up with making his appearance visible as a manifestation of something else, more specifically as the natural expression of his historical significance. In this way, the portraits not only underscore what the figure stands for but also serve to reinforce the historian's authority by substantiating the particular significance that he attaches to the figure in his narrative. What Robespierre stood for was patently obvious and there for everyone to see; just look at the man himself.

The "something else" reflected in Robespierre's appearance can take a variety of more or less abstract, more or less historically specific forms— even within the same text. Robespierre's image may be constituted as an expression of his character (in Blanc, his self-abnegation and honesty in working for the people; in Michelet, his sterility and rigidity). It may also be seen as the embodiment of a principle or ideal: in Lamartine, his exemplary lifestyle at the Duplays; in Esquiros, his spiritual values (he had "the face and the shape of Christian nations" as opposed to the "pagan beauty" of the Girondins and the sensual materialism of the corpulent Danton).[20] Finally, Robespierre's image may be seen as the individual incarnation of a particular historical force: in Michelet, the force of sterile reaction as opposed to the spontaneous renewal that brought about the Revolution; in Esquiros, the force of spiritual renewal as opposed to the materialism of the preceding age. (The image serves not only to manifest a particular historical force but also to show how Robespierre envisions the future. Blanc, as we have seen, portrays him with his eyes constantly fixed on the horizon; Michelet presents him as myopically straining to see beyond his own nose; and Esquiros, in an elaborate exegesis of Robespierre's use of two different pairs of spectacles, suggests that they indicated his capacity to see both what was close by and what was in the distance [1:197–98]). The range of meanings with which Robespierre's physical image is thus invested suggests that, in representing "Robespierre," the historians seek to "figure" a particular ideological program by attaching it to the will, the actions, and the person of the particular individual identified as its principal spokesman.

At the same time, the different portraits of Robespierre also play an important role in establishing or clarifying the nature of that individual's relationship to the theoretically sovereign *peuple*. Blanc, as we have seen, represents Robespierre as having "come forth to represent" a program for universal political equality. The fact that his image is constituted as a sign of his integrity, commitment, and lack of personal ambition serves both to explain his rhetorical force and to justify the privileged role which the narrator openly accords him as the true representative and defender of the people's interest. In Michelet's account, by contrast, the fact that Robespierre's image reflects his moral sterility and rigidity means that it also functions as the living, manifest proof of his alienation from the *peuple*. Michelet defines the *peuple* precisely by its "fecund and warm" instinctual life (1:869), qualities that Robespierre patently lacks but that are found instead in Danton, that "powerful, productive being" (1:1024) "in whom there was such a powerful life, with whom all life vibrated."[21]

IV

The leader's relationship to the *peuple* is not merely inscribed in his portrait, but in the public "recognitions" of him at the time of the Revolution—as represented, of course, by the different historians. Public recognition may take the form of scenes of enthusiasm in which collective figures, taken as representatives of the *peuple* at large, react spontaneously and enthusiastically to the presence of the leader: in Blanc, for example, the Jacobins stretching out their arms swearing to die for Robespierre (1:698); in Michelet, the crowd's immediate response to the patriotic eloquence of Danton (1:1024); in Esquiros, the public's elation at Robespierre's speech on the Etre Suprême (2:399). Such scenes are supplemented by general statements regarding the popularity of the man within society at large and his capacity to evoke personal loyalty within his immediate circle. Whereas Michelet presents the devotion of the Duplays to Robespierre in terms of an unnatural deification (2:59), Blanc and Esquiros foreground that devotion and also refer in more general terms to his enormous popularity within society. Lamartine also recognizes Robespierre's popularity, but in effect limits it to the Duplay family and their friends, taken as representative of the "revolutionary, but honest, mass of the people of Paris" (1:795).

The different accounts of the death of the representative figure illustrate in a particularly clear manner the way in which the public recognition of his significance is inscribed in the narrative representation itself: Who grieved for him? In Lamartine's representation of Robespierre's death, the

only reference is to a jubilant mob: the living proof that Robespierre had
failed to extend his personal influence beyond the Duplay sphere in such
a way as to realise his dream of the "calm and regular reign of the *peuple,*
personified by its representatives" (2:469). But in Esquiros' representation
of Robespierre's death, the mass of spectators are identified as jubilant
bourgeois, and members of the *peuple* are conspicuous by their scarcity:
"In contrast, one saw only a few, mournful members of the *peuple,* personified in Robespierre" (2:468). Blanc relates how the streets were lined
with jubilant counterrevolutionaries and then goes on to quote the grieving complaint of a peasant woman, representative of the poor, who cried
out when she heard the news: "Oh! it's all over for poor people [*le pauvre
peuple*], they have killed the man who loved them so much" (3:83). Finally,
Michelet's account of the death of Robespierre focuses exclusively on the
frenzied jubilation of the counterrevolutionaries at his fall. In narrating the
death of Danton, however, he relates both the jubilation of the royalists
and the grief of the *patriotes* and, like Blanc in the case of Robespierre,
ends his account with the direct quotation of a grieving cry: in this case,
the patriots' lament that "They have decapitated France" (2:809). In thus
appealing to the *vox populi* of 1794, the narrators can be seen attempting
to legitimize their own claim that the death of the individual represented
the death of the Republic and, more generally, to legitimize their own role
as faithful spokesmen for the collective past.

In an article published in 1850, the liberal Baudrillart surveyed the recent
historiography of the Revolution and complained of the insurrectionary
dimension of Michelet's history in the following terms: "The people dictate, he writes; the people delegate him, he represents them. I ask you,
what is that but the democratisation of history-writing, already declared
a republic in 1847." [22] The treatment of Robespierre in the four histories
considered here illustrates the extent to which the symbolic reconstruction
of collective political events could involve questions of political representation or, to use Baudrillart's terms, "the democratisation of history-
writing." In representing the national past in discourse, the historians
constitute certain individual and collective figures as representatives of
the *peuple* and as spokesmen for the particular agendas that the *peuple* is
shown to have embraced. But if the "democratisation of history-writing"
may be common to the four histories, the evidence presented here also
indicates the historians' lack of consensus in the years preceding and following 1848. Who was the *peuple* whose lives the historians reconstruct
for the latter-day public? Was it the *pauvre peuple,* the "revolutionary
but honest *peuple,*" or the *patriotes*? What were its aspirations? Political
and social equality, national unity, or religious renewal? Which individual

figure, which "representative man" best voiced those aspirations and what is the nature of his "representational" relationship with his constituency? Michelet's Danton was like the *peuple*. Esquiros claims that Robespierre personified the *peuple*. Blanc's Robespierre is devoted to the *peuple* and acts on their behalf. Lamartine's hardworking, virtuous Robespierre is rather a model or exemplar for that segment of the *peuple* who consider him "the type of truth and virtue" (1:795).

In different and complex ways, then, the reader is invited to translate the figure of the "representative man" into the program and the constituency he stands for. Yet the individual figure—"the man himself"—remains the irreducible remainder of any such translation. Human interest, Lamartine once wrote, "never attaches itself to abstractions, but always to persons. The human mind seeks to give a face to ideas, a name, a heart, a soul, an individuality to things."[23] Whether humans can indeed become interested in events and ideas only through "individualizing" or personifying them is a moot point. But certainly the function of personification in these histories suggests that the historians were trying, in the absence of a king, to give an individual face to the different democratic programs that concerned them. The importance of individualisation and "human interest" suggests that it is not enough to see the different representations of Robespierre or Danton exclusively in terms of their signifying function—who or what he "stands for" in the public eye. The different narrative representations should also be considered in terms of their rhetorical, seductive function. The particular traits by which the individual's image is defined—his stature, his eloquence, his personal attractions, his ethical values or his pathos—all of these can be seen as so many ways to increase his rhetorical force as spokesman. They can be seen as ways of engaging the uncritical interest of the latter-day public for the man himself as a preparation for identifying with his program and with the particular collectivity he is shown to represent.

NOTES

1. Jacques Le Goff, "After *Annales:* the Life as History," *Times Literary Supplement* 4489 (14–20 April 1989): 394–405.
2. Alphonse de Lamartine, *Histoire des Girondins,* 2 vols. (Paris: Plon, 1984); Alphonse Esquiros, *Histoire des Montagnards,* 2 vols. (Paris: Victor Lecou, 1847); Jules Michelet, *Histoire de la Révolution française,* ed. Gérard Walter, 2 vols. (Paris: Pléiade, 1952); Louis Blanc, *Histoire de la Révolution française,* 3 vols. (Brussels: Meline, Cans et Cie. [vols. 1–2]; Lacroix, Verboeckhoven [vol. 3], 1847–62). Further references to these works will be given in the text. For an account of the

importance of the historians in the ideological preparation for 1848, see especially Maurice Aguilhon, *1848 ou l'apprentissage de la république 1848–1852* (Paris: Seuil, 1973), 6–9; Henri Guillemin, *Lamartine en 1848* (Presses Universitaires de France, 1948); Philippe Desan, "Poetry and Politics: Lamartine's Revolutions," in *Literature and Social Practice*, ed. P. Desan *et al.* (Chicago: University of Chicago Press, 1989), 182–210.

3. For an earlier, more extensive discussion of the issues treated in this paper, see Ann Rigney, *The Rhetoric of Historical Representation: Three Narrative Histories of the French Revolution* (Cambridge: Cambridge University Press, 1991).

4. Frank Ankersmit suggests a fundamental link between the theory of representative democracy and the practice of literary realism in *The Reality Effect in the Writing of History: the Dynamics of Historiographical Topology* (Amsterdam: Koninklijke Nederlandse Akademie van Wetenschappen, 1989), 36. In the light of this suggestion, it is interesting to recall Balzac's pronouncement that "French society was to be the historian, I was simply the secretary," *La Comédie humaine*, ed. P.-G. Castex, 12 vols. (Paris: Pléiade, 1976–81), 1:11. All translations from the French in this essay are mine.

5. Lamartine 2:922. As will become apparent in my analysis, the word *type* as it occurs in these texts has a variety of meanings: the model after which something is made or should be made; the figure symbolizing an idea or event; the person exhibiting the qualities typical of a particular temperament or sociohistorical class. The last notion of type, promoted by Balzac in his preface to the *Comédie humaine* (1842) and later elaborated and historicised by Lukács (see note 6 below), does occur in these narratives, but the first and second meanings of *type* are more dominant. The "great men" are often referred to as "typical" (of an idea or historical moment) in a way that recalls the idealist perspective of Charles Nodier more than the social perspective of Balzac. According to Nodier, the name of a "typical figure" was "the representative sign of a conception, a creation, an idea." *Oeuvres* (Geneva: Slatkine, 1968), 5:49.

6. Quoted in François Furet, *La Gauche et la Révolution française au milieu du XIXe siècle* (Paris: Hachette, 1986), 253–54. While the terms used are different, Blanc's "representative man" comes quite close to Lukács's account of the heroic types of "world-historical individuals" characteristic of Scott's novels; according to Lukács, "The great historical personality is the representative of an important and significant movement embracing large sections of the people" (*The Historical Novel* [Harmondsworth: Penguin, 1962], 38).

7. For a historical overview of the different modes of political representation, see Hanna Pitkin, *The Concept of Representation* (Berkeley and Los Angeles: University of California Press, 1967). For a reconsideration of the concept of political representation in the light of literary theorists' recognition that all (discursive/pictorial) representation involves construction and not simply reproduction, see Frank Ankersmit, "Politieke representatie. Betoog over de esthetische staat," *Bijdragen en mededelingen betreffende de geschiedenis der Nederlanden* 102.3 (1987): 358–79. For a succinct discussion of the different meanings of the term "representation" in its political and aesthetic applications, see Raymond Williams' *Keywords: A Vocabulary of Culture and Society* (London: Fontana, 1976), 222–25.

8. The term "cultural unit" is used here in the sense of Umberto Eco, *A Theory of Semiotics* (Bloomington: Indiana University Press, 1979), 159.

9. Alfred Nettement, *Les Historiens de la Révolution française. M. de Lamartine. Etudes Critiques sur les Girondins* (Paris: de Signy et Dubey, 1848), 587.

10. Of Robespierre Esquiros writes: "If the great mast of the Revolution broke when he was brought down by the storm, that was because he contained the religious idea of the Revolution. That man was predestined: but the sign of his predestination was not in him, but in a society which was being dissolved by the materialism of the aristocracy. . . ." (2:54).

11. 2:808. Although Danton is accorded a symbolic role here as representative of the Revolution, he is a much less dominant figure in Michelet's narrative than Robespierre is in Blanc's. The symbolic role Michelet accords him should be seen relative to his foregrounding and celebration of the direct intervention of the *peuple* in the Revolution on such *journées révolutionnaires* as 14 July 1789, 5 October 1789, the *Fédérations* of July 1790, and 10 August 1792.

12. Consider, for example, Michelet's invitation to the reader to accompany him to one of the meetings of the Cordeliers: "What a crowd! Can we get in? Citizens, make some room; comrades, can't you see I've brought a stranger along. . . . The noise is deafening; on the other hand, it's hard to see anything at all. . . . The first impression is bizarre, unexpected. The crowd is a real mixture, with well-dressed men, workers, students (among these, you can see Chaumette) . . ." (1:499).

13. Exemplifying this poetics, Carlyle's 1832 essay on "Biography" stresses the importance of graphic powers for historical writing and suggests that memorability depends both on the events narrated being "real" and on their being "really seen." See Thomas Carlyle, *Critical and Miscellaneous Essays*, 7 vols. (London: Chapman and Hall, 1895), 4:62. For a more detailed account of this poetics, see Rigney, *The Rhetoric of Historical Representation*.

14. For an overview of the different literary portraits of Robespierre, organised by feature, see Roger Vilfroy, "Le Personnage de Robespierre dans la littérature française du XIXe siècle." Dissertation, Paris, Université de la Nouvelle Sorbonne, 1975. For an account of the extant pictorial images of Robespierre, see Hippolye Buffenoir, *Les Portraits de Robespierre; étude iconographique et historique* (Paris: Leroux, 1910). Debate concerning the physical appearance of Robespierre and Danton seems to have reached its peak in the years following the publication of Aulard's *Danton* (1881) and his *L'Éloquence parlementaire pendant la Révolution française* (1886). That Robespierre's physical appearance long remained a hot historiographical (and ideological) issue is exemplified by such publications as Robert Petitgrand, "Un portrait de Robespierre," *La Révolution française* 10 (1886): 704–07; Albert Mathiez, "Un portrait inconnu de Robespierre," *Annales révolutionnaires* 4 (1911): 206–13; Pierre Marcel, "Contribution à l'iconographie de Robespierre," *Annales révolutionnaires* 5 (1912): 37–40; Albert Mathiez, "Sur les portraits de Danton et de sa famille," *Annales révolutionnaires* 9 (1916): 533–37.

15. As an illustration of the extent to which Robespierre was known by his clothes, see Balzac's reference, in *La Vieille Fille*, to a "waistcoat in the style of Robespierre" and, in *La Ténébreuse Affaire,* to "a brown velvet waistcoat in the style of Robespierre" and to "a velvet waistcoat with floral stripes [*à raies fleuretées*] in a style reminiscent of those worn by Robespierre," in Balzac, La *Comédie humaine,* 4:829; 8:544, 655.

16. Quoted in Vilfroy, 25–26.

17. Albert Mathiez, *Girondins et Montagnards* (Paris: Firmin-Didot, 1930), 26.

18. The biographer Ernest Hamel went one step further—almost, but not quite, into the unrecognizable. Attacking the "caricatures" of Robespierre that had shown him as "pale" and "bony," he claimed that the lawyer from Arras was "not without" a certain "embonpoint" and a certain "freshness of complexion." *Histoire de Robespierre*, 3 vols. (Paris: Lacroix, Verboeckhoven, 1865), 3:295.

19. In his account of the same *Fête*, Lamartine describes Robespierre's face as "radiant with his idea" (2:827), while Esquiros writes that his "pale face, his twisted features, stuck out clearly against the blue sky" and moved the onlookers to tears: "An old shoemaker, a silent spectator lost in the crowd, told me of his impressions: 'I'm no more sensitive or religious than any one else; but when I saw that man lift up his hand towards heaven as if he were inspired, I felt something move here (he showed me his heart), and tears of tenderness ran down my cheeks'" (2:451).

20. "Since generally men have a face like the idea they represent, the Girondins were handsome in the classical manner," unlike the Montagnards who had "the face and figure of a Christian nation" (2:339). As Esquiros' narrative proceeds and Danton moves into opposition with Robespierre, more and more emphasis is placed on Danton's "taste for sensual pleasures and good food" (2:306); if Robespierre finally saw the necessity of opposing him, this was because he feared that Danton's "materialism" might lead him to indulge in "a purely sensual compassion for the victims" (2:417).

21. Michelet, 1:907. As Lionel Gossman pointed out in his helpful comments on an earlier version of this paper, Michelet's foregrounding of Robespierre's paleness against Danton's energy can be seen as a perpetuation of the late eighteenth-century debate regarding line and colour, a debate that went on to acquire a specific ideological charge at the time of the Revolution, when Winckelmann could be cited to legitimize the austere idealism of the Jacobins, while Diderot and Lessing valued the variety and energy of life in the here and now.

22. Henri Baudrillart, "Les Historiens de la Révolution française et la Révolution de février," *Revue des deux mondes* 20e année, no.4 (1850): 813.

23. Alphonse de Lamartine, *Cours familier de littérature*, 28 vols. (Paris, 1856–69), 2:53.

Representing the Body Politic: Fictions of the State

CAROL BLUM

On 9 Thermidor (27 July 1794) Saint-Just rose to speak, his last attempt to master the assembled deputies of the nation. On his speech hung, literally, his life. His words at that desperate moment reveal the archangel of the Terror grappling with a failing instrument, his own words: "Que langage vais-je vous parler?" he asks his fellow deputies, suddenly transformed into his judges; "Comment vous peindre des erreurs dont vous n'avez aucune idée, et comment rendre sensible le mal qu'un mot décèle, qu'un mot corrige?" [What language shall I speak to you? How can I depict for you errors of which you have no idea, how can I make you feel the evil that a word reveals, that a word rectifies?].[1] It was not surprising, but rather appropriate, that Saint-Just's final plea for the legitimacy of the Committee of Public Safety and his own should be couched in terms of a crisis in words, for it was through his command of the politically dominant language of his generation that Saint-Just, in concert with Robespierre and their Jacobin colleagues, had seized control of the government. The language that now lay prostrate in his mouth had gained definitive ascendancy less than two years earlier, in the fall of '92 and the winter of 1793, when the accused was Louis XVI and Saint-Just the accuser.

Saint-Just, the voice of the absolute radical Republic, now faltered in this last speech as he found himself finally incapable of representation (how to depict) and rhetoric (how to move). In the presence of an evil that threatened the existence of the Fatherland and yet was susceptible to words, an evil that a "word reveals, that a word rectifies," Saint-Just lost his command of both language and men.

Thermidor marked the final exhaustion and collapse of the particularly dynamic Manichaean discourse that had characterized the Terror, the positive feedback-loop of polarizing language translated into lethal force in the form of executions in France and the concept of total war at the front.

Both aspects of terror owed much to Saint-Just's revolutionary discourse. His comment demonstrates the extent to which the French Revolution was conceived and enacted as a discursive struggle in which fiction was pitted against fiction. From its inception in the authorial task of preparing *cahiers de doléances*, through the torrents of antagonistic language climaxing at Thermidor, the French were locked in an agony of *logos*. It is my contention that the corpus of Rousseau's work formed the arsenal from which revolutionaries at all points on the political spectrum drew their arms, that Rousseau's writings facilitated certain essential tasks for those wishing to destroy the monarchy and found a new polity, and that by far the most ardent and adept of Jean-Jacques' disciples formed the nucleus of the Jacobin organization during the period that François Furet refers to as *"dérapage"*[2] and Ferenc Fehér as "frozen"[3]: the period of the Jacobin Republic. Finally, I contend, the internal logic of Rousseau's state could only create a body politic in constant purge. For the twentieth century left, the Jacobin era—the period running from the trial of Louis and the outbreak of war until Thermidor—came to epitomize the true Revolution, what Albert Soboul calls "la revolution dans toute son efficacité" [the revolution in all its efficacy].[4] For Western moderates, on the other hand, the same period came to embody demagogic democracy run amok. This radical split between interpretations of the Jacobin era has long problematized the very discussion of the struggle for representation that raged within it.

In various papers and publications I have spoken about the Rousseauvian contribution to radical language in the trial of Louis XVI,[5] not only because I view this event as politically crucial but also on account of its decisive nature in determining the direction and consequences of future discourse. The arguments over Louis' fate, especially in the formulations of Saint-Just, clearly reveal the emerging rhetoric of "Virtue and its emanation Terror." At this point I would like to attempt to integrate these arguments, beginning with some remarks on the politically charged nature of the French language itself.

Although the establishment of a privileged language generally accompanies a given group's successful domination over subdued populations, the case of France is extreme. There is perhaps no nation on earth so exquisitely sensitive to its own tongue as France. The peculiar intensity with which the French have invested all aspects of their language is demonstrated in such phenomena as the rigid rules regarding grammar and syntax, the nearly hysterical attitudes toward pronunciation and intonation, the question of whether certain words may be admitted into the realm of official discourse, and the necessity of protecting its purity against foreign intrusion while at the same time imperiously urging its adoption abroad. These manifestations of aggressive linguistic narcissism are scarcely present, if at all, among other peoples; the Italians, Germans, Swedes, and English, in comparison with the French, take an almost slovenly attitude toward their native tongues.

One might trace the origins of what could be termed a national obsession to the middle of the sixteenth century and Du Bellay's *Défense et illustration de la langue française*. Yet the fullblown phenomenon of the French hypercathexis of oral communication really emerges in the seventeenth century as part of a deliberate, conscious, and remarkably modern campaign to solidify the absolute monarchy. The inordinate power vested in French discourse is a consequence of its role in the self-aggrandizing monarchy. Richelieu put money, time, and effort into harnessing the French language to the Sun King's chariot. In so doing, he institutionalized monarchical authority over both written and spoken French through the Académie française, repudiating words alien to the ideal of Versailles, words evoking "le village, le vieux, et le bas." The purity of French was not only enforced by royal police; its very utterance required the king's permission. The Comédie française alone was privileged to speak French on stage; popular entertainments were restricted by law to silence, although this mutism was thwarted by endless ingenious strategies. The will to absolute power extended to a linguistic theological police state that could never completely silence the impudent voices from below. As Jeffrey Merrick has described it, "The laws of the Ancien Régime protected the sacred character of times, places, and objects consecrated to God by . . . punishing sacrilegious acts . . . by a graduate scale of penalties for repeated blasphemies, culminating with the amputation of the incorrigible tongue."[6] The dire nature of the punishment corresponds both to the immense power attributed to the tongue and to the difficulties of controlling it.

The great achievement of this linguistic dictatorship consisted of two literatures: one, the neoclassical flowering of dramatists and moralists, which did so much to further French cultural imperialism in Europe, and second, the corpus of monarchical apologies directly commissioned by Richelieu starting in the 1620s. These latter writings were by no means on the artistic level of Racine and Pascal, nor were they intended to be. They consisted of hundreds of little stories and homilies, told in a simplified language, that presented some piece of justification for the absolute monarchy. This is not the serious political philosophy of the era, but a specific genre of simple, pious stories explaining the legitimacy of the French monarchy and its connection to a Catholic God: stories intended for the widest possible audience, including the youngest and the marginally literate.

Two tales in particular were central to legitimizing the power of the king. The best known received its eventual definitive form in Robert Filmer's *Patriarcha* (1680), and was thoroughly savaged by Locke in his two *Treatises of Government*. Like many of the other tales, this one depicted the institution of monarchy as an addendum to Genesis, the *Ur*-text of authenticity, because God was alleged to have endowed Adam with sovereignty over creation and all kings were directly descended from our first father. This appropriation of the God of Abraham and Isaac as guarantor of Bourbon legitimacy was not new in the seventeenth century, but the breadth and sophistication of its dissemination were unprecedented. The condescendingly childish nature of the story being flogged linked it to the tradition of popular hagiography.

The analogy of God and King explained the origins of authority, for in this variation on Thomistic sources, God had delegated his righteous power to the temporal sovereigns through the flesh.[7] In a material and imperfect way they resembled him, sharing to some degree his omniscience, his omnipotence, and even, as works on the King's body have emphasized,[8] his spiritual omnipresence within the nation. In this theory of correspondences, the Catholic Church was welded to the Bourbon monarchy, and whatever disparities resulted had either to be repressed or denied. The ideal total acceptance of the formula may be illustrated by L'Estoile's assertion of total Catholic monarchism in a statement addressed to Richelieu: "Etre votre ennemi, c'est l'être de mon Roi, et l'être de mon Roi, c'est l'être de Dieu même." [To be your enemy is to be the enemy of my King and to be the enemy of my King is to be the enemy of God himself].[9]

As the king was a material representation of an immaterial God, so the "bon père de famille" was a still less perfect representation of the King. Nonetheless the father was a figure of metaphysical importance. In this way authority was explained and validated from top to bottom and from bottom to top as each patriarchal chief reinforced the others. Disobedient children were not merely challenging father but the state, the religion, and the Almighty himself. Even in the 1740s, for example, Diderot's father could have his thirty-year-old son incarcerated against his will in a monastery because the young man wished to marry and had spoken to him disrespectfully on the subject. As intellectually derisory as this model of monarchical authority may appear to the modern observer, it offered a consistent and comprehensible, if oppressively simplistic, account of familial, national, and supernational origins.

The second crucial story recounted the specific act linking the French monarchy to the divinity, given official narrative form in 1628 by Louis and Scevole de Sainte Marthe, royal *historiographes*. At the moment of

Clovis' conversion in 496, the Holy Ghost appeared as a dove carrying an ampoule filled with sacred oil; this vessel had remained full even though used to anoint each King of France. Its significance as a sign of God's special grace for France was symbolized by the anointed King's power to cure scrofula.[10]

"Religious mysteries," a distinct genre of implausible fictions, were invoked in Catholic theology when belief in an important manifest contradiction was required—in this instance the divine origins of a bottle of oil. This story not only guaranteed the King of France's legitimacy, but conferred upon him a sacerdotal role. In this respect competition among sovereigns took precedence over monarchical solidarity, for the kings of France took communion in both forms (dans les deux espèces)—both bread and wine—a privilege not granted lesser princes. Thus Louis's second legitimizing narrative was not a defense of monarchy, but only of the French monarchy. Although within France God, King, and Father reinforced each other, there was no solidarity among the temporal powers sanctioned by the master fiction. In fact, the kings of France were thought to resemble God even more than other sovereigns did. Jacques Cassan expressed it in 1632: "Sur tous les Rois qui commandent dans l'univers, Dieu a choisi par prérogative les Rois de France, pour graver en leurs majestés des traits et linéaments plus augustes de sa Divinité." [Of all the Kings reigning in the universe, God has chosen by privilege the Kings of France to inscribe in their majesties the most august features and traces of his Divinity].[11]

A third narrative central to Louis XVI's definition of himself was used not to bolster the monarchy but to denigrate it in favor of the aristocracy. Generated to contradict the absolutist *apologia* inspired by Richelieu, this tale put forth the claims of what Louis XVI would innocently refer to as his aristocracy. Like the stories of Adam's royal heirs, the Sainte Ampoule, and the royal touch, this one had a long past. But it was given full-dress treatment by Henri de Boulainvilliers, and like the other stories it attempted to provide a material basis for legitimizing the exercise of force. According to this tale, the "immemorial nobility" too held a material and not merely conventional ascendancy based on the blood of conquerors running in their veins, for the rightful members of the second estate were a Teutonic race apart in France, both naturally and divinely formed to rule the Gallo-Roman races they had permanently subdued. Unfortunately for the monarchy, however, Boulainvilliers "refused to ascribe any electoral or hereditary legitimacy to the three 'races' of French kings."[12] In this tale, the absolute monarchy is represented as the enemy of true aristocracy and has corrupted the flower of the nation by manipulating access to noble status. Absolutist France produced abundant pious monarchical materials and some impressive propaganda for the nobility, but none of the important seventeenth-century works of political history or theory. In Etienne Thuau's words, "La philosophie politique du régime de Richelieu est moins le fruit de la réflexion désintéressée que le masque de la volonté de l'Etat et un instrument de la domination" [The political philosophy of Richelieu's regime is less the fruit of disinterested reflection than the mask of the state's will and an instrument of domination]. Eventually, however, the controversies spawned by royal apologies and nobiliary counterclaims entered the mainstream of Enlightenment political debate. For Louis XVI, by no means a theoretician, royal consciousness remained at the level of self-contradictory anecdotal justification.

Much of the energy of Enlightenment was channelled into casting a great Cartesian doubt over the whole Catholic-monarchical "métaphysico-théologo-cosmolonigologique" structure of France. If the prose of Richelieu's propagandists has a peculiarly gelid quality, it had the merit of evoking the most splendid destructive texts of modern times. On the one hand, Encyclopedists and their allies challenged seriously and at length every tenet of the hegemonic discourse; on the other, a constant stream of anecdotal ridicule poured over the labored pieties of the monarchical fictions.

The definitions of key terms of political theory received elaborate treatment in the two great compendia of doubt, Pierre Bayle's *Dictionnaire* and the *Encyclopédie* of Diderot and d'Alembert. The techniques used to undermine both divine-right monarchy and Catholic ascendancy were substantially the same. The most effective strategies were the enormous multiplicity of divergent views challenging the windy but hollow *ex cathedra* voice of the single monarchical author, and the citation of prestigious authorities followed by expressions of dubiety or frank contradiction. This plurality of texts diffused the tremendous authority of the printed word. Diderot learned from Bayle the capacities for intellectual sabotage inherent in the construction of a reference work. He also inherited from Bayle the mélange of impressively meticulous scholarship, with quotations from both ancient and modern sources, often in Latin and Greek; a running commentary alternately friendly and dismissive; interjections of witty (and as frequently as possible scabrous) material; and provocative cross-references.

Bayle's critique of absolute monarchy, for example, does not appear in any one entry but darts in and out through the entire four volumes, in hundreds of different entries. Under the rubric *Religion* in the index, one reads: "Religion soumet les souverains aux peuples, bien loin de soumettre les peuples aux Souverains" [Religion submits sovereigns to people, far from submitting people to sovereigns]. In a footnote to an article on Arnisaeus (and one of Bayle's peculiarities was footnotes much longer than their entries, "Arnisaeus" taking up 8 lines, the notes 35), he says: "Il a donné un catalogue de ceux qui ont soutenu que la souveraineté appartient au peuple; dogme qui, au jugement de Boeclerus, est très pernicieux, et le pivot de rebellions. Si on faisait un tel catalogue la présente anneé 1699, il serait beaucoup plus long; car le dogme de la supériorité du peuple est devenu à la mode depuis quelque temps." [He gives a catalog of those who claim that sovereignty resides in the people; a dogma which, according to Boeclerus, is very pernicious and the source of rebellion. If one were to make such a catalog this present year of 1699, it would be longer yet because the dogma of the people's superiority has been fashionable for some time now]. These techniques were devised to render the censor's work all but impossible, since the subversive matter was not within the articles, but intertextual or draped with preterition. One could gather the free-thinking gist, but one could not prove it. The vast quantity of these assaults, from one-liners to major pieces, endowed the reference works with a destructive efficacy superior to that of conventional political tracts.

The Encyclopedists developed Bayle's techniques yet further. Kingdom was defined as follows: "*Royaume:* Ce mot signifie (je ne dirai pas ce que disent ces républicains outrés, qui firent anciennement tant de bruit dans le monde par leurs victoires et leurs vertus) un tyran et des esclaves; disons mieux qu'eux, un roi et ses sujets" [*Kingdom:* this word signifies (I won't go so far as to say what those exaggerated republicans used to say, the ones so highly acclaimed for their victories and their virtues) a tyrant and slaves; let us do better than they, and say a king and his subjects]. This flippant barb was one of innumerable entries attributing moral value to republics ancient and modern while denying it to monarchy. Such typical ludic needling of the official word has been described by Starobinski as "le non-recevoir que l'on oppose par le rire ou le mépris aux formes aberrantes ou fallacieuses du discours"[13] [The nonreception that is opposed, by means of laughter or contempt, to fallacious or aberrant forms of discourse]. Royalty was defined thus: "Les républicains sont ennemis de la royauté" [Republicans are enemies of royalty.] Whatever one's political opinions, that this should be the definition of royalty in a reference work published in a kingdom marks a lethal level of disengagement between official ideology and high-culture opinion.

As effectively destructive as the philosophic endeavor had been, however, it offered very little of positive value to shape opinion for a reformulated polity. Most of these texts presuppose the philosophic fantasy of a sovereign enlightened enough to introduce reform from above; the vision of the nation with a royal head is nowhere truly supplanted by a powerful alternative metaphor.

It was Rousseau who offered what the Encyclopedists had not, a startling new picture of the state as a whole, as an organic creature sufficing unto itself in all regards, as what Novalis would call "the beautiful individual." Rousseau's contribution to the imaginative linguistic pool from which revolutionaries drew their most effective terms of discourse may be divided into three main categories: (1) his conclusion and metamorphosis of the process of redefining fundamental political vocabulary, a process stimulated by Locke and developed by the *philosophes,* to restructure the body politic; (2) his model of the state as a projection of an idealized, virtuous self with which many revolutionaries reported a gratifying, energizing, and reciprocally binding identification linked to a politically valuable eloquence; and (3) his deliberate introduction of frank, vulgar words into serious discourse, so that the sovereignty of elevated diction established under the absolute monarchy was definitely destroyed in favor of the popular, the vulgar, the common.

All three of these major Rousseauvian revisions of old-regime verbal conventions were bolstered by moral rationales; all three incorporated hostile assaults on, respectively, the monarchy, the aristocracy, and the dominant intellectual culture of the Enlightenment. Although Rousseau denied aggressivity in himself, he analyzed the pugnacious virtualities of language most perceptively. The words of the Spartans, Rousseau's privileged example of virtue, were as injurious as their blows: "Toujours faits pour vaincre, ils écrasoient leurs ennemies en toute espèce de guerre, et les babillards Athéniens craignoient autant leurs mots que leurs corps" [Ever ready to conquer, they crushed their enemies in every kind of war, and the blabbering Athenians feared their words as much as their bodies].[14] It was from a vantage point of moral superiority that Rousseau announced the authentic meanings of such words as *sovereign* and *state,* that he described a "republic of virtue," and that he valorised the plebeian tongue. All three innovations were generated against existing structures of the old regime and contained destructive capacities realized only during the Revolution. In the process, however, "le village, le vieux, et le bas" were rehabilitated at the expense of the court, the modern, and the elite.

Systematically, though not always consistently, Rousseau organized and energized this transvaluation of values in the political works, especially the *Contrat social.* Where the *philosophes* had conducted a kind of linguistic guerrilla warfare out of sporadic sarcasms against the monarchical fortifications, Rousseau erected a total new city that, by its very existence, challenged the old order's right to be. That revolutionaries did not all know or understand the contents of the *Contrat social* has been widely accepted; however, as Roger Barny and others have shown, they were aware of the work's existence and of its fundamental revolutionary premise: namely, that regardless of history and contemporary reality, sovereignty was claimed to reside in the people.[15]

The Encyclopedists had defined the word "sovereign" in the traditional way, as the human being to whom the state delegated authority. While defining him thus, they used every opportunity to cast doubt on the institution of kingship and to press royal reform on crowned heads. According to the *Encyclopédie*, sovereigns were those "à qui la volonté des peuples a conféré le pouvoir nécessaire pour gouverner la société. L'homme, dans la nature, ne connaît point de souverain; chaque individu est égal à un autre . . . il n'est pas dans cet état d'autre subordination que celle des enfants à leurs pères. Un souverain, quelque absolu qu'il soit, n'est point en droit de toucher aux lois constitutives" [. . . those on whom the people's will has conferred the power necessary to govern society. In nature man knows no sovereign; each individual is equal to any other . . . in that state there is no subordination other than that of children to their fathers. A sovereign, no matter how absolute, has no right to touch the constitutive laws].

In the *Contrat social* Rousseau not only dismissed the idea of natural parental authority altogether but made the conceptual leap into political modernity: the sovereign was not a person at all, but the whole body politic. In this way the nation itself now constituted a moral person, sovereign over itself. As each individual surrendered to the group, the group became "un corps moral et collectif composé d'autant de membres que l'assemblée a de voix, lequel recoit de ce même acte son unité, son *moi* commun, sa vie et sa volonté" [a moral and collective body composed of as many members as the assembly has voices, which now receives from this very act its unity, its common *ego*, its life and its will] (3:361). Having thus defined the state as a collective fusion of identity, a modern mystery story, he went on to reveal that the ancient European vocabulary differentiating one political term from another was fallacious. Understood correctly, all the old political words referred to the same thing: the body politic, the "public person," seen under different lights.

Rousseau then elaborated: "Cette personne publique qui se forme ainsi par l'union de toutes les autres prenait autrefois le nom de *cité*, et prend maintenant celui de *république* . . . *état* quand il est passif, *souverain* quand il est actif, *puissance* en le comparant à ses semblables. A l'égard des associés ils prennent collectivement le nom de *peuple*; . . . *citoyens*

comme participans à l'autorité souveraine, et *sujets* comme soumis aux
lois de l'Etat. Mais ces termes se confondent souvent et se prennent l'un
pour l'autre; il suffit de les savoir distinguer quand ils sont employés dans
toute leur précision." [This public person formed by the union of all other
people used to take the name of the *city*, and now takes that of the *republic . . . state* when it's passive, *sovereign* when it's active, a *power* compared
to its peers. As to the associates, they collectively take the name *people; . . .
citizens* when participating in the sovereign authority and *subjects* when
submitted to the laws of the state. But these terms are often confused
and mistaken for one another; it suffices to be able to distinguish them
when they are used in all their precision] (3:361–62). Thus the science of
government was reduced to a taxonomy understood by Rousseau and his
disciples virtually alone. In all of France, for example, he permitted only
d'Alembert to understand the word "citoyen" correctly: "Nul autre auteur,
que je sache, n'a compris le vrai sens du mot" [No other author, to my
knowledge, has understood the true meaning of the word] (3:362). This
Gleichschaltung eliminating difference, this radical, *ex cathedra* reorder-
ing of political vocabulary, did away with king and kingdom. Rousseau
did not argue against monarchy here; he semantically liquidated it. The
old European words that had distinguished one thing from another were
now seen to signify the same object, the undifferentiated body politic,
viewed in varying light. In a complementary argument, Rousseau formulated the new demographic basis of the new polity, the simple theory that
one equals one. The "people" constituted the nation, people signifying the
third estate, and what was not the "people" was numerically so insignificant that it might as well not exist. "C'est le peuple," he wrote in *Emile*,
"qui compose le genre humain; ce qui n'est pas peuple est si peu de chose
que ce n'est pas la peine de le compter." [It is the people who compose the
human race; what is not the people is so insignificant it's not worth count-
ing] (4:509). A legitimate government would be based on the mathematics
of population. Understand that your species consists "essenciellement de
la collection des peuples," he continued, emphasizing the potential power
of numbers, "quand tous les rois et tous les philosophes en seraient ôtés, il
n'y paroitroit guère, et que les choses n'en iront pas plus mal" [. . . composed in essence of the collection of peoples, that if all the kings and all the
philosophers disappeared it would scarcely be noticed, and things would
be no worse] (4:511). By using the word *peuple* to mean human in some
places, the masses elsewhere, and ethnic collectivities elsewhere yet, Rousseau maximalized the radical potentialities of his pronouncements. He
announced a world at which the *philosophes* only hinted, a world where
quality, as in "un homme de qualité," was replaced by quantity.

It was this Rousseauvian language that was used to obliterate Louis XVI during the factional struggles of his trial. Laclos, for example, supporting regicide, pointed out that according to Rousseau in the *Contrat social*, "qu'en présence de l'assemblée le prince n'existait point" [. . . in the presence of the assembly the king ceased to exist],[16] a reference instantly understandable to the assembled deputies. Laclos's remark was only one of many texts urging the semantic destruction of Louis in advance of his corporal execution.

Saint-Just, arguably the most conscious and lucid of Rousseau's disciples, borrowed his mentor's definition of sovereign to render the King nonexistent. Since "sovereign" signified the state and the state was synonymous with the "people," Saint-Just demonstrated the necessity for executing Louis by defining the "people" as the Parisian mob that invaded the Tuileries on 10 August. "Depuis que le peuple français a montré sa volonté, tout ce qui l'oppose est hors le souverain, tout ce qui est hors le souverain est l'ennemi . . . entre le peuple et ses ennemis il n'y a rien de commun que le glaive." [Since the French people has demonstrated its will, everything opposing it is outside the sovereign, everything outside the sovereign is the enemy . . . between the people and its enemies there is nothing in common but the blade] (Saint-Just, 2:479). Louis was defined out of existence before being guillotined.

In the eighteen months of Terror leading from his trial to that of his accuser Saint-Just, juridical procedure underwent a sort of demonic acceleration. The radical simplification that had redefined the body politic without its traditional head was used, in the months following Louis' decapitation, to eliminate one group after another from the body politic in words before their destruction in the flesh.

Saint-Just spent the hours preceding Thermidor preparing a long discourse, but he was interrupted during the first paragraph by the panic-stricken deputies, his voice drowned in the noise of opposition, and he never spoke the words that would have deflected the evil from him onto others. In the speech he had not been allowed to finish, he expressed the injustice of the accusations against him: "C'est au nom de la patrie que je vous parle: j'ai cru servir mon pays et lui éviter des orages en n'ouvrant mes lèvres sincères qu'en votre présence. C'est au nom de vous même que je vous entretiens . . ." [I speak to you in the name of the fatherland: I believed I served my country and I steered it away from misfortune by never opening my sincere lips except in your presence. It is in your own name that I speak to you now . . .] (2, 533). Terrified terrorists did not let him have his word, and the deadly confusion of a body politic without a head expressing its will entered a new phase.

NOTES

1. Saint-Just, *Oeuvres complètes* (Paris: Charpentier and Fasquelle, 1908), 2:478. Hereafter cited as Saint-Just.

2. Furet's discussion of the Terror from the perspective of Thermidor stresses the Convention's need to produce an acceptable narration of 1792–94 that would distance the deputies from events in which most had participated or which they had at least tolerated. *La Révolution: 1770–1880* (Paris: Hachette, 1988), 161–167.

3. In *The Frozen Revolution* (Cambridge: Cambridge University Press, 1987), Fehér analyses the political significance of the complex historiographical arguments about Jacobinism. His treatment of the relationship between nineteenth-century historicism and Marxist representations of the "Republic of Virtue" is especially revealing.

4. Albert Soboul, *Le Proces de Louis XVI* (Paris: Juillard, 1966), 132.

5. *Rousseau and the Republic of Virtue: the Language of Politics in the French Revolution* (Ithaca, N.Y.: Cornell University Press, 1986); "Rousseau and the Democratization of Language in the French Revolution," *Studies in Eighteenth-Century Culture* 17 (1987): 309–317.

6. "The Religious Police of the *ancien régime* and the Secularization of Jurisprudence in the Eighteenth Century" (article in press).

7. For a discussion of Aquinas's contribution to the synthesis of divine will and human institutions within the concept of natural law, see Thomas Gilby, *The Political Thought of Thomas Aquinas* (Chicago: University of Chicago Press, 1958).

8. See particularly E. H. Kantorowicz, *The King's Two Bodies* (Princeton: Princeton University Press, 1957).

9. *Le Sacrifice des muses*, cited by Etienne Thuau, *Raison d'état et pensée politique à l'époque de Richelieu* (Paris: Colin, 1966), 245.

10. *L'Histoire généalogique de la maison de France* (Paris: 1628); see Marc Bloch, *Les Rois thaumaturges* (Paris: Colin, 1961).

11. *La Recherche des droits de Roy* (Paris, 1632), 2. Alexander's 1812 Holy Alliance among Christian kings would seem to fulfill the royal conspiracy theory only after the fact, its utility curiously obvious to Revolutionaries before crowned heads.

12. Harold Ellis, *Boulainvilliers and the French Monarchy* (Ithaca, N.Y.: Cornell University Press, 1988), 84.

13. "La Chaire, la tribune, le barreau," *Les Lieux de Mémoire: la Nation* (Paris: Gallimard, 1987), 430.

14. Jean-Jacques Rousseau, *Emile*, in *Oeuvres completes*, 4 vols. (Paris: Gallimard, 1959), 4:362. Henceforth I cite this edition for all of Rousseau's works.

15. Roger Barny, *Rousseau dans la Révolution: le personnage de Jean-Jacques et les débuts du culte révolutionnaire* (1787–1791) (Oxford: Voltaire Foundation, 1986).

16. Laclos cites Rousseau in "De la déchéance du roi," *Oeuvres complètes* (Paris: Gallimard, 1959), 617.

Performing Arts: Theatricality
and the Terror

MARIE-HÉLÈNE HUET

During the debates of June 1791 on the death penalty, a deputy declared: "Interest the hearts of all citizens in the fate of the unfortunate who will come under the sword of Justice so that he will be offered solace, on every side; and let their miserable remains receive the honors of burial."[1] We don't know with any certainty where most of the victims claimed by the guillotine were buried, least of all where the body of the king finally came to rest.[2] But in recent years, a grandiose memorial has been dedicated, if not to the king himself, then to the images of kings brutally destroyed in the violence of revolutionary iconoclasm that followed the execution of Louis XVI.

Set in a remote area of the Cluny Museum in Paris, the Eighth Gallery (fig. 5) displays a remarkable collection of Gothic sculpture, the last remains of the statues removed from Notre Dame in 1793 and 1794. To the left of the entrance, twenty-one heads rest on high pedestals; to the right, twenty headless bodies stand erect, many of them, we are told, still unidentified. The gallery, a large space contained on the north and west by the ruins of the Gallo-Roman baths, on the east by the sixteenth century Chapel and on the south by a recent, nineteenth century addition, thus offers the most ambitious reconstruction of the Gothic sculpture that originally decorated Notre Dame.

Fragments of the statues destroyed by the Revolution were recovered in the nineteenth and twentieth centuries, but no occasion was more dramatic than the discovery, in 1977, of the twenty-one heads of the Galerie des Rois de Judah, at the headquarters of the Banque Française du Commerce Extérieur, rue de la Chaussée d'Antin. These heads had belonged to the Tree of Jesse that stretched horizontally across the main entrance to Notre Dame.[3] As both images of kings and religious symbols, they had represented a double affront to the revolutionary ideal and were taken down, along with more than one hundred other sculptures.

The dramatic distribution of the fragments in the gallery, the careful placing of the kings' heads "at an appropriate height" on the one hand, and the display of truncated bodies on the other (fig. 6), present the visitor, to quote the Museum brochure, with "an important testimony to the stylistic revolution that took place brutally in the years 1230–1240."[4] The historical significance of this testimony is further enhanced by the arrangement of the statues in chronological order, and the suggestion that the mutilated bodies to the right of the visitor were executed at a later date than the heads that first greet the spectator at the entrance to the gallery. Clearly, several executions are at stake here. While the Eighth Gallery may be the most eloquent depository of the Gothic statuary, it also presents the spectator with a powerful rebuke to the excesses of a regime that sought with equal violence the execution of Louis XVI and the metaphorical beheading of the Kings of Judah. It could be said of this display that it represents the last and most dramatic staging of a death penalty, thought of as a spectacle, and fit for a king. For the theatricality of the guillotine came to symbolize in the eyes of Europe the frightful determination of a government eager to do away with the secrecy of the old regime and to provide the people with new emblems of patriotic virtue. "If you want the death penalty to retain all its exemplary effectiveness," said Dutau in 1791, "make the punishment of the guilty into an imposing spectacle; link the execution to a painful and most touching display; let that terrible day be a day of national mourning; let the general suffering be depicted strikingly. Imagine the forms that are most compatible with a tender sensibility. . . . Let the magistrate robed in black crepe announce to the people the crime and the sad necessity of legal retribution. Let the different scenes of this tragedy make an impression on all the senses."[5] Another deputy added: "The spectator must return home filled with terror."[6]

The Revolution thus meant to stage both the erasure of the old regime and the emergence of the new order, using what the *Révolutions de Paris* called "the powerful language of images."[7] The desire for a public revolution was further enhanced by a series of decrees regulating all levels of performance, permitting the unchecked proliferation of theaters, the simultaneous rehabilitation of the actor and the executioner, and the decision, by the Convention, that a selection of patriotic plays be produced, at no cost to the public, for the education and benefit of all citizens.[8] The use of Paris as stage for the revolutionary project was extraordinarily successful, and observers could not help seeing the events of 1789 and 1792 as a powerful, if mixed, theatrical genre: "A monstrous tragi-comic scene" for

Burke, a farce or a tragedy for others, a spectacle for all. If the theatrical model underlined the desire for a public regime, a regime devoted to the people and free of plotting behind the curtains, it also suggested a dramatic fusion between actors and politicians on the one hand and spectators and the revolutionary crowds on the other. For years during the *ancien régime,* a series of oppressive measures had been imposed upon the little theaters that thrived under the auspices of the Foire Saint-Laurent and the Foire Saint-Germain. Anxious to protect its domination and exclusive use of the classical repertory, the Comédie-Française got several decrees proclaimed against rival theater companies. The actors, first prohibited from reciting texts, took to singing them; prohibited from singing texts, they began to carry placards displaying their lines; prohibited from using a text in any form, they turned to mime. Finally, they were required to act with a veil suspended between them and the spectators during the entire performance. It is said that upon learning of the fall of the Bastille, Plancher-Valcour, director of the Délassements-Comiques, ripped down the notorious veil to the cry of "Vive la Liberté!" In other versions of the incident, after official permission had been given to all theaters to reopen their doors, the curtain was torn to shreds by a mob of impatient spectators. The theater thus provided models for public disclosure. The desire to "tear away the veil," the forceful and passionate search for unmediated action, was a constant theme of revolutionary rhetoric. The explicit requirement of public virtue, and of virtue dedicated to the public welfare, was that no one should be allowed to conspire behind the curtain. Similarly, just as the text and the right to speak had been conferred upon popular theaters as a revolutionary victory, the "prise de parole," the right and obligation to speak up, was to remain one of the enduring principles of revolutionary ideals and philosophy. It was illustrated by public speeches at the Convention and at the political clubs and by an important innovation in the judicial process: the public voting of the Jury at the revolutionary tribunal.

Yet the creation of a public stage where the Revolution would unfold its destiny was not without danger. "How could Liberty ever have established itself among us?" asked Marat in July 1792. "At several nearly tragic scenes, the revolution has only been a web of farcical representations."[9] Furthermore, the effectiveness of the theater as pedagogical instrument came to be questioned as well. The right to produce classical repertory that had been denied them for so long was first seen as a victory for the small theaters, and the success of plays representing the major events of the Revolution—the fall of the Bastille and the death of Marat, for example—gave them an undeniable patriotic aura. But the theatricality of the Revolution could not be contained in the narrow confines of the playhouses. The changing values of the regime, the constant suspicion that the most revolutionary proclamations only served to hide or mask aristocratic plots, all this generated a political drama that was too chaotic to be represented within the theaters. In the spring of 1794, Plancher-Valcour renounced the classical repertory entirely with these words: "Plays recalling the old regime should no longer be produced even if they attack it, recall its vices, its follies, its monstrous abuses. It is not enough to decree that counterrevolutionary plays must not be given. We should dispense with all classics for at least half a year." [10] Censorship was officially reinstated on 2 Floréal Year II (21 April 1794); about this time (a few weeks before what has been called the Great Terror), Joseph Payan, a member of the Committee on Public Instruction, declared: "The theaters are still encumbered with the rubbish of the old regime. We must sweep this chaotic mass out of our theaters. We must clear the stage." [11] This last appeal, "we must clear the stage," signals a break in the Revolution's attitude toward all spectacles, whether inspired by faith, justice, or revolutionary virtue. I would like to show how the Terror, as it was conceived by Robespierre, was both furthered and undermined by a determination to "clear the stage," to renounce entirely the dramatic closure of the Revolution. The Terror was a war against spectacles and images, performance and representations; ultimately, it was a war against language itself.

The Unspeakable Terror

On 18 Floréal Year II (7 May 1794), Robespierre outlined the necessity for a new religion, the Cult of the Supreme Being, and moved the celebration of the festival that would take place a few weeks later, on 20 Prairial (8 June). The Festival of the Supreme Being inaugurated a new cult that repudiated both the Catholic Church and the recent and more profane Cult of Reason dedicated on 10 November 1793. The Cult of Reason had been deliberately theatrical: an intricate ceremony took place at Notre Dame where an actress from the Opera, dressed in tricolor garb and surrounded by two groups of young women in white, was paraded around the aisles and up to the altar. "The entire ceremony had been performed by artists of the same theater," notes F. A. Aulard.[12] By contrast, the Festival of the Supreme Being was to be a festival without images or representations. After having set fire to gigantic statues representing Egoism, Atheism, and Nothingness (a powerful dismissal of idols and the vices they represent), a large procession unfolded from the Tuileries to the champ de Mars (then called champ de la Réunion), according to a plan staged by David. The burning of the statues was symbolic: when Robespierre proposed the Cult of the Supreme Being, he explicitly sought to bring the Revolution back to a form of worship that would owe nothing to previous religions or their images. "When it comes to defining the Supreme Being," wrote his friend Claude Payan, "our idea of Him will be so *sublime* that we shall not degrade Him by giving Him a face or a body similar to ours."[13] The word *sublime* should be understood here in the sense of the *Third Critique*, in which Kant writes: "We have no reason to fear that the feeling of the sublime will suffer from an abstract mode of representation like this, which is altogether negative as to what is sensuous. For though the imagination, no doubt, finds nothing beyond the sensible world to which it can lay hold, still this thrusting aside of the sensible barriers gives it a feeling of being unbounded; and that removal is thus a presentation of the infinite." And Kant adds: "As such, it can never be anything more than a negative presentation—but still it expands the soul. Perhaps there is no more sublime passage in the Jewish Law than the commandment: Thou shalt not make unto thee any graven image, or any likeness of any thing that is in heaven or on earth."[14] The Cult of the Supreme Being, as it was proposed by Robespierre in his speech of 18 Floréal, sharply criticized the idolatry of false religions and abusive powers: "What do priests and God have in common?" he asked, "How different the God of nature is from the God of priests! He knows nothing so resembling atheism as the religion they have made. By *disfiguring* the Supreme Being, they have destroyed Him to the best of their abilities. They have made Him into a globe of fire, an ox, a tree, sometimes a man, sometimes a king. The priests have created God in their own image."[15] The exclusion of images was closely linked to the exercise of virtue. Not only was virtue also disfigured in the worship of idols, but it had no place in it. At the same time that Robespierre asked for a cult without images, he also argued that "All virtues compete for the right to preside over our festivals" (p. 281). They are the expression of "a *sublime abandon* to the Fatherland," and, he added: "Woe betide him who seeks to erase this *sublime* enthusiasm, and to destroy with devious doctrines the people's moral strength, which moves it to the greatest deeds" (p. 282).

Robespierre thus tried to create a form of religion that, like revolutionary virtue, would be sublime and would wrest itself away from all sensual representations of its ideal. The Festival of the Supreme Being meant to erase idolatry and do away with all the images that would degrade its sublime ideal. The Festival of the Supreme Being was like a brief pause in the last spring of the Revolution. The guillotine disappeared from the place de la Révolution (today's place de la Concorde), and the people are said to have believed that the new cult also signaled an end to the executions.

Yet, two days later, the Convention adopted the Law of 22 Prairial, submitted by Couthon but inspired by Robespierre, which led to what was
later called the Great Terror. The Law of 22 Prairial eliminated the judicial
system of the defense and left the Tribunal with but two options: liberty
or death. In the two months that followed, there were 1,376 executions
in Paris.[16] The contrast between the peaceful glory of the Festival of the
Supreme Being and the onset, two days later, of the Great Terror has not
failed to puzzle witnesses, critics, and historians.[17] I would like to show
how the Law that led to so many deaths constituted a new measure of the
sublime, that is, a measure *against representation,* be it that of God, crime,
or punishment.

It may be useful to specify here that the theoretical Terror proposed by
Robespierre was a principle of justice and government that had nothing
to do with the excesses of the revolutionary Tribunal headed by Fouquier-
Tinville. The word *terror* had acquired a second meaning for the *sans-
culottes*—the simple elimination of the enemies of the Republic. "Terror
alone can secure our Liberty," wrote the *Journal Universel* on 24 Brumaire
Year II (14 November 1793), "No more leniency. Let the blade of the law
graze upon all the guilty heads." But Robespierre denounced "the false
terrors" and played a crucial role in putting an end to Carrier's infamous
drownings in Nantes. Robespierre's negative Terror, as we shall see, is
precisely the reverse side of the monstrous theatricality that would endow
death with a parodic ceremonial in the last two months of the Revolution.

In his discourse of 18 Pluviôse Year II (5 February 1794) on "The principles of political morality that must guide the Convention in its administration of the Republic," Robespierre stated: "If the mainspring of popular
government in peacetime is virtue, the mainspring of popular government
in time of war is both *virtue and terror:* virtue without which terror is fateful; terror without which virtue is helpless. Terror is nothing but prompt,
severe and inflexible justice; it is thus an emanation of virtue" (p. 221).
What this discourse conveyed more forcefully still is that if the Revolution
is to realize the sublimity and virtue that make up its very definition, then
it must transcend not only the sensible presentation of ideas, but also the
representation that is part and parcel of language itself; it must transcend
"the abuses of language," which are always capable of betraying the meaning and truth of the sublime. The Law of 22 Prairial gets rid of all those
who would speak *in the name of* the suspects, testify for them, in short,
represent them. This reduction of the rhetorical system of the defense aids
and abets a tragic simplification of the trial's outcome; there are no more
degrees of innocence or guilt. "Liberty or Death," which had been one of
the great slogans of the year 1792, takes on its most literal meaning. This

absolute reduction of the *sentence* (which should be understood here as both a judgment and a unit of discourse) should also be seen in the context of what Robespierre sought to define as *purity*. "We have just presented, in all its purity," he said, "the moral and political principle of popular government" (p. 217). "Purity" is opposed to the most serious form of treason, that which stems from language itself. "How easily we are misled by words!" (p. 225) says Robespierre (who started his career as a defense lawyer). The judicial system that allows for the representation of the suspects also allows for the representation of crime, for one to speak *in the name of* crime. Describing the old system of justice, Robespierre notes: "Some want to govern revolutions through legal cavil. Some treat conspiracies against the Republic as one would an individual trial. Tyranny kills and liberty pleads; and the code made by conspirators themselves is the law by which they are sentenced. When the safety of the Fatherland is at stake, testimony from the entire world cannot supplement a testimonial proof, nor can evidence itself replace literal proof." (p. 225) Liberty, this sublime idea, should not have to defend its own cause. Language cannot be trusted; of the "false revolutionaries" who spread false rumors, Robespierre declares: "Let us not judge by the difference in words but by the identity of results." (p. 230) For Robespierre, the suspicion that taints all sensible representation spreads in turn to the intangible and thus more powerful representation of language and words. Language is suspect, and the Law of 22 Prairial is also a law against words. Just as the old religion had worshipped images, the previous form of justice in its wordiness spoke for tyrants and treason: "It is so much more convenient to put on the mask of patriotism to *disfigure the sublime* drama of the Revolution with insolent parodies, to compromise the cause of Liberty with hypocritical moderation and studied extravagance. How many traitors interfere with us to ruin our efforts! Do you want to try them, to ask them true services instead of oaths and declamations? Is action needed? They make speeches instead" (p. 231—emphasis mine).

Robespierre tried to define the Revolution as sublime, as an ideal that would transcend all representation and escape all misrepresentation, as a rhetorical purity that could only be expressed in a negative form. Once again, Kant, rather than Rousseau, may offer the best assessment of Robespierre's sublime: "The safeguard is the purely negative character of representation. For the inscrutability of the idea of freedom precludes all positive representation." [18] The concept of Law, like the concept of Liberty that Law expresses and protects, also transcends all representation, even linguistic representation. "Laws," said Robespierre, "have not been etched in marble or stone, but in the hearts of all men" (p. 211). The Mosaic prohibition of images is carried to its absolute negation, that is, to the denial of its engraving on the tables of the Law. Robespierre's words on the Revolution and its laws also echo Kant's description of the experience of the sublime: "This *astonishment* amounting almost to a terror, the awe and thrill of devout feeling that takes hold of one when gazing upon the prospects of mountains ascending to heaven, deep ravines and torrents raging there . . . all this when we are assured of our own safety, is not actual fear." [19] It should be emphasized that Robespierre's Terror, contrary to traditional interpretations, meant to pose no threat to virtuous citizens. Virtue was, quite precisely, the safeguard of Terror. In Robespierre's conception of a political morality rescued from writing and representation, virtue protects the honest citizen—"It is the terror of crime that guarantees the security of innocence." [20]

The decision not to provide a tangible representation of the Supreme Being and the decision not to provide a legal representation of the crime expressed the same teleological concern that led to the adoption of an "inscrutable justice," to quote Robespierre, and that no doubt helps to explain the successive displacements of the guillotine. No execution took place on the day of the Festival of the Supreme Being. On that day, the guillotine was taken from the place de la Révolution to the Faubourg Saint-Antoine; a few days later, it was moved again, to the Barrière du Trône Renversé (today's place de la Nation) far away from the stage of the Festivals. The tragic and popular festival of death would be temporarily removed from its daily audience. Shortly after Robespierre's discourse of 5 February 1794, Payan protested publicly against the regular habit of bringing benches and renting seats for the spectators surrounding the guillotine. "The scaffold would no longer be pressed by the crowd," Michelet would later write, "it was the emancipation of the guillotine. She was to take a deep exterminating breath, outside the civilized world, having nothing more of which to be ashamed." [21] Terror and the sublime both transcended material representations and allowed for no spectacle. In one of his last public acts, Robespierre proposed that the place de la Révolution, where the guillotine had so long remained, now be reserved for the exclusive use of revolutionary festivals. The stage was cleared. Terror and justice, like the sublime, disclaimed any form of representation.

But Robespierre's explicit desire to create a sublime Revolution, his attempts to denounce what he saw as a parody of Liberty, also sustain a more radical decision to denounce treason and words, or words that themselves speak for treason. Decrying what he calls "the abuses of language" and the disguises of virtue, he claims: "A King, a vain Senate, a Caesar, a Cromwell must above all cover their project with a religious *veil*" (p. 210)

Robespierre's last discourses are entirely fraught with the paradox that consists of disclaiming all material and sensible representation of the Revolution, all suspicious verbal rhetoric, while using nothing but words to unmask words, a last performance to denounce all performances, a final testimony to unveil all testimonies. "This great purity which founds the French Republic, the very sublimity of its project, is both our strength and our weakness" (p. 220). Such is the dilemma of a language, a rhetoric that would no longer be the "dupe of words" but would be driven by "the ascendancy of truth over imposture." Robespierre was an avid reader of Rousseau. Given his expressed desire for a language of transparency, it would be tempting to see his last discourse as yet another symptom of the Rousseauvian aspiration to tear away the veil and to remove all masks, to achieve a purity that stems from a language spoken directly by the soul. The contrast between a law that is fallacious and etched in stone and the pure, incorruptible law written in the hearts of men seems to repeat Rousseau's suspicion of *écriture*, of writing considered as a threat to the authenticity of an interior, and finally unattainable, language.[22] But Robespierre makes the immanent perversion of language more absolute still: "Everything you say," he warns his colleagues, "will be turned against you, even the truth we have just put forward . . . false terrors are misleading and paralyzing the Convention" (p. 234). In this general betrayal of language, in the dramatic failure of language and representation to make truth prevail, what will be the last recourse of words? What will be their final referent? "Quel est le remède de tous ces maux?" asks Robespierre. The written form *maux* means "evils," but to the ear it can mean both "words" (*mots*) and "evils." What then is the remedy to all these evil words? . . . "We know of none other than the development of the main force of the Republic: Virtue." (p. 236) Virtue comes to mean not only what drives and motivates revolutionary discourse, but also, in its sublimity, what would elevate such discourse beyond all possible misrepresentation.

Death Told

Robespierre delivered his last speech before a hostile assembly a few hours before his arrest. It has been said that the discourse also caused his arrest, for it denounced a conspiracy without naming anyone, thus implicating the entire Convention. But more simply and urgently, Robespierre claimed that the right to speak, the pure necessity of telling the truth at the risk of one's life, *is the sublime.* The right to speak, the duty to speak when death will follow, the conviction that death will result when truth is spoken—such is the absolute guarantee that words, on the edge of ruin and silence, on the shores of negation, have finally reached the sublimity that defies all representation, hence all misrepresentation. "What objection can be made", he asked, "to him who wishes to speak the truth and agrees to die for it?" (p. 307) Death then becomes the referent of truth, and the one and only truth, guaranteed by the knowledge of his imminent death, is that he who is about to die *may* speak, *is entitled to* speak. "I shall conclude," continues Robespierre, "that principles are outlawed, and that tyranny reigns among us, *but not that I should remain silent*, for what objection can be made to a man who is right and is willing to die for his country?" (p. 308—emphasis added). The repetition of the sentence "What objection can be made?" posits the absolute character of this last discourse. It underlines the fact that language can no longer betray its purpose, that truth (which is nothing else than the right to speak the truth on the threshold of death) reveals its final purpose, its value as testament. Robespierre says: "I promised some time ago to leave a fearsome testament to the enemies of the people. I shall publish it now with the independence which suits the situation in which I have placed myself. I bequeath them the dreadful, the terrible truth and death" ["Je leur lègue la vérité terrible et la mort"] (p. 292) The dreadful and terrible truth is the truth that brings terror, terror without which virtue is helpless, and death in which truth alone mirrors itself.

It could be said that Robespierre's desire to define and further a sublime revolution failed twice. Robespierre had tried to impose a cult devoid of all sensible representations, a religion worthy of its sublime project, but in that regard, the Festival of the Supreme Being was a spectacular failure. The theatrical nature of the procession staged by David, of the symbolic mountain built on the Champ-de-Mars, and even the sacrifice of idols publicly burned at the onset of the ceremony all framed a stage where Robespierre became an unwilling actor, and for some, a high priest. Several historians have even seen Robespierre's physical isolation at the head of the procession as an obscure prefiguration of his downfall. Thus Madame de Staël, who had not witnessed the event, wrote in her *Considérations sur la Révolution Française*: "At the procession of this impious festival, Robespierre dared to go first, to claim preeminence over his colleagues, and from then on, he was lost."[23] Not only did the festival fail to avoid the theatricality of all the great revolutionary events, but it survived the death of Robespierre in a parodic form that was associated with the feminine and idolatrous Cult of Reason it had sought to erase. These two forms of worship mixed, and Charles Nodier would later decry the "scandalous orgies of the atheists . . . the stupid emblems of this absurd idolatry."[24] Not only did Terror fail to purify the language or the Justice of the Revolution, but it was to be drowned in an excess of morbid spectacles that culminated with Robespierre's own death. His death was organized as an impromptu festival with actors performing along the route and crowds of inebriated spectators. "The crowd was vast," said the *Journal de Perlet*, "The sounds of rejoicing, the applause, the cries of: 'Down with the tyrant! Long live the Republic!' the curses resounded all along the way." The *Annales de la République Française* of 11 Thermidor add: "Never had there been so large a crowd as for this execution. Women, children, old people, all of Paris was there."[25] The day after Robespierre's death, the guillotine was returned to the center stage of Paris, Place de la Concorde, for the largest number of public executions ever ordered in a single day. Theaters reopened. The Law of 22 Prairial was voided. "After 9 Thermidor," wrote Paul Thureau-Dangin, "everything was diminished, events and men. The stage was given to walk-ons, things fell so low that creatures like Tallien and Barras became characters."[26] The sublime revolution died along with Robespierre in the parodic displays of democratic merriment that followed 9 Thermidor.

We are all familiar with Marx's comment that history always repeats itself twice in its own theatricality, "once as tragedy, and again as farce." In his presentation of the collective volume entitled *Du Sublime*, Jean-Luc Nancy writes: "It may appear that our era is once again rediscovering the notion of the *sublime*, its name, its concept and the questions it entails; such is not the case of course, as one never returns to anything in History."[27] That the sublime should be precisely that which, in history, eludes repetition seems particularly appropriate here. Furthermore, the double concept of a history that never returns to its past, and a history that is always repeatable, also shows in what sense history is profoundly theatrical. Or rather, it illustrates that if history should repeat itself, it can do so only insofar as it already is, like theater, a performance. The symptomatic character of this performance, its tendency to repetition, the betrayal of its own project, was further illustrated in the spectacles that slowly replaced the stage of the executions. On 18 Fructidor Year II (4 September 1794), the Cité-Variétés of Paris gave a play entitled "The Fall of the last Tyrant or the 9th Thermidor." An anonymous letter to the *Abréviateur Universel* complained: "Citizens, shall we ever refrain from turning everything into an opera, a fantasy, a drama, a scenic play?" But Robespierre's own person was reappropriated by a legend that started to weave its fiction just a few months after his death. Charles Nodier described him as half bird of prey, half hyena. Madame de Staël wrote: "I talked once with Robespierre at my father's house in 1789. Then, he was known only as a lawyer from the Artois, very exaggerated in his democratic views. His features were repulsive, his complexion pale, his veins a shade of green."[28] Romanticism reinterpreted history as a scenic drama.

"Western historiography," writes Michel de Certeau, "battles with fiction. . . . Not that it tells the truth. No historian has ever claimed to do so. Rather, with the critical apparatus of discourse, the scholar removes error from 'fables.' The historian gains ground by diagnosing falsehoods. He cuts through accepted language, to make room for his discipline . . . as if he devoted himself to hunting down lies rather than establishing the truth, or as if he could only determine truth by determining error."[29] As presented by Michel de Certeau, the historian's work curiously overlaps Robespierre's desire to rid language of all false representations, and to reach truth through the negative sublime that contrasts so sharply with the symbolic output of the Revolution. It has been shown that romantic historiography was shaped by its own fiction, the necessity of narration, and the desire to connect past and present, to set up causalities and a continuous sequence of dates and events.[30] But this historiography also met its 9 Thermidor. And if the fall of Robespierre has supplied the material for so many books and plays, the conclusion to so many narratives, it is also because history testifies repeatedly to the failure of the sublime and the staying power of representations.

As we know, the Museum was the paradoxical creation of a revolutionary regime anxious to do away with all symbols of the past.[31] Thus it may be fitting that the twenty-one Kings of Judah, beheaded in the early days of the Terror, found their final resting place in the quiet splendor of the Hôtel de Cluny. In its repetition of the iconoclastic violence of the Terror, the Eighth Gallery also offers a performance, the ultimate staging of a failed Revolution. The Cluny Museum brochure tells its own dramatic version of a tale of murder and recovery: "As early as the classical age, serious damage was done to this exceptional ensemble, before the Revolution would strike the fatal blow."[32] The effectiveness of the exhibition stems from its emphasis upon the mutilation that took place, rather than the sculpture that was mutilated. As the spectator's gaze slowly discovers the decapitated heads, the fragmented torsoes and the scattered fragments of still unidentified bodies, the serenity of Gothic statuary is shattered by an unparalleled sense of inarticulate violence, silent and frozen in time. A stone requiem for kings.

By contrast, the most appropriate epitaph to Robespierre's sublime dream may be this footnote to Michelet's *History of the French Revolution*. It is signed Gérard Walter, and it reads in very fine print: "Robespierre and his companions were buried in a plot adjacent to the Parc Monceau. During the Restoration, a public Ball was set up on this spot. After the

Revolution of 1830, a group of admirers undertook excavations there in order to find his remains. These efforts yielded no results."[33]

NOTES

1. Session of the National Assembly, 3 June 1791, in *Le Moniteur,* no. 154. Unless otherwise indicated, all translations in this essay are my own.

2. The remains of the King were transferred to Saint-Denis after the Revolution, but there is considerable speculation as to whether the body removed from the cemetery of La Madeleine was indeed the King's body. See Michelet, "Des Cimetières de la terreur," in *Histoire de la Revolution française* (Paris: Gallimard, 1952), 2:922–29.

3. In *Signs and Symbols in Christian Art* (New York: Oxford University Press, 1961), George Ferguson gives the following description of the Tree of Jesse:
The genealogy of Christ, according to the Gospel of St. Matthew, is frequently shown in the form of a tree which springs from Jesse, the father of David, and bears, as its fruit, the various ancestors of Christ. Usually the tree culminates with the figure of the Virgin bearing her Divine Son in her arms. The representation of the Tree of Jesse is based upon the prophecy of Isaiah II:1–2, "and there shall come forth a rod out of the stem of Jesse, and a Branch shall grow out of his roots: And the spirit of the Lord shall rest upon him. . . ." The presence of the Crucified Christ in the Tree of Jesse is based on a medieval tradition that the dead tree of life may only become green again if the Crucified Christ is grafted upon it and revives it with His blood. (p. 39)

4. *Les Sculptures de Notre-Dame* (Paris: Editions de la Réunion des Musées Nationaux), 12. The brochure also offers a short history of "revolutionary destructions" (p. 2).

5. Session of 3 June 1791, *Le Moniteur,* no. 154. On this text and the motion voted by the Assembly on the following day, see Marie-Hélène Huet, *Rehearsing the Revolution: The Staging of Marat's Death, 1793–1797* (Berkeley and Los Angeles: University of California Press, 1982), 28–45.

6. Session of 4 June 1791, *Le Moniteur,* no. 155.

7. On the question of politics and the press, see Gérard Walter, *La Révolution Française vue par ses journaux* (Paris: Tardy, 1948).

8. On the theater of the French Revolution, see Marvin Carlson, *Theater of the Revolution* (Ithaca, N.Y.: Cornell University Press, 1966); Jacques Herissay, *Le Monde des theatres pendant la Revolution* (Paris: Perrin, 1922).

9. Quoted by Joseph Butwin in "The French Revolution as *Theatrum Mundi,*" *Research Studies* 43 (3) (September 1975): 147. The original French text compares the Revolution with a *pantalonnade,* an act in the *Commedia dell'arte* tradition.

10. Quoted by Frederick Brown in *Theater and Revolution: The Culture of the French Stage* (New York: Viking, 1980), 71.

11. Brown, 80. Joseph-François de Payan was born in 1759; he became a member of the Committee on Public Instruction in March 1794. His brother Claude-François de Payan was a close friend of Robespierre and died with him on 10 Thermidor.

12. F. A. Aulard, *Le Culte de la Raison et le Culte de l'Etre Supreme, 1793–*

1794 (Paris: F. Alcan, 1909), 55. See also F. A. Aulard, *Christianity and the French Revolution* (Boston: Little, Brown and Company, 1927), and Marie-Hélène Huet, "Le Sacre du Printemps: Essai sur le Sublime et la Terreur," *MLN* 103/4 (September 1988): 788–99.

13. Quoted in F. A. Aulard, *Le Culte de la Raison et de l'Etre Suprême, 1793–1794*, 287, emphasis added. See also Carol Blum, *Rousseau and the Republic of Virtue: The Language of Politics in the French Revolution* (Ithaca, N.Y.: Cornell University Press, 1986), 238–59; Lynn Hunt, *Politics, Culture and Class in the French Revolution*, (Berkeley and Los Angeles: University of California Press, 1984), 52–119; Mona Ozouf, *La Fête révolutionnaire, 1789–1799* (Paris: Gallimard, 1976), 125–39.

14. Immanuel Kant, *The Critique of Judgement*, trans. James Creed Meredith (Oxford: Clarendon Press, 1952), 127.

15. Maximilien Robespierre, *Discours et rapports à la Convention* (Paris: Union Générale d'Editions, 1965), 274. Further references are cited in the text.

16. This is the number given by Georges Lefèbvre in *The French Revolution from 1793 to 1799* (New York: Columbia University Press, 1964), 125. "In all, the 'Great Terror' cost the lives of 1,376 persons, while only 1,251 had been executed in Paris from March, 1793, to 22 Prairial. Public opinion was shaken, and the practices of repression abetted the fear. The tumbrils slowly transported the condemned across the Faubourg Saint-Antoine as far as the Trône-Renversé gate, the new emplacement for the scaffold." It may be worth noting that the "Great Terror" did not spread to the provinces, and that the only other city to have known a sudden increase in the number of executions in the spring of 1794 was Nîmes.

17. See Blum, 257–59.

18. Kant, 128. For a recent commentary on Kant and the Sublime, see *Du Sublime*, edited by Jean-Luc Nancy (Paris: Belin, 1988), more specifically, Philippe Lacoue-Labarthe's "La Vérité sublime", pp. 97–101.

19. Kant, 121.

20. Robespierre's last discourse, 8 Thermidor, Year II (26 July 1794), in Robespierre, 297.

21. Michelet, 882.

22. On the question of Rousseau's suspicion of *écriture*, see Jean Starobinski, *La Transparence et l'obstacle* (Paris: Plon, 1958); Jacques Derrida, *De la Grammatologie* (Paris: Minuit, 1967), 318–26; Thomas Kavanagh, *Writing the Truth: Authority and Desire in Rousseau* (Berkeley and Los Angeles: University of California Press, 1987), 51–77; Marie Hélène Huet, "Ecriture et Paternité chez Rousseau," *MLN* (1989). On Rousseau and the Revolution, see Jean Starobinski, *1789: Les Emblèmes de la Raison* (Paris: Flammarion, 1976), 175–79; Carol Blum, *Rousseau and the Republic of Virtue;* and all biographies of Robespierre, particularly, Gérard Walter, *Robespierre*, 2 vol. (Paris: Gallimard, 1961). See also *Robespierre: Ecrits presentes par Claude Mazauric* (Paris: Messidor/Editions Sociales, 1989).

23. Germaine de Staël, *Considérations sur la Révolution Française*, (1818; Paris: Charpentier 1862), 1:452.

24. Charles Nodier, *Portraits de la Révolution et de l'Empire* (1829; Paris: Tallandier, 1988), 1:189.

25. See F. A. Aulard, *Paris pendant la réaction thermidorienne et sous le Directoire* (Paris: Quantin, 1898), 1:1–15; and Walter, 356–69.

26. Paul Thureau-Dangin, *Royalistes et républicains* (Paris: Plon, 1888), 1.

27. Jean-Luc Nancy, 7.

28. Germaine de Staël, 1:449.

29. Michel de Certeau, *L'Ecriture de l'histoire* (Paris: Gallimard, 1978), 312.

30. See Lionel Gossman, *Between History and Literature* (Cambridge: Harvard University Press, 1990); Hayden White, *Metahistory: The Historical Imagination in Nineteenth-Century Europe* (Baltimore: Johns Hopkins University Press, 1973); and Linda Orr, *Headless History: Nineteenth-Century French Historiography of the Revolution* (Ithaca, N.Y.: Cornell University Press, 1990).

31. On the relationship between iconoclasm and the Museum, see Stanley J. Idzerda, "Iconoclasm during the French Revolution," *American Historical Review* 60 (1954): 13–26.

32. *Les Sculptures de Notre-Dame*, 2.

33. Michelet, 1138.

The Rights and Wrongs of Woman:
The Defeat of Feminist Rhetoric
by Revolutionary Allegory

MADELYN GUTWIRTH

The vicissitudes of women and their representation in the Revolution might have been prefigured by Diderot's prophetic raptures over their endowments in his *Sur les femmes:*

Woman carries within her frame an organ subject to terrible spasms which domi-nate her and arouse fierce phantoms of all kinds in her imagination. In her hysterical delirium she recapitulates the past, and throws herself into the future: all time becomes present for her. It's in that organ specific to her sex that all her extraor-dinary notions begin. The woman who was hysterical in youth becomes devout in old age; the woman in whom there is still some energy into advanced years was hysterical in her youth. Her head still speaks the language of the senses, when the latter have become mute. Nothing is more contiguous in her than ecstasy, vision, prophecy, revelation, fiery poetry and hystericism. . . . The woman dominated by hysteria feels infernal or celestial powers I cannot know. Sometimes she makes me shiver. I've seen or heard her possessed at moments by all the fury of a wild animal: how intensely she felt! And how she expressed herself! Her speech was in no way that of a mortal being. . . . It was a woman who walked out into the streets of Alexandria with bare feet, her hair unkempt, a torch in one hand and a ewer in the other, proclaiming, "I want to burn the heavens with this torch, and extinguish hell with this water, so that man may love God for his sake alone!"[1]

For Diderot, the female embodies a potential for representing—and what is more, expressing—what surpasses cultural enunciation. His prose steams with longing for the inexpressible qualities of fervor and emotional power he describes. Yet the awesome intensity he ascribes to woman is tellingly linked with fanaticism. Such gifts spring from woman's uterine (*hysteri-kos*) alterity; an alterity fundamental, precultural, ineradicable. Attraction and dread for this specter of female ardor cancel each other out in this text.

   This is not, however, by any means Diderot's only species of discourse in speaking of women. No more than a few pages beyond these remarks he asks, "What then, is woman?" only to give his celebrated reply: "Neglected by her spouse, abandoned by her children, a nonentity in society, religion is her last and sole recourse. In almost all countries the cruelty of civil law has been added to nature's own against women; they have been treated like so many idiot children" (10:44).

Paul de Man has observed with respect to the surplus meaning in allegory that "it is part of allegory that, despite its obliqueness and innate obscurity, the resistance to understanding emanates from difficulty or censorship in the statement and not from the devices of enunciation. . . . The difficulty of allegory is rather that this emphatic clarity of representation does not stand in the service of something that *can be represented*."[2] Dictionaries of iconography like Ripa's or Gravelot and Cochin's[3] have nonetheless reassuringly systematized conventions that actually enshrine a practice fraught with obfuscation. A key that ties de Man's statement to Diderot's is their common stress on the emphatic character common to the putative expression of female hysteria as well as to allegory: both insistently embody the inchoate, the unsayable. Yet the two phenomena differ at the core. Allegory is conservative; it is eternal recapitulation, the established, culturally sanctioned, rigid assimilation of phenomena or qualities to a predetermined sign, whereas the wild female speech Diderot evokes is spontaneous invention, dealing dangerously with the newly spoken. Still, both allegory as de Man envisages it and those inspired hysterical outbursts Diderot evokes are masculine constructions crafted largely out of attributes consecrated by male culture as female. The Revolution would witness the sudden explosion of allegory resuscitated: an ambiguous repetition of old signs freshly charged with formerly repressed male passion, political and sexual. This torrent of male allegory's superfluity of meaning would meet tides of female energy as yet quite unheard from and quite unexpected. The resultant conflict between the discourses of myth and of rights cannot be reduced to a binary opposition; it looks more like a free-for-all, one of those examples of turbulence, of the generation of uncontrollably multiplying eddies, that physics has shown us to be the characteristic of meetings of matter with energy.

Neither visual nor literary allegory was any longer a potent form in the decades preceding the Revolution: rather, its continued presence gave evidence of a vapid, sentimental aesthetic attraction to the monarchical prestige of the departed baroque. Cochin's drawing for the frontispiece to the *Encyclopédie* (figure 7), which Diderot describes in his 1765 *Salon*, is, for all its erudite pretensions, an excellent example of fallen rococo allegory. Truth stands poised awkwardly at its apex between what I take to be the sole male allegorical figure in the scene, crowned Reason, who tries to unveil her, and Imagination, who offers to deck her with her garland.

"Proud metaphysics seeks less to see than to divine her," writes Diderot, whereas Theology simply turns her back upon Truth and "awaits enlightenment from on high." The various arts and sciences throng busily below her, while a mob of philosophers, their eyes fixed upon Truth, worshipfully awaits her illuminations (6:243–44). Though not without charm as a visual edifice,[4] Cochin's design shows us a too purely graceful Truth lacking majesty of posture or repose. This Truth seems more vulnerable than the members of her court, but all its members are endowed with the schematic and slightly juvenile cast of feature and form of the rococo. The visual intentness of the massed philosophers, while strong, is placed too low to compensate for the loss of focus here. If Cochin had striven to portray Truth as embattled, he might have proceeded no differently. Allegory, if we are to judge by Cochin's effort, would seem to be in a state of transition: even in the service of a great enterprise like the *Encyclopédie*, it is a weakened genre.

By the latter decades of the century, allegory had become a merely nostalgic form, associated, as in the case of royal emblems, with the more unambiguous power of the previous century. The "new" bourgeois art of Greuze, as well as the older bourgeois art of Chardin, resolutely shuns the representation of myth for that of contemporary life. If allegory is on the decline in the visual arts, it has been virtually absent from literature for more than a century. Mythology too, where present, figures largely as a joke in Voltaire's *Pucelle* or Piron's anacreontic, salacious verse.[5] Mythology's language still holds sway as sarcasm about the euphemisms of love. This irony points to a near-consciousness of the yawning gap in the dominant discourse about eros, characterized alternatively as courtly ideal or as swinish impulse. If the visual arts maintain the courtly mythological fiction as long as they do, it is because of their closer relationship to aristocratic patronage, whereas literature has become the virtual monopoly of the bourgeois aesthetic. The neoclassical period's subsequent return to visual allegory must be viewed as a decided renewal of the need or desire to allegorize, precisely so as to lend greater visual prestige and authenticity to the attempt to alter the system of values.

Marina Warner writes, "Onto the female body have been projected the fantasies and longings and terrors of men and through them of women, in order to conjure them into reality or exorcise them into oblivion." But as Warner acknowledges, despite the universalizing claims made for them, the woman consumer of female allegorical images has a quite different relationship to them than the man. As she points out, "Often the recognition of a difference between the symbolic order, inhabited by ideal allegorical figures, and the actual order, of judges, statesmen, soldiers, philosophers, inventors, depends on the unlikelihood of women practicing the concepts they represent." She concludes that "the representation of virtue in the female form interacts with ideas about femaleness and affects the way women act as well as appear," in that intermingling that Aristotle termed *mathexis*.[6] In the case of women, I would contend, that exchange may be one either of consonance or of dissonance, or of both at once. The power of allegory for women is palpable, for who would deny its charge of mimesis, of identification? And yet this very charge is steeped in ambiguity, in the ambivalences women must perforce experience in responding to the reading of themselves by others, their masters, implicit in it. For women, the abstract representational force of female allegory must always be mitigated in some measure by its mimetic power as prescription.

The use of allegory as an arm of ideological propaganda about women is exemplified by an emblem (fig. 8), one of a set devoted to the newly married Marie-Antoinette as Dauphine. A baroque courtly mood is conjured up in the rhyme, which calls the Princess an amiable wife full of virtue as well as the very incarnation of the courtly, virtuous Astrea.[7] This graceful print shows us an Athenalike figure, armored and helmeted, seated leaning lightly on her shield, with pacific farm animals plowing and grazing behind her. Its legend tells us that this image of a benevolent goddess [une Déesse bienfaisante] has been inspired by the "wise, pious, enlightened Dauphine, who is to be France's greatest boon in her Wisdom, Justice, Humanity, Vigilance, Mercy, Conjugal Fidelity and Moderation." As poignantly as one could imagine, this delicate rococo emblem exemplifies the cooperation of word and image in an allegory striving to transfigure royalty's own self-conception. Within its gracious lightness, the emblem seeks to inscribe upon Marie-Antoinette's person, *as* emblem, both the elegance of the old courtly idyll and the placid new ideal of sage sobriety and devotion to family ties dictated by the emergent bourgeois idyll. If the princess was able, in her youthful heedlessness, to resist such allegorical imperatives, they would nonetheless eventually submerge her.

Implicit in the appeal to the familial is a revulsion of taste and hence of values. Identified especially with the rise of the bourgeoisie but not confined to that class, this revulsion was provoked by the ethical and aesthetic slipperiness of the rococo.[8] The treatment of the female figure in a whole series of works reveals the complex process by which artists broke the royal stranglehold over aesthetics. David's *Brutus* (fig. 9) is perhaps the most instructive example from his work. The much-discussed gender split that we find in the earlier *Horatii* recurs distinctly here: the wife and daughters of Brutus, occupying two thirds of the canvas, serve as choral weepers for their dead sons and brothers, who are borne home by the

Lictors at left. While Brutus, who has sacrificed them for the state,[9] sits meditating in the shadows, the ghostly effigy of the goddess Roma hovers over him as his mentor. Incised into Roma's seat is the image of the Lupa, the wolf with pendant teats who suckled the infants Romulus and Remus.

Jean Clay has noted how columns and drapes separate the women from the men.[10] Reasons of state are implicitly, if sorrowfully, defended in this work by the protective goddess of the Roman city-state. By seating himself before her, Brutus has arrogated to himself this symbol of female nurturance as foundation for his statecraft. As in the *Oresteia*'s judgment of Athena that the child's parent is its father, not its mother, David's canvas equally conveys the gender cleavage inherent in Republican power. Both Roma and the principle of female fecundity upon which her throne rests are on the side of the legislator, Brutus. As much as it expresses funereal pain, therefore, the female figures' open-handed show of powerless dismay signifies their own dispossession and exclusion.

As we move into the thicket of Revolutionary iconography, we find a stripped-down neoclassical image of overthrown royalty (fig. 10) writhing on her couch, with the symbols of her former preeminence strewn about on the ground. She is a figure of desperation not only in her aristocracy— menaced by the Phrygian bonnet and the carpenter's level suspended like a Damoclean sword just above her breast—but also in her sex. As allegory, she gains emotive as well as dramatic impact from her sexual vulnerability, her bared breasts and abandoned posture, the hand tearing at her hair as her body twists and writhes. The aura of sexual menace is underlined by the figure of the satyr functioning as handle of the ewer, whose lip points toward Royalty from the left.

The political cartoon (fig. 11) demonstrates that commonplaces never bore an allegorist. A commemoration of the "Glory of the French of 14 July 1789" now offers us Royalty as maiden in distress, saved by common soldiers from death in the abyss as a *sans-culotte* throng stands in the wings. Hatred for the royal figure still seems to lie in abeyance here: royalty is an inept power, but perhaps salvageable. Aristocracy is viewed far more critically but still rather benignly in an engraving titled "Last words and death of the aristocracy" (not illustrated). As the skeleton of death hovers with its scythe and hourglass, Aristocracy mouths to her confessor, the Abbé Maury, an eloquent advocate of counterrevolution, her words of aristocratic bad faith. If her speech is hypocritical, she remains in her aspect a stolid figure, not in the least viscerally upsetting. The legend bears all the animus in this cartoon, as the victim is, in a sense, allowed to choke to death on her own words, but in her own bed. In a drawing of "The Dying Aristocracy" (fig. 12), the emotional pitch is higher. Even in her death throes, this matron, stripped of all noble trappings, wearing the simplest bourgeois garb, prostrate and in distress—indeed reminding us of David's stripped-down sketch of Marie-Antoinette on her way to the guillotine— still holds in her left hand the serpents of discord, illustrative of her poisonous potential, as the legend tells us: "Friends, mistrust her to the death. You know the blackness of her perfidy well enough to rightly fear that even at death's door, she may spring some fatal trick."

Those verbose inscriptions, added to the caricatures, mimic what Judith Schlanger has searchingly explored,[11] the Revolution's tendency to inundate visual texts with a flood of words. Such verbally augmented images betray a lack of confidence in pictorial powers of edification: the allegorical tendency toward ambiguity becomes suspect for its lack of drive toward a desired political signifier. Some of the vicissitudes of uncontrollable allegory may be most strongly felt in less sophisticated, verbally guided works. A cartoon of 1791 ostensibly illustrates Liberty handing the scarf of municipal office to Péthion, mayor of Paris (fig. 13). Except for her lack of a matron's cap and her unbustled draped garment, this figure, despite her pike tipped with a Phrygian bonnet, looks distinctly like a lady on the town, no different in her stature or comportment from any of the figures about her. How could some among the real women, then, not find their own reflection in her? How could some men not be reminded of Liberty or some other widely represented goddess in women's persons? We see this tendency confirmed by sardonic references in police reports and elsewhere to the *déesses* in the streets, often an allusion to prostitutes.[12]

A print of a fine relief by the sculptor Moitte, also from 1791, shows us Aristocracy and its agents buried beneath the ruins of the Bastille as Liberty with her sword kills the Hydra of aristocracy (fig. 14). Winged Liberty's sister goddess, at left, flails strongly about, abetting the nation's vengeance against its "petty tyrants." A sweeping strength and energy in these forceful female figures, though somewhat austerely contained by their neoclassical framework, dominates the work and even threatens to overrun it. The effect of such representations of armed women acting for the renewal of the nation could not be easily contained, even by such classically distanced figures as these, at a time when flesh-and-blood women were massing in the streets, marching to Versailles, agitating, meeting in clubs, writing *cahiers*.

Simply put, these emblematic acts now menace the fragile order of the Revolution's art. Once released from their allegorical poses, women can hardly be made to serve a stable symbolic system, especially that of an order antedating the Revolution. As Lynn Hunt has seen, "The proliferation of the female allegory was made possible . . . by the exclusion of women from public affairs. Woman could be representative of abstract qualities and collective dreams because women were not about to vote or govern." [13] But many women were understandably unaware of what might keep them from participation in the state; in the effervescence of the moment's raised aspirations, they agitated on behalf of their national political beliefs and needs, and even, in the case of one group, for their interests as women. This latter group was the one that most disrupted traditional conceptions of order.

Condorcet, mathematician, technocrat, and humorless disciple of Voltaire, was also a marquis. He would throw in his lot—tragically—with reason, whose case he tried to make in his *Sketch for a Historical Portrait of the Progress of the Human Mind*, published posthumously after he poisoned himself to death in prison in 1794. For Condorcet as for other supporters of the Revolution, the juridical and political realm is the place of election of the rational.[14] According to Schlanger, such a view rearranges all human history by positing a past that has led inexorably to the present moment, in which the prospect of renewal is possible: "this spent past," as she tells us, "ends with the present as ending to the past and dawn of the future;" for this species of revolutionary mind has today "ended its voyage through limbo, that prehistory of freedom that is history: the age of emancipation has arrived" (Schlanger, 104). In the eyes of Condorcet, Emancipation is a civilized version of Apocalypse that will result from legislation.

Condorcet's belief would lead him to the fantastic proposal made in his 1788 *Lettres d'un Bourgeois de New-Haven*,[15] written as if from America (already, for Europe, the imaginary locus of improbable innovation), advocating full civil rights for women, including the right to vote and to legislate.[16] Seemingly starting from a Rousseauvian premise—that we call rights natural when they appear to arise from the original nature of man— he rushes on to a most un-Rousseauvian conclusion: If men are sentient and sense-making beings, capable of reason and judgment, hence worthy of rights, then, by virtue of sharing these endowments, so are women. Yet, he points out, never in any so-called free constitution have women been granted rights as citizens. What is more, he notes that the civil laws operate precisely to deny women such rights. With huge daring, Condorcet applies to the context of women the proposition that citizenship is "the acting out of one's will," and proposes that women ought to have this capability. Finally, what were seen in Condorcet's time as women's deficiencies were for him nothing but the result of what we now call socialization: "the species of constraint in which opinion and custom imprison the souls and minds of women virtually from childhood, and especially at that moment when genius begins to develop, must hamper their progress in every realm." He concludes that "the law ought not to exclude woman from any role" (Condorcet, *Lettres*, 286). Condorcet's rhetoric eschews bombast and strives for the sobriety of logic as it spurns polarization by gender to posit a single prior human nature possessed by both sexes. The end result of such reasoning as this would be the overthrow of those idols of alterity, the allegories.

A quiet rhetoric of abstract reason like the marquis,' however, would have great difficulty in being heard once political revolution was under way. The problem surfaces almost immediately. Take, for example, an account by "a man of letters" of the October Days. On the one hand, he thanks the women for their "immortally glorious" act in shoring up liberty by their march to Versailles, capturing the king and the royal family and bringing them triumphantly to the capital. On the other, he advises them to live up to this "role" by practicing abstinence from drink and using their feminine wiles to keep the men from drunkenness and disrespect for authority.[17] The efficacy of women's direct political action, for this gentleman, suggests that if united, women might control every male excess through the traditional forms of sexual pressure and good housekeeping. For him, women's alterity, rather than being undermined by their acts as members of the national community, is ratified by those acts. The sheer force women have demonstrated makes him wish to see them not as subversives, but as keepers of moral order—a function that in no way could they have assumed effectively. Even among the women's own partisans, we find other obstacles to forging any new paradigm for women. In June of 1791, Etta Palm d'Aelders' reception speech to the National Assembly defending the political rights of her sex is couched in the inflated jargon of revolutionary cliché:

You have restored man to the dignity of his being in recognizing his rights, you will not let women groan longer beneath arbitrary authority; to do so would be to overturn the fundamental principles of that majestic edifice you are building in your tireless efforts for the happiness of the French people: it is no longer time to shilly-shally; philosophy has drawn truth out of the shadows; the hour has rung: justice, sister of liberty, demands that all individuals have rights to equality, without distinction of sex: the laws of a free people must be equal for all beings, like the air and the sun.[18]

Even granting the necessity of figurative speech in the task of persuasion the speaker has set herself, we see readily that her argument is bombast. Imitating the simplistic tropes required of revolutionary discourse, d'Aelders personifies truth, philosophy, justice, and liberty. Only equality, the central term of her speech, retains its unpersonified character as abstract noun. She elaborates her argument as if it could be represented by a pictorial allegory. In fact, it would seem that only this mode—of philosophy drawing truth out of the shadows and so on, in replication of the skein of allegory in Cochin's frontispiece for the *Encyclopédie*—possessed the requisite weight of embodiment to recommend it to the revolutionary mentality. The *Sainte Liberté* d'Aelders appeals to does after all become for a time the godhead of the nation.

The force of Olympe de Gouges's *Déclaration des Droits de la Femme* lies in the simplicity of its outraged imitation of the "Rights of Man," as it tries, like Etta Palm d'Aelders' speech, to make the Revolution extend its egalitarian principles to women. "Woman," says de Gouges, "is born free and remains equal to man in rights. Social distinctions can only be founded on their usefulness to society." But even de Gouges feels constrained to echo some of the Revolution's commonplaces of female alterity: Women are "the sex superior in beauty as in its maternal suffering."[19] And we note the allegoristic phraseology she employs in her *Postambule*: "The powerful realm of nature is surrounded no longer with prejudice, fanaticism, superstition and lies. The flame of truth has dissipated all clouds of folly and usurpation" (2:12).

The discourse of the feminists, then, was weakened by two imperatives arising out of its derivative status in male, even if revolutionary male, culture. The first was the requirement that all discourse, even when it affirmed the basic human equality or resemblance of the sexes, had to be couched in terms that would appear sufficiently gentle and feminine to be heeded. Hence the frequent references to women's vulnerability, to their groans. It is noteworthy how much more profoundly this stratagem marks the *vindication* of Mary Wollstonecraft, who repeatedly admits women's present weakness and even immorality in order to plead more effectively for the improvement that might be wrought in *the lot of men* by women's ameliorated status and education. Her enunciation of the turn of the century's materialist familial ideal is more coaxing and promising of peace in intimacy than that of the French sexual egalitarians, although their final domestic goal is similar. She writes, "Would men but generously snap our chains, and be content with rational fellowship rather than slavish obedience they would find us more observant daughters, more affectionate sisters, more faithful wives, more reasonable mothers—in a word better citizens. We should then love them with true affection, because we should learn to love ourselves; and the peace of mind of a worthy man would not be interrupted by the idle vanity of his wife, nor the babes sent to nestle in a strange bosom, having never found a home in their mothers'."[20]

A second paradoxical characteristic of revolutionary feminist discourse, as we have seen, lay in its use for dramatic emphasis of the same personifying clichés used in all political speech and writing. Because these visualizable figures, nearly all female, represented ambiguous abstractions, they clouded over the language of sexual equality. One might even claim they submerged it in the metaphoric force of association. Besides, the activities of women, as in the celebrated illustration of the march on Versailles (fig. 15) or Olympe de Gouges's July 14 1792 march with armed women, distilled their own brew of irrational anxiety. Pierre Guyomar, in his *Partisan de l'Egalité politique entre les individus*, published in April of 1793, during the heyday of revolutionary feminism, similarly mixes genres. First he is rationally linear: "I submit that one half of the individuals in a society has not got the right to deprive that other half of its inalienable right to express its own desires. Let us free ourselves at once of the prejudice of sex just as we did of the prejudice against the color of the negro." But this soberer tone, once he is carried away, will give way to every commonplace of revolutionary parlance, to such an extent that it becomes a virtual paraphrase of the words of the *Marseillaise*: "As to myself, I would like to wipe out this crime against humanity with my blood, this crime that soils the very ground of equality and liberty. *Sincere love of nation [amour sacré de la patrie]*, deep feelings of justice, holy voice of humanity, break this talisman that enchants us, destroy the prestige of this feudal barbarism!"[21] In his apostrophies, Guyomar personifies justice and humanity, female figures of male construction, who not unsurprisingly return to their pitiless stony inertia when invoked to serve as liberators of real women.

Ruth Graham has stressed the underlying consensus among nearly all political parties in 1793 and 1794 for the view that women's participation in public life was "unnatural."[22] Although certainly no faction fully espoused women's collaboration, the Jacobins' antagonism toward them would culminate in the attack against some of the Jacobins' own women, members of the Club des Citoyennes Républicaines Révolutionnaires and its leader Claire Lacombe. The pretext for their fall was a quarrel about symbolism: after the women had fought for and wrested the right to wear the tricolor cockade, a privilege of citizenship accorded the women in September, the militants pressed their right to wear the Phrygian bonnet, which they now saw as the more palpable, less merely decorative badge of full citizenship.[23] Their enemies accused them of trying to force other women, the women of the market, to adopt it as well. Whether incited to do so by instigators or on their own, these "outraged" women attacked the militants and whipped Lacombe, dragging her through the mud on October 28 of the Year II. Following this riotous scene, the Comité de sureté acted on the very next day to ban all women's associations.

The wearing of these insignia would have been the visual signifier of an equality between women and men that the Revolution's men were not prepared to accept. For Robespierre, these activist women were "unnatural" because, as he saw it, they lacked modesty in wanting men to make room for them in assemblies and even on rostrums. His distaste was neither reasoned nor abstract, but visceral: he considered women who claimed rights "as sterile as vice" (Graham, p. 249). In evoking this menace to his Republic of Virtue,[24] the Incorruptible could have used no more alienating term. Fired at women who acted on their claim to equality, the charge of female sterility expressed the Revolution's ultimate anathema for women, consigning them to an absolute state of negativity in Otherness.[25]

L. P. Dufourny, president of the Department and Sections of Paris, quivering with inner contradiction, published his advice to the Revolutionary Republican Women on June 30, 1793. In this proclamation he charges them with large tasks of preserving sexual and civic virtue: with tasks, that is, both of liberating sensuality and containing it, in a spirit of selflessness without limit. Yet in assigning to women this role as inspirators and guarantors of victory he uses terms that recall Diderot's effusions on female hysterias. Dufourny postulates entirely separate essences and hence separate roles for women and for men. His text exudes equal measures of wish fulfillment and sexual anxiety as he once more attributes near-magical powers to women:

Courage, Citoyennes, the Magistrates of the people recognize the rights of the Magistrates of nature; they confirm that power of persuasion with which it has endowed you; they place under the protection of the Law that mission you have received from your passions and your virtues. Sex insatiable in desire, sex impregnated with an immense love, no, your heart does not deceive you when it is never satisfied; and if satiated with pleasure, it still desires, this is because it is saying to you: Mothers of one generation, you are still mothers of generations to come; their lives exist in you, and from the bottom of your soul these generations already lay claim to your tenderness, make you feel you were born to prepare their happiness. . . . It is for you revolutionary Republican Women to run to the public places, fire up your youth, promise it victory, and guarantee it will be worthy of glory and crowns. You *will* accomplish this, it would be slander to doubt it; you will do this and the desperate tyrants, unable to sustain the glances of virtue, will dry up in their rage and shame. (*Les Femmes*, vol. 2, item #68)

Dufourny's proclamation articulates the view of women generally adopted by revolutionary men—a view that Serge Bianchi sums up thus:

As long as they remain within the limits assigned by nature, women are the vestals of the *fêtes* symbolic of virtue and fidelity; the allegorical goddesses of grace and beauty. Wives must reign over their households, direct the children's education in early childhood as indispensable auxiliaries and subordinates to men. They may play a civic role: "embroider police bonnets and belts," make bandages, give care. But they must desist from trying to do more for compelling biological reasons (Bianchi, 246).

Women's biology now comes to the fore, defining their "nature" and obscuring in them all else that might allow them to be perceived as civic beings.

Bianchi adds that it was a simple step for Amar, the Deputy who pronounced women's banishment from the public space in October 1793, to move from a regretful lament for women's biological weakness to decry their putative moral and political defectiveness (Bianchi, 245–46). This attack on women was not a merely theoretical one. In the same month that saw women banished from public life, and within a month after the execution of Marie-Antoinette on October 16, Olympe de Gouges and Manon Roland would also be beheaded.

Perhaps the Frenchmen's Revolution, in its own iconography, had raised the very specter it now strove to exorcise. One such specter is a fairly typical cartoon figure picturing the aristocracy as a nefarious rococo harpy cursing the Revolution (fig. 16). Her grimacing frown, her tensed, muscular arms, her tiny, compressed waist, her furbellows—all are subordinated to those aging pendulous breasts emblematic of the body of sterile Discord. The fury compressed in her figure reflects a felt charge of fury *toward* her figure. She is all naked, impotent will.

Two examples, one each from the political left and the political right, show how the consecrated iconographic use of the female figure as Discord or Fanatacism transcends our traditional political categories. The legend beneath a caricature of the conduct of the clergy in 1790 (fig. 17) tells us how "fanaticism, armed with a crucifix, is bringing discord to France, but the Genius of the Realm discovers their maneuvers and threatens them with his sword." Disorder here, holding her flaming brand, marches forward with bared breast and stares hypnotically before her as if in one of Diderot's trances. Together with her serpentine, Medusalike hair, a phenomenon that Neil Hertz reads as threateningly phallic,[26] the breast aggressively protruding from her chiton lends this figure, in her alliance with the churchly forces of reaction, a fearful, visceral currency.[27] Allegories such as this feed the ancient dread of woman's wild, uncontrollable, sexually grounded alterity. And if the anticlerical Jacobins could represent the church as a fanatical Medusa, Jacobinism itself could be treated the same way. In one cartoon of the Terror (fig. 18), the republic is represented as Liberty gone mad, a deranged crone brandishing snakes, skulls, and dagger as she tramples crown and miter underfoot. Of course, the features of both Disorder and the Republic replicate those in Gravelot and Cochin's

Iconography (1791), the artist's textbook of allegory. But it is not hard to imagine how such traditionally ratified images might have struck the popular imagination in the wake of the passage of real armed women, like the militant Théroigne de Méricourt who promenaded about wearing her plumed hat and had proposed that a battalion of women be formed to go to the front, or the red-bonneted revolutionary Republican women, who marched provocatively through the city streets. Gorsas would refer in his newspaper *Les Quatre vingts départements* to the "organ of the furies" drunk with blood, their "pistols and their daggers" bearing forth the flag of license." [28]

Three final examples of how an inadvertent, unconscious use of allegory lends attributes of power to women verging on delirium show further why this kind of allegory paradoxically impeded the cause of women's rights. On the surface, all of these images are benign. The Monnet-Helmann print of the Fountain of Regeneration, from the Fête of 10 August 1793 (fig. 19), bears a suggestive date, preceding as it did by two months the repression of women's right of association. In this work a giant statue of Hathor sits enthroned high over the gathering of the people, symbolically feeding the assembled legislators from the streams spurting out of the breasts she presses with her crossed hands. The literal meaning here is accentuated in the print by the family whose mother with child gestures at bottom center, by the two kneeling young future mothers at right, and the nursing mother seated together with her family on the stones at the left. But the difference permeating the analogy between the two kinds of motherhood, the state's and the private woman's, could never have been more plainly put. Hathor is deliberately conceived as a hieratic, schematized figure wrested from antiquity so as to dehumanize and generalize her nurturant gesture, and restrict it to serving the male republic. The French nation would be revived by the thin milk of this distant, foreign mother: as it subsumed biological maternity under this aegis, its new government would be, like Brutus's Rome, a "better" mother than any biological one. The inner ring of adult male spectators, those receiving sustenance here, are the active participants in statecraft. Beyond their rim is the people, arrayed as families, whose women are to recreate in their humble sphere the visibly huge power of birth and nurturance. This Hathor represents, perhaps, all that men find terrifying in women's powers. From such a specter, as Lynn Hunt has shown, the Jacobin government recoiled, proposing that the figure of Hercules rather than the omnipresent effigies of Liberty or Reason henceforth represent the Republic.

For it was in November of 1793 that David unveiled his project to erect a colossal, twenty-four foot high statue of Hercules, holding tiny effigies of Liberty and Equality in the palm of his right hand (Hunt, *Politics*, 94–8). We see a similar configuration in a drawing by Augustin Du Pré (fig. 20) that shows the curiously foreshortened Hathor dwindling beside Hercules. As Hunt has seen it, "In the eyes of the Jacobin leadership, women were threatening to take Marianne as a metaphor for their own participation. . . . Hercules put the women back into perspective, in their place and relationship of dependency. The monumental male was not the only active figure" (*Politics*, 104). Hunt points to the polyvalence of this resuscitated male symbol, which was capable of being at one and the same time " 'popular,' fraternal, parricidal, and antifeminist," despite its history as a symbol of monarchy. We find a verbal parallel to this move by David in an outburst by Payan, Robespierre's disciple, who denounced the monumentalizing of the female figure: "A mythology even more absurd than that of antiquity, or of the priests, and more corrupt than those we'd just overturned, goddesses more degraded than those of fable were about to rule over France. The Convention saw these conspirators. . . . They are no more." [29]

But in fact, though the women went home to stay, the Hercules did not capture the fancy of the nation. Even placing him at the pinnacle of the mountain could not guarantee that minds would assent to his unproblematic supremacy. For had not the folklore peddled by the sellers of the Bibliothèque bleue (a traveling bookshop) spread it about in the villages of France that a woman had tricked Hercules out of his club and handed him a distaff instead? [30] At any rate, after the Jacobins' defeat at Thermidor, their aesthetic program foundered along with their politics, and female effigies reappeared. A muted but powerful female allegory is found in an antirevolutionary print from after 1795 (fig. 22). It depicts a huge proto-Marianne atop a Trojan horse, dragged forward into Paris by *sans-culottes*, as bourgeois citizens, one of whose pockets is being picked by a woman of the people at bottom left, look on helplessly. Its Virgilian legend reads: "Yet on we press, heedless and blind with rage, and set the ill-omened monster in our hallowed citadel" (*Aeneid* 2:244–45). The massive, passive figure in herself, so bosomy and stalwart, does not threaten, yet her very size and the context of trickery evoke fear of a monstrous, unwelcome presence. This figure, like the Hathor and a host of others, may well have evoked the disquiet that object-relations psychology locates in the female figure, the looming love-hate object of the child in infancy. [31] The tranquil threat of this huge, mute female specter is a warning to the populace against its complacency toward apparent female harmlessness.

As Maurice Aguilhon has described it, the figure that would eventually become Marianne, an image of Liberty transformed into that of nation, would disappear only to return another day in other revolutions. But the Revolution's proto-Marianne is frequently a far cry from allegorical stateliness. In an obviously very popular print of Republican France offering her breasts to all Frenchmen (fig. 21), we have taken a long trip from the elevated representation of abstraction to the pin-up. Despite such consecrated symbols of equality as the level she wears between her breasts, her cockaded bonnet, and the national rooster, her supremely vapid facial expression and her eloquent bosom convey their charge of sexual invitation, which pruriently mocks even as it celebrates the very symbols she wears. Her carpenter's level signifying equality is not for her; rather it represents the sharing of her. We can rest assured that this Marianne is not thinking about her rights. She retains nothing of the complex sibylline otherness of Diderot's hysterical prototype. She is France as pure object of male desire.

Ernst Gombrich suggests that "what even the advocates of natural religion and natural symbolism did not foresee and could not . . . was the waning appeal of reason itself, the increasing ambivalences mobilized by the fair, bright and exalted divinities which stood for Light, Beauty and Stern Duty. They took it too easily for granted that our Semantic Space is fixed and the good and the light will always triumph and defeat the dark and the monstrous. Alas," he sighs, "this is a most dubious proposition." [32] Those wildly irrepressible ambivalences, while submerging reason, nearly submerged iconography as well. The more violently the Robespierre party insisted on its own simple rightness, the more fiercely it repressed the complexity of allegory. In advocating the cult, not of Reason, not of the People, but of a supreme unrepresented Being, as in the Mosaic law, Payan insisted that the Revolution had wrought not a religion but a simple set of eternal principles which could not be adequately represented. Yet, he went on, despite the declaration of men's rights, the superstition of atheism still threatened the nation, in the form of the bloodied but powerfully hideous monster of fanaticism (quoted in Aulard, 191). In what must be nearly one of the very last evocations of the French nation as Apollo, Louis XIV's fetish, a small but elegant revolutionary sculpture by Chinard (fig. 23) celebrates the victory of the god of Reason over superstition—the same rank, dread enemy evoked by Payan. This seemingly classical work represents the Revolution in such a way as to provoke Gombrichian ambivalences. Aesthetically, the *gloire* (or sunburst) that crowns Apollo and his effete elegance bespeak aristocracy. And the victim he has trampled into submission despite the power of her heavy cross is the Church. In the name of the Revolution, this work amazingly recapitulates the traditional churchly sculptures of Christianity's victory over despised and defeated Synagogue. The cloud on which Apollo stands so lightly all but crushes her. Reason's enemy, Superstition, is female in her deceit, her vulnerability, and, like the Synagogue formerly, her sheer defeatedness.

Rarely a woman of the people, but most often a "goddess of antique lineage" representing universalist values (Hunt, "Engraving," 17), the allegorized female of the French Revolution visually signifies its aesthetic and political anachronisms: caught on the cusp of momentous alterations in our conceptions of human rights, the Revolution was mired in Rousseau-esque nostalgias and hopes for reincarnation of past classical glories. It can scarcely surprise us that it was to end in the reign of a Caesar. The relentless hold of allegory on the art of this era ensured that women remained a class apart, available to personify every classification and every abstraction needed for personification by the male mind.

Simplification, reiteration, and redundancy in the speech and the images of the Revolution left little space for the emergence of a female individuality that could lead to women's equality or parity with men. Insofar as women came forth from their relative retirement into the public sphere to demand bread or soap, to press their venal sexual favors on the populace, to cheer at executions, or to demand jobs, inheritances, education, divorce, and the vote, their very noisy activity aroused age-old male terrors also embodied in ready-made allegory. There were fears of their disorderliness, of their rejection of men's rules, of their readiness to contribute some of their own, of their speaking out in prophecy and blasphemy. In these guises they were viewed as "them," the class of women. The Girondist Buzot would speak of "lost women coming out of the mud of the capitol whose effrontery is equalled only by their absence of modesty, female monsters with all the cruelty and weakness and all the vices of their sex" (Quoted in Rosa, 218).

This ancient atavistic male distrust would carry the day. Herzen has written, cogently for us here, of woman as that other *peuple*: "As carriers of civilization, the people and woman . . . are represented as victims, castrated, without desire; as creatures of desire, their role is immediately reversed. They became objects of terror, furies, castrators, destroyers of civilization."[33] Women's unself-conscious, unsuspecting self-exposure of their desires in the effervescence of the Revolution could, at that point in human history, have met only with frightened rejection.

Allegory, then, helped press women after 1800 back into a too-tidy form of the ancient dualism, one perhaps even more pronounced than the one preceding the Revolution. This gender dispensation would produce many fewer female effigies, and those would be so magniloquently stylized, so lifeless and so carefully crafted (see fig. 24), that no woman would ever want to see herself in one of them.

NOTES

1. Denis Diderot, "Des Femmes," *Oeuvres complètes* 17 vols. (Paris: Club Français du Livre, 1971), 10:41–43. Further references are cited in the text. All translations mine unless otherwise indicated.

2. Paul de Man, "Pascal's Allegory of Persuasion," in *Allegory and Representation—Selected Papers from the English Institute*, 1978 (Baltimore: Johns Hopkins University Press, 1981), 80.

3. Gravelot and Cochin, *Iconographie par figures* (Paris, 1791).

4. Diderot felt that its planes did not stand out or back sufficiently, and hoped that another phase of this print might rectify this "defect" (6:243–44).

5. From the Pucelle, for example, we have this satire of the gallant mode:

Just conjure up youth's very Flower—
Her wood nymph's form and gentle airs
Like Venus's enchanting power—
And see fair love's seductive mien,
Arachne's art, the siren's chant.   (I, 33–37)

See Jeroom Vercryusse, ed., *La Pucelle d'Orléans* in *Les Oeuvres complètes de Voltaire* (Geneva: Institut et Musée Voltaire-Les Délices, 1970), 7:260.

6. See Marina Warner, *Monuments and Maidens—The Allegory of the Female Form* (New York: Atheneum, 1985), 37.

7. *L'Astrée* was the title of a long and popular novel by Honoré d'Urfé (1568–1625) that deals with the love of Celadon and Astrea.

8. On resentment against the rococo style, see Robert Rosenblum, *Transformations in Late Eighteenth Century Art* (Princeton, N.J.: Princeton University Press, 1967).

9. See Carol Duncan's important study, "Fallen Fathers and Images of Authority in Revolutionary French Art," *Art History* 4 (June 1981): 200.

10. Jean Clay, *Romanticism* (Milan: Chartwell Books, 1981), 54.

11. Judith Schlanger, *L'Enjeu et le débat—l'Invention intellectuelle* (Paris: Denoël Gonthier, 1979). See Chapter 6, "Le Peuple au front gravé."

12. See Richard C. Cobb, *The Police and the People, French Popular Protest 1789–1851* (Oxford: Clarendon Press, 1970).

13. Lynn Hunt, "The Political Psychology of Revolutionary Caricature," in *French Caricature and the French Revolution, 1789–1799* (Los Angeles: Grunwald Center for the Arts and Wight Art Gallery, University of California, Los Angeles, 1988), p. 39. I should like to indicate my deep indebtedness to Lynn Hunt's fine research and her sagacious findings in her readings of revolutionary representations of female and male figures in popular iconography. See "Engraving the Republic—Prints and Propaganda in the French Revolution," *History Today* (October 1980): 11–17, and *Politics, Culture and Class in the French Revolution* (Berkeley and Los Angeles: University of California Press, 1984), especially Chapter 3. What

I seek to do here is to extend her major insight into the gender dynamics of the Jacobins' rejection of the Marianne figure and its subsequent decline into passivity and rigidity. I wish to consider what verbal as well as visual allegory in the Revolution implied about women, and to set these implications within the framework of the Revolution's ideology of femininity.

No work dealing with the female figure during the Revolution can fail to owe much to Maurice Aguilhon's *Marianne au combat* (Paris: Flammarion, 1979).

14. See Schlanger, 104. She couples Condorcet with Volney as exemplars of this somewhat dissident view.

15. Marie-Jean Antoine Nicolas de Caritat, marquis de Condorcet, *Lettres d'un bourgeois de New-Haven à un citoyen de Virginie (Mazzei), sur l'inutilité de partager le corps législatif entre plusieurs corps* (Paris, 1788).

16. In "Sur l'admission des dames au droit de cité," *Journal de la Societe de 1789* 5 (July 3, 1790), pp. 1–13, Condorcet argues at first that the vote should be granted only to widows and unmarried women lest mothers be distracted from their maternal duties; in the end, however, he decisively endorses the inclusion of mothers among the enfranchised.

17. "Les Heroines de Paris, le 5 Octobre 1789," item #16 in L. P. Dufourny, ed., *Les Femmes dans la Revolution Francaise*, 2 vols. (Paris: Edhis, 1982), 1:7.

18. Etta Palm d'Aelders, "Appel aux Francaises sur la regeneration des moeurs, et necessite de l'influence des femmes dans un gouvernement libre," item #33 in *Les Femmes*, 2:38.

19. Olympe de Gouges, "Les Droits de la femme. A la Reine," item #36 in *Les Femmes*, 2:7.

20. Mary Wollestonecraft, *A Vindication of the Rights of Women* (New York: W. W. Norton, 1967), 224.

21. On Revolutionary feminism see Serge Bianchi, *La Revolution de l'An II— Elites et peuples, 1789–99* (Paris: Auber-Floreal, 1982), 109–151. For Guyomar's work see *Les Femmes*, vol. 2, item #45.

22. "In Paris, distrust grew of all politically active women during the struggle between the more conservative faction, the Girondins . . . and the more radical Jacobins." Ruth Graham, "Women in the French Revolution," in *Becoming Visible—Women in European History*, ed. Renata Bridenthal and Claudia Koonz (Boston: Houghton Mifflin, 1977), 247.

23. This struggle around emblems is illuminated by Naomi Schor's study, *Reading in Detail—Aesthetics and the Feminine* (New York: Methuen, 1987). "For the archeology of detail, the sexism of rhetoric is of crucial significance. Neo-classical aesthetics is imbued with . . . a sexist imaginary where the ornamental is inevitably bound up with the feminine. . . ." (p. 45). With this "logic" of the ornamental in mind, I conclude that the battle over the cockade could be conceded to women. Men's use of it might be interpreted as their seizure from women of a "feminine" detail, which the women then insisted be restituted to them. The red bonnet, on the other hand, is a cap: the symbolic equivalent for men as a symbol of shared sovereignty to the overthrown crown. Its adoption therefore constituted a far more blatant confrontation of authority by women than the affixing of the cockade.

24. For the most thoroughgoing discussion of the concept of virtue for the Revolution, see Carol Blum's *Rousseau and the Republic of Virtue* (Ithaca, N.Y.: Cornell University Press, 1982).

25. In a related metaphor, L. P. Dufourny's proclamation of June 1793 indicat-

ing to women the proper use of their energies reports that the Convention itself had been on the brink of producing an abortion or a monster (*Les Femmes*, vol. 2, item #68).

26. See Neil Hertz, "Medusa's Head: Male Hysteria under Political Pressure," *Representations* 4 (1983): 27–54.

27. See Marina Warner's extended discussion of the iconography of the "slipped chiton" in her chapter of that title in *Monuments and Maidens*.

28. Quoted in Annette Rosa, *Citoyennes* (Paris: Messidor, 1988), 218.

29. Quoted in Alphonse Aulard, *Le Culte de la Raison et le culte de l'Etre suprême* (Paris: 1892, reprint Aalen: Scientia Verlag, 1975), 191.

30. See Delacroix's *Portrait des femmes ou les femmes traitées comme elles le méritent* as cited in Arlette Farge, ed., *Le Miroir des dames* (Paris: Montalba, 1982), 359.

31. I refer to the works of psychoanalyst Melanie Klein as well as Dorothy Dinnerstein, *The Mermaid and the Minotaur* (1977), and Nancy Chodorow, *The Reproduction of Mothering* (1978).

32. Ernst Gombrich, "The Dream of Reason," *British Journal of Eighteenth Century Studies* 2 (1979): 204.

33. Quoted by Lionel Gossman, "Augustin Thierry and Liberal Historiography," *History and Theory*, Beiheft 15, 4 (Middletown, Conn.: Wesleyan University Press, 1975), 70.

Swordplay: Jacques-Louis David's Painting of Le Peletier de Saint-Fargeau on His Deathbed

DONNA M. HUNTER

During the entire course of the Terror, Jacques-Louis David's painting of Le Peletier de Saint-Fargeau on his deathbed hung directly before the eyes of the assembled members of the Convention. This meant that it was viewed from time to time while other things were happening or being said, rather like a prominent feature in a landscape that is always there to be seen even if it is seldom noticed by those familiar with the terrain. These viewing conditions were, I will argue, integral to the meanings that the painting was capable of producing. The painting, which is either lost or destroyed, is known through a stunning engraving and a rather faint drawing that is squared for transfer and that probably served as the model for the print (see figs. 25 and 27).[1] The engraving survives in only a single ripped proof; it was evidently not completed before Le Peletier's death ceased to be of public interest, or, to be more precise, ceased to be a politically correct thing to remember. The lost painting is known to have measured approximately five and a half feet high by a little over four feet wide. In the painting, therefore, Le Peletier's body must have been life-size and the sword about three feet long.

Several features of the engraving and drawing are noteworthy. Foremost are the wound in Le Peletier's side and—in the drawing—the sword hanging from a single hair (the strand is very obviously a hair and not a thread since there is a definite curl to it). The hilt of the sword is shaped like a cockerel's head, then a symbol of the French monarchy. A fleur-de-lis and the words "PARIS / GA . . . / DU ROI" are inscribed on the blade; it was a man named Pâris, former bodyguard to Louis XVI, who assassinated Le Peletier. The sword pierces a fairly large piece of paper on which was written—the words have been erased—"I vote for the death of the tyrant" [Je vote la mort du tyran]. The words refer to the sentencing of Louis XVI after he was found guilty of treason in January 1793. (The votes were spoken, however, not written, and Le Peletier, unlike more verbose or emphatic colleagues, simply said "Je vote pour la mort."[2]) Finally, blood drips from the tip of the sword as if the paper or the vote could bleed.

These features of the engraving and drawing reveal two different but related aspects of David's lost painting. The first is its political aim, a topic that has not been discussed at any length in the literature on the artist.[3] The second is the operation of shifters in what Roman Jakobson calls "duplex structure"—a structure that overlaps code and message, sender and receiver, event and participants. The painting was meant to be an unambiguous piece of Jacobin propaganda, a specifically Jacobin interpretation of the events of 1793. But it exceeded that political intention not only because the meaning of Le Peletier's death was contested, but also because the play of meanings generated by representation subverts any effort to fix meaning or lay down the law. Jakobson's categorization of those elements in language that economically introduce complexity offers a valuable model for an analysis of how an image, or rather the viewing of an image, can compound its meaning.

I wish to consider what can variously be called authority, orthodoxy, or the law, forces that righteously claim to represent what is best for those under their control. During the Terror, these forces did their work with great precision and seeming neutrality, with an objectivity that dispassionately split subject from object. But the very pretense of objectivity prompts us to look closely at the constraints imposed by this sort of authority, at the process whereby it was legitimated, at its simultaneous invocation of terror, virtue, and reason, and at the dizzying turns it took to condense, displace, or transfer subject positions and objects of knowledge even as it claimed to be a stable, unified order.

For example, in a speech on political morality delivered to the Convention in February 1794 (a speech given in the presence of David's painting), Robespierre plainly identified terror with justice:

If the strength of popular government in peace time is virtue the strength of popular government in revolution is simultaneously *terror and virtue* [emphasis in the original printing]: virtue without which terror is deadly; terror without which virtue is impotent. Terror is nothing but justice which is prompt, severe, inflexible; it is thus an emanation of virtue; it is less a specific principle than a consequence of the general principle of democracy applied to the nation's most pressing needs.[4]

A policy of terror masquerades as a policy of reason. Using the kind of sentence structure that is typically deployed for the statement of facts (the only verb joining subjects and predicates is the verb "to be" in the present tense), the speaker—who speaks as the government—separates himself clearly from the course of action he defines as well as from those who would become bloodied objects of such action. In other speeches, particularly those in which counterrevolutionary plots were invoked, swords mentioned, or David's painting singled out, the identity of the subject or object could veer wildly, depending on the alignment of certain variables or shifters. The play of signifiers simply could not be quashed by the effort to promulgate a single and incontrovertible message; in fact, the effort to do so produced the opposite result.

The peculiarities of Jacobin rhetoric can be partly explained by reference to what Freud calls "dream-work." If, as Freud argues, dreams operate through such mechanisms as condensation and displacement of meanings unacceptable to the conscious mind, the conscious mind can often suggest meanings unacceptable to itself or its audience through those same mechanisms, mechanisms that can also be described in terms of the ordinary and fairly overt operations of language. These operations or mechanisms are both a consequence of censorship *and* a means to avoid it, as has frequently been noted. Furthermore, if "dream-work is under some kind of necessity to combine all the sources which have acted as stimuli for the dream into a single unity,"[5] the same economy is at work in speeches that refer to blades that have killed Jacobins, could kill Jacobins, were once wielded by agents of royal authority, and have since been appropriated by patriots to execute a king and his supporters. The patriots surely had qualms about their own right to dispense such terrible justice even if such a thought was vociferously excluded from their own pronouncements. The sword in David's painting is precisely the sort of "single unity" that combines disparate and contradictory sources.

Robespierre himself implicitly recognizes this point. After flatly asserting that terror is synonymous with justice, he raises a question that must have occurred to his listeners: "It has been said that terror is the strength of despotic government. Does your government then resemble despotism? Yes, as the sword [*glaive*] that shines in the hands of the heroes of liberty resembles that with which the creatures [*satellites*] of tyranny are armed."[6]

The problem with this formulation is that it is impossible to tell the two swords apart. If Robespierre meant to suggest that a sword is the only thing shared by the heroes of liberty and the creatures of tyranny, his rhetorical stratagem—a comparison designed to accentuate a contrast—fails. And in failing, it points to the impossibility of dissociating terror from despotism, at least of doing so categorically. The sword with which the Jacobin "heroes of liberty" threatened their enemies was the same as the sword that David represented as the instrument of Le Peletier's death in a painting that Robespierre might have pointed to even as he spoke.

The painted sword was the weapon of what Robespierre called a *satel-*

lite. By the end of the eighteenth century, this word, which in medieval French meant "bodyguard" or "man charged with carrying out the orders of his superiors," had come to denote someone who was less than fully human, someone who was neither a free man nor a republican. But if the painted sword of a *satellite* cannot be distinguished from the free man's *glaive,* neither can the "heroes of liberty" be divided from the "creatures of tyranny." Robespierre's desire to separate the two by confidently admitting what he regarded as a trifling or misleading similarity reveals his own grave unease and that of the Jacobins as a group. Terror, it turns out, is also synonymous with fear, an emanation of doubts about one's own identity and purpose.

Quatrevingt-Treize

Victor Hugo's novel *Quatrevingt-treize,* an impassioned and partisan representation of the French Revolution in 1793, invites us to read the speeches and paintings made during the Terror as representations of the Revolution in progress, as the only means by which participants in the Revolution could give a larger meaning to its events.[7] Among the notes that Victor Hugo took as he prepared to write his novel is a statement that he attributes to Robespierre without giving the date or occasion: "Up until today the sword of the law has been only vertical; it falls from top to bottom; I wish it to be horizontal." Hugo commented, "This tragic formula sums up '93." [8] What does it mean for justice to operate horizontally? Why was this the tragic summation of 1793? In the novel itself Hugo maintains, "Events dictate, men sign," and he has Robespierre sign on 21 January.[9] Why should 21 January, the day Louis XVI was executed, be so clearly signed *Robespierre?*

These questions lead in turn to a further question: Can the decisive role played by the Jacobins in the execution of the king be linked to the painting that David, a Jacobin and a member of the Convention, painted to commemorate the death of Le Peletier, a Jacobin who, like all the members of that political club, had voted for the death of the king? Since a vertical sword figures prominently in David's painting and since the painting hung in the Convention, in front of men who had reason to fear for their lives, the remark imputed to Robespierre and Hugo's comment upon it may help to reveal the full meaning of David's work.

In another statement that Hugo's novel imputes to Robespierre without giving an exact source, Robespierre invokes a suspended sword. At the end of a long diatribe against Danton, he concludes, "We know the schemers, we know those who corrupt and those who have been corrupted, we know the traitors; they are in this assembly. They hear us; we see them and we will not take our eyes off them. Let them look above their head, and there they shall see the sword of the law [*glaive de la loi*]." At this point in Hugo's novel, Danton falls backward in his seat, one arm hanging straight down and his face looking up toward the ceiling, eyes half-closed—very much the posture of a man who had been mortally wounded, and very like the postures of Le Peletier and Marat (figs. 26 and 27) in David's paintings.[10]

David painted Marat expiring in his bathtub shortly after his assassination in July 1793. The two paintings hung in the Convention on either side of the tribune or speaker's platform, *Marat* to the viewer's left, *Le Peletier* to the right.[11] Although it is well-known that *Marat* is the pendant to *Le Peletier*, which was painted about five months earlier, most of those who have written on *Marat* have not seriously treated its relation to its predecessor—a relation that is political as well as formal.

To see this relation fully, we must further examine Robespierre's references to the *glaive*. He comes closest to expressing the wish that the sword of justice cut horizontally in a speech he delivered to the Convention in November 1793. Exhorting his fellow deputies, Robespierre says,

Applaud yourselves not only for having annihilated royalty and punished kings, for having pulled down the guilty idols before which the world prostrated itself; but above all for having amazed the world by an act of justice, such as it had never seen, cutting down with the sword of the law [*glaive de la loi*] those criminal heads which rose up in your midst, for having crushed thus far all factions under the weight of the national level [*niveau*].[12]

The *glaive de la loi* symbolized a form of justice that enforced a choice between liberty or death, with no other options; the *niveau* (carpenter's level) symbolized equality.[13] In 1793 the sword of the law, which protected liberty by meting out death, was conflated with the level, which not only verified equality but enforced it by crushing factions. In a print entitled *The Triumph of Equality,* published in 1794, Equality balances, like Victory, on a very large carpenter's level that has forced some arrogant men to bend their necks (fig. 28)—"Prideful ones, bow down" is written on the cross-piece. In one hand Equality holds a sword—called a *glaive* in the legend—that bears the inscription, "Equality or Death." In her other hand she holds the scales of justice fused with a small carpenter's level.[14]

The sword of the law that had traditionally operated vertically—from on high to those below—now supposedly worked like an instrument that had to be horizontal in order to do its job. In 1793, the year the Jacobins first dominated the Convention and the year the Terror became governmental policy, the sword and the level were conflated in the interests of a form of justice, i.e., the Terror, which had no respect for persons. But the "triumph of equality" also meant the downfall of Robespierre and his associates, for it is they who are shown being laid low in the print representing this triumph. Specifically, the two legs of the level and the lead weight at the end of the plumb-line do the work of a guillotine, for as the legend says, Equality crushes the heads ("écrase les têtes") of Robespierre, Couthon, and Saint-Just. If the spirit of Equality favored by the Thermidorean reaction brandishes a very large sword, Robespierre and Couthon are shown clutching knives or daggers, the insidious weapons long associated with counterrevolutionaries. The *glaive* and the *poignard* are now in different hands.

The fate of Robespierre and his associates suggests a third term, however, that was contraposed to liberty and equality. The Constitution of 1793, very much a Jacobin document, bore the motto "Liberty, Equality, Fraternity, or Death".[15] In a painting dated "l'an 3me" (1794–95), J.-B. Regnault shows how absolute this choice could be by representing the genius of the French people hovering between personifications of Death and the Republic (fig. 29).[16] In David's painting of Le Peletier, and in the later painting of Marat, this same choice is signified without the use of allegory. Instead, the meaning of each is derived from historical particulars and a careful adjustment of the painting's mode of address, with verisimilitude or seeming transparency preferred. Even while eschewing conventional symbolism, David subtly invokes the particular physical and political context in which each painting would be seen.

Consider what the deputies saw along with the paintings themselves (see figs. 26 and 27). During the Terror, a Jacobin version of the Declaration of the Rights of Man hung in the Convention; it was inscribed on a tablet whose two halves were separated by a fasces, symbol of unity and absolute equality. Also facing the deputies were tablets inscribed with the articles of the Jacobin Constitution: tablets separated by a sword hanging point down. The painting of Le Peletier is thought to have hung beneath the Constitution (the two swords lining up), that of Marat beneath the Rights (Recall its motto, "Liberty, Equality, Fraternity, or Death"). Ironically, the Constitution and the revised version of the Rights, both of which physically hung in the Convention, were officially suspended during the Jacobin Republic because of a national emergency. One of the principal reasons for the state of emergency was the counterrevolution, two of whose 300,000 victims (by Robespierre's count) were Le Peletier and Marat.[17]

A Constitution drafted chiefly by the Jacobins was approved by the Convention on 24 June 1793, a short three weeks after the Jacobins had eliminated the Girondins. The Jacobin campaign to destroy as well as unseat this group of rival politicians began in earnest after the trial and execution of the king. The Girondins, along with the vast majority of the Convention, had found Louis guilty of treason, but they would have preferred to put the verdict to the vote of the people or, barring that, to postpone his execution until certain conditions had been fulfilled. But according to the Jacobins, these tactics created the climate in which Le Peletier's assassin was emboldened to strike. (Since Le Peletier was a former aristocrat, his vote for the death of the king must have struck a royalist as a particularly heinous act.) Le Peletier's last words, or the version circulated less than twenty-four hours after his death, refer specifically to liberty, equality, and the disclosure of the enemy within. He said, or is reported to have said, "I am satisfied to shed my blood for my country. My only hope is that it will serve to consolidate liberty and equality and cause its [my country's] enemies to be known."[18]

On the night before Louis XVI was scheduled to be executed, Michel Le Peletier de Saint-Fargeau was killed while eating dinner in a Paris restaurant, run through by one of the king's former bodyguards. In various prints issued shortly after his death and during the course of the nineteenth century (fig. 30), the assassination weapon is a long sword, which in fact it was, even though the legends that accompany these prints usually say that Le Peletier was killed by a dagger (the verb is *poignarder*).[19]

Ever since February 1791, when the *chevaliers du poignard* (the knights of the dagger) had attempted to abduct the king from the Palace of the Tuileries, aristocrats, and by extension all counterrevolutionaries, were said to stalk true patriots with daggers that they concealed on their persons. Patriots, on the other hand, publicly drew their swords and manfully delivered the death-blow for all to see. Their swords were definitely *glaives de la loi*. In 1794, at the height of the Terror, David made a drawing that represents "le Triomphe du peuple français" (fig. 31). It shows two young, strapping representatives of the people about to kill a king with huge swords while behind them advances the triumphal chariot of the people, followed by a group of persons famous for having chosen between liberty and death— Brutus, William Tell, and, at far right, Le Peletier and Marat displaying their wounds.[20]

Since the sword had come to signify true patriotism, David's use of a sword to represent the assassination of Le Peletier—even though historically accurate—generated contradictions that I will explore in the second part of this essay. For now I wish to consider another spectacle evoked by David's depiction of the wounded Le Peletier. On 24 January, four days after he was assassinated, Le Peletier was laid to rest in the Panthéon, the church that had recently been converted into a memorial and mausoleum for the nation's great men. The ceremonies began with the display of the body in the place des Piques, formerly and now once again the place Vendôme. In a scene that appeared in the Paris press within days (fig. 32), the corpse was artfully arranged atop the pedestal where a statue of Louis XIV had stood until the storming of the Tuileries on 10 August 1792, the day that sealed his descendant's fate. The king's body was treated very differently. Just three days before Le Peletier was laid to rest, the head of Louis Capet had been dangled before the crowd and his body tossed, without the least ceremony, into a mass grave. One of the most visually startling and politically concise images of the entire Revolution is a print showing just the executioner's hand grasping the decapitated head by the hair (fig. 33).[21]

While the ceremonies in the place des Piques sharply contrast with the disposal of the king, they invite comparison with David's painting of Le Peletier, especially since the artist may have had a hand in arranging them. Like David's painting, the print of the ceremonies shows a half-draped body recalling Hector or Meleager, an exposed wound, and a lethal sword. Le Peletier's last words, or supposed last words, were inscribed on the side of the pedestal: the wish, quoted above on page 175, that his death consolidate liberty and equality and make the nation's enemies known. A banner with those same words was carried in the procession from the place des Piques to the Panthéon, tellingly positioned in the midst of the *conventionnels*. Those who had equivocated during the king's trial or sentencing were thus in a sense publicly humiliated, if they did not stand accused.

At the place des Piques, Le Peletier was crowned with oak, the civic crown, by the president of the Convention, Vergniaud, the Girondin who had done most to promote the appeal to the people that might have saved the king's life. The death of Le Peletier required nonpartisan grief even though the Jacobins were exploiting the assassination as part of their campaign to uncover, impugn, and punish all counterrevolutionaries. At the Panthéon, while the eulogies were being read, a common soldier grabbed the death weapon and swung it above his head while promising to avenge the loss. Thus even at his funeral the instrument of Le Peletier's demise became what it also could very easily be, the insrument of his revenge: not only the sword of justice or of the law, the Terror of the revolutionary government, but a naked blade in the hand of a disorderly person, a source of simple terror.[22]

On 29 March 1793, just two months after the funeral, David presented his painting to the Convention. It was not unusual for artists to offer patriotic works to the legislature, but when such an ambitious canvas is presented by an artist of David's stature, who was also a member of the legislature, we need to ask what the motive might have been. It is highly unlikely that David was acting alone to express his own views; it is far more likely that he, as a Jacobin, discussed the project with other members of that Club or with the Mountain in general, the deputies who sat on the upper benches of the meeting hall. Hung in the Convention, the painting was meant to admonish the legislators as they conducted their daily business. Since the Jacobins frequently insinuated that a good number of those present were guilty of intrigue if not downright crimes against the state, the painting can be seen as the visual complement to their verbal campaign.

Swordplay

David's painting can be read not only in light of the Jacobin quest for power but also in terms of the linguistic phenomenon called "duplex structure," the shifter that causes a code to be comprehensible only in terms of the message it encodes.[23] For simplicity's sake, the analysis that follows will center on the sword, or rather on the effects of the sword, that hangs exposed in the middle of David's composition. Though the hanging sword obviously evokes the sword of Damocles, its significance is hardly limited to or really even coincident with that one figure of speech. Instead the painting refers to many speeches and to one figure of speech in particular, "the sword of the law."

The crucial part the sword plays in establishing the meaning of the painting is confirmed by the fact that it was painted out during the Restoration. In 1826 the canvas was purchased from David's estate by Le Peletier's daughter, "Mlle Nation," a ward of the former Republic who was then married to an ultraroyalist. Although some feared that she would destroy the painting, what she did instead was to have the sword, the dripping blood, and the piece of paper painted out. At the time of the sale, and attendant upon it, the plate for the engraving was broken in her presence and assurances given that all proofs had been destroyed.[24] One, of course, survived.

As a painted reference to a figure of speech, a hanging sword is an unusual feature in a painting by David, for the artist rarely broke with what passed for verisimilitude (*vraisemblance*) in later eighteenth-century French painting. Not that verisimilitude does not have its code and its conventions, but one needs to acknowledge that the code is motivated by the objects it represents. To use Peirce's terminology, such a painting is an "icon" since it resembles what it represents; or, to be more accurate, it "exhibits" or "exemplifies" some aspect of its object.[25] To use Jakobson's terminology, which explicitly builds on Peirce's, one could say that the code of mimetic art is made up of "indexical symbols." (Jakobson's prime example of an indexical symbol is the shifter.) Such signs are indices because, like a pointing finger, they are existentially related to the object they represent (needless to say, the "object" need not be an actual object); and they are symbols because they are associated with that object by a conventional rule.

To see how Jakobson's work on shifters can illuminate David's painting, we need to understand his vocabulary. Technically speaking, shifters are "a particular class of grammatical units" whose "general meaning cannot be defined without a reference to the message." To be more specific, shifters include the first- and second-person pronouns *I, we,* and *you:* words that shift their meaning as they pass from one speaker to another. Shifters also include certain "verbal categories"—categories that characterize one or more "narrated items" while referring the item or items to the "speech event" (the communication itself) or to its participants, the "sender" or "receiver." A narrated item may be an event or one of its participants, the "performer" or "undergoer." A verbal category that characterizes only one narrated item is called a "designator"; a verbal category that connects one narrated item to another is called a "connector." Both designators and connectors can act as shifters if they link the narrated event or its participants to the speech event. Designators that shift express the grammatical concepts of *person* and *tense;* connectors that shift express the grammatical concepts of *mood* and *evidential status.*

Examples make these concepts clearer. In the sentence, "We stared at the painting," the first *person* form of the verb indicates that the performers of the narrated event (staring at a painting) are the same as the senders of the speech event (the full sentence). (Since English verb forms seldom indicate person unambiguously, it must also be indicated by pronouns.) Using a third person in a sentence like "They stared at the painting" is a concise and in fact subtle way to indicate that the performers of the narrated event are not the same as the senders of the speech event. The performers of the narrated event are obliquely inscribed as undergoers in the speech event, as the objects, knowingly or unknowingly, of someone else's attention. The past *tense* informs the reader that the narrated event took place before the speech event, a simple formulation that subtly reveals our existence in time, our willed construction of sequence and consequence.

Further examples illustrate the meaning of *mood.* In a sentence such as "If Robespierre named the conspirators, his audience would explode," the mood of the verb characterizes the relation between the narrated events (naming conspirators, reacting violently) and its participants (Robespierre and his audience) while referring to the speaker's view of the connection between those events and the participants and between those same events and any results the participants may have wanted to achieve or avoid. The absence of any reference to the *speaker* lends the sentence the sort of authority that third-person narration affords, but this objectivity is a fiction, if not a fraud, for there is never an object without a subject. As well as the potential subjunctive, mood includes all the other forms of the subjunctive as well as indicative and imperative constructions. What makes all these modes of predication shifters is their capacity to relate a narrated event or its participants to a speech event. Such doubling or reflexivity is analogous to the complex relations involved in being or thinking, if it does not constitute all we can know of them.

"In language and in the use of language," Jakobson writes, "duplicity plays a cardinal role. In particular, the classification of grammatical, and especially verbal, categories requires a consistent discrimination of shifters."[26] Yet it is not only language but representation, and of course the *use* of representation, that is at least double and frequently duplicitous. And it is not only the classification of various categories within representation that calls for "a consistent discrimination of shifters," but also the everyday decoding of representation. I introduce these concepts into a discussion of painting because linguistics, or the translinguistic project of semiology, to paraphrase Barthes, can help us not only to see but, more pertinently, to explain how paintings make their meaning.[27] In the last twenty years, paintings have been analyzed in terms of icons and symbols, but the debate over what is and is not conventional has perhaps caused another mode of signification to be overlooked. The indexical symbol, in particular the shifter, not only offers a way out of this dualistic bind but also suggests a way to link concepts drawn from linguistics or semiology to key elements in the current discussion of the gaze.[28]

How then do shifters work in David's image of Le Peletier, and what work do they do? Since any history painting is concerned with a narrated event, one can liken its various elements, or their operation, to grammatical concepts that are implemented verbally or syntactically. (This is also true of David's portraits, since they turn the sitting into an event, just as *Le Peletier* combines history and portraiture.) To begin with *tense,* the simplest of the four verbal shifters, David's image characterizes not only Le Peletier's assassination and funeral but also what preceded them: the trial, execution, and summary burial of the king. It does these things *while* referring to the event that is the painting, the single static image that hung in the Convention while the Jacobins rose to power and then directed the Terror. In addition to references to past and present, there is also a clear projection into the future: the painting will continue to instill its message as long as the nation is in danger. (This is how David described its desired effect in the speech that he made when presenting the painting to the Convention.)²⁹ In a reproduction of the torn print, the various tenses that the painting employed are mixed with those that the print has employed and those specific to the reproduction. Such shifts are the product of our being situated in time and our enduring in time, a state of affairs equally true for persons, things, cultural memories, and history itself.

As for *person*, the painting gives a Jacobin characterization to the participants in the events just mentioned—participants who included not only Le Peletier and his assassin, but Louis XVI, the crowds who witnessed first the execution and then the funeral, the men who sentenced the king, and any and all counter-revolutionaries. It does this *while* referring the participants in those events (performers and undergoers alike) to the participants (senders and receivers alike) in the event that was the painting. David explicitly sent or addressed the painting to Le Peletier, for it bore the inscription "à Pelletier [sic]/David".³⁰ Further, as he indicated in his presentation speech, David also addressed the painting, or rather the painting addresses itself, to the French people, to the unborn as well as to the living.

To be more specific, the painting addresses all the members of the Convention, those who voted for the king's death and those who either opposed it or proposed conditions that were said to have heightened the danger in which true patriots lived. In its address the painting works both personally (it is the first person and its viewers the second) and impersonally (statements are made in the third person or in the passive voice).³¹ The second person is both any imaginable viewer and certain specific viewers. All these viewers can be identified according to each one's decoding of the message, or rather, of the messages. One can imagine the painting saying: "I remind you (the regicides) of the risk you run, and I cause you to reflect on what it means to decapitate a king"; "I embolden you (all those the Jacobins would describe as patriots) to prosecute counterrevolutionaries"; "I threaten you (any one the Jacobins would describe as counterrevolutionary) with a similar fate"; "I legitimate your (Jacobin) use of the sword, i.e., the guillotine." In the third person the painting assumes the character of a report or document: "He (Le Peletier, a *conventionnel* and a Jacobin) died for voting for the death of a king." But the air of incontrovertible fact cannot mask the attempt to control the possible meanings of an event, the attempt to prevail. "The banishment of polysemy," writes Barthes, "serves the Law."³²

It is the work of shifters to refer one characterization to another and thereby double, if not further multiply, its significance. Owing to this, the single element of the sword is too little understood if we do not hear both the message intended by the Jacobins and the messages that proliferated once the sword was set in play. This proliferation of messages also involves the verbal sparring, figuratively called "swordplay," that went on in the Convention, the press and the political clubs after the death of Le Peletier. Such swordplay, or in French *glaive de la parole* (sword of the spoken word, sword of eloquence) is the fantasized power of speech to dumbfound if not slay its opponents. Therefore, before considering the last two verbal shifters, mood and evidential status, which are more complex, we must examine two swords: the sword of Damocles and the sword of the law.

By the eighteenth century the expression "sword of Damocles" had come to mean little more than "imminent danger," although the details of the story were certainly known to the many deputies with a classical education, David among them. Damocles was a courtier of Dionysius, the tyrant who ruled Syracuse in the fourth century B.C. Damocles imagined that Dionysius was the happiest of men; to disabuse him, and to exercise his lawless power, Dionysius had a sword hung over his head at a banquet prepared expressly for the envious courtier. At some point during the meal, Damocles looked up, changed his mind about the pleasures of kingship, at least of sovereignty illegally obtained, and asked that the sword be taken down.

Clearly, Le Peletier cannot be put in the place of Damocles; at least he would not have been consciously put in that place by David, a committed Jacobin who had also voted for the death of the king. Le Peletier did not envy the king or wish to be king, although one might say that he and all the regicides aspired jointly to the king's power on behalf of the nation. Their consciously expressed intention to abolish kingship was surely mixed with the repressed desire to enjoy it. One should remember as well that the regicides often called the king a "tyrant," that is, "one who seizes the sovereign power in a state without legal right." It was not Louis XVI who threatened them, for he was dead; rather it was the living who constructed a dead man's threat, a threat that they directed against themselves as well as others.

One could say, however, that it was a tyrant, or the creature of a tyrant, who used the suspended sword to kill Le Peletier and threaten other regicides with the same fate. One could also say that the crowned heads of Europe were using the sword in an effort to undo the Revolution. But if one makes Louis XVI Le Peletier's assassin, or the crowned heads of Europe the only ones who wield the sword, a great number of other meanings are cut short. In revolutionary iconography, as we have seen, the sword signified true patriotism, and counterrevolutionaries were said to use daggers. Consequently, though the sword that was hung over Le Peletier in David's painting is identical to the one used to kill him, David as a Jacobin could not have left the sword, the preeminent instrument of justice, in the hands of tyrants or their subordinates. If that particular sword was literally the weapon wielded on their behalf, metaphorically it had to be the force that patriots used to eliminate those who they believed sought to knife them in the back. It goes without saying that this conflation gives rise to patent contradictions, but those contradictions are a fair equivalent of the opinions, doubts, and fears that the painter dealt with.

In short, the regicides, and chief among them the Jacobins, occupied a number of subject positions as they negotiated a difficult moment in French history and in their own ascent to power. I would argue that in this "confused" use of a clear reference to what was for its audience a fairly well-known story, the confusion was meant to operate productively. It allowed several meanings, contradictory meanings, to be made explicit. And all of this confusion took place under the cover of a seemingly fixed and limited figure of speech, a cliché that could be reduced to the simple and fairly uncontroversial notion of "precariousness" or "imminent danger." Since David used literary sources carefully, the fact that this painting seems to make such superficial or even sloppy use of its source is one reason it calls for explanation. But the confusion cannot be resolved into a set of meanings that express or reinforce a Jacobin intent. On the contrary, the painting derives a great part of its power from the fact that it exceeds and contravenes the meanings the Jacobins consciously wanted it to have.

To turn to the other sword, the sword of the law, one first needs to consider the meanings of *glaive* in French. Literally, this literary word means the same thing as the more common word *épée:* a long sword with one or two cutting edges. Figuratively, however, the words mean different things. The sword of Damocles is always an *épée,* for a tyrant's sword, especially when used sadistically to simulate the quality of a tyrant's life, could never be called a *glaive.* As a figure of speech, *glaive* has four basic meanings: (1) an instrument wielded by God, monarchs, ancient peoples, or destiny; (2) war or combat; (3) the right over life and death exercised by a sovereign; and (4) the *glaive spirituel* that signifies the jurisdiction of the Church, in particular its power to excommunicate.

Since a *glaive* and an *épée* are visually identical, David's sword can also function as the sign, the usurped or appropriated sign, of the *noblesse d'épée.* For centuries this branch of the aristocracy, and only this branch (unlike the nobility of the robe), had had the right to wield the sword to defend not only France but their own personal honor. By 1793, however, the French army was staffed and directed by men who had not been born to the sword, men whose swords were simply called *sabres* (sabers) or *sabres démocratiques* (democratic sabers).[33] Furthermore, the instrument of the Terror was the guillotine, not a symbol that those who made use of it cared to emblazon on their letterheads or invoke in their speeches. In place of the guillotine, the symbol used to refer to the Terror, as a synonym for justice and virtue, was the *glaive de la loi*. This translated the *couperet* or cutting edge of the guillotine (*couperet* also means a butcher's chopper) into a context that made its operation more acceptable.

The phrase *glaive de la loi* was used frequently after the death of Le Peletier. It had been used earlier, but after Le Peletier's death and after David's painting came to hang in a room where speechmaking was the order of the day, the phrase took on a particular meaning. Earlier I quoted from two speeches that Robespierre made in the Convention: a speech equating virtue with terror and a speech praising France for administering justice horizontally. Both speeches referred to the *glaive* or *glaive de la loi,* and in one of them Robespierre said that the terror of despotism resembled that of revolutionary government only insofar "as the sword [*glaive*] that shines in the hands of the heroes of liberty resembles that with which the creatures of tyranny are armed."[34] So certain was Robespierre of the difference between revolutionary government and despotism that he could frankly acknowledge their similarity. So certain was David of the difference between the sword that slew Le Peletier and the *glaive de la loi* that he could conflate them. But this certainty would unravel before the Terror was over.

Reading excerpts from several speeches made between the night Le Peletier was assassinated and the day David was called upon to memorialize Marat, we can note that the discourse on death is highly labile even when speakers try to state a "simple" policy of "liberty or death" or spell out the lessons to be learned from the assassination of Le Peletier and Marat. That policy and those lessons were, however, neither simple nor easily accepted. The rift between the professed certainty and the actual polyvalence of the Terror, or of terror in general, is the motor force of what I call "swordplay."

A few hours after the fatal attack, the news was announced at the Jacobin Club by a member who had just come from Le Peletier's bedside.

The knights of the dagger (*chevaliers du poignard*) are in full swing. I fear that a bloody night may deprive us of the fruits of the most glorious triumph for the true friends of liberty [the king's execution that was slated to occur later that same day].

Already, as I speak to you, one of our members, a virtuous citizen, a man (Le Peletier de Saint-Fargeau) who served the public interest with courage ever since the Constituent Assembly (there was a stir in the room at this point) perhaps no longer exists. . . . We need all the calm and tranquility possible in order to frustrate our enemies' plan. We must be aware that for the last four months all manner of means have been calculated to save the tyrant; there are those who wish to stir up a riot in order to prevent him [the king] from speaking. The schemers fear that their complicity will be revealed and punished. . . . We must sacrifice our own blood to make sure that the tyrant climbs the scaffold.[35]

As the voice of authority, Robespierre reiterated and expanded upon each of these points, and others took their cue from him. When a soldier proposed that an armed force be constituted to protect the members of the Club, an unnamed citizen declared that no one present dreaded the daggers. "Besides," he shouted, "it would be glorious to die for such a beautiful cause; we all envy Le Peletier's fate."[36] Like the early Christians who yearned for martyrdom, the Jacobins were more than half in love with death.

This same heady death-wish can be seen in an exchange that took place at the Club two months later. Swearing that his country would not be the slave of a Brissot (a leading Girondin) or a Brunswick (the Prussian general who invaded France), Robespierre exclaimed, "We will know how to die, we will die everyone of us!" This was greeted by applause and cries of "All of us, all of us!" Then Marat coldly responded, "I do not at all approve of the alarms raised by a deputy of the people [meaning Robespierre] in whom fear has inspired a patriotic delirium. No, we will not die, not at all; we will put our enemies to death, we will crush them." Those words met with applause as well.[37]

The evening after Le Peletier's death was announced to the Convention, a speaker at the Jacobin Club observed that the Mountain had "to deploy all its force in order to obtain the honors that Le Peletier so justly deserved." Immediately after saying that, with little or no transition, the same speaker claimed that it was the roll-call votes at the conclusion of the king's trial that had caused the true friends of liberty to be known. He also expressed his displeasure at the fact that the significance of Le Peletier's death had been diminished when Barère blandly said that the sovereignty of the people had been wounded or that Le Peletier had died a martyr of liberty. What needed to be said, the speaker declared, was that Le Peletier had died for voting to execute a tyrant.[38]

On 21 February, a bust of Le Peletier was presented to the Convention. To Le Peletier's brother, who presented the bust, the presiding officer declared: "Citizen, if ever the representatives of the people strayed from their duties, the bust of Michel Le Peletier, placed in their midst, would recall them to those duties and remind them that between sacrificing the people's interests and death, there can be no hesitation."[39] On 3 April, Robespierre pointed to this bust as he mounted an attack on Brissot.

I do not wish to convince the conspirators, no, not at all. (Someone whose last name began with "N" called out, "You're summoning the daggers!") I only wish to speak the truth; and when the men who talk of daggers have assassinated liberty and the last of her defenders, as they assassinated that man (Robespierre pointed to the bust of Le Peletier), then it will at least be said, at that moment when they think they have consummated their plots to kill liberty [*complots liberticides*], . . . [that] I spoke the truth. . . .[40]

Ten days later Robespierre pointed to David's painting of Le Peletier while countering accusations that had been leveled against Marat.

I know what side the conspirators are on; yes, the conspirators are on this side; yes, on this side are the traitors and the crimes! (He [Robespierre] points to the left [*sic*] of the presiding officer. Foot-stomping. Acclamations from the galleries. Someone shouts out, "The decree of accusation against Robespierre!") You can crush, you can slaughter, but you will not stifle my voice! There you see the man slaughtered by the dagger [*fer*] of the assassins (said while pointing to the painting of Le Peletier. Foot-stomping in the galleries.)[41]

A counterrevolutionary could use a weapon that clearly looked like a sword, but to a committed Jacobin it was a dagger (*poignard*) or an iron (*fer*), never the sort of sword that administered justice. But was there any real difference between the two sorts of blades? Could even a Jacobin consistently liken a guillotine to a *glaive*? The fact that the single sword in David's painting represented the implement used to kill Le Peletier, the implement that a tyrant used to threaten someone desirous of his place, and the implement used to eliminate counterrevolutionaries indicates two things: the Jacobins consciously paraded their incapacity to recognize the Terror for what it was, and they unconsciously admitted that their fears caused them to question their own publicly professed certainty about the justice of their cause and its means.

On 14 July, the day after Marat's assassination, a spokesman for the section where Marat had lived addressed the Convention as follows:

Our soul begins to free itself from this state of prostration [that the assassination had caused], our eyes still search for Marat. (The speaker scans the Mountain [where Marat had sat]. He sees the picture of Le Peletier facing the bar and says): Oh fearful spectacle! A picture, a bloody body, a legislator stretched out on his death bed! Is it you, Marat? No, it's Le Peletier. David? Where is David? (David answers, "Here I am." The orator continues:) Take up your brush, you must paint another picture . . . (The artist replies, "I will not forget." The orator continues:) And you, representatives of the French people, witnesses of our profound sorrow, you who cannot return Marat to us, give us a law, decree the most horrible punishment: there is none cruel enough to avenge our loss (voices in the galleries: "No! No!"); wipe out federalism and crime forever; teach the madmen what life is worth and, instead of cutting it [their life] like a thread, let the torments that the assassins [*sic*] of Marat shall experience forever stay the parricidal hands that threaten the head of our representatives.[42]

The slender thread of life, or the single hair that holds up a sword, can easily be cut. What is more effective is not to cut the thread but rather to instill a fear of torment that will disarm those who menace the friends of the people. This is what the painting of Le Peletier did, and did even more forcefully when paired with the *Marat*. With the two paintings hanging to the left and the right of whoever was speaking in the Convention, they bracketed, literally and figuratively, whatever was said. (It is not irrelevant to note that left and right are also powerful indexical symbols.)

A final light on David's painting is shed by Jakobson's concept of *evidential status:*

[It] takes into account three events—a narrated event, a speech event and a narrated speech event, namely the alleged source of information about the narrated event. The speaker reports an event on the basis of someone else's report (quotative, i.e., hearsay evidence), of a dream (revelative evidence), of a guess (presumptive evidence), or of his own previous experience (memory evidence).[43]

In David's *Le Peletier* the three events, in particular the narrated speech event, or, to be more precise, the pictorial representation of numerous speech events, are based on just the sorts of evidence Jakobson describes. The narrated events are Le Peletier's assassination and his funeral; the narrated speech events include the voting at the trial of Louis XVI, Le Peletier's supposed last words, the announcement of Le Peletier's death, the speeches and banners at his funeral, and the attacks on the Girondins made while David worked on the painting. (For anyone who viewed the painting after its completion, the narrated speech events would also include what was said in front of the painting after it was hung in the Convention.) The narrated speech events are based on quotations, fearful guesses or predictions of what might happen next, memories (visual or auditory) of what had occurred, and the associations attached to the sword. What makes the painting so effective is that this evidence is presented with a very keen sense of the relations among the narrated events, their participants, and the participants in the "speech event" that was the painting.

On 9 Thermidor (27 July 1794), the men who had wielded the sword of the law were put *hors la loi;* overnight they became "outlaws." Four months later the Jacobin Club was suppressed. On 9 February 1795, the paintings of Le Peletier and Marat were removed from the Convention. The previous day a report had been delivered on recent threats to public order. Who was to blame? According to one speaker, it was "the partisans of the odious and deadly regime of terror." In one of the Paris prisons men were said to have paraded a bust of Marat while cursing what the speaker called "the constitutional authorities and the true republicans, friends of justice and the laws."[44] At a clandestine gathering, the speaker went on, other men, armed with daggers, had supposedly revealed which deputies they meant to strike. After these and other reports of a similar nature, a proposal was read recommending that no citizen be accorded the honors of the Pantheon or have his bust placed in a public place until ten years after his death.

The next day, as the session was about to begin, David's paintings were removed. Some women who regularly frequented the galleries tried to disrupt the operation. Their shouts were drowned out by cries of "Vive la république!" and "Down with the furies of the guillotine!"[45] The swordplay of 1793 and 1794 was at an end even if, and just because, plots were supposedly rife and the appellations, "true republican" and "friend of the laws," were still disputed.

NOTES

I would like to thank the University of California at Santa Cruz for the research grants that enabled me to prepare this chapter. Specifically, I would like to acknowledge the support received from the Academic Senate Committee on Research, the Division of the Arts, and the Junior Faculty Development Award Program.

1. On the drawing, see *Le Néo-classicisme français. Dessins des musées de province* (Paris: Grand Palais, 1974–75), no. 32. On the engraving, see page 177 and note 24 below.
The spelling of the name Le Peletier varies in eighteenth-century texts as well as recent ones ("Le Pelletier," "Lepeletier" and "Lepelletier" are also common). This paper favors the version used by Le Peletier and his brother Félix.

2. *Archives parlementaires de 1787 à 1860*, 1st ser. (1787–1799), 57: 382 (16–17 Jan. 1793, *séance permanente*)—hereafter cited as *Arch. parl.*.

3. To my knowledge, no one except for Régis Michel has noted that the painting was intimately involved with a partisan purpose and a partisan way of thinking; see "Bara: du martyr à l'éphèbe," in the exhibition catalog *La Mort de Bara* (Avignon: Musée Calvet, 1989), 49. And to my knowledge no one has discussed the implications of the sword at any length. Like me, Jörg Traeger has noticed that the sword of Damocles works two ways: the tyrannicide is as much at risk as the murdered tyrant. See *Tod des Marat: Revolution des Menschenbildes* (Munich: Prestel, 1986), 141.
I wish to thank Robert Simon for lending me the text of a paper he gave at the *David contre David* colloquium in December 1989 ("A Contribution towards the History of a Missing Icon: *Le Peletier de Saint-Fargeau*"), forthcoming from the Editions des Musées nationaux. I was unable to consult an essay Simon cites:

Jeannine Baticle, "La seconde mort de Lepeletier de Saint-Fargeau," *Bulletin de la Société de l'Histoire de l'Art français*, 1985.

4. Maximilien Robespierre, "Sur les principes de morale politique qui doivent guider la Convention nationale dans l'administration intérieure de la République," report delivered on behalf of the Committee of Public Safety, *Arch. parl.* 84:333 (17 pluviôse an II [5 Feb. 1794]). All translations in this paper are the author's own with the invaluable assistance of Sylvia Goldfrank. Parentheses have been placed around supplementary material that occurs in the original French; brackets set off the author's own interpolations.

5. Sigmund Freud, *Interpretation of Dreams*, in *The Standard Edition of the Complete Psychological Works of Sigmund Freud*, ed. and trans. James Strachey (London: Hogarth Press and the Institute of Psychoanalysis, 1953), 4:179.

6. *Arch. parl.* 84:333 (18 pluviôse an II [5 Feb. 1794]).

7. A great many nineteenth-century French writers sought to defend or vilify the Revolution through representations of 1793; see Dominique Aubry, *Quatre-vingt-treize et les Jacobins. Regards du 19ᵉ siècle* (Lyons: Presses Universitaires de Lyon, 1988).

8. Gustave Simon, ed., "Reliquat de *Quatrevingt-treize*," *Quatrevingt-treize*, in the *Œuvres complètes de Victor Hugo* (Paris: Imprimerie nationale de la Librairie Ollendorf, 1924), 396 (this edition is hereafter cited as *Quatrevingt-treize*). On Hugo's use of sources, see pp. 454–56 of the "Sources historiques" in Simon's edition of the novel and Paul Berret, "Comment Hugo prépara son roman histo-rique de *Quatrevingt-treize*," *Revue universitaire*, 1914. I have been unable to find Hugo's source for Robespierre's remark in the *Œuvres de Robespierre*, ed. Marc Bouloiseau and Albert Soboul (Paris: Presses universitaires de France, 1967) or in either of two recent annotated editions of Hugo's novel, Jean Boudout's (Paris: Garnier, 1957) and Yves Gohin's (Paris: Gallimard, 1979).

9. Hugo, *Quatrevingt-treize*, 146.

10. Hugo, *Quatrevingt-treize*, 145. The source for this speech was also sought in the above mentioned edition of Robespierre's speeches.

11. *Le Peletier* and *Marat* were paired once David presented the latter to the Convention (24 brumaire an II [14 Nov. 1793]). For information on the layout and decoration of the meeting hall, see Traeger, 46–56 (figs. 26 and 27 of the present book indicate the approximate layout).

12. *Arch. parl.* 79:384 (27 brumaire an 2 [17 Nov. 1793]).

13. On the symbolism of the level, see James A. Leith, "Les étranges métamor-phoses du triangle pendant la Révolution Française," *Les Images de la Révolution Française*, proceedings of a colloquium held at the Sorbonne 25–27 Oct. 1985, ed. Michel Vovelle (Paris: Publications de la Sorbonne, 1988), pp. 251–59—hereafter cited as Vovelle. A different version of this essay has been published in English with many more illustrations in *Symbols in Life and Art/Les Symboles dans la vie et dans l'art*, ed. James A. Leith (Toronto: McGill-Queen's University Press for the Royal Society of Canada, 1987), 105–17.

The Jacobins, who had previously called themselves the "Amis de la Consti-tution, séants aux Jacobins" ("Friends of the Constitution, sitting at the former convent of the Jacobins"), changed their name to the "Société des Jacobins, Amis de la Liberté et de l'Egalité" ("Society of Jacobins, Friends of Liberty and Equality") on 21 September 1792, the day that the Convention met for the first time and the day that was designated (retroactively) day one of *an I*.

14. On the print, see the exhibition catalog *French Caricature and the French Revolution, 1789–99* (Los Angeles: Grunwald Center for the Graphic Arts, UCLA, 1988), no. 149 (hereafter cited as *French Caricature*). The date of "ca. 1793" given in the entry is incorrect; a date in the weeks or months following 9 Thermidor (27 July) 1794 would be more accurate.

15. As early as the monarchic period of the Revolution (1789–92), the Jacobins had used the motto "Vivre libre ou mourir" on their letterhead and publications (F.-A. Aulard, "Introduction," *Recueil de documents pour l'histoire du club des Jacobins de Paris* [Paris, 1889], 1: xxiii)—hereafter cited as Aulard. If the date of ca. 1793 assigned to a print by P. Lélu is correct, the motto was still in conspicuous use at a later date (*French Caricature*, no. 148, "Le Triomphe de la Montagne").

16. On Regnault's painting, see the exhibition catalog *French Painting 1774– 1830: The Age of Revolution* (New York: Metropolitan Museum of Art, 1974–75), no. 150. Although the work is dated *an III* (22 Sept. 1794–22 Sept. 1795), the author of the catalog entry (Jacques Vilain) maintains that it was finished in 1793 (a year that spans *an I* and *an II*), that is, while the Jacobins were either rising to power or in full control. If one accepts the date on the painting, Regnault completed the canvas after the fall of Robespierre (which took place two months before *an III* began); in this case, the artist probably meant to indicate that the French people had wisely chosen Liberty over Death.

In support of Vilain's date is the criticism Regnault received when he exhibited the painting at the Salon in fall 1795 (he was accused of flattering Robespierre and his henchmen). In support of a later date is the fact that the artist offered a larger version of the painting to the post-Thermidorean Convention on 3 February 1795 (*Réimpression de l'ancien Moniteur* 23:381 [18 Pluviôse, an III]). The government of the day would hardly have been thought to be interested in a painting that celebrated the fallen leader of the Jacobins. For the deputy who presented the work, Death was heroic, not horrific, a fate that all defenders of the Republic could bravely contemplate. To complicate matters, however, he made favorable mention of David's paintings of Le Peletier and Marat, works that were to be removed within the week. This range of interpretations points to the ambivalence or multivalence of visual images, particularly in times when opinions change rapidly and symbols are unstable. Further proof of this mutability lies in the fact that Regnault's painting hung in the Council of the Five Hundred during the Consulate (1799–1805).

17. *Arch. parl.* 62:38 (13 April 1793). To be strictly accurate, Robespierre's count does not include Marat, who was still alive; the speech was, however, made in defense of Marat who, as Robespierre emphasized, was regularly the target of counterrevolutionary threats.

18. Various versions of Le Peletier's last words circulated in the hours and days after his death. Félix Le Peletier, the dead man's brother, reported that he exclaimed, "Je meurs pour la liberté!" (Aulard 4:691 [21 Jan. 1793]). (Unlike others who quoted the dying man, Félix was present when Le Peletier died—which is not to say that he did not invent what he supposedly heard.) The version employed in this paper was used on a banner carried at the funeral and in certain commemorative prints (e.g., that by Vérité).

19. The legend in the print by Brion de la Tour reads "l'assassin le poignarde après lui avoir demandé s'il a voté pour la mort de Louis XVI." This same use of *poignard* or *poignarder* to describe a weapon or the use of a weapon that was,

by the speaker's or writer's own admission, much larger crops up in numerous sources. For example, in his biography of his brother, Félix Le Peletier refers to Pâris's saber as his dagger ("Ce poignard était son sabre de la garde du roi") and says that a *poignard* was displayed at the funeral (*Vie de Le Peletier*, written in 1794 and revised for publication in F. Le Peletier's *Œuvres de Michel Le Peletier* [Brussels, 1826], 61, n. 1, and 63 respectively).

20. On the drawing, see Antoine Schnapper, "A propos de David et des martyrs de la Révolution," in Vovelle, 111–12; for several plausible reasons, Schnapper proposes a date between 16 April and 7 May 1794. See also the entry by Arlette Sérullaz in the exhibition catalog *Jacques-Louis David, 1748–1825* (Paris: Musée du Louvre and Versailles: Musée national du château, 1989–90), no. 124.

21. On the print, see *French Caricature*, no 90.

22. *Révolutions de Paris*, no. 185 (19–26 Jan. 1793), 228. The soldier was one of the patriots from Marseilles who had come to Paris to protect the city, and the members of the Convention in particular, from the counterrevolutionary forces.

23. Roman Jakobson, "Shifters, Verbal Categories, and the Russian Verb," (first published 1957) *Selected Writings*, vol. 2 (*Word and Language*) (The Hague: Mouton, 1971), 130–47. For clarity in demonstrating the usefulness of shifter theory for the interpretation of a visual image, I shall adhere very closely to the language that Jakobson uses. Since his article is short and I am using relatively few pages (133–4, 136–43), page references will not be given unless specific passages are quoted at length.

The idea for treating David's painting of Le Peletier as I do was sparked by Roland Barthes' remarks on "second-order language" and shifter theory in *Elements of Semiology* (New York: Hill and Wang, 1968), 11 and 22 respectively. See also Rosalind Krauss, "Notes on the Index: Seventies Art in America," *October: The First Decade, 1976–1986*, ed. Annette Michelson, Rosalind Krauss, Douglas Crimp, and Joan Copjec (Cambridge: MIT Press, 1987), 2–15.

24. For the history of the painting and the print, see Maurice Tourneux, "Notes pour servir à l'histoire d'un chef-d'œuvre inconnu: *Le Peletier sur son lit de mort*, par David," *Nouvelles archives de l'art français*, 3rd ser., 5 (1889): 52–59; see also two articles by Jean Vallery-Radot, "A propos du centenaire de David. Un tableau disparu depuis cent ans: Le *Lepeletier de Saint-Fargeau*," *Revue de l'art ancient et moderne*, 49 (January 1926): 54–60, and "Autour du portrait de Lepeletier de Saint-Fargeau sur son lit de mort, par David (d'après des documents inédits)," *Archives de l'art français*, n.s., 22 (1950–57): 354–63.

25. On "exhibitive import," see Douglas Greenlee, *Peirce's Concept of Sign* (The Hague: Mouton, 1973), 79–83. On the triad icon-index-symbol, see Charles S. Peirce, *Collected Papers*, ed. Charles Hartshone and Paul Weiss (Cambridge: Harvard University Press, 1932), 2:247 ff.

26. Jakobson, "Shifters," 133.

27. Barthes, *Elements of Semiology*, 11.

28. On "spectatorship" in recent discussions of the visual arts, see Michael Ann Holly, "Past Looking," *Critical Inquiry* 16 (Winter 1990): 371–395.

29. *Arch. parl.* 60:695–96 (29 March 1793).

30. The inscription, which was apparently cursive and small in scale, was located in the lower right-hand corner. See the sketch made by E.-J. Délécluze before the painting was sold in 1826 (Robert Baschet, *E.-J. Délécluze, témoin de son temps, 1781–1863* [Paris: Boivin, 1942], 272–73. In his biography of David,

written years after he had last seen the painting, Délécluze reversed the inscription to read "David à Lepelletier" and included the date "20 janvier 1793" (*Louis David, son école et son temps. Souvenirs par E.-J. Délécluze* [Paris: Didier, 1855; Paris: Macula, 1983], 153). Délécluze's credibility is furthered weakened by his recollection of a crown of laurel on Le Peletier's head.

According to P.-A. Coupin, who also probably saw the painting in 1826, it bore a long inscription "au haut du portrait": "L'an 1793—2me de la République/A Michel Lepelletier/assassiné pour avoir voté la mort du tyran/J.-L. David son collègue" (*Essai sur J.-L. David* [Paris: Renouard, 1827], 27). By "au haut du portrait" might Coupin have been referring to a cartouche that formed part of the frame rather than the top of the canvas?

31. On pronouns and shifters, see Emile Benveniste, "La nature des pronoms," *Problèmes de linguistique générale* (Paris: Gallimard, 1966), 1:251–57. Jakobson himself refers to this study in his article on shifters. It is also worth noting that Benveniste's piece originally appeared in a volume entitled *For Roman Jakobson* (The Hague: Mouton, 1956).

32. Roland Barthes, "Writers, Intellectuals, Teachers," *Image, Music, Text*, trans. Stephen Heath (New York: Hill and Wang, 1977), 191.

33. On the *sabre démocratique*, see Gérard Sabatier, "Une imagerie emblématique du soldat citoyen: «Les petits Montmorency à coquilles»," in *Images de la Révolution*, 215.

34. *Arch. parl.* 84: 333 (17 pluviôse an II [5 Feb. 1794]).

35. Aulard, 4:685 (the speaker was Thuriot). The closely spaced periods may simply indicate a break in thought or a missing phrase or sentence that served as a transition in the original speech.

36. Aulard, 4:687.

37. Aulard, 5:89 (13 March 1793).

38. Aulard, 4:690 (the speaker was Monestier).

39. *Réimpression de l'ancien Moniteur* 15:526 (23 Feb. 1793; the presiding officer was Bréard).

40. *Discours* (4th Part: September 1792–27 July 1793), vol. 9 of the *Œuvres de Robespierre*, ed. Marc Bouloiseau (Paris: Presses universitaires de France, 1959), 367.

41. *Discours*, 430 (13 April 1793).

42. *Arch. parl.* 68:710 (14 July 1793; the speaker was Guirault).

43. Jakobson, "Shifters," 135.

44. *Réimpression* 23:415 (the speaker was Mathieu, a member of the Committee of General Security).

45. *Réimpression* 23:421.

Obscene Humor in French Revolutionary Caricature: Jacques-Louis David's *The Army of Jugs* and *The English Government*

JAMES CUNO

French revolutionary caricatures offer a rich and provocative index to the events and polemical issues of the Revolution. And, in their very functioning—in the way they disfigure and exaggerate their subjects—they embody the violent disregard for authority that came to characterize the revolutionary spirit itself.

The purpose of this essay is to examine two caricatures commissioned by the Committee of Public Safety in 1793—Jacques-Louis David's *The Army of Jugs* and *The English Government* (figs. 34 and 35)—in light of the revolutionary spirit's delight in obscene and scatological metaphors as figures of carnal assault upon its enemies. This is what distinguishes David's prints from other official caricatures of the Revolution: they exhibited, indeed *exploited,* what Neil Hertz has described in another context as a frequent turn of mind in revolutionary imagery—the representation of a political threat as an obscene, sexual one.[1]

To understand the role and character of humor in *The Army of Jugs* and *The English Government,* we must first consider the *official* qualities of these prints. For it is within this context—the manner and style of their official presentation—that David intended their humor to work. On 12 September 1793, the Committee of Public Safety asked David to "employ his talents and all the means in his power to augment the number of caricatures which could arouse the public spirit and make it perceive precisely how atrocious and ridiculous are the enemies of liberty and the Republic."[2] By May of the following year, David submitted designs for two prints, *The Army of Jugs* and *The English Government,* and a projected budget for printing each in black and white and in color. The Committee accepted the proposal and on 18 May decreed that he produce the caricatures in editions of one thousand each.[3]

Each print is a large-scale engraving, ruled along the platemarks and accompanied by a detailed explanation printed below. The language of the explanations is straightforward; the action is described and the satirical depictions identified, and the *Army of Jugs* even includes a kind of key, as small numbers are printed next to the figures described in the caption below. Nothing, or very little, is left open for further or especially contradictory interpretations. The prints' rich and irreverent imagery is circumscribed by the specificity of the caption's language. We are meant to see in these prints their official meanings: The English army is weak and led by fools, and like all monarchies, the English government is evil and unnatural. The clarity of their compositions and the refinement of their engraved lines only further emphasize the directness of their meanings. These prints are the products of a deliberate and analytical mind set to a specific task.

The same is true of other caricatures commissioned by the Committee of Public Safety. Dubois's *The Great Royal Knife-Sharpening Establishment for English Daggers,* for example, commissioned on 30 May 1794 in an edition of one thousand copies, five hundred each in black and white and color, depicts the English king George III as a squirrel turning a wheel that drives a grinder's stone.[4] Seated at the stone is the prime minister William Pitt, who is sharpening his knife; the caption makes it pointedly clear that he intends to murder the defenders of the people's liberty with it. Roughly the same size as David's caricatures (320 by 500 millimeters), Dubois's print is a lampoon of surgical precision: George III is made to look like a fat, dumb animal who can be made to run ceaselessly without direction; Pitt, drawn razor-sharp like the daggers he works on, is dressed like a vain and self-possessed fop. The print's point is clearly stated and made in the most economical of terms: it had to be understood instantly and without controversy, for the threat of English assassination plots in 1794 was very real.

A second print by Dubois, *The Republican Punishment,* commissioned by the Committee of Public Safety on 1 August 1794, depicts two victorious French generals administering a "republican punishment" to their military rivals (Cuno, no. 158). To the right, General Jean-Baptiste Jourdan spanks the bare bottom of the Duke of Coburg, whom he defeated at the Battle of Wattignies on 15–16 October 1793. To the left, General Jean-Charles Pichegru does the same to the Duke of York, whose forces were defeated in January 1794. York here appears as a young boy with the ears of an ass. Equal in size and comparable in economy to Dubois's other print, *The Republican Punishment* displays a more subdued humor and thus illustrates the Committee of Public Safety's new ambitions following the defeat of Robespierre on 9 Thermidor. The Committee was now concerned only with the conduct of war and diplomacy; the controversial violence of its domestic policies, which informed the more violent and scatological imagery of David's prints, is nowhere apparent in this caricature. Dubois depicts the French generals as handsome and virile young officers embarrassing their enemies by making them seem like little brats. He does so, however, without really disfiguring the foreign dukes; they are almost as handsome, or at least as clearly depicted, as the generals themselves, and are ridiculed without being caricatured. The point of Dubois' prints is simply put and painfully clear.

As with David's caricatures, Dubois's are finely engraved, ruled along the plate mark, and accompanied by a caption of clear, readable, official-looking script. A fifth caricature, by an unknown artist, is similarly ruled and captioned. Entitled *The Congress of the Allied Kings; or the Uncrowned Tyrants*, it may have been commissioned by the Committee of Public Safety from Charles-Jacques Mailly in December 1793 (Cuno, no. 112). A document in the Archives nationales identifies a commission for a print of this title from a *citoyen* Mailly and stipulates production of nine hundred copies, six hundred in black and white and three hundred in color.[5]

Unlike the prints of David and Dubois, however, *The Congress of the Allied Kings* is burdened with complex references and emblematic allusions. It shows the European monarchs of the First Coalition gathered around a table in a manner reminiscent of the Last Supper, consulting a map and planning the invasion of France. Over the map appears a Phrygian cap, symbol of the indivisible French Republic, and from it emanate blinding rays of light. Above the door, the Gallic cock clutches a triangle, the symbol of equality, as bolts of lightning strike the crowns of the European monarchs. Peering from behind a curtain at the far left is King Stanislav II of Poland, who has been excluded from the coalition because his country has been partitioned by Prussia, Russia, and Austria. Next to him his former lover, Catherine II of Russia, attempts to mount the table and attack the Phrygian bonnet, but is stopped by a bolt of lightning. At the foot of her throne, futile plans are symbolized by the ship that has run aground and a mound of straw that has caught fire and gone up in smoke.

At the center of the table, the Holy Roman Emperor Francis II raises the map in a figurative attempt to overthrow the French Republic. His double-headed eagle is struck by lightning and falls, clutching the emperor's crown and inadvertently revealing the double-headed snake of his malicious leadership. At the far right end of the table, George III of England throws down the gold of corruption at the urging of William Pitt, who tries to steal the city of Toulon, the scene of Napoleon's victory in 1793 over the English, Spanish, and French royalists. Finally, Pope Pius VI sits condemning the godless revolutionaries while the dove of the Holy Spirit lies dead at his feet; and King Ferdinand IV of Naples, referred to in the caption as the Neapolitan Monkey, emerges from under the table to join the Coalition.

By contrast to the far simpler prints by Dubois, this caricature is burdened with complex references and emblematic allusions. The all-powerful triangle recalls the Christian Trinity or the Masonic triangle of past, present, and future embodied in the deity—only to become by the following year the symbol of the Supreme Being. All of this suggests that the revolutionary violence to which these figures are subject is a vehicle for the dispensation of divine justice.

Whether the average republican would have understood the point of this print is doubtful, even with its detailed caption. Pedestrian and not at all compelling, its design is fussy, awkward, and surprisingly static for such a dramatic scene. A more popular alternative must have been the anonymous *Bombardment of all the Thrones of Europe/and the Fall of the Tyrants for the Happiness of the Universe*, of ca. 1792 (fig. 36). It shows Liberty atop three tiers of bare-bottomed deputies of the National Assembly, igniting a cannon that fires into the ass of Louis XVI and forces him to vomit vetoes that rain down upon the crowned heads of Europe, the pope, and William Pitt. Liberty's cannon bears the inscription "violent emetic" and is transported on wheels bearing the words "Free Arbitrator of the French People." From the bare bottoms, "liberty" streams forth as urine—perhaps a tongue-in-cheek reference to Liberty's authority, which originates "from below" unlike that of monarchical rule, which is imposed from "on high"—while a gigantic Prussian eagle departs with a crown that might have shielded the monarchs from the stain of "liberty" but, as the bird confesses, "for these dogs of *sans-culottes.*" Only one monarch rises above the assault. She is the monstrously bare-breasted Catherine II of Russia, who shouts at her fleeing fellow monarchs, "Return you cowards and I will make you all bite the dust . . . how I regret my poor rubles," a reference to her lone support of the French *émigre* army in its efforts to invade France.

In both the official caricatures and the more popular anonymous one just described, the European monarchs are rendered impotent and silly, making weak and futile attempts at military strategy and looking confusedly in all directions to escape the streams of urine falling down upon them. Clearly, however, the anonymous print is more compelling than the official ones. Even if one cannot read the remarks of the figures left and right, one can understand the meaning of this image and join in its obscene assault on the European monarchs and on the poor, powerless Louis XVI.

The five official caricatures I have described—from David's to the anonymous *The Congress of the Allied King*—represent just under one third of the prints commissioned by the Committee of Public Safety between 15 October 1793 and 5 October 1794. In all, as Claudette Hould has noted, eighteen prints were commissioned, including fourteen caricatures, ranging in price from twenty-five sous to one and a half livres; of the five I have described, all but Dubois' *The Republican Punishment* were sold for one and a half livres. Of the fourteen caricatures, the greater majority were directed against England, with the others directed against the Coalition.

This, then, is the context within which to consider the caricatures of David: they were commissioned by the Committee of Public Safety as part of its campaign to secure public safety and influence public opinion; their manner and style of presentation was consistent with other commissioned caricatures; and they were expensive, selling for one and a half livres at a time when a laborer could eat a hearty meal in a tavern for six to ten sous. Indeed, like the other official caricatures, they were intended both for exhibition in official and public spaces throughout the Republic and for sale to print collectors, who almost certainly comprised the market for which the *Journal General des Gravures de Paris* was published at a subscription price of fifty-one livres per annum, and who followed the advertisements for *tableau historiques* in the *Moniteur*, prints depicting the most important events of the Revolution and selling for between one and six livres in editions of one to two thousand.[6]

The peculiar and most interesting aspect of David's caricatures is that they were at once prints of the highest quality—*des gravures savantes*— and prints that exploited a sense of humor of the most popular kind, the humor of *des gravures populaire* or *des caricatures*. In other words, in *The Army of Jugs* and *The English Government* David mixed the style and format of official prints with the popular humor of more spontaneous satiric responses to the Revolution. Their manner of presentation was no doubt intended to enhance the obscene and scatological charge of their humor, just as their clarity of execution was meant to drive home a simple point: the English government is foolish, weak, unnatural, and evil, an enemy against which all Frenchmen can and should defend the Republic at this moment, 1793–94, when tensions are at their highest and when domestic and foreign threats are at their most grave. We may now look more closely at David's obscene humor and the traditions on which it drew.

Albert Boime has pointed to the numerous verbal and visual puns at work in *The Army of Jugs* (*L'Armée des cruches*).[7] George III is depicted as a potbellied pot or crackpot, leading the British troops (also depicted as jugs or *cruches*) and being led in turn by a turkey—"Milor Dindon," My Lord Turkey—identified in the caption as William Pitt. The French word *cruche* can mean not only "pitcher," "jug," or "crackpot," but also "blockhead" or "dolt," just as to behave like a crackpot is to utter *crucheries*, or utter nonsense. Similarly, the French word for "turkey," *dindon*, recalls the verb *dindonner*, literally "to dupe," and is associated with several popular expressions that suggest a pompous, conceited fool; it also suggests the word *dandin*, which can be used to mean a "blockhead." Further, at the rear of the English army is "My Lord Goose," Charles James Fox, a chief parliamentary opponent to George III's Tory party. His position at the opposite end of the troops represents his position on the opposing bench from which, through a trumpet in the ass of his English mount, he (to quote the caption) "sounds the call to retreat from the rear out of prudence." As the French word for "Goose," *oie*, also means a "simpleton" or "ninny," David depicts the inane Goose-Fox breaking wind as a warning to Pitt and George III, who proceed unperturbed toward their inevitable defeat as one blockhead being duped by another.

The English defeat is secured by bare-bottomed *sans-culottes*, who crouch atop the gate through which the troops must pass. They have dropped their trousers and are defecating on the English advance guard, which has been reduced now to chamber pots, the targets of the French *sans-culottes'* "colic," as the caption describes it, punning on the term which in both French and English refers to abdominal and intestinal disorders and their accompanying temperament. To this end, the English army counterattacks with a row of well-aimed artillery in the rear center of the print. The attack weapons are described in the caption as "the new English artillery which has the virtue of being able to extinguish fires and delay fortifications," and they appear to be powerful siege cannons. Yet they are giant syringes or clysters typically used to administer enemas for the purpose of extinguishing "intestinal" fires and breaking up "fecal" fortifications. Typically, David exploited a verbal pun, since the "pump" of the clyster was in French a *canon* and the word *siege* or "siege" literally meant "seat," or ass, the target of the clyster cannon. Thus the enema siege cannons are poised to backfire, as it were, and to encourage rather than diminish the excremental assault that is tumbling and cracking the pots of the English advance guard.[8]

David was not the first to make verbal and visual puns in caricature or to exploit his public's delight in scatological humor. Both are central to the way caricature works. Freud wrote of this in his study of *Jokes and Their Relation to the Unconscious* when he noted that "where a joke is not an aim in itself—that is, when it is not innocent—there are only two

purposes that it may serve . . . it is either a hostile joke (serving the purpose of aggressiveness, satire, or defence) or an obscene joke (serving the
purpose of exposure)."[9] In hostile as well as in obscene jokes—and political caricature, as evidenced by David's *The Army of Jugs,* is often both
hostile and obscene—humor makes possible the satisfaction of a desire
in the face of a barrier imposed by an outside authority. It allows the ex-
ploitation of "something ridiculous in our enemy which we could not, on
account of obstacles in the way, bring forward openly or consciously . . .
the joke will evade restrictions and open sources of pleasure that have
become inacessible" (Freud, 98).

This would suggest, on the one hand, that humor in caricature works
to circumvent restrictions on publication or distribution, such as official
censorship. But the question of such censorship during the French Revolution was complicated. On 12 July 1789, Mailly, the mayor of Paris, signed
an order establishing a censor—a M. Robin, member of the Academy
of Painting and Sculpture—to judge if a print or printed pamphlet was
in opposition to the good order and tranquility of citizens.[10] Throughout
the early years of the Revolution, this new censorial power was executed
against prints or pamphlets that were judged obscene and dangerous to the
purity of public morals. Acts by the Committee of Public Safety on 8 June
1793 and 13 January 1794 reaffirmed the position of the censor just as the
revolutionary Commune des Arts was constituted in July 1793 to encourage the representation of republican virtues in the visual arts. Thus, at the
same time as it was approving David's *The Army of Jugs,* the Committee
of Public Safety was condemning other images as obscene for failing to
represent sufficiently the virtues of the new republican morality.

In other words, the Committee of Public Safety seems to have had two
standards: one for high art, as it were, and another for the indecorous art
of caricature or satirical propaganda. The latter could be obscene precisely
because it was popular. The authority its humor sought to circumvent was
not official censorship but the threat of foreign invasion. If the French did
not have the military might to defeat the English, it had the vicious and
popular wit to imagine that defeat as one of public humiliation—of obscene, scatological assault upon the pride of England, its king and army.
In this way, humor opens what Freud calls "sources of pleasure that have
become inaccessible."

In describing the mechanisms of obscene humor, Freud wrote that "[i]t
compels the person who is assailed to imagine the part of the body or the
procedure in question and shows her [or him] that the assailant is himself [or herself] imagining it" (Freud, 96–97). Thus, in *The Army of Jugs,*
David meant for his public to participate in the imaginative assault upon
the English army by acknowledging the fear King George was meant to

feel as he saw himself exposed and vulnerable: exposed not only to ridicule but to an imagined and desired physical assault upon his person and office. More to the point, with regard to tendentious jokes such as this one, Freud claimed that humor permits the joke-teller and his public to experience together the belittling of their enemy as if they were actually, physically carrying out the implied assault: the joke is at once a mechanism for building community between the teller and his public and a means of assaulting its subject. Thus, at a time when the young Republic was trying desperately to defend itself against attack from without as well as from within, the citizens of France were invited by David and his *Army of Jugs* to participate in the excremental assault on George III and his army and to experience the pleasure of that assault as if they were actually making it.

This is, of course, to overstate the case, to make conscious and deliberate something that is experienced unconsciously and instantly, in the laughter that rises from seeing the *sans-culottes* defecating on the English army and George III as a crackpot being led toward the *sans-culottes* by a turkey. But I overstate the case to make a point: David used scatological humor in official caricature because it draws us into its very working, into the disfiguring and humiliation of its subject. David knew this from the countless other obscene and scatological caricatures that had appeared in Paris over the previous four years. And he knew from the other official caricatures that a more sophisticated or prosaic image would not be as effective as a humorous one. For an artist who otherwise showed little capacity for humor in his work, David was fully aware of the value of humor in *Army of Jugs,* and even more so about its place in his second print, *The English Government.*

The English Government depicts its subject as a "flayed devil" whose monstrous Medusa-like head is enveloped in snakes and whose bare buttocks assume the likeness of George III. Through his mouth (the devil's anus), the king spews taxes on English citizens. The caption below explains that the English government is "personified by the figure of the Devil skinned alive . . . The portrait of the king is located at the rear-end of the government which vomits on its people a myriad of taxes which overwhelm them." The imposition of taxes as an excremental assault upon the people is an ironic twist on two anticlerical caricatures of 1789. One (fig. 37) shows a bishop of the *ancien régime* vomiting up the benefices and canonries he had consumed before the Revolution; in the other (fig. 38), an enema administered by an apothecary of the Third Estate relieves a priest of his privileges. While both of these prints show privileges expelled through the mouth or the anus, *The English Government* shows privileges derived from impositions defecated on the people.

In representing George III as a cruel joke plundering the resources of

his citizens, David was alluding to a caricature by William Hogarth of
some thirty years earlier, entitled *The Political Clyster*.[11] It shows the Lil-
liputian ministers of the English government running a clyster up the anus
of John Bull; alluding to sodomy as well as to the eighteenth-century tradition of *galanterie* that shows young men leering lasciviously as young
ladies are given enemas by their maids, it suggests that the English people
are being buggered by their government. Originally, Hogarth's print was
meant to illustrate Jonathan Swift's *Gullivers Travels*.[12] In Part IV, the bestial Yahoos are fascinated with their own excrement, which carries magical
and ritualistic powers, and at one point they discharge their excrement
from high in a tree onto Gulliver's head. Turning the story around, David
gives George III the excremental power to manipulate the fortunes of his
Yahoo subjects, who turn and flee from the fiery feces being discharged
upon them. *The English Government* is indeed a remarkable image, rendered all the more powerful by the pigments of its colored version, in which
the devil who represents the English government is painted a hideously
bright red.

To associate power and privilege with excrement is also to associate
them with gluttony. Two caricatures of 1790 and 1791 depict Louis XVI
as the gluttonous Gargantua. In the first (fig. 39), *The Gargantua of the
Century, or the Oracle of the Divine Bottle*, a corpulent Louis XVI sits
astride a tiny horse, having come to hear the "Oracle of the Divine Bottle"
foretell his future. The King, soft, flabby, and red-faced, is in the company
of bizarre creatures dressed in clerical garb, who, as the caption tells us,
are "very dirty, stinky, conceited, and voracious" (one holds a document
bearing the words, "Live for Yourself"). As the King approaches the oracle,
he is stunned by the words on the tablets that hang on the trees before
him: "The yoke of the oppression of France will be opened," says one; and
"A people, fully free to win its Liberty," says the other. According to the
caption below, the King persists and asks to know the secrets of the bottle.
After a frightful boom, the bottle pops its cork and pronouces "Trinck," an
onomatopoeic pun on *trinque*, meaning "drink" or, in the familiar sense,
"to get the worst of it"; clearly not what the monarch had hoped to hear.

In the second caricature, titled *The Ci-devant Great Family Feast of the
Modern Gargantua*, 1791 (fig. 40), Louis XVI is portrayed at table about
to eat an entire pig as his many subjects struggle to satisfy his appetite for
the kingdom's plentiful produce and game. He turns to the Marquis de
Bouillé and asks if there is not enough to fill his great gullet for a year.
Marie-Antoinette interrupts, however, pushing the King away, thrusting
her glass to the neck of the young soldier, and asking if the blood spilling
from his neck and filling her glass will not also serve as her bath. (Bouillé

is identified in the caption as the "Butcher of Nancy" for his role in the violent repression of the mutiny that occurred in that city in 1790; thus his attack on the neck of the young soldier.) The implication here is that the blood the royal family has sucked from its subjects in the forms of goods and currency will lead to its own violent downfall and bloodbath, the effect of a gluttonous appetite gone mad.

Ironically, then, this print shows that when power becomes gluttonous, it becomes powerless, unable to act or discharge the duties of office and the apparatus of power. The more one takes in, as it were, the less one can give out. One becomes bloated and immobile, the subject and not the agent of assault. In *The Ci-devant Great Family Feast of the Modern Gargantua*, this is further emphasized by the intervention of Marie-Antoinette. The foreign-born queen was often portrayed in revolutionary caricatures as manipulating and cuckholding. In *He hu! Da da!* of 1791, for example, the King is portrayed as a child riding a toy stag with the horns of a cuckold and being pushed along by the shrewish queen (Cuno, no. 77). They approach Montmédy, represented as a kind of childish rebus of a mountain (*mont*) with a clock labeled only with noon (*midi*). As the king spies his illusory goal and rides innocently to his humiliation and eventual demise, he is reduced to making the infantile sounds, "*He hu! Da da!*," which roughly translate to "Gee gee! Haw haw!," a verbal play on the infantilization of the king by Marie-Antoinette.

In a second caricature, also of 1791, entitled *I'll make better use of it, and I'll know how to keep it*, the king is again portrayed as a child—this time being pushed along in his walker by the queen (Cuno, no. 76). He has dropped his royal scepter and has picked up the dauphin's paper windmill or whirligig, which he seems to prefer.[13] Meanwhile, the dauphin has secured the fallen scepter and, in a frankly oedipal gesture, holds it erect and asserts arrogantly, "I'll make better use of it, and I'll know how to keep it." It is an image with a sharp barb, indeed. Not only has the king been humiliated by the continued cuckolding he has endured from his manipulating queen and his ignoble arrest following the flight to Varennes, but he is now being ridiculed and dismissed by his own son and made to seem a child. Stripped of his manliness and no longer interested in the phallic symbol of his power, he slips further into infancy, it would seem, into the anal phase of his development, when his excrement assumed symbolic importance and was associated with power, pleasure, and property, discharged then as it is now ingested in his "Gargantua" phase.[14]

The infantilization of the king by the queen was a popular subject of revolutionary caricatures. It allowed caricaturists access to Marie-Antoinette, whom they subjected to ridicule of the most obscene kind.[15] In an anonymous print of 1789, for example, which was widely accepted as portraying the queen, Marie-Antoinette is represented as a kind of Arcimboldesque composite of male and female genitals: her face is made of dismembered phallusses, one of which—the nose—appears to penetrate a pair of bare buttocks that forms the queen's forehead, with a leg falling down to touch the queen's cleavage (Cuno, p.18, fig. 6). It is a grotesque portrait, one that deforms the queen's physiognomy into a melange of body parts for the purpose of "revealing" her true, evil, licentious nature. Her face is not only an ass, like George III's in David's *The English Government*: it is an ass and phalluses at play.[16]

Such humor links David's caricatures to the same world of popular discourse as Jacques-René Hébert's populist Jacobin journal, *Le Père Duchesne*.[17] The sobriquet "Père Duchesne" was associated with a common figure of the popular imagination who, like Hébert himself, was celebrated for his coarse, candid, and jocular character; a figure not unlike the *sans-culotte* in the anonymous caricature of 1790 (Cuno, no. 46), who applauds while a soldier of the Gardes Françaises, formerly a royal regiment, squats on the rue de la Liberté and defecates on the nobility and clergy as they are swept by in the gutter along with the other sewage. His coarse features, muscular stature, and salacious glee made this figure readily identifiable in revolutionary caricatures, where he came to represent a typical *sans-culotte*.

Hébert used his colorful language to appeal, as he said, to the *sans-culottes* and to knock down the pretended superiority of the elite, especially if the elite were the less radical revolutionaries opposed to Hébert and the Jacobins. In fact, he often used many of the same figurative devices as David—such as *sans-culottes* urinating on soldiers, kings being led by the nose, and George III as a stupid *dindon*—once calling Pitt "the Seeing Eye Dog for the blind King Georges Dandin." But above all it is *Père Duchesne*'s obscene imagery that links Hébert's world to that of David's caricatures. At one point Hébert sarcastically pleads with the court physicians to clyster Louis XVI, purge him, and heal him quickly. Later he admonishes the lawmakers of the National Assembly to "purge France of all the excrements of despotism and aristocracy." Meanwhile, the "chronic indigestion" of the enemies of the people have made the Constituent Assembly "belch up and throw up these stinking excrements of the Club of '89 and the *Feuillants*," who "have been discharged through the anus of nobility."[18] Ironically, it was perhaps the clarity of Hébert's language that led to his execution by the Jacobins themselves just two months before David submitted his designs to the Committee of Public Safety. For the revolutionary government was anything but stable; civil wars were being fought, mass conscription was being violently opposed, and food prices were rising to unprecedented levels. It was not the time for Hebert's unbridled criticism of the government from the far left. While his obscenity aroused passions against the unstable revolutionary government, David sought to excite rage against the government's foreign enemies and, it could be argued, to distract the people from the grave domestic crises of 1794.

Of course, David could have taken his colorful, obscene, and scato-logical language from the tradition of French caricature as well as from the example of *Père Duchesne*. For such images as those described above were part of a fertile tradition of scatological caricature in France long before the Committee of Public Safety made its commissions. Indeed, in a lexilogical study of more than six hundred caricatures published between 1789 and the death of the king in 1793, Antoine de Baecque has found that 60 percent emphasized the mouth eating, devouring, and vomiting, while 30 percent emphasized the body's lower half—the ass, belly, feces, and genitals.[19] In other words, a full nine out of every ten revolutionary cari-catures published between 1789 and 1793 exploit the public's delight in the exhibition of the "corporeal circuit," as de Baecque calls it, the complex similarities between the oral and anal orifices, the taking in and throwing out of food matter that each enjoys. It is a delight that lies at the very heart of caricature, which in French is a *portrait-chargé,* or a loaded portrait that charges or overloads a singular trait or feature of its subject in order to reveal his or her hidden character—the true person behind the mask of respectability. In numerous cases, the face is made to resemble an ass, or vice versa. For instance, in a Swiss caricature of 1773 by Jean-Jacques Foulquier entitled "All seeing me, laughed at me," odd and exaggerated faces loom large as an animalized figure approaches a peasant seated on a wall. The faces grimace and grin in a visual cacophony of ridicule, re-ducing the peasant to an easy target for the wild boar approaching him. A close look at the print's center, however, reveals one face to be a broad, bespeckled ass whose anus or mouth spews the fecal matter of hideous assault.[20]

This play of ass-as-face occurred simultaneously in French and English as well as in Swiss caricature and lay at the origins of political caricature in Germany during the Reformation. There, in the so-called Pope-Ass de-signed by Wenzel von Olmutz for a pamphlet with texts by Luther and Melancthon published in 1523, a pope is depicted as a monster with a don-key's head, a woman's naked torso, a scaled body, one human hand and one hoof-hand, one griffin's foot and a hoof, and an ass with a face from whose anus/mouth emerges the head of a griffin or dragon. The compound image was meant to unmask the pope by revealing his true nature to be that of an ass, harlot, or dragon.[21]

The play of ass and face occurred well into the nineteenth century and appears not only in the caricatures of Daumier but also in those of the Mexican artist, José Guadalupe Posada. In a particularly moving woodcut, Posada depicts a young boy bending over and revealing his ass to be a large, grimacing face. Writing about this image and of the recurrence of its central motif throughout history, Octavio Paz noted: "When we say that the ass is like another face, we deny the soul-body dualism; we laugh because we have resolved the discord that we are. But the victory of the pleasure principle does not last long: at the same time that our laughter celebrates the reconciliation of the soul and the body, it dissolves it and makes it laughable. Once again . . . when we laugh at our ass—the caricature of our face—we affirm our separation and bring about the total defeat of the pleasure principle. Our face laughs at our ass and thus retraces the dividing line between the body and the spirit."[22]

Thus Paz interprets the ass-face motif as pointing up the vulnerability of human identity, the narrow line between repressed and explosive behavior, human and bestial nature, and our continuing need to reestablish the delicate line between the soul and the body. In the hands of a caricaturist like David, the ass-face motif is a powerful weapon used to undermine the authority of the English government and the English king George III.

We have considered such obscene metaphors as figures of carnal assault. In a recent study of the role of obscene language in Attic comedy, Jeffrey Henderson has defined obscenity as "reference to areas of human activity or parts of the human body that are protected by certain taboos agreed upon by prevailing social custom and subject to emotional aversion or inhibition."[23] The use of obscenity is thus tantamount to exposing what should be hidden. It is by nature extroverted and its target is social taboos; pornography, on the other hand, is introverted, and its target is autoeroticism and private imaginings. The pleasure afforded by the latter lies in our escape into private fantasy, while that of obscenity lies "in our enjoyment at exposing someone else or seeing someone else exposed without having to effect the exposure physically" (Henderson, p.7).

This is what I meant above when I stated that in *The Army of Jugs* David invited his public to experience the pleasure of excremental assault on George III as if they were actually making it. The same is true of *The English Government*, which encouraged David's public to enjoy the pleasure of disfiguring and humiliating the king by transforming his face into the fiery ass of a devil. It is the mark of David's talent that he understood the value of obscene humor and that he introduced it into the rather sober and prosaic genre of official caricature. For obscenity had long been the province of more popular and spontaneous forms of satire. Official caricatures, such as those I have described above, tended to employ more didactic or tendentious devices, such as the squirrel's wheel or knife-sharpening stone, or multiple and specific references to contemporary politics or the appropriation of religious symbols. Even the anonymous anti-*émigré* caricature of 1791, *The Great Army of the Ci-devant Prince de Condé* (fig. 41), which is as competent in its design and execution as David's prints, was hesitant by comparison in its use of obscene humor.

The Great Army shows the Prince de Condé in his chateau at Worms reviewing the troops—in the form of toy soldiers—recently sent him by his supporters in Strasbourg. It is a lampoon of the *émigré* army threatening to invade France and restore the monarchy. Here the army is reduced to toy soldiers for the prince's daughter and grandson, who delight in setting them in their ranks, only to find them knocked down by a stream of urine let loose by the unruly dog to the right. The dog, it should be noted, wears a collar that identifies him as belonging to Père Duchesne, a sign of the close and mutually supportive relationship between revolutionary caricature and the language and images of Hébert's journal, *Père Duchesne*. In the anonymous caricature of 1790 cited above (p.000), a coarse and hook-nosed *sans-culotte* is accompanied by a barking dog like the one of *The Great Army*, leading one to see in the *sans-culotte* a reference to Hébert's *Père Duchesne* himself. In any case, he has the same rough features and crude sense of humor as the fictional character of Hébert's journal, as he laughs vigorously and applauds a soldier defecating on the members of nobility and clergy. The obscene joke of the print is upfront and central and cannot be missed.

So is that of the anonymous anticlerical caricature of 1790 entitled *The Two Infuriated Devils* (fig. 42). It depicts two of the most outspoken opponents of the National Assembly's refusal to recognize Catholicism as the state religion, the Abbé Maury and Jean-Jacques d'Eprémesnil, a former deputy of the nobility to the Estates General. Here they are shown being shat into existence by winged devils, the Abbé Maury feet-first and d'Eprémesnil head-first, as the verses below describe the humiliating scene:

> On 13 April 1790 two flying devils
> Made a bet
> Who would shit most foul
> On Human nature
> One shat the Abbé M. . .y
> The other paled
> And dropped D'E. . .y
> And his entire clique.

Its joke is an assault on refined taste and the conventions of decorum.[24]

How different these images are from *The Great Army of the Ci-devant Prince de Condé*, which marginalizes its obscenity and forces it to compete for our attention with the numerous other references in the print. More like the anonymous images, David places his jokes in the center of his prints, both literally (within their compositions) and figuratively (in terms of their meaning). *The Army of Jugs* lampoons George III by depicting him front and center as a crackpot being led by a blockhead to the excremental assault by French *sans-culottes*, and *The English Government* presents George III as the ass of a giant flayed devil from which the call for more taxes is like a blast of excrement.

Centrally placed, these jokes are like a pun, which, as Freud noted, provides pleasure precisely because of its economy (Freud, 120). In its concentrated, graphic shorthand, the visual pun works as a kind of psychological short-circuit to allow its public to make connections that are usually more difficult to establish. That is what distinguishes David's caricatures from the others commissioned by the Committee of Public Safety: their obscene humor works as a kind of explosive device in the center of their imagery, detonating an abusive response that is pleasurable in its overcoming of inhibitions at the expense of another's self-image. In this respect, David drew upon the example of popular caricatures and gave official sanction to the use of obscenity in defense of the Republic. At a time when it did not have the military might to overcome its enemies, the radical government of the Terror employed caricature in its defense.

Elsewhere I have considered whether or not David succeeds in synthesizing the popular and obscene anticlerical caricatures of the early years of the Revolution with the sophisticated and far more refined anti-*émigré* caricatures of 1792. I concluded that he did not, that his attempted syntheses were actually compromises.[25] But among the official caricaturists, David alone understood the value of popular and obscene humor and introduced such humor into his prints. That he did not fully succeed at this is less a criticism of him or his art than it is of the Committee of Public Safety and its official ambitions for the caricatures it commissioned.

Ironically, the radical Committee seems to have misunderstood its public. Indeed, in 1793, Detournelle complained about the prints after designs by David—the heads of Marat and Le Peletier—which were selling for six livres each. They were too expensive for the laborer and the field worker, who, he complained, were left to decorate their rooms with cheaper prints of inferior quality. He then called for the end of such extravagances and for replacing them with engravings designed by the people for distribution to the Departments, the popular societies, and to families.[26] At the same time, Jacques Roux was denouncing the government for allowing runaway inflation. It was, he declared, "the shame of the eighteenth century . . . that the representatives of the people had declared war on external tyrants but had been too cowardly to crush those within France [the rich]. Under the old regime it would never have been permitted for basic commodities to be sold at three times their value."[27]

Little wonder that the Committee of Public Safety chose not to commission caricatures aimed at the considerable domestic crises it was facing and chose instead to concentrate on the threat of foreign invasion: it meant to distract its public from their dissatisfaction with the government. The Committee must also have felt, however, that prints close in spirit and image to the obscene popular caricatures of the day were just too hot to handle. Thus it turned to the greatest and most sophisticated artists of the day and commissioned from them the caricatures I have described above. Under these conditions, David's famous contrary nature allowed at least a bit of popular humor into the official caricatures of the Revolution. It is a measure of David's talent that he alone among the official caricaturists of the Revolution engaged his public's taste for the wicked delights of gross humiliation and obscene humor.

NOTES

This essay has had a long history and along the way I have benefited from the advice and criticisms of many friends and colleagues, particularly Laure Beaumont-Maillet, Cynthia Burlingham, T. J. Clark, James Heffernan, Klaus Herding, Lynne Hockman, Regis Michel, Ronald Paulson, Margaret Sullivan, and Ann Wagner.

1. Neil Hertz, "Medusa's head: Male Hysteria Under Political Pressure," *Representations* 4 (1983): 25–55.

2. André Blum, *La Caricature révolutionnaire* (Paris: Jouve, 1916), 195. Translation by Albert Boime.

3. Archives nationales, AF II, 66 dossier 489, fol. 17, 29 floréal an II. Also see Claudette Hould, "La Propagande d'état par l'estampe durant la terreur," in Michel Vovelle, ed., *Les Images de la révolution française* (Paris: Publications de la Sorbonne, 1988), 29–37.

4. Reproduced in James Cuno, ed., *French Caricature and the French Revolution, 1789–1799*, exhibition catalog (Los Angeles: Grunwald Center for the Graphic Arts, UCLA, 1988), cat. no. 113. Hereafter cited as Cuno.

5. Archives nationales, AF II, 66 dossier 489, fol. 3, 2 nivose an II.

6. See Claudette Hould, *L'Image de la révolution française*, exh. cat. (Montreal: Musée du Quebec, 1989), 80–90. Also see Claudette Hould, "L'Image des images de la Révolution française dans les annonces de journaux," *Nouvelles de l'estampe* 106 (July–August, 1989): 14–24.

7. Albert Boime, "Jacques-Louis David, Scatological Discourse in the French Revolution, and the Art of Caricature," in Cuno, 67–82.

8. For a similar use of the clyster in French caricature of the July Monarchy, see my "Charles Philipon and La Maison Aubert: The Business, Politics, and Public of Caricature in Paris, 1820–1840," Ph.D. dissertation, Harvard University, 1985. Revelvant material on this subject can also be found in my "Charles Philipon and 'la poire': Politics and Pornography in Emblematic Satire, 1830–1835," in *Proceedings of the Consortium on Revolutionary Europe* (Athens, Ga., 1984), 147–56.

9. Sigmund Freud, *Jokes and Their Relation to the Unconscious*, trans. James Strachey (New York: W. W. Norton, 1960), 96–7.

10. Claudette Hould, *L'Image de la révolution française*, 73–5. Daniel Roche notes that Article II of the declaration of the Rights of Man circumscribed the freedom of speech thus: "Free communication of thought and opinion is one of man's most precious rights: therefore, every citizen may speak, write, and print freely . . . except that he must answer for the abuse of that freedom in such circumstances as the law may provide." See his "Censorship and the Publishing Industry," in Robert Darnton and Daniel Roche, eds., *Revolution in Print: The Press in France, 1775–1800* (Berkeley and Los Angeles: University of California Press, 1989), 3–26.

11. Ronald Paulson, *Hogarth's Graphic Works*, 2 vols. (New Haven, Conn.: Yale University Press, 1965), 1:132–3.

12. It was printed in 1726 and originally entitled *The Punishment Inflicted on Lemuel Gulliver*. On scatological humor in Swift's writings, see Jae Num Lee, *Swift and Scatological Satire* (Albuquerque: University of New Mexico Press, 1971).

13. Since the seventeenth century, the whirligig was a common symbol of foolishness and useless activity. See Ella Snoep-Reitsma, "Chardin and the Bourgeois Ideals of His Time," *Nederlands Kunsthistorisch Jaarboek* 24 (1973): 211–2, cited in Vivian P. Cameron, "The Challenge to Rule: Confrontations with Louis XVI," *Art Journal* 48 (1989): 150–4.

14. *Père Duchesne* often lampooned the king by exploiting the double entendre, *impuissance,* which can mean both powerlessness and impotence. Hébert used the word often to represent the breakdown in political control as the physical deterioration of the king himself. Often portrayed in *Père Duchesne* as drunken and lazy and a cuckold pig, "fat Louis," sneered Père Duchesne, "is too flaccid to be a monk." See Elizabeth Colwill, "Just Another *Citoyenne?* Marie-Antoinette on Trial, 1790–1793," *History Workshop* 28 (1989): 72.

15. For a discussion of why the caricatures subjected the queen to such violent calumny and not the king, see Lynn Hunt, "The Political Psychology of Revolutionary Caricatures," in Cuno, 33–40. See, also Colwill, 63–87, and Nancy Davenport, "Maenad, Martyr, Mother: Marie-Antoinette Transformed," in *Proceedings of the Consortium on Revolutionary Europe* (Athens, Ga., 1985), 66–84.

16. In almost every case, Arcimboldo's composite portraits are allegorical and panegyric. An exception is his portrait of 1566, *The Jurist*, in the collection of the Statens Konstsamlingar Gripsholm Slott, Sweden. Long thought to be a satirical portrait of Calvin and now considered by some a depiction of the imperial jurist, Johann Ulrich Zasius, the painting may also correspond to one ordered by Maximilian II from Arcimboldo: the painting of a doctor of laws whose face was ravaged by the "French pox." See Thomas DaCosta Kaufmann, *The School of Prague: Painting at the Court of Rudolf II* (Chicago: University of Chicago Press, 1988), cat. no. 2.8. In any case, it is clear that Arcimboldo's intentions in

this painting were satiric, as the berobed figure's face is a grotesque mélange of fish and poultry. Though I once thought that the image of Marie-Antoinette was unprecedented (Cuno, 22, n. 26), I have recently seen a reproduction of a round bowl dated 1536 and decorated with an image of a male head made entirely of phalluses. [Unfortunately nothing is known about this unattributed piece of Faience; see Pontus Hulten, et al., *The Arcimboldo Effect: Transformations of the Face from the 16th to the 20th Century* (New York: Abbeville Press, 1987), 382.] There is also a caricature of Abbé Maury, which depicts the hated Abbé as a Medusa's head composed of phalluses and coupling figures (Cuno, 17–18). Such images were fairly common during the Revolution: two variations on these caricatures are reproduced in Kirk T. Varnedoe and Adam Gopnik, *High and Low: Modern Art and Popular Culture*, exhibition catalog (New York: Museum of Modern Art, 1990), 137. Subsequent to these Revolutionary prints, the German artist Johann Michael Voltz designed a popular caricature of Napoleon with a face composed of naked corpses, the refuse of his military defeats; see Gerhard Langemeyer et al., *Mittel und Motive der Karikatur in fünf Jahrhunderten: Bild als Waffe*, exhibition catalog (Munich: Prestel Verlag, 1984), cat. no. 146. By the middle of the nineteenth century the joke of depicting a human head as a composite of naked figures was a commonplace, surfacing even in *Ukiyo-e* prints such as those by Utagawa Kuniyoshi; see Hulten, 235–9.

17. This point was first made by Albert Boime in "Jacques-Louis David," (Cuno, 76–79). *Père Duchesne* was one of the three or four most influential newspapers of 1790–94, perhaps even more influential than Marat's *L'Ami du peuple*. More than 40,000 copies were sold in France and to the republican armies between July 1793 and March 1794; see Colwill, 64–65. On Hébert's use of language see Jacques Guilhaumou, "Les milles langues du Père Duchesne. La parade de la culture populaire pendant la Révolution," *Dix-huitième siècle* 18 (1986): 143–54.

18. *Père Duchesne*, nos. 42, 153, and 134, respectively; see Boime, "Jacques-Louis David," Cuno, 77–78.

19. Antoine de Baecque, "Image du corps et message politique: la figure du contre-révolutionnaire dans la caricature française," in Vovelle, ed., *Les Images de la révolution française*, 177–83.

20. Reproduced in *Caricature and its Role in Graphic Satire*, exhibition catalog (Providence, R.I.: Rhode Island School of Design Museum, 1971), cat. no. 73.

21. See Cuno, 18–21. Luther and Melancthon explicitly used the period's fascination with monsters as a tool of religious polemic in their pamphlet of 1523. The pamphlet (and its two images, the *Pope-Ass* and *Monk-Calf*) was very influential, being frequently reprinted in the sixteenth and seventeenth centuries and translated into French, Dutch, and English. See Katherine Park and Lorraine J. Daston, "Unnatural Conceptions: The Study of Monsters in Sixteenth-Century France and England," *Past & Present* 92 (1981), 25–30. For a sixteenth-century painted example of the devil with a face for an ass, see Michael Pacher's painting, *St. Wolfgang with the Devil*, 1483 (Bayerische Staatsgemäldesammlungen), reproduced in Enrico Castelli, *Il Demoniaco nell'arte* (Milan: Electa Editrice, 1952) 89. For an extraordinary variation on this theme, see Master L. CZ's engraving, *The Temptation of Christ*, reproduced in Castelli, *Il Demoniaco nell'arte*, 124; it depicts the devil with faces on both his ass and his abdomen, in such a way that the spikey tongue of the latter is clearly a sign for the devil's penis. The depiction of a face on the ass of the devil may derive from the tradition of the "obscene kiss," or

osculum infame, of witchcraft. In this tradition, witches or their followers would kiss the naked posteriors of their leader, each other, or cats in a gesture of dark communion with the devil, "an eating of the god, a total taking into oneself of the devil," as Jeffrey Burton Russell has written of witchcraft in the Middle Ages. But it may also have been an allusion to the Judas kiss and thus to betrayal in general; see Russell, *Witchcraft in the Middle Ages* (Ithaca, N.Y.: Cornell University Press, 1972), 285–6. Both allusions would have been appropriate to the image of George III's face on the ass of a devil, an image which, without direct reference to a specific tradition, conjurs up notions of evil and betrayal.

22. Octavio Paz, "Metaphor," in his *Conjunctions and Distortions*, trans. Helen R. Lane (New York: Seaver Books, 1982), 5.

23. Jeffrey Henderson, *The Maculate Muse: Obscene Language in Attic Comedy* (New Haven, Conn.: Yale University Press, 1975), 2. Also see Amy Richlin, *The Garden of Priapus: Sexuality and Aggression in Roman Humor* (New Haven, Conn.: Yale University Press, 1983), especially 57–80 and 86–96.

24. There is an interesting precedent for this image in the form of an anonymous sixteenth-century woodcut entitled *The Origins of Monks*. It shows three cackling devils defecating monks who fall into a soft and pliant mound in an open field, their robes tossed up and revealing, at least in one case, an equally soft and pliant—indeed, flaccid—phallus [repr. Christine Megan Armstrong, *The Moralizing Prints of Cornelis Anthonisz* (Princeton, N.J.: Princeton University Press, 1989), fig. 101]. In a second Lutheran precedent, a she-devil gives birth to popes through her anus as witches tend and suckle them [repr. Robert Hughes, *Heaven in Hell in Western Art* (New York: Stein and Day, 1968), 230]. This precedent is evidence, too, of the learnedness, as it were, of revolutionary caricatures—something further illustrated in Cuno, 16.

25. James Cuno, "En Temps de guerre: Jacques-Louis David et la caricature officielle," in *David contre David: Acts du colloque David* (Paris: Musée du Louvre, forthcoming).

26. See Claudette Hould, *L'Image de la révolution française*, 80–90.

27. Quoted in Simon Schama, *Citizens* (New York: Alfred A. Knopf, 1989), 754.

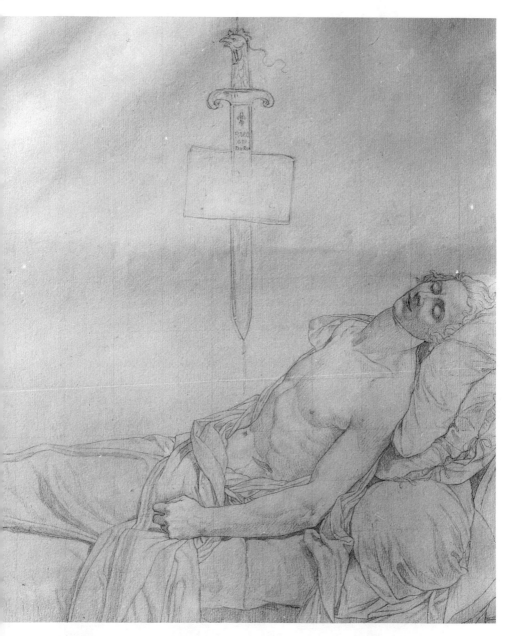

25. Anatole Devosge after J.-L. David, *Le Peletier de Saint-Fargeau on his Deathbed*, 1794. Musée des Beaux-Arts, Dijon.

26. The placement of
David's work in the
Convention. Right:
Declaration of the Rights of
Man. Below: J.-L. David,
The Death of Marat, 1793.

Musées royaux des Beaux-Arts de

Belgique, Brussels.

27. The placement of David's work in the Convention. Above: Tablets inscribed with articles of the Jacobin Constitution and divided by a sword (artist's rendering). Below: P.A. Tardieu after J.-L. David, *Le Peletier de Saint-Fargeau on his Deathbed,* 1794. Cabinet des Estampes, Bibliothéque Nationale, Paris.

28. Villeneuve, *Equality Triumphant; or, the Triumvirate Punished,* 1794. Cabinet des Estampes, Bibliothèque Nationale, Paris.

29. J.-B. Regnault, *Liberty or Death,* 1794–95. Hamburger Kunsthalle, Hamburg (Elke Walford Fotowerkstatt, Hamburg).

30. Brion de la Tour, *Assassination of Le Peletier*, 1793 (?). Cabinet des Estampes, Bibliothèque Nationale, Paris.

31. J.-L. David, *The Triumph of the French People*, 1794. Musée Carnavalet, Paris. © 1991 ARS N.Y./SPADEM.

32. Anonymous French, *Honors rendered to the memory of Le Peletier,* from *Révolutions de Paris,* nº 185 (19–26 January 1793), 226. Cabinet des Estampes, Bibliothèque Nationale, Paris.

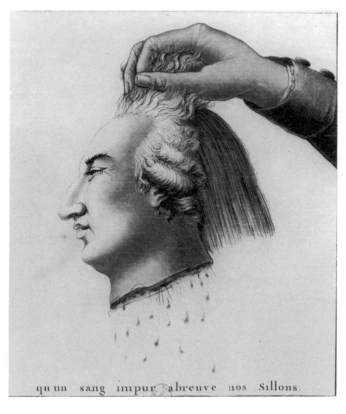

33. Villeneuve, *Matter for Thought for Crowned Jugglers,* 1793. Cabinet des Estampes, Bibliothèque Nationale, Paris.

34. Jacques-Louis David, *The Army of Jugs*, 1793–94. Bibliothèque Nationale, Paris.

35. Jacques-Louis David, *The English Government*, 1793–94. Bibliothèque Nationale, Paris.

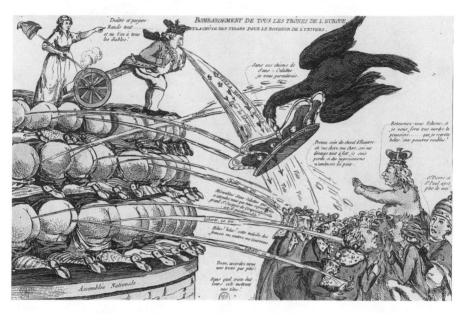

36. Anonymous French, *The Bombardment of All the Thrones of Europe*, ca. 1792. Bibliothèque Nationale, Paris.

37. Anonymous French, *Monsignor after such a long and severe indigestion, the Nation's doctors prescribe a diet*, 1789. Bibliothèque Nationale, Paris.

38. Anonymous French, *Ah! Monsignor! It seems that they want us to give everything back, yet while in the game I had advised you to play trumps*, 1789. Bibliothèque National, Paris.

39. Anonymous French, *The Gargantua of the Century, or The Oracle of the Divine Bottle*, ca. 1790. Bibliothèque Nationale, Paris.

40. Anonymous French, *The Ci-devant Great Family of the Modern Gargantua,* 1790. Bibliothèque Nationale, Paris.

41. Anonymous French, *The Great Army of the Ci-devant Prince de Condé,* ca. 1791. Bibliothèque Nationale, Paris.

42. Anonymous French, *The Two Infuriated Devils*, 1790. Bibliothèque Nationale, Paris.

43. (Opposite page, top) P. Le Sueur, *Club patriotique de femmes.* Musées de la Ville de Paris. © SPADEM 1990.

44. (Opposite page, bottom) Amazon-Cannibals. Illustration from Levin Hulsius, *Die fünfte Schiffahrt. Kurze wunderbare Beschreibung des goldreichen Königreichs Guianae in America oder neuen Welt.* Frankfurt, 1612. Herzog August Bibliothek, Wolfenbüttel.

45 and 46. South American Cannibals. Illustrations from Hans Staden, *Warhaftig Historia vnd beschreibung eyner Landtschafft Wilden/Nack-eten/Grimmigen Menschenfresser Leuthen in der Newenwelt America gelegen.* First edition, Marburg, 1557.

47. Giovanni Battista Tiepolo, *America* (1750–52), detail from fresco in the Bishop's Residence, Würzburg. Bayerische Verwaltung der Staatlichen Schlösser, Gärten und Seen.

48. Giovanni Battista Tiepolo, detail from *Queen Zenobia Addressing her Soldiers* (c. 1730). National Gallery of Art, Washington, D.C. Samuel H. Kress Collection.

49. Amazons. Frontispiece
from Pierre Petit, *De
Amazonibus dissertatio*
(Amsterdam, 1687). Courtesy
of the John Carter Brown Library at
Brown University.

50. *The Contrast* (1792). Anonymous print, England. Professor Isaac Kramnick, Cornell University.

PART THREE

Crossing the Border

*

The French Revolution in the

German Imagination

Crossing the Border:
The French Revolution in the German
Literary Imagination

SUSANNE ZANTOP

I just received a letter from B[eulwitz]. Of the Parisian women he tells me strange stories which I hope are untrue; some of them are said to have gathered around a slain Garde du Corps, torn out his heart, and drank his blood in goblets, toasting each other. Things must have gone far if they have so utterly forgotten their sex.

(Charlotte von Lengefeld to Friedrich Schiller, 12 November 1789)

Analyses of the French Revolution's impact on German writers never fail to make two central claims: first, that many German intellectuals initially supported the Revolution enthusiastically but changed their attitude in 1792-93, when Robespierre's Reign of Terror revealed the bloody nature of the revolutionary battle, a battle that was carried across the border into Germany; and second, that these intellectuals developed philosophical and aesthetic approaches that channeled revolutionary energy away from the political and into the aesthetic and moral realms to produce, in Herder's words, a *Revolution der Denkart,* a revolution in the way of thinking. The French Revolution, many scholars maintain, served Germans as an "incitement for spiritual rebirth" (Gerhart Hoffmeister), as a stimulus to create their own intellectual revolution—idealism—without getting their hands dirty in revolutionary practice.[1]

Scholars who argue this way base their optimistic conclusion on philosophical, political, or aesthetic manifestos—for example, by Friedrich Schlegel, Hegel, Hölderlin, or Novalis—and find evidence for an aesthetic revolution in the Romantic fragment, the concept of Romantic irony, or generic hybridization.[2] But as Norbert Oellers has recently argued, to concentrate exclusively on the opinions of a few canonized individuals or on so-called high literature distorts the picture insofar as it ignores the interaction of "higher" literature and "lower," more popular forms of writing, their mutual indebtedness, and their collaboration in creating a "spirit of the Revolution."[3] My own research supports Oeller's contention. Indeed, representations of revolutionary moments in a variety of genres, by a variety of authors writing at various times from a variety of ideological backgrounds, reveal coincidences, constants, and shared preoccupations rather than differences. Apparently, the proximity to the events in France, the horror stories related by émigré nobles and foreign correspondents, and the confluence of two related but different insurrections—that of the Paris masses and of the slaves in Santo Domingo—mobilized residual anxieties in German observers, who proceeded to articulate these anxieties by recurring to classical and not-so-classical myths. As Germany received the news that masses of "unbridled" women were marching to Versailles to demand bread from the king and that "black hordes" were massacring their masters, depictions of revolutionary scenes abounded with references to "amazons" and "cannibals," who, transgressing gender and moral taboos, declared war on the established order and patriarchal authority. A close reading of newspaper reports and of both popular and "high" literature indicates that many German intellectuals, irrespective of their political bent, feared that the bare-breasted "Liberty"—in whom the images of fury and antique goddesses are fused with that of the New World warrior woman[4]—would not only walk over dead bodies, but cross the borders, literally and metaphorically.

The Revolution as Spectacle

One of the earliest German responses to the storming of the Bastille was an article by the Enlightenment author Christoph Martin Wieland— an article that appeared in September 1789 in his journal *Deutsche Merkur* under the pedantic title "Über die Rechtmäßigkeit des Gebrauchs welchen die Französische Nation dermalen von ihrer Aufklärung und Stärke macht" [On the legitimacy of the use the French Nation is currently making of its enlightenment and strength].[5] The article is structured as a dialogue between two men, Walther and Adelstan, who debate a recent French newspaper attack on moral corruption in revolutionary France. Walther, a bourgeois liberal, is appalled at this denigration of a nation which, he maintains, "has been astounding all of Europe for several weeks now with its demonstrations of patriotism, wisdom, courage, and endurance, unparalleled in history." Whereupon Adelstan, a conservative aristocrat—as his name indicates[6]—insists on the justness of the French self-critique: "A whole great nation in upheaval is a spectacle that will undoubtedly arouse and retain general attention: but unless I am completely mistaken, dear Walther, these horrendous and cannibalistic scenes we see acted out in and around Paris and in some of the provinces are the strongest proof that the unnamed writer whose words you just read to me did not exaggerate the corruption and licentiousness [die Verderbniß und Zügellosigkeit] of his fellow citizens. In my view the extraordinary pretensions of the National Assembly on the one hand and the notorious eruptions of popular wrath on the other are the logical consequence of that licentiousness which the author lamented. . . ." (Wieland, 7).

This apparent confrontation between two diametrically opposed positions, a liberal and a conservative one, turns into an amiable and somewhat academic disagreement about how the current explosion of popular energy can best be controlled. Walther opts for the National Assembly, whose "manly spirit" will guide the irrational, immoral, impetuous people; Adelstan, afraid that the nation risks being submerged in an "unfortunate state of complete anarchy, . . . soon to become the setting for the wildest passions [wildtesten Leidenschaften], the most licentious brutality of marauding brigands" (p. 11), prefers to rely on monarchical authority. He fears that while the "the gentlemen demagogues," as he calls the representatives at the National Assembly, are busy planning the New Republic, the "poor patient" [the French nation], "whom they wanted to regenerate in Medea's magic cauldron, may very well die and rot, unless some Deus ex machina comes to its aid" (p. 11). The exchange ends on a conciliatory note. Walther, who has the last word, prophesies a happy solution to what are actually just family squabbles: Father King, who would rather rule over happy subjects than over slaves, will no doubt recognize the legitimate claims of his nation and will cede to it some of his authority for the sake of familial harmony and a happily-ever-after outcome.

I have quoted Wieland's article at length because it contains in an embryonic form the elements that characterized the attitude of most German intellectuals toward the events in France. As Wieland indicates, the French Revolution was a fascinating spectacle to the German onlooker. France, or rather Paris, appeared as the stage for scenes of horror or delight, which the German spectators could comment upon, applaud, or boo from what appeared to be a safe distance.[7] The stage effect was underscored by the Revolution's own self-conscious theatricality[8] and by the representation of the Parisian "drama" on German stages and in printed texts. Literary reenactments of the revolution in Germany often took the form of comedy, which distanced the events as it represented them. After 1792, when the Revolution was carried across the border, the German auditorium became, so to speak, center stage, which made detached, amused spectatorship no longer possible, and comedy turned to tragedy.[9]

Since the German audience—the writers and readers of political journals and the theater public—were a relatively homogeneous group, comprising mostly the bourgeoisie and lower nobility, their responses to the drama enacted before their eyes had a limited range. A more diversified response in the first phase of the Revolution gave way to uniform skepticism after 1792.[10] Fear of the "Pöbel" (the rabble), violence, and political chaos now reunited the Walthers and Adelstans behind the banner of monarchism. In fact, even those intellectuals who continued to believe in some form of "democratic rule" preferred utopian visions of a people's monarchy to republican experiments. It is probably safe to say that after 1792, despite scattered remnants of Jacobinism, the majority of German intellectuals rejected a bloody revolution as a means toward political emancipation. (Saine, 328ff.)

As Klaus Träger and others have convincingly argued, this reversal of allegiance even among radical supporters of political emancipation was due to a totally inadequate vocabulary or conceptual apparatus, which hindered German intellectuals from understanding and appreciating the true nature of the revolutionary process.[11] Since their language was the moral and rational language of Enlightenment, it proved incapable of representing and making sense of the "immoral," "irrational" outbursts of violence everyone witnessed. Mostly accustomed to small court residences and rural environments, German intellectuals could not comprehend either the "dynamics of scale" or the economic roots of large-city mass riots. (Saine, 329). Their language served as a screen that obfuscated or distorted the political and economic power struggles instead of illuminating them.

This conceptual inadequacy is already apparent in Wieland's dialogue. In his attempt to explain the relationship between the people and their rulers and the breakdown of that relationship, Wieland evokes four rhetorical figures, or "allegorical keys," as Jameson would call them,[12] in the form of binary oppositions.

There is first the slave-despot dyad, wherein the nations, the "slaves," have broken or will break their chains, freeing themselves from the despotism of their rulers. Rooted in classical antiquity, this model was expressed in Rousseau's apocalyptic vision of revolutionary upheaval.[13] It acquired a colonial connotation in the late eighteenth century through Abbé Raynal's and Diderot's immensely popular *Histoire des Deux Indes*, which appeared in numerous editions in Germany,[14] and it gradually supplanted the "subject-tyrant" model typical of Storm-and-Stress discourse.

The second figure, the kind father-obedient children dyad that Walther proposes, benevolently revises the slave-despot/subject-tyrant configuration. It connotes a "natural" relationship between ruler and ruled based on love, protection, and obedience. As head of the Fatherland, the benign *Landesvater* caring for his *Landeskinder* provides an attractive, because peaceful, alternative to both tyranny and revolutionary conflict, a kind of "German solution" to which German commentators continuously re-sorted.

When either the slave-despot or the child-father models showed cracks or broke down (as they did, for example, in 1792 and 1793), a third figure was evoked, which I will call the cannibal-victim model of social inter-action. In the fear of being cut up, roasted, and devoured by "savages," archaic terror of demonic possession merges with sexual and territorial-colonial anxieties. It is therefore not surprising that "cannibalism" became a code-word for all forms of violent appropriation in 1789, when savage masses in Paris and masses of "savages" in the colonies attacked the bas-tions of European civilization, wealth, and political control.[15] References to "cannibalism" that mobilize archaic fears thus served to articulate a rudimentary perception of economic or class struggle, for which a proper vocabulary was still lacking in late eighteenth-century Germany.

In Wieland's text, the cannibalistic model is extended and given par-ticular poignancy by his reference to "Medea's cauldron." The sorceress Medea, the myth goes, herself no stranger to dismemberment, had taken revenge on Pelias by persuading his daughters to cut him into pieces and boil the limbs in a cauldron, claiming that the king would emerge rejuve-nated. As was to be expected, he remained dead, victim of a parricide committed by the unwitting female accomplices of a vengeful, vicious, du-plicitous woman. The image of the *Hexenkessel,* the witches' cauldron, in which the dismembered man perishes at the hands of women, introduces a fourth, overriding construct, gender: while the slave-despot/child-father dyads focus on the patriarchal male and his dependents, the images of the cannibals or witches devouring their victims clearly involve women.[16] Whereas the former two models are invoked to rationalize an incompre-hensible process, the latter emerge whenever rationality breaks down and violence and chaos erupt. Together, these four models inform and orga-nize the revolutionary imagination of German writers and many German representations of the Revolution. As I shall try to show with concrete examples, they operate both synchronically and diachronically; they over-lap, clash with each other, or collapse into one another, revealing in and through their interaction the ambiguities in the "political subconscious" of the spectators across the Rhine.

Trouble in the Father-Land

As mentioned before, German writers felt the need to contain, harmo-nize, or divert the conflicts they saw erupting in France by casting them in the comic mode.[17] A particularly apt example of this tendency is August von Kotzebue's farce *The Female Jacobin Club,* which appeared in 1792, about the same time as Le Sueur issued a gouache called *Club Patriotique des Femmes* (fig. 43).[18] Kotzebue had the dual advantage of having been both an eyewitness to events in Paris in 1791 and the most popular German playwright in late eighteenth-century Europe. We can reasonably consider him *the* representative of popular opinion, an opinion he in turn shaped more than any of the so-called classic authors did.[19]

His "political *comedy in one act*," as *The Female Jacobin Club* is subtitled (wishful thinking, no doubt), centers around an aristocratic Parisian family in upheaval. While Monsieur Duport, who abhors the Revolution and all it stands for, worries about the family's finances, Madame Duport, an enthusiastic follower of the "goddess of Freedom" (p. 11), undermines the family's very foundations: she renames her son Louis "François" in honor of Mirabeau, cuts out paper gallows and dead aristocrats for him to play with, and, worst of all, founds a female Jacobin Society that meets in her dining room, "tastefully" decorated with a painting of the destroyed Bastille, the women's march to Versailles, a portrait of Lafayette, and two life-size wax figures showing a National Guardsman about to chop off the head of a kneeling, enchained aristocrat. The seven aristocratic women who assemble in Madame Duport's dining room choose "Lucretia" as their secret password and a twisting of their hands, like "wringing a chicken's neck," as their conspiratorial signal. They swear an oath never to fall in love with a nobleman, or, in case they are already married to such a "monster"—and all of them are—"to plague, torture, martyr, flay, squeeze, tease, annoy, scold and ridicule" their aristocratic husbands "until they surrender" [bis sie zu Kreuze kriechen, 44].

The parallels between public life and private life and between state and family are made obvious from the start. "Mother" nation's rebellion, her attempt to gain equality with the father, is squelched by a "counterrevolution" initiated by the King-father and carried out by the cunning former modiste Antoinette, who has lost her business because of the Revolution, and by Duport's future son-in-law, the marquis de Rozières. Aristocracy, clergy, and the dispossessed entrepreneurial class engage in this counterrevolution with the express approval of Duport's completely apolitical, chaste, and naturally submissive daughter, who bears, appropriately, the Rousseauian name Julie. Upon her father's request that Julie "freely" choose her government ("the aristocratic rule of your parents or your relatives? the democratic rule of all your admirers? or the monarchic rule of a husband?"), she opts for a "monarchy in which the monarch is linked by the bonds of love to his subjects,"[20] despite her mother's interjection that monarchy and traditional marriage are by definition despotic. This "loving" relationship between husband and wife, king and subject, master and slave, is reestablished in the end, when all the husbands, in a reversal of the storming of the Bastille, storm the female Jacobin Club and bend their knees to their "queens." In the final words of the play, the Jacobin ladies say to each other: "Code word: *amour;* secret signal: a kiss" (p. 52).

In Kotzebue's snug familial farce, female transgression is the cause of all evil. Wives, in defiance of patriarchal authority, break with traditional political acquiescence by founding their own separate political society. Claiming a voice and share in revolutionary "history," they seek alliances with the lower classes, as the text suggests when it associates the mother's rebellion with the women's march to Versailles, the *poissardes'* street demonstrations, and the servants' demands for equal rights. The text links women even with actual "savages," as when Duport, responding to his wife's plea for a new, egalitarian relationship between masters and servants based on the "proud self-consciousness" of the lower classes, exclaims: "And I'd rather be a missionary and convert the savages of Hudson Bay to Christianity than try to change the preconceived opinions of a woman" (p. 18).

Kotzebue tries to belittle the threat posed by those who want to break their "chains"—women, the lower classes and other "slaves"—by reducing the revolt to a family squabble among the privileged and declaring it a frivolous entertainment. The childish members of the Female Jacobin Club "play" at revolution because it is fashionable, and because they want to appear in history books; their discussions of politics degenerate, as is to be expected, into chatter about what to wear: Amazon costumes are "out," as one of the women declares at their first meeting, and overcoats with steel buttons are "in" (p. 45). Their rebellion is therefore easily contained when, in a reversal of the slave-despot model, the husbands profess their slavish devotion to their "domestic despots," to whom they concede "complete power" in the home, thus putting women back into the place Rousseau had created for them.

The obsession with transgressive femininity, with women who cross the boundaries between the private and the public sphere and become advocates of change, is not limited to such conservative German observers of the Revolution as Kotzebue. The tendency to feminize the Revolution and to perceive "public women" as the major threat to family and state can be found among liberal commentators as well. Kotzebue can, for example, rely on observations made by the famous educator and revolutionary sympathizer Joachim Heinrich Campe, who had rushed to Paris in August 1789 to witness the "funeral of French despotism" and whose *Letters from Paris* became a bestseller in 1790.[21] Campe claims that it is the Parisian women, and particularly the market women, not the men, who have created "unlawful disorders" and committed "acts of barbarism" (p. 186), and he blames these excesses on (French) women's cultural inferiority, their lack of "modesty" and "moral sense." This inferiority, Campe explains, is caused by a variety of factors: women's physical weakness ("As we all know, the weaker person tends to be the more cruel one"); a deficient or misguided education; the French men's gallantry and courtesy, which spoils women of all stations and renders them arrogant and haughty; and the desire of the female sex, "particularly in France," to "use every opportunity to meddle in public affairs, to express a male desire for power, to grasp and hold on to that power, and to use it licentiously" [bis zur Ausschweifung zu benutzen] (pp. 188–89). Campe's careful rhetorical buildup and his repeated allusions to women in general reveal that women's public activism, their intrusion into a "male" sphere, and their challenge to patriarchal rule in the state and at home constitute a threat to both French and German men, that is, to the European family at large.[22] Although he insists that the excesses he claims to have witnessed are peculiar to France, the message to German "heads of households" is clear: female licentiousness and drive for power are universal—therefore: *principiis obsta!*

Like Kotzebue, Campe believes the remedy to be "love." Addressing his patron, the Duke of Brunswick, in the dedicatory foreword to his *Letters*, he writes: "Doubly and triply will posterity praise the sacred memory of that rare monarch who has been a guardian angel to the Germans both on the battlefield and in his cabinet and who, at a time when all despots tremble before their slaves, can peacefully look down on his happy, grateful people like a father on his children, and can permit them to express their delight that other peoples in other countries will soon be able to enjoy the same blessings as the happy Brunswickian" (Foreword, v–vi). Love keeps the family—parents and children, "masters" and "slaves," monarchs and subjects—happily united. Love keeps history at bay.

Both the liberal Campe and the conservative Kotzebue thus resort to the "benign father-obedient children" model in order to contain, repress, and neutralize the rebellion. Kotzebue's cannibalistic metaphors, however, reveal the seriousness of the threat, not only to France but to the extended European family. Responding to his wife's remark that he is in such a "biting humor," Duport answers: "These days, everybody either bites, or is bitten. No wonder that I'd rather be among those who bite than among those who get bitten" (p. 19). Food metaphors, such as "the sweet fruit of freedom" (p. 18), "the milk of freedom," the "porridge of equality" (p. 22) and preoccupation with devouring masses ("they devoured the decrees," p. 26), although they stay within the familial model, introduce an element of violence that subtly subverts it. The German spectators are literally left with these "nagging" questions: Will "love" suffice to satisfy the "children's" hunger? Can the Duports preserve their "Einnahmen" [income], literally their intake, by feeding the have-nots the rhetoric of symbolic submission? Will the slaves not only bite, but devour their masters? What if the French cannibals want more?

The Cannibals' Progress

In the second phase of the Revolution, from the 10 August massacres onward, the paranoia among German spectators clearly rose, along with the number and shrillness of allusions to what one antirevolutionary pamphlet would call "the cannibals' progress."[23] As the French King proves increasingly unable to restore order in his own "house," as the scene is taken over by violent, "despotic" throngs who do not love but "enchain" and eventually kill their *Landesvater,* and as these "cannibalistic" masses prepare to "gobble up"[24] all of Europe, the gendered discourse of cannibalism gains increasing prominence in German rhetoric, competing with, and at times even replacing, that of the "good father." The four-volume collection of responses to the French Revolution in the Rhineland (ed. Hansen), for example, lists only one reference to "cannibals" for the years 1789–1791, while for 1792-93 there are twelve. What had appeared in embryonic form in Kotzebue's play, namely the combined attack by women and other savages on their masters' rule, becomes the central focus of many writings after 1792.

This "feminization" of the masses, although no new phenomenon, responded, I would argue, to a particular German need in 1792–93. As the French armies crossed the borders into German territory, reducing Germany to a "body" about to be invaded and violated, "femininity" needed to be displaced onto the French nation in order to save face and restore the authority of the European monarchs.[25] This process is clearly visible in the German press, where the description of the Jacobins as sly, cowardly, frivolous, vain—characteristics generally reserved to the "weak" sex[26]—is extended onto the National Assembly after the Jacobins' takeover and then to the whole French nation after the king's execution. It was as if by devouring their gluttonous, corpulent, effeminate King, the French masses themselves had turned into a cannibal queen.[27] French national character, which until 1792 had abounded with "manly" qualities in the eyes of sympathetic German observers, returned to its former tempestuousness, frivolity, and licentiousness as the sympathy waned. Even liberal writers feared that Marianne, the Goddess of Unbridled Liberty, was out to get the German Michel. The question was, would he surrender, seduced by her charms, or would he resist?[28] Would she devour him, or would he be saved?

Referring to the atrocities in Avignon and the September massacres, the poet Klopstock, one of the five German honorary citizens of the French Republic,[29] states that "the Germans are fixated on those horrors, and devoured by atrocious, heart-rending contemplations [verschlungen in diese gräßlichen, herzzerfleischenden Betrachtungen], they forget everything that once attracted them to the French Revolution."[30] Similar metaphors appear in so-called eyewitness reports. "Don't be surprised if my present letter reflects the disorder in my heart; ground up, or rather: ripped to shreds [wundgerieben oder vielmehr zerfleischt] by a series of terrifying scenes, whose end, unfortunately, remains to be seen. . . ."—so begins the 14 August 1792 "Letter from Paris" by the German Girondin Konrad Engelbert Oelsner, printed in the Hamburg newspaper *Minerva*. Oelsner's choppy, or should I say chopped-up, relation of the events is cast in the "witches' cauldron" mode, as the narrator registers processions of "decapitated heads" (p. 516), piles of dead bodies (p. 518), and blood baths in streets (p. 518) that are taken over by hordes of savages (p. 520) and raging, foaming furies (p. 521)—an environment that feels like "a burning oven" (in einem glühendem [sic] Ofen, p. 517), like "fiery jaws" [Feuerrachen, p. 518] about to swallow everybody: "The rejoicing of the women muffles the groans of terror. They slurp, with brutal lust [mit brutaler Wollust] the women slurp up the moans of the dying, and through their mouths, a devilish drunkenness mocks the last quivers of agony" (p. 522).[31] Oelsner's sexually charged language reveals his own ambivalence about the Revolution, his "male fantasies" in which raging women and streams of blood form a red flood threatening to spill over into Germany.[32] Oelsner's misogynist agenda becomes evident when he moves from his cannibalistic metaphors for the violence of French revolutionary women to generalizations about the female sex:

And though it disgrace all womanhood, I must say that it is the women who, in all the stormy scenes of the Revolution, have always been the first to invent and execute atrocities, or to incite men to commit new tortures and bloody deeds. During the night following that horrible day, they reportedly denuded themselves on the dead bodies, roasted the limbs of the killed men, and offered them as food. Even the morning after, I have seen women clawing among the dead, mutilating their limbs. This tendency toward excess was noticable even among the educated class of women. I have always found that the weaker half of society has the greatest inclination to commit desperate and horrendous acts, and I could abhor women, were not that very same excitability, which in an eruption of hatred and revenge transforms them into repulsive monsters, almost the sole mainspring of their virtues. (pp. 522–23)

Clearly, Campe's or Kotzebue's few misguided French ladies who engaged in political activism in the first phase of the Revolution have turned into "de-natured women," bacchantic Furies who castrate men and devour their victims like ferocious beasts. These incidents of female excess that writers "report" or evoke are not the exception, but the rule.[33]

Schiller's famous epic poem, *Das Lied von der Glocke [The Lay of the Bell]*[34] echoes, almost a decade later, the theme of revolution as female transgression. It is a theme with which he had been familiar since his fiancée's letter of 12 November 1789, reproduced as epigraph to this essay.[35] The corporate patriarchal idyll that Schiller evokes in this poem—an idyll based on complementary male-female roles and cheerful acceptance of one's God-given social station—is almost destroyed: first by a natural catastrophe, fire, then by a man-made catastrophe, the Revolution. Natural forces are equated with human violence: the fire, red as blood, searing "like the breath of an oven" [wie aus Ofens Rachen] is as destructive to culture as are people in revolt. Yet while fire, "the free daughter of Nature," devours property, unbridled revolutionary women devour their enemies—whoever they may be. When it comes to ferocity, Schiller implies, man transcends nature—and women, it seems, transcend men:

> Freiheit und Gleichheit! hört man schallen,
> Der ruh'ge Bürger greift zur Wehr,
> Die Straßen füllen sich, die Hallen,
> Und Würgerbanden ziehn umher,
> Da werden Weiber zu Hyänen
> Und treiben mit Entsetzen Scherz,
> Noch zuckend, mit des Panthers Zähnen,
> Zerreissen sie des Feindes Herz.
> Nichts Heiliges ist mehr, es lösen
> Sich alle Bande frommer Scheu,
> Der Gute räumt den Platz dem Bösen,
> Und alle Laster walten frei.

> "Freedom! Equality!" the calls
> Have quiet burghers reach for swords;
> Packed tight with throngs are streets and halls
> And roamed at will by murdering hordes.
> Then women turn to wolves from shepherds,
> Commit atrocities for sport;
> Still pulsing, with the fangs of leopards
> They lacerate the foeman's heart.
> No sanctity survives, the altars
> Of pious reverence are stained,
> The wicked triumph, goodness falters,
> All vice pursues its course unchained.[36]

Walter Arndt's translation reproduces the anguish, the hysterical pitch of this depiction that confronts the "ruhige Bürger," the composed, quiet citizen, with "Würgerbanden," bands of marauders. His choice of the word "wolves" for hyenas, however, while aptly rendering the idea of the protector of life turned ferocious destroyer, does not convey the same associations as "*die* Hyäne": a vicious, devious, impure "female" animal that lives off rotting carcasses.

In Schiller's poem, as in Kotzebue's play and the many press reports cited, women become the emblem of chaos and licentiousness. Unlike Kotzebue, however, Schiller does not suggest a model in which paternal love serves to tame the beast. Without transition, the poem switches from a depiction of horror and destruction to one of bliss: "Freude hat mir Gott gegeben!"—"God has given me joy!" The bell in the poem's title, a cultural artifact produced by the community of men, tolls in peace; God-given patriarchal order is literally "saved by the bell."

By redirecting revolutionary energy—fire and knowledge—into the cultural form of a bell that praises the glory of the Lord, Schiller's poem, like Kotzebue's previous play, attempts to "contain" [aufheben] and ward off revolution, the female threat to male law and order. His shift from a chaos generated by ecstatic, "de-natured" women to peace and *Brüderschaft* under the Lord's protective umbrella is, however, a leap of faith away from political reality into utopia: only with the help of higher powers, the great Father's, can the original brotherhood of men be restored—in art.[37]

The Revolt of the Slaves

In the image of the cannibal-amazon who threatens to overturn the moral and political order not only of France, but of the German monarchies as well, anxieties about the loss of sexual and political identities are intertwined. As Neil Hertz and Ronald Paulson have argued, "castration anxiety," fear of the "phallic mother," or of "excessive," "insatiable" female sexuality conflate with or give metaphorical expression to territorial anxieties, to anxieties about control and about invasion of the body.[38] While "cannibal" stands for violent physical appropriation and incorporation (of bodies, property, and territory), the word "amazons" represents revolution as a "female" attack against patriarchy. Women warriors, *Männinnen*, who join the masses on the streets instead of staying at home, destroy not only the fabric of society but the "natural" and "holy" order. As they transgress the boundaries of the house, they overstep all other boundaries.

There is, however, another element of the cannibal-amazon fantasy that Kotzebue's aside had already hinted at: the link between the rebellion of the metaphorical "slaves" in Paris (women, the lower classes) and the rebellion of actual slaves in the colonies.[39] The parallels between German descriptions of cannibalistic orgies in Paris and contemporaneous representations of slave rebellions in Santo Domingo permit us to understand the global dimensions of the anxiety that the French Revolution aroused: the fear of a "Verwilderung," of a return to a state of moral and cultural savagery,[40] the fear that a European civilization based on the wealth accumulated through the possession of colonies will go under if the "savages" have their way. The revolutionary couples (slave-despot, cannibal-victim) must therefore be understood not only as a metaphorical reference to the class struggle taking place in France; they also literally address a global confrontation between colonizer and colonized. "Four issues were of major concern to the [French] nation," *Minerva* reports in January 1792, "the terrible situation in St. Domingo, the increasing turmoil in the provinces because of the priests, the finances, and the measures against the hostile powers."[41]

Throughout the revolutionary years, the journal reports events in the West Indies side by side with events in Paris, often in the same article. On the page and in the minds of the German readers, the French people, "rising from the most profound morass of slavery" (Campe, 21), are thus associated with colonial peoples demanding political rights. This association was prepared by allegorical depictions of the New World in the form of bare-breasted cannibalistic amazon queens—for example in Tiepolo's Würzburg fresco—who metamorphose directly into bare-breasted goddesses of liberty wearing a Phrygian cap instead of feathers (figs. 47 to 50). It is manifest in descriptions of the September massacres in terms of Aztec human sacrifices.[42]

Germany, although not directly involved in colonial activity, partakes of Europe's colonial anxiety. Even when reports in the liberal press openly favor the demands of the slave population against the French colonists, the actual depictions of atrocities focus on those committed by the slaves, not their masters, undermining the overt political message.[43] The associations between revolutionary riots and slave riots in the liberal press are exploited by conservative writers. H. A. O. Reichard, the editor of the antirevolutionary *Revolutions-Almanach*, for example, describes the Revolution as "a battle of civilized Europe against a gang of usurpers and thieves, . . . a battle of self-preservation and self-defense, a battle of right against wrong, of property against robbery, of culture against the return of the savagery of the feudal wars [Fehdealter]."[44] Reichard identifies the aggressors as "the inhabitants of other states and nations, the rabble, the poor, the true sans-culottes" (p. 28), who would take the French *sans-culottes* as their example and start their own revolution. "With this kind of predisposition," he warns, "one needs only the slightest incident, the smallest spark, and the volcano erupts, and the lava stream of insurrection and the overthrow of culture and society will advance unimpeded." According to the most conservative observers, in the battle between the European allies and France, nothing less than the decline of Western civilization is at stake.[45]

One of the most profound and disturbing representations of the Revolution, Heinrich von Kleist's *The Betrothal in Santo Domingo* [*Die Verlobung in San Domingo*],[46] published in 1811, highlights the links between the revolution in France and the one in the colonies.[47] In a way, Kleist's novella can be interpreted as a German metastory of the Revolution, since it thematizes precisely the ethical dilemma of the not-so-innocent bystander who is trapped in the slaves-tyrant/children-father model and its female cannibal/witch counterpart and is therefore unable to understand fully the nature of the revolutionary process.[48] Kleist's story takes place in 1803, "at the time when the blacks were murdering the whites" (231), as the narrator bluntly states. Although both the narrator and the protagonist of the story, Gustav, a Swiss mercenary in French services, describe the revolutionary conflict in terms of the two patriarchal models mentioned, they avoid any overt reference to "slavery," which would have supposed a willingness to recognize the real structures of oppression. Unwilling to do so, narrator and white protagonist couch their remarks in a "black-and-white" discourse of morality, according to which "innumerable favours and kindnesses" on the part of the white master, a kind of father figure, are met with treachery and an "inhuman thirst for revenge" by the blacks, his children. When the mestiza Toni asks Gustav why the whites had incurred such a hatred among blacks, Gustav explains "that situation"—as he refers to slavery—in moral, not economic or social terms: "It is one which has lasted for many centuries. The mad lust for freedom which has seized all these plantations has driven the negroes and creoles to break the chains that oppressed them, and to take their revenge on the whites for *much reprehensible ill-treatment they have had to suffer at the hands of some of us who do our race no credit*" (p. 241) [das aber schon seit vielen Jahrhunderten auf diese Weise bestand! Der Wahnsinn der Freiheit, der alle diese Pflanzungen ergriffen hat, trieb die Neger und Kreolen, die Ketten, die sie drückten, zu brechen, und an den Weißen *wegen vielfacher und*

*tadelnswürdiger Mißhandlungen, die sie von einigen schlechten Mitglie-
dern derselben erlitten,* Rache zu nehmen] (p. 195, emphasis mine). Clearly
Gustav's need to individualize guilt and to avoid the term "slavery" shows
his inability, or unwillingness, to understand the systemic causes of the
outbreak of violence and his own involvement in them.

While Gustav's frame of reference is the patriarchal model of the kind,
moral father, another model informs his subconscious, that of the threatening "witches' cauldron," in which destructive sexual women figure prominently. In the tales of two women in revolutionary situations, the two
models appear side by side: the story of an unnamed "treacherous" slave
woman who, suffering from yellow fever, takes revenge on her abusive
master by luring him into her contaminating embrace, is juxtaposed with
the heroic story of Marianne Congreve, "the most faithful creature on
earth," who sacrifices herself on the revolutionary scaffold to protect Gustav's life from the "bloodthirsty band of (his) pursuers" (p. 246).[49] While
Gustav tells the mestiza Toni the story of the white woman's heroic sacrifice in order to convince her not to act like the black slave woman, he fails
to understand the "third" story, the "love story" he and Toni are currently
living, which is constructed over an abyss of violence and fear. The white-
or-black, saint-or-whore stories Gustav relates reveal his inability to grasp
a "mixed," that is "historical" situation, where skin color or sex cannot be
equated with a particular moral stance. Not only does Gustav misinterpret
Toni's actions, but he remains unconscious of his own ambiguous feelings
toward her and toward the revolutionary struggle: the mixture of fear and
attraction he is experiencing. The "remote resemblance" Gustav perceives
between Marianne and Toni thus seems to reside less in physical or moral
likeness than in the parallels between Gustav's two fateful misapprehen-
sions: his reckless naïveté during the French Revolution, which led to the
execution of Marianne, and his blindness during the Haitian Revolution,
which leads to the destruction of Toni. The final eruption of violence,
when Gustav literally blows his brains out, is the "logical" consequence
of a series of violent misperceptions arising from categories that no longer
correspond to lived realities—or never did.

The *Betrothal in Santo Domingo* is thus—among other things—a story
about false perception, about violence through language, about the abyss
behind the signs. Gustav's attempt to represent revolutionary reality as
female transgression blinds him not only to the complexities of the revolutionary moments he is witnessing, but to his own investment in them.
He has to discover that while he thought he was safe, a morally superior

outsider, he was in fact, and in his language, the accomplice of the counter-revolution—a discovery that German intellectuals would face in the years to come.

NOTES

My thanks to the John and Eliza Howard Foundation and the National Endowment for the Humanities for providing me with the time and funds to carry out research for this paper in Germany.

1. The literature on the topic is, of course, immense and still growing. The most informative recent study is Thomas P. Saine's *Black Bread, White Bread: German Intellectuals and the French Revolution* (New York: Lang, 1988). On the repercussions of the Revolution in European literature see Gerhart Hoffmeister's essay, "Rhetorics of Revolution in West European Romanticism: How to Get the Schlegels, Victor Hugo and Wordsworth under One Hat," forthcoming in *The French Revolution and Literature in the Age of Goethe* (Hildesheim: Olms); *Deutsche Literatur und Französische Revolution. Sieben Studien* (Göttingen: Vandenhoek, 1974)—hereafter cited as *DLFR*; and Gerhard Schulz, *Die deutsche Literatur zwischen Französischer Revolution und Restauration* [de Boor-Newald VII, 1] (Munich: Beck, 1983). See also the anthology by Klaus Träger, *Die Französische Revolution im Spiegel der deutschen Literatur* (Leipzig: Philipp Reclam, 1975)—hereafter cited as Träger; and Inge Stephan, *Literarischer Jakobinismus in Deutschland 1789–1806* (Stuttgart: Metzler, 1976), 33–37, which contains an extensive bibliography.

2. Although this assessment has been substantiated through many careful, learned studies, it reproduces the split between politics and aesthetics established by idealism—a split contemporary critics lament—and tries to mend it in a tour de force by declaring the aesthetic political. The claim that reactionary politics can coincide with revolutionary aesthetics in the same work had already been expressed by Novalis when he stated: "Many *anti*revolutionary books have been written *for* the Revolution. Burke, however, has written a revolutionary book against the Revolution" (*Schriften*, ed. Richard Samuel [Stuttgart: Kohlhammer, 1960], 2:464). Likewise, Karl Heinz Bohrer defines as "revolutionary" a text infused with the perception of a "categorical newness," of rupture, irrespective of its ideological message ("Zeit der Revolution—Revolution der Zeit," *Merkur* [February 1989]: 13–28). Revolution in this context becomes a mere metaphor for drastic change; and change, or "newness," it is implied, is in itself already revolutionary.

3. Norbert Oellers, "Literatur für die Mehrheit? Notizen über Heinrich August Ottokar Reichard und seinen 'Revolutions-Almanach,'" *Aufklärung. Interdisziplinäre Halbjahresschrift zur Erforschung des 18. Jahrhunderts*, 1–2 (1986):26–27.

4. See Susanne Zantop, "Liberty Unbound: Heine's 'Historiography in Color,'" in *Paintings on the Move: Heinrich Heine and the Visual Arts*, ed. Susanne Zantop (Lincoln: University of Nebraska Press, 1989), 31–49, especially p. 43.

5. In Christoph Martin Wieland, *Meine Antworten. Aufsätze über die Franzö-*

sische Revolution 1789–1793, ed. Fritz Martini (Marbach am Neckar: Deutsches Literaturarchiv, 1983), 7–24—hereafter cited as Wieland. (Unless otherwise stated, all translations from the German are mine, with my colleague David Ward's expert help).

6. Saine (p. 48) makes a convincing case for using the terms "liberals" and "conservatives" in the German context rather than "royalists" or "Jacobins." Apropos the name Adelstan, *Adel* means aristocracy.

7. See Herder: "We are in a position to keep our German common sense, to watch and examine everything, to adopt the good things with reason, and to reject the bad things after careful, measured judgment." [Da bleibt es uns erlaubt, unsern deutschen gesunden Verstand zusammenzuhalten, alles prüfend zu sehen, das Gute vernünftig zu nützen, gerecht und billig das Verwerfliche zu verwerfen]. Quoted in Träger, 59.

8. See Joachim Heinrich Campe, who speaks of "the great, marvellous spectacles that were staged here during those days and continue to be staged every day" and describes Paris as "the stage on which one of the greatest political dramas our world has recently seen is now being performed." *Letters from Paris* (*Briefe aus Paris zur Zeit der Revolution geschrieben*, 1790; reprinted with afterword by Hans-Wolf Jäger [Gerstenberg: Hildesheim, 1977]), 1, 3—cited hereafter as Campe. On the continuation—or actually expansion—of theatrical activity proper in Paris see, for example, the anonymous "Briefe aus Paris, über den neuesten Zustand des dortigen Theaters," *Minerva* (Jan. 1793): 35 ff.. See also the essay by Marie-Hélène Huet, "Performing Arts: Theatricality and the Terror" in this volume.

9. For samples of commentary on the Revolution as spectacle (*Schauspiel*) and tragi-comedy see Wieland (Träger, 37; Wieland, 98–99), Herder (Träger, 57); and Christoph Girtanner, who called the Revolution "The great European Tragedy" [*Politische Annalen* 2 (April 1793): 3]. See also Jäger in Campe, 86.

10. The skeptical responses included Goethe and Schiller (see Claude David, "Goethe und die FR," and Walter Müller-Seidel, "Deutsche Klassik und Französische Revolution" in *DLFR*); the enthusiastic ones included Joachim Heinrich Campe, Georg Forster, and Klopstock. But even the latter reverted to theoretical support for the "idea" of revolution and abhorrence of its reality during Robespierre's terror; see, for example, Campe's "recantation," quoted in Campe, 57–61, and Klopstock's response to the execution of Louis XVI, quoted in Joseph Hansen, ed., *Quellen zur Geschichte des Rheinlandes im Zeitalter der Französischen Revolution 1780–1801* (Bonn: Hanstein 1931–33), 2:708—hereafter cited as Hansen.

11. See Träger, 15; Claude David, in *DLFR*, 64; and Kurt Wölfel, in *DLFR*, 161. Although I completely agree with their assessment, I do not think that these authors probe deep enough in their analyses of the German discourse of the Revolution. None of them, for example, seem to notice the gendered nature of this discourse.

12. Fredric Jameson, *The Political Unconscious: Narrative as a Socially Symbolic Act* (Ithaca, N.Y.: Cornell University Press, 1981), 28.

13. *Rousseau's Political Writings*, ed. Alan Ritter and J. Bondanella trans. Julia Conaway Bondanella, (New York: Norton, 1988), 55: "From the midst of this disorder and these revolutions despotism, gradually raising its hideous head and devouring all that it had perceived to be good and sound in every part of the state, would finally succeed in trampling the laws and people underfoot and in establish-

ing itself upon the ruins of the republic. . . . Wherever despotism reigns . . . , it admits no other master; as soon as it speaks, neither integrity nor duty is considered, and the blindest obedience is the only virtue left to slaves."

14. On the universalization of the slave terminology see Hans-Jürgen Lüsebrink, afterword to Guillaume Raynal und Denis Diderot, *Die Geschichte beider Indien* (Nördlingen: Greno, 1988), 336.

15. See Goethe, *Die Campagne in Frankreich*, quoted in Träger, 249; Girtanner, 2: 207; and my discussion below.

16. While cannibals are of course not necessarily female, they are, in European representations, often associated with the female witch. In the witch of Hansel and Gretel, for instance, the ancient tradition of night-flying female cannibals (*strigae*) merges with stories of the malevolent sorceress (*malefica*), a common combination during Reformation Europe; see E. William Monter, *Witchcraft in France and Switzerland: the Borderlands during the Reformation* (Ithaca, N.Y.: Cornell University Press, 1976), p. 17.

17. Examples include Goethe's *Der Groß-Cophta* (1791), *Der Bürgergeneral* (1793), *Die Aufgeregten* (1793), *Hermann und Dorothea* (1796-97), and *Die natürliche Tochter* (1799-1803); August von Kotzebue's *Der weibliche Jakobiner-Clubb* (1791); Iffland's *Die Kokarden* (1791); and Schiller's *Die Jungfrau von Orleans* (1801), and *Wilhelm Tell* (1804). Although Schiller's plays do not address the French Revolution directly, they have to be read against the backdrop of the events in France. Gonthier-Louis Fink ("Das Motiv der Rebellion in Kleists Werk im Spannungsfeld der Französischen Revolution und der Napoleonischen Kriege," *Kleist-Jahrbuch 1988–89*, ed. Hans Joachim Kreutzer [Berlin: Erich Schmidt, 1988], 64–95) points out that although prorevolutionary plays existed, strict censorship kept them largely off the stage.

18. August von Kotzebue, *Der weibliche Jakobiner-Clubb* (Frankfurt and Leipzig, 1792). All page numbers in parentheses refer to this edition. Since I was unable to procure the English translation (*The Female Jacobin-Club: A Political Comedy in One Act*, trans. J. C. Siber [Liverpool: Coddington, 1801]), all translations of this comedy are mine. The popular play was translated into French as early as 1792.

19. On Kotzebue's popularity see Oellers, 39ff.; Geiger, *Allgemeine Deutsche Biographie* (1882, rpt. Berlin: Duncker u. Humblot: 1969), 16:780; and Ludwig Böhm and Herbert Meyer, introduction to their exhibition catalog *August von Kotzebue 1761–1819* (Mannheim: Reiss-Museum, 1961-62).

20. Kotzebue, 20–21. It may be worth noting that Duport's reference to "Eltern" includes the rebellious mother. In Kotzebue's presentation, the mother's rebellion against paternal monarchic rule is but a recent fad, a stray from the proper female path.

21. As Jäger reports, the "Letters" had three editions in 1790 alone, and two Dutch editions by 1792 (Campe, Appendix, 75).

22. A similar solidarity with the fatherly king attacked by ferocious women is expressed, for example in "Geheimer Briefwechsel zwischen den Lebendigen und den Toten" (Koblenz, 1789), printed in Hansen 1:456–58: "The King appeared; he received those women deputies with benevolence—and what else could he have done! Ah, fate of those who bear the crown! a King of France!" [Der König erschien; emfing diese Weiberdeputation mit Güte, und was konnte er besser tun? O Schicksal der Gekrönten! ein König von Frankreich!]. It seems that the women's

march to Versailles unleashed deep anxieties also among German spectators. See the responses to the October events printed in Hansen 1: 522–25.

23. *The cannibals' progress; or the dreadful horrors of French invasion; As displayed by the Republican Officers and Soldiers, in their perfidy, rapacity, ferociousness and brutality, exercised towards the innocent inhabitants of Germany,* trans. Anthony Aufrer (Walpole, N.H.: Thomas and Thomas, 1798).

24. A remark attributed to Frau v. Stein (cf. George P. Gooch, *Germany and the French Revolution* [New York: Longmans, 1920], 363). In the pamphlet "The Cannibals' Progress," the French armies are described as hordes of male savages engaged in the "desecration" of female bodies.

25. Lynn Hunt ("Engraving the Republic," *History Today* 30 [1980]:15f.) describes the familial relationship in terms of European "uncles" who replace the French "father/tyrant" in his battle against the combined sons and daughters. The "feminization" of France may, of course, also relate to the self-representation of the French Republic in the form of a female allegorical figure; see Maurice Agulhon, *Marianne into Battle: Republican Imagery and Symbolism in France 1789–1880,* trans. Janet Lloyd (Cambridge: Cambridge University Press, 1981), 16–30.

26. I have used the term "weak sex" rather than "female sex" on purpose, for "cowardice", "slyness," and devious behavior are attributes or weapons of the weak, as Campe tells us, and "the weak," as the term "weak sex" suggests, are generally associated with "the female." The tendency to designate the "other" in a power struggle as savage, devious, and, by implication, as "female" (or rather "effeminate") is also addressed by Tzvetan Todorov, *La Conquête de l'Amérique: La question de l'autre* (Paris: Seuil, 1982), 159ff.

27. Hansen 2:220–21, 318–19; Saine, 346f. See also Campe, 18, who claims that the French national character has been purified by recent events and shed some of its lightheartedness, frivolity, and arrogance. On the "effeminate" image of the French king see Sara Maza, "The Diamond Necklace Affair Revisited: The Case of the Missing Queen," *National Humanities Center Newsletter* 10.2 (Winter 1988-89): 4.

28. In April 1793, Girtanner raised the question in sexual terms: "Behold, dear citizens of Mainz, the all-devastating stride of Revolutionary Violence; announced, and certainly not depicted in too black colors, by herself; and you should embrace this foreign Fury out of your own free will [Triebe]? You should voluntarily introduce her into your fatherland, despite all the atrocities she committed with temples, schools, matrimonial bonds and all other relations in her own? She invaded your territory with the war torch in her hand; can this invasion, with all its devastations, be as pernicious as her embrace?" (Girtanner 2:79).

29. The others are Anarcharsis Cloots, his uncle Cornelius de Pauw (actually not a German by birth), J. H. Campe, and Schiller.

30. *Minerva* 5 (Jan. 1793): 13.

31. See also Saine, 342–343, and *Revolutions-Almanach* (1794,) 232–243.

32. I borrow the phrase "male fantasies" from Klaus Theweleit's *Male Fantasies,* trans. Stephen Conway (Minneapolis: University of Minnesota Press, 1987).

33. Similar occurrences are reported in the May 1793 issue of *Minerva,* 191; in Hansen 2:320 and 705–06; and in Wieland (Sept. 1792), 116. See also Altstätten's poem to B. F. v. Gerolt (Hansen 2:218), in which earth has been "desecrated by

cannibalistic orgies" [durch kannibalische Feste geschändet]; and Fichte, "Zurück-forderung der Denkfreiheit von den Fürsten Europas, die sie bisher unterdrückten," 1793, where, although Fichte seems to criticize the representations of cannibalistic excesses in reactionary newspapers as a manipulative move, he in fact accepts them as true and justifies them historically and politically (Johann Gottlieb Fichte, *Werke 1791–1794* [Stuttgart: Frommann, 1964]1:184). This language of cannibalism is, incidentally, also used to discredit the aristocrats; see, for example, Dorsch's speech before the Mainz Jacobin Club on 4 November 1792, quoted in Hansen 2:542.

34. Schillers *Werke. Nationalausgabe* 2. 1 (Weimar: Böhlau, 1983): 237.

35. For a discussion of the Amazon myth in Schiller and Kleist see Inge Stephan, " 'Da werden Weiber zu Hyänen . . .' Amazonen und Amazonenmythen bei Schiller und Kleist," in *Feministische Literaturwissenschaft. Dokumentation der Tagung in Hamburg vom Mai 1983,* ed. Inge Stephan and Sigrid Weigel (Berlin: Argument, 1984), 23–42.

36. My thanks to Walter Arndt, Dartmouth College, who translated Schiller's passages specifically for this essay.

37. See Gerhard Kaiser, in *DLFR,* 90.

38. See Neil Hertz, "Medusa's Head: Male Hysteria under Political Pressure," *Representations* 4 (Fall 1983): 27–50, the responses by Gallagher and Fineman in that same issue, and Inge Stephan's more feminist-historical analysis in Feministische Literaturwissenschaft, 29–40, especially 39. Klaus Theweleit's *Male Fantasies* provides an even more convincing argument for the linkage of cannibals and women by demonstrating how hatred of women is linked to the fear of being swallowed up, engulfed, or annihilated by them. See also Ronald Paulson, *Representations of Revolution 1789–1820* (New Haven, Conn.: Yale University Press, 1983) 9f., 22–42. The connection between contemporary depictions of transgressive femininity and Greek mythology (Bacchae, maenads, etc.) is established by Ines Lindner, "Die rasenden Mänaden: Zur Mythologie weiblicher Unterwerfungsmacht," in *Frauen, Bilder, Männer, Mythen. Kunsthistorische Beiträge,* ed. Ilsebill Barta *et al.* (Berlin: Reimer, 1987), 282–303.

39. This link was repeatedly established, for example, in Olympe de Gouges's *Déclaration des Droits de la Femme.*

40. Campe (16 May 1793), 57ff. "Continued lawlessness led to a sad decline [*Verwilderung*] in thought, the passions, and morality."

41. *Minerva* 1.1 (January 1792): 123.

42. Ines Lindner (299ff.) calls attention to this transfer of symbolic representations from Greece and Europe to the New World.

43. "Historische Nachrichten vom neuern Frankreich," *Minerva* 1 (January-March): 125–26: "There were deputies of the rulers of St. Domingo in Paris to ask for the immediate dispatch of troups and for official approval of some illegal measures. Their depiction of the terrors they had experienced was horrendous. The negroes had carried as their banner the body of a child on a spike. Not just the mean masters and their families were doomed to die, but even the most peaceful ones! 'I have done you nothing but good,' said a colonist to his slave who threatened to kill him. " 'This is true,' responded the latter, 'but I am bound by an oath to kill you.' . . . Another one of these kind men was murdered by his house-negro, and his wife was thrown onto her husband's dead body, where she had to suffer the bestial lust of these monsters, before she was strangled, too." etc.

44. *Revolutions-Almanach* (1795), 15–16.

45. "The Cannibals' Progress" (fn. 23) stresses the association between revolutionaries and colonial hordes. The French soldiers, who are supposedly violating German women at random, pillaging houses, and destroying crops, break out into "war whoops" (p. 23); they destroy altars, pollute the communion table with their ordure, desecrate the host, roast their meat on spikes on which they had formerly exposed the corpses of the beheaded; they "placed a crucifix before the fire, and amidst shouts of most indecent mirth, turned it round like meat roasting upon a spit" (p.10). And they spread syphilis, the disease which was supposedly brought over to Europe from the West Indies. Clearly, the author(s) of this pamphlet try to arouse, among other things, racist passions in their fight to preserve "Western culture" from heathens. In a curious inversion of the slaves-master model, they declare the revolutionary imperialists "slaves" who want to become masters by enslaving the rest of Europe. And in a further inversion, the text refeminizes the savage hordes when it refers to France's seductive but treacherous offering to other countries: a liberty "pregnant with mischief."

46. Henceforth I cite the German original of Kleist's narrative from Heinrich von Kleist, *Sämtliche Erzählungen* (Stuttgart: Reclam, 1984), 183–224, and the translation from *The Marquise of O—and Other Stories*, trans. David Luke and Nigel Reeves (London: Penguin, 1978-83), 231–269.

47. This parallel is explored by G.-L. Fink ("Das Motive der Rebellion in Kleists Werk . . .") and Ruth Angress ("Kleist's Treatment of Imperialism: 'Die Hermannsschlacht' and 'Die Verlobung in St. Domingo,' " *Monatshefte* 69 (1977): 17–33). As Angress points out, Kleist's novella "anticipates" C. L. R. James's analysis of the interrelatedness of the two revolutions; see *The Black Jacobins, Toussaint L'Ouverture and the San Domingo Revolution*, 2d ed. (New York: Random House, 1963). In the argument between Fink and Angress (*Kleist-Jahrbuch* [1988-89]: 89–95), I agree with Ruth Angress, since it appears that Fink does not take into consideration Kleist's narrative strategies that radically undermine, even shatter, any traditional positions on the Revolution.

48. Sander Gilman's analysis of Kleist's novella ("The Aesthetics of Blackness in Heinrich von Kleist's 'Die Verlobung in St. Domingo,' " *MLN* 90 (1975): 661–672) overlaps with mine as far as he also insists on the problem of limited perceptions. However, I do not agree with his exclusive focus on the black-white aesthetics at the expense of an "aesthetics of gender"; nor would I support his claim that Kleist is raising a universal question rather than a specific historical one. In fact, Kleist's general questions emerge from a very specific historical and economic situation, which I would define as the confluence of three very different kinds of "liberation movements" in the years 1789 to 1810, a confluence he is trying to reproduce in his narrative. Kleist's historical specificity is stressed both by Angress (fn. 52) and by P. Horn ("Hatte Kleist Rassenvorurteile? Eine kritische Auseinandersetzung mit der Literatur zur 'Verlobung in St. Domingo,' " *Monatshefte* 67. 2 (1975): 117–28.

49. Marianne Congreve's name, which couples the allegorical freedom goddess or republic Marianne with ("con") the Place de la Grève, aptly conveys Kleist's ambivalence toward a revolution that betrayed its own emancipatory goals on the guillotine.

PART FOUR

Crossing the Ocean

*

The French Revolution in the

Caribbean Imagination

Haiti's Tragic Overture: (Mis)Representations of the Haitian Revolution in World Drama (1796-1975)

VÈVÈ A. CLARK

Centennials inspire a curious mix of unquestioned restatement and skeptical reinterpretation when memory demands lavish, public celebration of major historical events. Whether bi-, tri-, or more, as in the case of the quincentennial of Christopher Columbus's explorations of the "New World," these occasions have become in the twentieth century a measure of Western civilization's progress and domination over time. Euro-American methods of periodizing history in contrasting and exclusive categories— B.C. and A.D., medieval and modern, modern and postmodern—eliminate world cultures from traditional chronologies. Euro-Americans have every right and duty to rememorize significant achievements, but to comprehend the full significance of the French Revolution, scholars of world history must challenge and enlarge the narrow focus on its representations as a purely European phenomenon. Oppositions between royalists and their upstart brethren during the French Revolution were not strictly an internal affair confined to the Continent. Since the late seventeenth century, France had been a prosperous colonial power, particularly in St. Domingue, soon to become independent Haiti in 1804. At the close of the eighteenth century, Revolution included not only class conflict in France but also slave revolts in the Caribbean.

Colonial rule does not begin abroad; initially the phenomenon accumulates power and acquires the skills of subjection at home. Control originates with the deletion of cultural memory among the peasantry living in the so-called provinces. When the ruling French elite succeeded in diminishing the importance of a provincial language such as *langue d'oc*, and, moreover, standardized correct speech through the offices of academies and dictionaries, they subjected the lower classes to a form of internal colonization.[1] Subsequently, a similar technique of control was applied to slaves providing labor and resources exported from the colonies to the home country. Such was the case in seventeenth-century France, and any evaluation of the Haitian Revolution must consider the patterns of domination that prevailed during that period and had originated centuries before.

French citizens who indicted monarchy and the rule of a minority ensconced in the Île-de-France were reacting in part to centuries of erasure of all but aristocratic and bourgeois definitions of French culture. Their rebellion, although focused on the seat of power in Paris, ultimately dismembered the network of French nobility that supported autocratic rule in the provinces.[2] Erasure of provincial cultural memory in seventeenth- and eighteenth-century France meant that regional peasant culture was denied its place in history and was effectively excised from the official written record even though local histories and cultures have survived, transformed no doubt, to this day.[3] Before the Revolution, the part spoke for the whole. Richelieu and the Louis had established a center-to-periphery relationship with peasants living within the country's borders. During the reign of Louis XIV two important documents—the Code Noir (1685) and the Treaty of Ryswick (1697)—forged a similar center-to-periphery relationship with St. Domingue. The Ryswick Treaty granted France dominion over the western portion of Hispaniola, wresting the area from former Spanish control; the Code Noir set standards for the importation of African slaves and the rules of behavior these subjects were bound to follow.

Throughout the eighteenth century, French rule in St. Domingue was presented as a near-legendary record of success. Because of its phenomenal production and exportation of sugar and coffee to the metropole, the island became known as the Pearl of the Antilles, and St. Domingue was considered the capital of colonial culture largely because the classics were periodically staged there by visiting French theater troupes invited to perform for the colonists in the theatres of Cap-Francois.[4] Were the story to end in 1791 before the Haitian revolt erupted, one might accept the benign depictions of colonial French behavior on the island and perhaps dismiss the abuses documented in historical records as infrequent and misguided aberrations. But the details of the Haitian Revolution and the circumstances demanding reform on the plantations contradict revisionist views that all was well. Representations of colonial progress by planters and travelers before, during, and after the Haitian Revolution distorted reality as the slaves knew it to be[5] and also failed to portray life on the plantations as a system of production and oppression invented long before disinherited French nobles, indentured servants, missionaries, and African slaves arrived on the island.

French colonization and settler practices in the New World followed a pattern the Spanish and Portuguese explorers and colonists had designed during the fifteenth century. Two centuries before France took control of St. Domingue, Spanish entrepreneurs had exhausted one of the island's attractions, gold, a commodity that the Tainos, the original inhabitants, were forced to mine for European rather than indigenous profit, and at the cost of their lives. By 1517, twenty-five years after Christopher Columbus's expedition established the first colonies in the New World, African slaves replaced the indigenous labor force, which by then had nearly disappeared.

The original inhabitants of the Caribbean—the Tainos, Arawaks, and Caribs—were not only made to perish but also deleted from historical memory by European cultural and political hegemony and its tacit rule of silencing those who serve the economic needs of colonialism. The silence prevails despite the existence of documents from the period that refute exalted portrayals of conquistador lore and settlers' versions of history. Bartolomé de Las Casas, writing in 1542 against settler abuses and in defense of the Indians, is supported by Tzvetan Todorov's recent critical studies of conquest. Both texts distinguish *invisibility* and *cultural dismemory* as phenomena associated with the less recognized side of Europe's overseas policies during the prerevolutionary era.[6] When the perspective of the silenced majority of mulattos and slaves living and working in the Caribbean emerges as countertext, the bicentennial of the French Revolution becomes a restricted representation, or *lieu de mémoire*, as Pierre Nora has defined the term.[7] Examining how colonial history has been largely constructed from a ruling-class perspective provides sufficient distance from received opinions that documented, albeit forgotten areas of world history might be restated, and our shared cultural memory thereby expanded.

Established memory is hierarchical and generally privileges northern over southern cultures. During the bicentennial of the French Revolution, some enlightened scholars included Latin American revolutions in scholarly discussion. Consistently, however, the southern subject came last, if not to imply least, in the chronology of events. In the case of the Haitian Revolution, that tendency reflects our habit of misrepresenting history as a stream of influence flowing from north to south, as though Caribbean history were but a by-product of northern development rather than an essential component of it. Ultimately, this view of history obscures the interrelationships between the French and Haitian revolutions.

In *real time* the Haitian Revolution (1791–1804) began two years after the French uprisings and lasted three years longer. The Trinidadian historian C.L.R. James demonstrated in his 1938 study, *The Black Jacobins, Toussaint L'Ouverture and the San Domingo Revolution*, that in 1794, when Jacobins approved full emancipation for the free *and* the enslaved in the colonies, they were responding to radical ideas proposed notably by some of the St. Domingue delegates to the Convention. After the abolition of slavery (4 February 1794), groups of mulatto freedmen vehemently opposed French revolutionary legislation that accorded equal status to freedmen and slaves, mulattos and blacks. During the Haitian Revolution, mulattos and blacks waged two different and, in a sense, separate wars against the French, determined by class and color antagonisms that the French Revolution helped to bring more clearly into focus. Although colonial in character, the Haitian conflict resembled similar socioeconomic upheavals occurring at the time in France. The pattern of dominance was not only comparable but reflexive. Both revolutions ultimately deposed an aristocratic elite—a number of whose sons had sought to revive their diminished financial status in the colonies; and both emancipated a suppressed majority—the peasant societies of France and St. Domingue.[8] Revolution in Haiti was far more closely linked to the French Revolution and more simultaneous than the recent celebrations would lead us to believe.

Performing the Other Side of History

From 1796 through 1975, a total of sixty-three plays concerned with the Haitian Revolution were either performed or published. Playwrights from Africa, the Caribbean, Europe, Scandinavia, and the United States have provided diverse interpretations of the event and its principal leaders, the Black Jacobins.[9] I have chosen four plays to discuss here as representative of the corpus. Each focuses on a single revolutionary figure—Toussaint Louverture or Henri Christophe. Moreover, the texts illuminate problems common to representation in historical and political theater, principally historicity and its reflection in mise-en-scène, characterization, and discourse. Dramas by Lamartine, Brierre, O'Neill, and Césaire demonstrate varied, original approaches to black liberation in the New World.[10] By focusing attention on Toussaint Louverture and Henri Christophe, the playwrights examine universal motifs associated with armed resistance and postindependence strategies during the years from 1791 to 1820. In this period of Haiti's tragic overture, Toussaint died in a Swiss prison, and his two most trusted lieutenants, who became his successors, each died abruptly. Dessalines, who ruled from 1804 to 1806, was hacked to death; Christophe, who ruled from 1807 to 1820, committed suicide. The tragic endings of these three leaders from Haiti's revolutionary era established an ambiguous code of behavior that during the 1960s provided a cautionary tale for future heads of decolonized states in the Third World.

The four plays I will examine belong to a tradition of political theatre. Largely designed to reflect or radically alter political realities, they celebrate *lieux de mémoire* and present the other side of mainstream history. By so doing, they show how decolonization, like the period of original settlement, promoted cultural invisibility and dismemory.

Representation is a central issue in political drama because of the playwright's often partisan approach to an event or problem.[11] The four plays discussed below illustrate successively three modes of interpreting and dramatizing historical events: *representation* or mimesis, *misrepresentation*, and *re-presentation*. These categories are neither mutually exclusive nor immutable; rather, they reveal the spectrum of ideologies and forms evolving within Haitian historiography and its dramatization over a period of 167 years. The mimetic dramas recreate the sequences of documented history. In these plays, Toussaint and Christophe generally appear as members of a formerly colonized elite imitating Jacobin political views, strategies, and even dress. Moreover, their characterizations emphasize military prowess and the cult of the persona, which survives to this day as *personalismo* in the Caribbean. Mimetic plays include Jean Brierre's *Adieu à la Marseillaise* (1934). Published the same year that American Marines were finally called home after almost two decades of occupation in Haiti, it tries to be representational in order no doubt, to correct previous deformations of the historical record, and perhaps also to reawaken the revolutionary spirit among Haitians. In *Adieu*, mimesis is intertextual. The ideology of the text implies revision of dismemory contained in previous dramas and dialogue with contemporary political affairs.

Misrepresentation in drama occurs when the ideology of performance either serves as polemic supporting solely one side of a political debate or deforms the historical record in order to reflect a preconceived construct. Eugene O'Neill's *The Emperor Jones* (1920) illustrates the latter tendency, as I shall demonstrate below. Mimesis was by no means the playwright's intent; adopting an expressionist approach, O'Neill confused personages and periods, transferred certain details of the Haitian Revolution to an Anglophone setting, and reframed the action in psychological rather than political terms. When an assuredly Francophone and Creolophone historical event is performed in standard English, French, or some other language, the drama distorts the bicultural environment in which the historical events unfolded. Many of the plays about the Haitian Revolution were written in French and, as a result, obscure the fact that the culture represented was then, as now, bilingual and diglossic—speaking both Haitian Creole and French, or Creole alone. Moreover, to recreate scenes of the Haitian Revolution in *alexandrins*, as Lamartine and Brierre do, misrepresents the bilingual landscape of the Revolution and the history of communication between colonials and African slaves beginning in the seventeenth century. This cross-cultural affiliation created among the peasants and the elite a common speech, Creole, that until the 1980s remained an unofficial mode of expression in Haiti.

A final category among these plays re-presents the Haitian Revolution in terms of indigenous Third World structures, notably the Creole language and Vodoun mythology. Edouard Glissant's *Monsieur Toussaint* (1961) relies on this kind of re-presentation. So does Aimé Césaire's *La Tragédie du Roi Christophe* (1963), which broke the convention of monolingualism by having peasants speak in *petit nègre*, a kind of colloquial French approximating Creole, with the elite conversing in a pompous, stylized French. Furthermore, Césaire's poetic evocation of Haiti's past departs from the Eurocentric, north-south mimetic tradition that treats Toussaint, Dessalines, and Christophe as black versions of the French Jacobins. During Christophe's reign (1807–1820), the accumulated prestige of Haiti's revolt, the threat of invasions, and internal class and color conflict led to excesses—invented by Christophe's ruling black elite—that were no longer modeled on the Jacobin example. Recognizing this fundamental difference, Césaire's re-presentation incorporates what is best understood as an east-west analogy between the leadership of elite Haitian generals and the theatre state, as anthropologist Clifford Geertz calls it, in nineteenth-century Bali.[13] The final word rests with Césaire's *Tragédie* because it illustrates *representation, misrepresentation* and *re-presentation* together more forcefully than do any of the other dramas.

The corpus devoted to the Haitian Revolution does not follow a predictable chronology from mimesis to misrepresentation to re-presentation. In fact the earliest text, *La liberté générale ou les colons à Paris* (1796) was a comedy glorifying abolitionist sentiments expressed by mulatto freedmen. The unidentified author, a certain Citizen B., defended emancipation of the slaves by ridiculing a *cabale* mounted from Paris by absentee colonists who sought to overturn the 1794 abolition of slavery and the very spirit of the French Revolution. Debate is strictly polemical; the colonists are caricatured in this drama and, as in several other works from the nineteenth century, the text engages overtly in misrepresentation. Abolitionism as an ideological posture among mulattos was double-voiced, as was their sociopolitical position at the time. The call for full emancipation by a single mulatto residing in Paris, where the play is set, thematically contrasts with mulatto opposition to this same principle in St. Domingue, where the play was first performed privately.[14] Lamartine's *Toussaint Louverture* (1848) belongs to this polemical tradition, but for different reasons described below. Subsequently, in plays performed after 1807, Haitian black and mulatto authors sustained a protracted debate over class and color dominance. Plays devoted to military exploits became political platforms, as the Haitian historian Henock Trouillot noted in the preface to his play, *Dessalines* (1967):

Antoine Dupré and Juste Chanlatte were among the first playwrights to rely on blocks of our history (for material). At the time, the type of history that attracted attention was alive and very close to them. General Lamarre, who after 1807 waged war against Christophe in the North, had scarcely died before Dupré celebrated him in drama as a national hero. In other words, the data of this fresh history had a polemic character, a quality of political propaganda to it. For the benefit of Port-au-Prince society and those living in other cities, one glorified Pétion's army, for instance, in order to disparage Henri Christophe's northern forces.[15]

During the midtwentieth century, such misrepresentation of the revolution was revised through mimesis and re-presentation by Jean Brierre and Aimé Césaire.[16]

Toussaint Louverture and *Adieu à la Marseillaise*

Lamartine's *Toussaint Louverture* (1848) and Jean Brierre's *Adieu à la Marseillaise* (1934) use different kinds of characters to treat a common problem. In one crucial scene in each of the dramas (Act 3.4 and 2.4 respectively), the playwrights dramatize what became in the 1930s the cultural dilemma of Négritude, and they anticipate the process of decolonization that occurred throughout the Third World in the 1960s. During this period, colonized subjects who had been alienated from their own culture by imported educational curricula were exposed to ritual practices, and through these developed pride in their indigenous origins.

In both of the plays, the conflict between imported and indigenous cultures reveals itself in characters representing Toussaint's sons—his stepson Placide Clerès and his natural son Isaac Louverture. According to historical record, Toussaint sent both young men to France before the revolutionary period to attend the Colonial Institute in Paris under the watchful tutelage of one Abbé Coisnon. The two were separated from their families in St. Domingue for six years. Once rebellion on the island became a demonstrable threat to French rule, Toussaint feared that his sons would be held hostage by Napoleon. Fortunately, the young men were sent home, but not simply as students. Accompanied by the Abbé and the French armed forces of General LeClerc, they had been given the task of assuring Toussaint that the French army had come to ensure peace—not to reenslave Toussaint and his people.

The playwrights present the homecoming in very different ways. From text to text, the reader must evaluate the playwrights' interpretation of historical events and their debt to literary history. In the case of Lamartine, who may have written *Toussaint Louverture* to express his anti-Napoleonic sentiments,[17] historicity gives way to invention at all levels of characterization. Though Brierre is more faithful to history, as we shall see, he was undoubtedly influenced by the Lamartine play. Most dramas of the Haitian Revolution written prior to the 1840s do not refer to Toussaint's sons. Lamartine's inclusion of them seems to have been original, and Brierre was content to follow his lead. Moreover, like Lamartine, Brierre wrote his drama in classic alexandrines, a form of versification that, after the seventeenth century in France, had become increasingly unsuitable for dramatic discourse and was well beyond the pale in 1934. Brierre's intertextual resources included as well a work by Massillon Coicou, another Haitian poet and dramatist, who wrote *Les Fils de Toussaint* (*Toussaint's Sons*) in 1895.

Dramatic contrast in *Toussaint Louverture* centers on the differing ideologies represented by Isaac Louverture and his brother—a character called Albert. When the two return to St. Domingue, the younger son, Isaac, who has been away from the colony for a shorter time, remembers the homeland fondly, and subsequently supports Toussaint's resolve to banish French hegemony from the island. Albert, the older, has assimilated French cultural norms to such a degree that he sides with the French against his own. Through the opposing perspectives of Isaac and Albert, Toussaint confronts his dual career as father and hero: must he choose St. Domingue over France, race before glory, flesh over destiny? For readers familiar with Haitian history, it is clear that Albert is a Lamartinian invention, for no such person appears in the historical record. Lamartine presents the character as a mediator between St. Domingue and France, father and hero, racial consciousness and assimilation. Albert's perspective is clear in Act 3, scene 4 when he declaims:

> Il est un plus beau sort, ah! laissez-nous le croire!
> C'est de confondre, enfin, dans un égal amour
> Le héros et le père à qui l'on doit le jour;
> D'être en les rapprochant le noeud qui les rassemble,
> D'aimer les deux en un, de les servir ensemble
> Et de faire à la fois, en les réunissant,
> Le bonheur de sa race et l'honneur de son sang . . .

> [There is a finer destiny, ah, let us trust
> That would finally merge into one equal love,
> The hero and the father to whom one owes one's life,

By bringing the two together, to be the knot that binds,
To love the two as one, to serve them together
And in uniting them, assure
The good fortune of the race and the honor of one's blood.] (118).

Lamartine's Albert illustrates both misrepresentation and re-presentation. The playwright has reversed the ideologically opposed positions of
the sons, for in fact it was Toussaint's assimilated natural heir, Isaac,
who refused to bear arms against France, while his elder stepson resolved to fight with Toussaint against the threat of occupation presented by
LeClerc's French forces. By casting Albert as mediator, Lamartine reforms
the passive role that the actual sons apparently played when Toussaint decided to fight LeClerc.[18] Through Albert's character, Lamartine portrayed
the phenomenon of double consciousness in 1848 well before W. E. B.
Dubois invented the term in 1903.[19] Moreover, Lamartine attempted to
reconcile the double consciousness of educated, colonial subjects in *Toussaint Louverture*. Albert's transnational consciousness was visionary and
would not be embraced and embodied by colonized individuals on a wider
scale until after the post-Independence period of the 1960s. At that time,
double consciousness developed not into an Hegelian synthesis, but into a
third point of awareness beyond dialectical representations of the very cultural dis-ease from which Toussaint's sons have suffered in both historical
accounts and in dramas.[20]

In *Adieu à la Marseillaise*, Brierre adheres more strictly to Haitian historiography. Following Lamartine and Coicou, he makes two central characters personify the opposition between race pride and alienation. But unlike
Lamartine, he correctly identifies Toussaint's sons as Placide and Isaac.
The true, attempted reconciler, according to Brierre, is none other than
the Abbé Coisnon who accompanied the Louverture *fils* on the mission.
Brierre has Coisnon say to Toussaint in Act 2, scene 4:

> Il faut croire, Monsieur, que Saint-Domingue, c'est
> Un morceau détaché de notre sol français.
> C'est la même fraicheur, la même mélodie
> Que sur les mamelons dorés de Normandie.
> Votre terre est aussi la terre des Héros . . .
>
> [Milord, you must realize that St. Dominique is
> A particle detached from our French soil;
> The chill of an evening, the same sounds
> Exist on the golden hillocks of Normandy.
> Your land too is a land of Heroes.] (91)
>
> Quand on est Louverture il faut qu'on se rallie
> Aux étendards français, où deja votre ciel

A l'avance hissa son azure immortel
Pour fixer son destin de Province Française.

[When you're a Louverture, you must rally
To the French banner, for your renown
Has already raised an immortal sign
Establishing its destiny as a province of France.]   (91)

Albert's apparent resolution of alienation and race pride in the Lamartine
drama suggests to Brierre a concession to commonwealth status or a form
of neocolonialism. It is a compromise more palatable when spoken by a
French citizen. Brierre makes this cogent point easily twenty-four years
before the debate over decolonization and neocolonialism preoccupied the
populace in France's remaining colonies of the African diaspora. Not until
1958 and DeGaulle's Referendum on African Autonomy would decolonization assume the magnitude it had in Haiti a century and a half earlier.
Brierre's *Farewell to the Marseillaise* adheres to the historical record in
mimetic style. Isaac Louverture was characterized, even at the time, as
righteously for France, and Placide Clerès as dedicated to a new St. Domingue. Their characterizations leave the dramatic contrast unresolved in this
particular scene.

The Emperor Jones

Eugene O'Neill's *The Emperor Jones* (1920) presented innovative approaches to mise-en scène and characterization. Although O'Neill does
not claim to represent the historical character of Toussaint, readers and
theatre goers have instinctively identified the play's protagonist with, if
not Toussaint, at least one member of the Haitian revolutionary triumvirate. Not unlike another drama in the corpus, Edouard Glissant's *Monsieur Toussaint* (1961), *The Emperor Jones* symbolically represents the fall
of a decolonized leader possessed by ghosts—the peasants whose revolt
prepared the way for one man's ascendancy. In both plays, the leader is
surrounded by admirers and threatened by enemies, yet cast as a solitary
individual besieged by the memory of failure. The playwrights' manipulation of time shows striking similarities. Isolated in the jungle, Brutus Jones
travels psychologically along the African-American emancipation trail in
reverse order from North America back to West Africa, while the action
of the play moves swiftly forward in the present tense toward his impend-
ing death. Jones's monologue at the center of the drama becomes a lyrical,
vertical departure bearing a perpendicular relationship to the horizontal
unraveling of the action. Using a similar configuration, Glissant sets the
four acts of *Monsieur Toussaint* on two planes: one horizontal—a com-

plex narration of the final hours Toussaint spent in his Swiss prison cell; the other vertical—a series of meditative confrontations between Toussaint and the gods (Act 1), the dead (Act 2), the people (Act 3), and the heroes (Act 4). At the level of structure, Glissant's debt to O'Neill seems apparent.

Scenic innovations in *The Emperor Jones* have been remarked upon often.[21] O'Neill rejected the conventional three-act format for a series of episodes in which dramatic contrasts were either suggested or demonstrated graphically. The action of the drama turns upon antithesis. Throughout, the Emperor's character is defined in opposition to the bush Negroes he has duped, ruled, and overtaxed—the same "ignorant" fellows who assassinate him in the final scene. The Emperor's rise to glory contrasts with his former low-life, prison existence and the fall from power portrayed visually in scenes where Jones is literally stripped of the regal, scarlet trappings of sovereignty, reduced to tatters and bare feet.

Characterization and setting have led to intriguing speculation about O'Neill's sources for *The Emperor Jones*. Since 1926, scholars have associated Brutus Jones with the regimes of three Haitian heads of state, namely Toussaint Louverture (1796–1802), Henri Christophe (1807–1820) and Vilbrun Guillaume Sam (22 March–27 July 1915). For evidence, critics have relied on O'Neill's remarks about the genesis of his work or on their familiarity with Haitian history. In a precise summary evaluation of the play, Margaret Ranald writes in *The Eugene O'Neill Companion* (1984): "The character of the Emperor Jones is modeled after Toussaint L'Ouverture, the Haitian revolutionary leader and former slave, treacherously mistreated by the French and also Vilbrun Guillaume Sam, of Haiti."[22] In a study first published in 1926, Barrett H. Clark quotes from a *New York World* interview of 9 November 1924 in which O'Neill is quoted as having said,

The idea of *The Emperor Jones* came from an old circus man I knew. The man told me a story current in Hayti [*sic*] concerning the late President Sam. This was to the effect that Sam had said they'd never get him with a lead bullet; that he would get himself with a silver one . . . This notion about the silver bullet struck me, and I made a note of the story.[23]

Finally, Horst Frenz, writing in 1971, elaborates upon the same story, and identifies Sam and Henri Christophe as inspirations:

A circus performer had told O'Neill the story of President Sam, dictator of Haiti, who spread the rumor that he was immune to ordinary lead bullets and could be killed only by a silver one, and who was finally hacked to pieces. O'Neill combined this figure with another Haitian dictator, a Negro slave named Henri Christophe who proclaimed himself emperor of part of Haiti and finally committed suicide.[24]

That Brutus Jones could represent three Haitian leaders of apparently different character who ruled during distinct historical periods and in a jungle
environment that had not existed on the island since the sixteenth century
is consistent with the expressionistic air of the drama.[25] The anachronisms
in the play do raise questions about the accuracy of O'Neill's reconstruction of the Negro collective unconscious in the Caribbean.

To clarify a number of misconceptions reproduced in the drama and in
subsequent critical response to its sources, one should note that O'Neill's
Brutus Jones is a composite based primarily on King Henri Christophe's
bravura statement that only a *silver bullet* would end his career and life.
The legend became for O'Neill the original inspiration and title of the
play.[26] Christophe was crowned *king* on 2 June 1811; the dubious title
of *emperor* never belonged to him, but rather to Dessalines, proclaimed
Emperor Jacques I on 8 October 1804.[27] As for the jungle setting, it was
inspired by O'Neill's negative encounters in Honduras,[28] a profound confrontation with his own 'heart of darkness' transformed into a Jungian
approach to Negro racial unconsciousness.[29] If, as rumor would have it,
President Sam resurrected in 1915 Christophe's nineteenth-century boast
about invincibility, his was a rather unoriginal restatement of legend; the
behavior is commonplace in Haitian political history.

By combining in Brutus Jones characteristics associated with three
heads-of-state, the text clearly misrepresents the historical record. It serves,
however, to remind the informed reader of the paradoxical scheme through
which Haiti's revolutionary tradition has been represented. On one hand
the noble deeds of Toussaint, and on the other dictatorial governance by
Dessalines and Christophe have defined the nation's political lore since the
early nineteenth century. Moreover, by including Sam in the portrait and
setting, *The Emperor Jones* implies that this peculiar, Janus posture persists residually among twentieth-century Haitian leaders. Three decades of
Duvalier rule (1957–1986)—*père et fils*—suggest ironically that O'Neill's
misrepresentations were prescient indeed. In his drama devoted to Henri
Christophe, Aimé Césaire would refigure the oppositions in other, more
cultural terms.[30]

More disturbingly, *The Emperor Jones* recalls nineteenth-century Haitian plays in which revolutionary figures appeared on stage for the purpose
of political persuasion. According to O'Neill, the drama "takes place on an
Island in the West Indies as yet not self-determined by White Marines."[31]
The play actually premiered five years *after* American marines occupied
Haiti (1915–1934). President Sam, deposed on 27 July 1915 by rival factions in Haiti, was replaced the next day by American forces. Speculation about possible political intentions on O'Neill's part seems far-fetched

and inconsistent with the playwright's characteristically dramatic intent. Nonetheless, the appearance of revolutionary heroes in fifteen plays written on the subject between 1915 and 1934 by Haitians and Americans alike suggests a dramatic contrast between life and literature worthy of attention. What effect, if any, did the *The Emperor Jones* and other plays of the period have on American sentiment regarding the invasion of a sovereign black state before Herbert Hoover's Forbes Commission (1930), under pressure from the Haitian opposition, advised the abandonment of what had become an ignominious intrusion?

La Tragédie du Roi Christophe

Glissant's *Monsieur Toussaint* (1961) and Aimé Césaire's *Tragédie* (1963), plays by two authors from Martinique, attempt to represent the Haitian Revolution in terms particular to the region. The life expectancy of such a radical change in ideology corresponds to a phenomenon defined by Geertz as the theatre state he observed in Bali. The analogies are fascinating despite the differences in cultural influences and native conflict operating in Indonesia and the Caribbean. Among the similarities are the ruling elite's need to imitate an exemplary code of behavior imposed by a foreign power, and the dependence of that same elite upon indigenous economic labor provided by a peasant underclass whose mores conflict radically with imported, upper-class behavior.[32] Toussaint and company, acting out French ideals of governing, contrast dramatically with their countrymen; in a theatre state as Geertz describes it, emulation and opposition measure the endangered order of the regime's limited existence. Like O'Neill, Glissant and Césaire question the value of emulating foreign behavior by causing Toussaint and Christophe to journey inward toward their indigenous ancestry.

Césaire's *La Tragédie du Roi Christophe* centers dramatic action outside the orbit of Toussaint's life, and by so doing shifts thematic concerns away, in part, from French-Haitian confrontations onto internal power relationships.[33] Under Dessalines and Christophe, major sociopolitical problems emerged following Toussaint's capture, the defeat of the French, and the subsequent metamorphosis of colonial St. Domingue into the Republic of Haiti. After 1806, the nation was divided by civil war, black North against mulatto Southwest. Alexandre Pétion, a mulatto freedman and military leader who had sided with the French at one point in his career, was the principal obstacle to black rule. Class and color antagonisms were intensified by the fundamental language division separating the ruling French-speaking elite from the Creolophone majority. Having written elsewhere on the rhetorical climate that existed in decolonized Haiti,[34] Césaire employs antithesis as the unifying principle shaping dramatic representation and discourse in his text. He accomplishes this strategy by juxtaposing oppositional behavior in contiguous acts or scenes expressed in language that reflects the (seeming) contradiction.[35] I would argue, moreover, that the political theory informing both the historical period and its representation in these dramas derives from the theater state ritual of emulation and opposition.

The incongruities of Dessaline's rule devolved under Christophe into a problematic atmosphere of outright political, social, and cultural opposition. After 1807, Haiti was divided; Christophe, the black former slave and cook, governed the North, and Pétion, the Paris-educated mulatto, ruled the Southwest. Each man headed a republic duly supported by his constituencies. During the thirteen years of his rule, Christophe's visions of progress and status were challenged simultaneously by mulattos and the masses.[36] He faced other challenges as well, particularly after he had the Citadel fortress built in Cap-Haitien to defend against the threat of French invasion. It is a symbol of black ingenuity and self-defense, and in 1820 became the burial place of King Henri Christophe I. Called the eighth wonder of the world, Citadel La Ferrière is said to have cost the lives of some 20,000 workers during its construction. The structure came to symbolize transcendence among the ruling elite and oppression of the peasantry, a sign of autocratic rule that reoccurs frequently in Haiti's history. To this day the Citadel remains an emblem of the sociocultural conflict that Césaire represented in drama.

Aimé Césaire's *Tragédie* plays upon antithesis. His version of Christophe's republic replicates the theatre-state model more closely than does Glissant's *Monsieur Toussaint*, primarily because King Christophe's reign exemplified the phenomenon far more demonstratively than Toussaint's did.[37] The fundamental antithesis between the center and the periphery (ruler and ruled) emerges in the prologue and the interlude between acts 1 and 2. From the prologue, the play builds in stages. Beginning with the disorderly rivalry among peasants at a cockfight, act 1 ends with Christophe at his apogee discussing with the architect Martial Besse plans for constructing the Citadel. From that point, the play descends into the disorder of act 3: in act 3.6, Christophe commits suicide using a silver (or gold) bullet; in act 3.9 his remains are buried within the confines of the fortress, La Ferriére.

Scenes juxtaposed at crucial moments in the drama reveal the antithetical relationships between peasant folkways and imported Jacobin culture. The prologue, for instance, consists of two parts, a cockfight and a commentary. In the initial disorderly scene gamecocks named for Pétion and

Christophe do battle, urged on by peasants dressed in customary blue denim. One of the cocks perishes, foreshadowing the death of one of the two leaders by the end of the play. Then, while the peasants remain on stage, a Commentator enters wearing period clothing of the French gentry. He interprets the preceding action and offers an historical précis by explaining the rivalry between Pétion and Christophe.

The Commentator: Fighting cocks used to have names like Drum Major or Peck-'is-Eye-Out; today they are named after political figures: in this corner Christophe, over there Pétion. It didn't appeal to me at first, but come to think of it, it's no more unreasonable than most fashions. A King and a President of the Republic are bound to tear each other's eyes out. And if they tear each other's eyes out, why not name fighting cocks after them? . . . But, you may argue, it's all very simple with fighting cocks, relations between men are more complicated. Not necessarily. The main thing is to understand the situation and to know the men the cocks were named after. Who is Christophe? Who is Pétion? That's what I'm here to tell you.

On the island of Haiti, formerly a French colony called Saint-Domingue, there lived, early in the nineteenth century, a black general. His name was Christophe, Henri Christophe, Henri with an i.

. . . At the death of Dessalines, of Dessalines the founder, the first Haitian chief of state, all eyes turned to Christophe. He was appointed President of the Republic. But as I have said, he was a cook, in other words, a shrewd politician, and as a cook, he felt that the dish they were offering him was short on seasoning, that this presidency was rather a hollow honor. Abandoning the city of Port-au-Prince to the mulattoes and to Pétion, their leader, he set himself up in the Northern Province. From then on, to make a long story short, two states coexisted in Haiti, and none too peacefully: in the South a republic, with Pétion as president, in the North a kingdom. There's the situation: Christophe and Pétion, two great fighting cocks, two calojies, as they say in the islands.

Yes, Christophe was King.

King like Louis XIII, Louis XIV, Louis XVI and a few others. And like every king, every true king, every white king I mean, he created a court and surrounded himself with a nobility.

But now I've said enough.

I give you Christophe, I give you Pétion. (8–10)

The Commentator as the solitary voice of History and Order literally upstages the collective, combative noise of the cockfight. His dispassionate discourse is metonymic, substituting eighteenth-century reasoned analysis for the impassioned, metaphoric speech and prophecies expressed during the peasant gaming scenario.

Césaire uses this contrastive strategy again at the end of act 1 and during the following interlude. In act 1.7 Christophe and Besse discuss their plans to build the Citadel (44–45):

Christophe: Ah, it's you, Martial Besse, the engineer, the builder. That's a good trade. That's what I want to be, the builder of this people. Well, Martial, haven't you anything to say? An idea? A suggestion?

Martial Besse: Majesty, to build up a patrimony for a people, its own patrimony of beauty, of power, of assurance! What task could be more worthy of a paraclete, of the man who calls a people to its outermost limits, who awakens them to their hidden powers.

Christophe: Thank you, Martial Besse . . . Thank you . . . Your idea is good: a patrimony. Except that I should speak of a patrimony of energy and pride. Yes, pride, why not? Look at the swelling chest of the earth, the earth stretching and tensing its loins as it shakes off sleep, the first step out of chaos, the first step to heaven.

Martial Besse: Majesty. These are terrifying slopes to build on.

Christophe: Exactly. This people has to want, to gain, to achieve something. Against fate, against history, against nature. That's it. Extravagant venture of our bare hands! Insane challenge of our wounded hands! On this mountain a solid cornerstone, a firm foundation. Assault of heaven or sun's resting place, I do not know—fresh troops charging in the morning. Look, Besse. Imagine on this very unusual platform, turned toward the north magnetic pole, walls one hundred and thirty feet high and thirty feet thick, lime and bagasse, lime and bull's blood, a citadel. No, not a palace. Not a fortress to guard my property. No, the citadel, the freedom, of a whole people. Built by the whole people, men and women, young and old, and for the whole people.
    Look, its head is in the clouds, its feet dig into the valleys. It's a city, a fortress, a battleship of stone. Impregnable, Besse, impregnable. Yes, Mr. Engineer, to every people its monuments. This people, forced to its knees, needed a monument to make it stand up. There it is. Risen! A watchtower! (Spellbound.)
    Look! . . . No, look! It's alive. Sounding its horn in the fog. Lighting up in the night. Canceling out the slave ship. Charging over the waves. My friends, the acrid salt we drank and the black wine of the sand, I, we, we who were flung ashore by the surf, I have seen the enigmatic prow, spewing blood and foam, plowing through the sea of shame.
    Let my people, my black people, salute the tide smell of the future.

A vision of the Citadel stands out, illumined, against a double chain of mountains.[38]

The polite tone of this conversation in the original French is followed by yet another antithetical Interlude. The dialogue is among peasants attempting to navigate Haiti's most arduous river. In contrast to the idealistic security reflected in the Christophe/Besse plan, the peasants' work is rough, unsteady, and filled with images of death. Death and imminent destruction in this scene encroach upon Christophe's notions of monumental triumph and mandarin court privilege.

Speech patterns provide a subtext for the play's antithetical structure. Césaire uses a multiplicity of voices in the scenes described above, where no less than five examples appear: Creole, *petit nègre*, French conversational, French precious, and a fifth that is stylistic rather than rhetorical— the incantatory, surrealist narration identified with Césaire's language in his epic poem, *Return to My Native Land* (1939). Creole appears prominently in the riverboat scene. When faced with the dangers of navigating safely through the last portion of their journey, the sailors implore Agwe, the Haitian Vodoun guardian of the waters, not to let their raft capsize: "Pas quitter bateau-la chavirer Aguay oh!" (67).

Meditations on death in 3.6–8 recall similar endings in *The Emperor Jones* and *Monsieur Toussaint*. Deeply troubled by his failure to unite the citizenry, Christophe approaches death in an environment borrowed from the Petro cult of Vodoun, where Baron Samedi crosses the ancestral waters to carry the deceased to the resting place. In this case, Hugonin—Christophe's former assistant—assumes the role of Baron Samedi. Even in these intimate scenes with Christophe, Madame Christophe, and Hugonin, the language is mixed: Creole, French precious, and surrealistic. The elite cannot separate itself from the cacaphony of surrounding voices. Through his use of language, Césaire suggests that antagonistic cultures and opinions invade Christophe's psyche and, in his weakened state, drive him to suicide.

Had the play ended here in scene 8, *La Tragédie* would simply have reproduced dramatic endings constructed by O'Neill and Glissant earlier. But by focussing in 3.9 on the burial of Christophe, I believe that Césaire created a theatre-state ceremony not unlike the Balinese example. Members of Christophe's court participate in the funeral along with peasants who carry the body to its tomb. The dialogue returns to the antithesis represented in the Prologue and Act I. Here peasants express their fears in *petit nègre* and the court speaks in polite French or Césairien poetic style. Opposition and emulation surround the body and memory of the deceased. The sure sign that the theatre-state model survives after a leader's death appears in the final speech declaimed by one of the courtiers, the African Page (3.8:152):

> Père, nous t'installons à Ifé sur la colline aux trois palmiers
> Père, nous t'installons à Ife dans les seize rhombes du vent
> A l'origine
> *Biface*!
> Ici patience et impatience défaite et victoire
> Faisceau d'écailles à contre-jour échangent leurs armes, leurs larmes.
> Force de nuit, marée du jour,
> Shango
> Je te salue, O . . . quand tu passeras par les promenoirs du ciel monté sur
> les beliers enflammes de l'orage. (Emphasis added)

> [Father, we enshrine you at Ifé on the hill of the three palm trees.
> Father, we enshrine you at Ifé in the sixteen rhombuses of the wind
> At the very outset
> *Two-faced*!

Here patience and impatience defeat and victory
Beams of tortoise-shells against the light
Exchange their weapons, then tears,
Power of night, tide of the day
Shango
I salute you, O . . . when you will pass through the arcades of the sky
mounted on the inflamed battering rams of the storm.]   (3:8–95)[39]

The principal oppositions of *La Tragédie* are accumulated in this ora-
tion. *Biface* is the key term describing both the state of political affairs and
its form of expression—the double-featured nature of Haiti's decolonization. In a departure from previous representations, *La Tragédie* transcends
the individual leader's wish to make peace with his past or, by embracing Africa as in *Monsieur Toussaint*, incorporate his persona into peasant
ritual practices. Dramatic action in scene 9 diminishes the role of the individual by focusing on his participation in a resurrected cycle of prestige
and privilege designed to dominate opposition—and never actually doing
so. Haiti's tragic overture is re-presented as a status ceremonial by Césaire,
and Geertz writing on Bali provides the grounds for comparison:

The whole (cremation) ceremony was a giant demonstration, repeated in a thousand ways with a thousand images, of the indestructibility of hierarchy in the
face of the most powerful leveling forces the world can muster—death, anarchy,
passion and fire. The king is annihilated! Long live his rank! (p. 120)

Rank and hierarchy do live on, even in contemporary Haiti as the regimes
of the Duvaliers and recent attempts at overthrow and free elections from
1986 to 1991 have illustrated.

Analysis of these four plays has revealed their construction of history, re-
assessed heroic characterization, and the discourse of radical social change.
As one would expect, historical dramas often distort documented evidence
in order to display the author's ideological perspective. Here we find a
tendency toward symbolic or psychological portrayals that represent, misrepresent, or re-present the accomplishments of a particular ruler's administration. Given the complexities of state rule, no three- to five-act drama
can pretend to be documentary; rather, these plays devoted to the details
of the Haitian Revolution provide a series of cautionary tales. By negative
example, the works suggest how one might avoid the tragic beginnings
that at once distinguished Haiti and led to the elaboration of an insidious
mode of governing. At this writing, the country has not yet successfully
replaced the theatre state with a more progressive model.

APPENDIX

Plays about the Haitian Revolution: A Preliminary Chronology [40]

1796	Haiti	Le Citoyen B., *La liberté générale ou les colons à Paris.*
1804	Haiti	P. Fligneau, *L'Haitien expatrié.*
1812	Haiti	Antoine Dupré, *La Mort de Lamarre.*
1812	Germany	Theodor Korner, *Toni.*
1818	Haiti	Juste Chanlatte, *L'Entrée du roi dans sa capitale.*
1819	Sweden	Frederick Cederborgh, *Toni.*
1820	Haiti	Juste Chanlatte, *La Partie de chasse du roi.*
n.d.	Haiti	Juste Chanlatte, *Nehri.*
1823	Haiti	Jean-Jacques Romane, *La Mort de Christophe.*
1824	Haiti	Anonymous, *L'Enfant de la Patrie au siège de Port-au-Prince.*
1832	Sweden	Andre Lindeberg, *Toni.*
1841	Haiti	Pierre Faubert, *Ogé ou le préjugé de couleur.*
1848	France	Alphonse de Lamartine, *Toussaint Louverture.*
1855	Haiti	Liautaud Ethéart, *La Fille de l'Empereur.*
1877	Haiti	Alcibiade Pommayrac, *La Dernière nuit de Toussaint Louverture.*
1893	U.S.A.	William Edgar Easton, *Dessaline.*
1894	Haiti	Massillon Coicou, *Liberté.*
1895	Haiti	Massillon Coicou, *Les Fils de Toussaint.*
ca.1896	Haiti	Vendenasse Ducasse, *1804.*
1896	Haiti	Vendenasse Ducasse, *Toussaint au Fort de Joux.*
n.d.	Haiti	Vendenasse Ducasse, *Noirs et Jaunes.*
1900	Haiti	Emil Domingue, *Guerre Civile.*
1901	Haiti	Verginaud Leconte, *Le Roi Christophe.*
1906	Haiti	Massillon Coicou, *L'Empereur Dessalines.*
1907	Haiti	Charles Moravia, *La Crête à Pierrot.*
1911	U.S.A.	William Edgar Easton, *Christophe, A Tragedy in Prose.*
ca.1917	Haiti	Isnardin Vieux, *La Fille de Geffrard.*
1917	Haiti	Isnardin Vieux, *Mackandal.*
1918	U.S.A.	William Dubois, *Haiti.*
1918	U.S.A.	Leslie Pickney Hill, *Toussaint L'Ouverture.*
1920	U.S.A.	Eugene O'Neill, *The Emperor Jones.*
1920	U.S.A.	John Matheus and Clarence White. *Ouanga* (opera).
1921	Haiti	Isnardin Vieux, *La Mort d'Ogé et Chavanne.*
1923	Haiti	Isnardin Vieux, *La Marche à l'Indépendance.*
1925	Haiti	Duraciné Vaval, *L'Apothéose.*
1925	Haiti	Dominique Hippolyte and Stéphen Alexis, *Soirée au Cap François avec Pauline Bonaparte.*

1931	Haiti	Annie Desroy, *La Cendre du passé*.
1931	Haiti	Jean F. Brierre, *Le Drapeau de demain*.
1932	Haiti	Jean F. Brierre, *Pétion et Bolivar*.
n.d.	Haiti	Jean F. Brierre, *Sur la Piste des géants*.
n.d.	Haiti	Christian Werleigh, *Tout pour le Roi*.
1934	Haiti	Jean F. Brierre, *Adieu à la Marseillaise*.
1935	Trinidad	C. L. R. James, *Toussaint L'Ouverture*.
1935	U.S.A.	May Miller, *Christophe's Daughters*.
1935	U.S.A.	Helen Webb Harris, *Genifrede, The Daughter of L'Ouverture*.
1935	U.S.A.	Langston Hughes, *Drums of Haiti* (rewritten as *Troubled Island* [1949], an opera with music by William Grant Still and later as *Emperor of Haiti* [1963]).
1939	Haiti	Dominique Hippolyte and Placide David, *Le Torrent*.
n.d.	Haiti	Dominique Hippolyte and Luc Grimaud, *Jour de Gloire*.
1942	U.S.A.	Selden Rodman, *The Revolutionists*.
1944	Haiti	Jeanne Perez, *Sanite Bélair*.
1946	Haiti	Languichatte, *De la Révolution à la liberté*.
1947	Haiti	Antoine Salgado, *La Rivière rouge*.
1940s	U.S.A.	Dan Hamerman, *Henri Christophe* (Federal Theater).
1950	St. Lucia	Derek Walcott, *Henri Christophe, A Chronicle in Seven Scenes*.
1954	Haiti	Marcel Dauphin, *Boisrond Tonnerre*.
1961	Haiti	Claude Vixamar, *Les Briseurs de chaînes*.
1961	Martinique	Edouard Glissant, *Monsieur Toussaint*.
1963	Martinique	Aimé Césaire, *La Tragédie du roi Christophe*.
1963	Haiti	René Philoctête, *Boukman*.
1967	Haiti	Hénock Trouillot, *Dessalines ou le sang du pont rouge*.
1973	Ivory Coast	Bernard Dadie, *Iles de Tempête*.
1973	U.S.A.	Percy E. Johnson, *Emperor Dessaline*.
1975	Haiti	René Philoctête, *Monsieur de Vastey*.

NOTES

My thanks to Judith Chazin-Bennahum and James Heffernan for their critical readings of this essay.

1. Suppression of Occitan actually began in 1539 with the Edict of Viller-Cotterets, which required that legal documents be written in French rather than Latin or any of the regional languages. Vincent Pollina kindly drew my attention to this document, but the analogies I am suggesting between internal and external colonization are my own. See also Pierre Bec, *La Langue occitane* (Paris: Presses universitaires de France, 1963).

2. Pierre Nora's stimulating essay, "Entre Mémoire et Histoire: la problématique des lieux" treats issues of memory and celebration. See *Les Lieux de Mémoires*, ed. Pierre Nora (Paris: Gallimard, 1984), xvii–xlii. An English version "Between Memory and History: *Les Lieux de Mémoire*" appeared in *Representations* 26 (Spring 1989), 7–25.

3. Studies of seventeenth-century peasant and provincial French societies have increased significantly since the 1950s. The range of approaches varies from comparative to case study. See, for example, Marc Venard, *Bourgeois et paysans au XVIIe siècle: recherche sur la vie agricole au XVIIe siècle* (Paris: S.E.V.P.E.N., 1957); E. Leroy Ladurie, *Les Paysans de Languedoc* (Paris: Flammarion, 1969); Peter Burke, *Popular Culture in Early Modern Europe* (New York: New York University Press, 1978).

4. Haitian historian Jean Fouchard has published several illuminating studies on colonial St. Domingue, all of which were reprinted in 1988 by Editions Henri Deschamps, Port-au-Prince, Haiti: *Les marrons du syllabaire*, 1953; *Plaisirs de Saint-Domingue*, 1955; *Le théâtre à Saint-Domingue*, 1955; *Artistes et répertoires des scènes de Saint-Domingue*, 1955; and *Les marrons de la liberté*, 1972.

5. For a description of colonial histories, see the annotated bibliography in C. L. R. James, *The Black Jacobins* (1938; New York: Random House, 1963), 379–389.

6. Bartolomé de Las Casas, *The Devastation of the Indies: A Brief Account*, trans. Herma Briffault (New York: Seabury Press, 1974). Perhaps not so ironically, it was Las Casas who suggested the importation of African labor to Hispaniola; see James, 4. See also Las Casas, *In Defense of the Indians*, trans. Stafford Poole (De Kalb: Northern Illinois University Press, 1974); Tzvetan Todorov, *The Conquest of America* (1982; New York: Harper and Row, 1984); and Hans Koning, *Columbus: His Enterprise* (New York: Monthly Review Press, 1976).

7. Nora, xvii–xx.

8. James compares the two revolutions in chapters 4 and 5 of *The Black Jacobins:* "The San Domingo Masses Begin," "And the Paris Masses Complete," 85–144. Patrick Bellegarde-Smith discusses Franco-Haitian nineteenth-century social policy in *In the Shadow of Powers: Dantès Bellegarde in Haitian Social Thought* (Atlantic Highlands, N.J.: Humanities Press International, 1985).

9. A chronological list of plays by authors from these countries appears in an appendix to this chapter.

10. The plays in question and the editions to which further mention refers are the following: Alphonse de Lamartine, *Toussaint Louverture* (Paris: Michel Levy

Frères, 1850); Jean Brierre, *Adieu à la Marseillaise*, bilingual edition in Spanish and French (Buenos Aires: Editorial Troquel, 1955); Eugene O'Neill, *The Emperor Jones* (New York: Boni and Liveright, 1921); Aimé Césaire, *La Tragédie du roi Christophe* (Paris: Présence Africaine, 1963, 1970). The original version of this study included Edouard Glissant's *Monsieur Toussaint* (1961) and Hénock Trouillot's *Dessalines ou le sang du pont rouge* (1967).

11. See for example Ronald Paulson, *Representations of Revolution, 1789–1820* (New Haven: Yale University Press, 1983). The representation of blacks and mulattos in French Romantic literature, including Lamartine's play, is addressed in Léon-François Hoffmann, *Le Nègre romantique: personnage littéraire et obsession collective* (Paris: Payot, 1973). Max Dorsinville's chapter, "Le Silence des commencements" discusses O'Neill's play and generally the theme of the Haitian Revolution in literature. *Solidarités* (Montreal: CIDIHCA, 1988), 135–144.

12. French is still Haiti's official language, but since the departure of Jean-Claude Duvalier in February 1986, Creole has become more accepted in primary education, publishing, and advertising.

13. Clifford Geertz, *Negara, The Theatre State in Nineteenth Century Bali* (Princeton, N. J.: Princeton University Press, 1980).

14. Robert Cornevin, *Le Théâtre haitien des origines a nos jours* (Québec: Leméac, 1973), 39–40; Jean Fouchard, *Le Théâtre à St. Domingue* (Port-au-Prince: Editions Henri Deschamps, 1988).

15. From the preface of *Dessalines ou le sang du pont rouge,* (Port-au-Prince: Imprimerie des Antilles, 1967), 4 (my translation).

16. Haitian playwrights have treated the theme of the Haitian Revolution more often than writers from other countries. Of the sixty-three dramas in the corpus, forty-two are from Haiti, twelve from the United States, four from elsewhere in the Caribbean, two from Sweden and one each from France, West Africa, and Germany. Through 1975, the subject has remained a decidedly New World concern, given that fifty-eight of the plays are by Caribbean and North American authors. Among the list appear the names of renowned writers such as C. L. R. James, Langston Hughes, Jean Brierre, Derek Walcott, Edouard Glissant, and Aimé Césaire. Descriptions of the plays by Haitians appear in Cornevin's detailed account of historical dramas; see *Le Théâtre haitien* (1973).

17. See, for example, Henry Cohen's "Lamartine's *Toussaint Louverture* (1848) and Glissant's *Monsieur Toussaint* (1961): A Comparison," *Studia Africana* 1.3 (Fall 1979): 255–269. For a discussion of Lamartine's abolitionist activities and his contribution to the genre known as "negrophile drama," see Ardell Striker, "Spectacle in the Service of Humanity: The Negrophile Play in France from 1789 to 1850," *Black American Literature Forum*, 19.2 (Summer 1985): 76–82.

18. Documentation of the sons' return to St. Domingue in the company of Abbé Coisnon is recorded in historical studies and biography: C. L. R. James, *The Black Jacobins*; Percy Waxman, *The Black Napoleon* (New York: Harcourt, Brace and Company, 1931); Ralph Korngold, *Citizen Toussaint* (Boston: Little, Brown, 1945).

19. W. E. B. Dubois, *The Souls of Black Folk* (Greenwich, Conn.: Fawcett Publications, 1961).

20. On the theory of a third non-linear, spiralist response to oppositions see Vèvè Clark, "Marasa: Images of Women from the Other Americas," *Woman of Power* 1.1 (1984): 58–61; Maximilien Laroche, *Le Patriarche, Le Marron et La Dossa: Essais sur les figures de la gémellité dans le roman haitien* (Sainte-Foy,

Québec: GRELCA, 1988); and Clark, "Developing Diaspora Literacy and *Marasa* Consciousness," in *Comparative American Identities: Race, Sex and Nationality in the Modern Text*, ed. Hortense Spillers (New York: Routledge, forthcoming 1991).

21. Notably, the constant drum rhythm throughout the play and its rise to a crescendo punctuating Jones's firing at imagined menaces were considered daring innovations.

22. Margaret L. Ranald, *The Eugene O'Neill Companion* (Westport, Conn.: Greenwood Press, 1984), 207.

23. Barrett H. Clark, *Eugene O'Neill, The Man and His Plays* (New York: Dover, 1926), 72.

24. Horst Frenz, *Eugene O'Neill*, (New York: Frederick Ungar, 1971), 30.

25. In the Wilderness Edition of O'Neill's plays, the playwright restates the story about the old circus man and identifies President Sam alone as the inspiration for *The Emperor Jones*. In addition, innovative staging was inspired by O'Neill's exposure to Congolese drumming and personal experiences in Spanish Honduras. *The Emperor Jones* (New York: Charles Scribner, 1934), 145.

26. Ranald, 208.

27. See, for example, Robert Debs Heinl and Nancy Gordon Heinl, *Written in Blood: The Story of the Haitian People 1492–1971* (Boston: Houghton Mifflin, 1978).

28. Louis Sheaffer, *O'Neill, Son and Playwright* (Boston: Little Brown, 1968), 151–154.

29. Ranald, 206.

30. The Janus posture to which I have alluded is not simply a question of personality or political expediency on the part of Toussaint, Dessalines, and Christophe. The paradox seems to be culturally constituted and embedded in Haitian peasant belief systems, which figure the *lwa* (ancestral spirits) as opposed forces representing benevolence and malevolence, good and evil at once. For ethnographic documentation of the phenomenon, see Maya Deren, *Divine Horsemen* (New York: Thames and Hudson, 1953); Milo Rigaud, *Secrets of Voodoo* (New York: Arco, 1969); and Alfred Métraux, *Voodoo in Haiti* (New York: Schocken Books, 1972).

31. Eugene O'Neill, *The Emperor Jones*, 145.

32. Clifford Geertz, *Negara, The Theater State in Nineteenth Century Bali*. Historians and literary critics have been content to define various Haitian governments as authoritarian. The label is accurate, but not nearly as revealing as the theater-state model. In precolonial Bali and nineteenth-century Haiti, the theatre state was an amalgamation of several political ideologies that *resemble* comparable forms in the Western world but do not correspond entirely to them. *Negara* may appear feudal because of the "sinking status relationship from lord to lord" (p. 32), although it is not a feudal society. As in Haiti, this is a unique response to statehood.

33. In the body of this text, I have not discussed historicity, but in the preface, Glissant does point out the degree of mimesis or lack of it in his play. In two articles, Henry Cohen has shown how Césaire distorted the historical record in *La Tragédie*. See "History, Invention and Césaire's Roi Christophe," *Black Images* 2.3–4 (1973), 33–36; and "The Petrified Builder: Césaire's Roi Christophe," *Studies in Black Literature* 5.3 (1974), 21–24.

34. Aimé Césaire's study of Toussaint, *Toussaint Louverture: La Révolution française et le problème colonial*, was originally published in 1960 by *Présence Africaine*.

35. In all probability, Césaire was influenced by three of Jean Genêt's postwar plays. In *The Maids* (1947), *The Balcony* (1956), and *The Blacks* (1958), Genêt dialectically presented power disputes concerned with class conflict, rebellion, and race. His method reproduced the conflicts thematically and theatrically by causing theme, structure, setting, and discourse to converge.

36. For the interested reader, the following provocative readings of *La Tragédie* are enlightening on the play's political perspective and discourse: Marc A. Christophe, "Totalitarianism and Authoritarianism in Aimé Césaire's *La Tragédie du Roi Christophe*," *CLA Journal* 22.1 (September 1978): 31–45; Serge Gavronsky, "Aimé Césaire and the Language of Politics," *French Review*, 55.2 (December 1982); 272–280; Bernard Mouralis, "L'Image de l'indépendance haitienne dans la littérature négro-africaine," *Revue de Littérature Comparée* 48.3–4 (July–December 1974); 504–535; Liliane Pestre de Almeida, "Christophe, cuisinier, entre nature et culture," *Présence Africaine* 105–106.1 and 2 (1978): 230–249; Daniel-Henri Pageaux, *Images et mythes d'Haiti* (Paris: L'Harmattan, 1984).

37. Geertz's descriptions of the theater state in Bali provide a useful comparison to Christophe's obsession with building a citadel. *Negara* is a Sanskrit loan word meaning "palace, capital, state, realm, and town." In precolonial Indonesia, *negara* represented high culture and classical civilization. Its opposite was the *desa* or countryside, the governed area or masses. Before *negara*, chaos existed; after *negara* perfection became the doctrine of an exemplary government that embodied the faultless, civilized world. Political power was an accumulation of prestige, including authority, virility, charisma, violence, service, and worship guided by hereditary leadership. The court was located in the city; its most sacred areas faced mountainward away from the tumult of the sea. It was opposed to the countryside of the masses, which derived its own control from trade routes leading seaward. Commercial alliance networks among the masses supported the center and were responsible for the state of the economy (Geertz, 4, 13, 32, 97, 109). The analogies to the Haitian situation from 1807 to 1820 deserve further examination, for they suggest a definition of statecraft that is also thespian.

38. The translation is by Ralph Manheim from *The Tragedy of King Christophe* (New York: Grove Press, 1970), 95. Manheim's version does not always follow the original; the interlude, for instance, has been omitted from the English translation.

39. This passage was translated by Keith Walker.

40. The Chronology has been compiled from information provided in the following sources: Robert Cornevin, *Le Théâtre haitien* (1973); Raphael Berrou and Pradel Pompilus, *Histoire de la littérature haitienne*, 3 vols. (Port-au-Prince: Editions Caraïbes, 1975–1978); Jean Fouchard, *Le Théâtre a St. Dominque* (Port-au-Prince: Imprimerie de l'Etat, 1955); Hénock Trouillot, *Les origines sociales de la littérature haitienne* (Port-au-Prince: Théodore, 1962); Duraciné Vaval, *Histoire de la littérature haitienne* (Port-au-Prince: Héraux, 1933), Harold Waters, *Black Theater in French, A Guide* (Sherbrooke, Can.: Editions Naaman, 1978); and Errol Hill, "The Revolutionary Tradition in Black Drama," *Theatre Journal* 38.4 (December 1986): 408–426.

Carpentier's Enlightened Revolution, Goya's Sleep of Reason

BEATRIZ PASTOR

In the midst of Alejo Carpentier's novel *El siglo de las luces,* Sofia opens the door of the family home to Esteban, her long-gone cousin. Summing up his four years of total immersion in the events of the French Revolution, his first words to her are: "I come from living among the barbarians" (Vengo de vivir entre los bárbaros). Since the time of the discovery, the Old World has always been associated with civilization and the New World with barbarism. Esteban's radical inversion of these terms expresses his global rejection of the realities of that same revolution to which he had sworn passionate allegiance four years earlier, of the same historical processes in which he had been totally immersed: first in Paris, then in northern Spain, and finally in the Caribbean where, following the gradual expansion of revolutionary ideals, he had sought to devote his whole life to the revolutionary transformation of society.

The paragraph that narrates Esteban's return to Havana further elaborates on the depth of his rejection of an experience that is characterized as a "nightmare":

The colors, the sounds, the words that still haunted him gave him a deep feeling of distress, not unlike the anguish that weighs heavily on our chests, in that same area where anguish becomes throbbing, pounding, arrythmia, and visceral convulsion in the early stages of recovery from an illness that could have been lethal.[1]

But the significance of Esteban's statement goes well beyond his deep malaise and his personal experience of the events of the revolution.

Within the context of modern Latin American history, the significance of the French Revolution transcends the impact of the actual ideas that shaped the revolutionary project itself. It symbolizes the very transition between an oppressed, backward, colonial Latin America, and an enlightened, dynamic, independent Latin America in search of an identity regenerated by the ideals of the French Enlightenment. To modern Latin America, the French Revolution signals Latin America's access to the modern world, its rejection of colonial obscurantism, its enthusiastic participation in the struggle for the light of independence, justice, and self-definition. But who formulated these ideas of the Enlightenment in Latin America? What social groups would import, disseminate, share, and articulate these ideas into individual national programs while controlling the record and weaving the story of their own rise to power into the historical narratives that became the new history of Latin America as opposed to the old, the colonial accounts spoken by the voices of the metropoli and invested with the authority of the crown?

I can answer these questions only in part. The philosophy of the Enlightenment nurtured all the great thinkers and leaders of the struggle for independence, but it also provided the ideological grounds and political rationale for the rise of an alliance between the new liberal bourgeoisie and the old Creole aristocracy. In the long power struggle of these social groups against Spanish domination, a struggle that would eventually lead to the independence of Latin American countries, the political discourse of revolutionary France provided models, rationales, and alternatives that helped legitimize the rise to power of a new oligarchy as a movement for the good of the people, that is, of all "Americans, of any state, profession, color, age and gender." [2] What was lost in this rise to power was precisely the revolutionary spirit and principles so often invoked rhetorically by the newly empowered social groups. During the nineteenth and twentieth centuries, they would shape the development and underdevelopment of Latin America not so much according to enlightened revolutionary ideals as to their own economic and class-determined interests. In this sense the history of the inscription of the ideals of the French revolution in Latin American culture and politics is also the history of their betrayal. [3]

Esteban's inversion of the terms *civilized* and *barbarian* explicitly questions the nature of the Enlightenment and the meaning of the French Revolution. At the same time, it implicitly undermines two historically different discourses. It not only challenges the traditional binary opposition between metropolis and colony instituted with the conquest of America and perpetuated through the colonial period; it also rejects the new version of that opposition that would be used by the thinkers and politicians of the process of independence to legitimize their growing economic, ideological, and cultural dependency on European countries—specifically France and England—and to provide models of race and culture that would rationalize the continued oppression of certain social groups (e.g., the gaucho) and the virtual genocide of some native populations. [4]

Within the Latin American context this challenge is far from marginal, for despite betrayals and contradictions, the quests for independence and the political programs launched throughout the nineteenth century, when Latin America's modern states were constituted, were inspired by the rationalism of the Enlightenment and by the ideals of the French Revolution. Consequently, any critical reevaluation of the meaning of the Revolution and its impact on Latin America inevitably becomes a critique and demystification of a chapter of history that, in many ways, has come to represent the birth of modern Latin America.

Who could be better equipped to deconstruct Latin American myths of independence and revolution than the Cuban writer Alejo Carpentier? Born in Havana of a European father in 1904, educated in France, a member of the European avant-garde in the twenties and thirties, a political exile from Batista's dictatorship in the fifties, a sacred figure of the Cuban revolution since the sixties and a central figure of Latin America's culture throughout his entire life, Carpentier embodies in many ways the systematic probing of the endless series of oppositions—civilized vs. barbarian, French vs. Spanish, European vs. American, white vs. black, capitalist vs. socialist, and so on—that shape the dynamics of self-definition in Latin American countries seeking autonomy and self-determination.

Carpentier's systematic probing of these oppositions provides a starting point for a reading of his novel *El siglo de las Luces* (1962), literally "The Age of Enlightenment,"[5] wherein the literary representation of the events of the French Revolution and of their impact on Latin America becomes simultaneously a meditation on Western culture, a critical reevaluation of revolutionary processes and historical narratives, and a lucid reflection on modern Latin American sociohistorical realities. *El siglo de las luces* is an extremely dense, richly textured, complex, and in some ways contradictory text, one that invites endless readings. In dealing with it here, however, I would like to show how Carpentier's version of the French Revolution becomes a global critique of its philosophical underpinnings.

The novel begins in Havana, in 1789, with the death of a wealthy Cuban merchant. He leaves two children, Sofia and Carlos, and a nephew, Esteban. After a year of mourning, which the orphans spend locked up in the family mansion, their isolation is broken by the visit of Victor Hughes. A French businessman from Port-au-Prince, Hughes also turns out to be a freemason and a revolutionary who will expose Sofia, Carlos, and Esteban to the ideals of the French Revolution. Fleeing from repression in Cuba, Victor and Esteban go to Paris and eventually return to the Caribbean as high representatives of the French revolutionary government. The novel narrates the processes of transformation brought about by the revolution first in Europe, then in the Caribbean. Catapulted to power during the Terror, Victor Hughes is subsequently demoted and purged, becoming a well-known pirate before being rehabilitated and named governor of Cayenne, his last high political position on this continent. Esteban, on the other hand, spends many years in prison on charges of conspiracy against the Spanish crown before being rescued by the efforts and influence of Sofia. The novel closes with the events of 2 May 1808, when the people of Madrid rose up against Napoleonic domination and Spain began its war of independence from the French.

In a way, the first few sections of the novel prefigure the revolutionary events that follow, but their relationship to these events cannot be called simply "expansion"—the term some critics have used to describe the development of Carpentier's account of the Revolution.[6] The death of the father initiates a series of cycles that anticipate, in the private and personal sphere in which the orphans are confined, the great public stages of revolutionary upheaval. In the first of these cycles, freedom takes the form of unrestrained creative imagination. All schedules are disrupted and all routines broken when the orphans turn their backs on the paternal order represented by the warehouse, with its perfectly classified merchandise grouped by kind, by price, by value, by demand. In the warehouse, even chaos and heterogeneity are rationally ordered. Beyond the stock of Spanish cheeses, the rows of flour sacks, and the barrels of oil or good wine is a vault reserved for odd and superfluous things, playing cards and umbrellas, gold leaf and Andean blankets. But the orphans reject the warehouse, spurning this emblem of a rational order determined by usefulness and profit. Out of their own unpredictable purchases of unpredictable things (either superfluous, useless, or made useless by the orphans' refusal to acknowledge their predefined function), the orphans create their own timeless space. It is a space of perfect freedom generated by the systematic disruption of accepted order and the imaginary transformation of the countless unopened crates, trunks, and cartons loaded with Sofia's French furniture, china, and art objects, Carlos' musical instruments, and Esteban's physics-laboratory artifacts. Implicitly turning values, functions, and rules upside-down, the orphans' play shapes their existence in an endless rhythm of constant transformation, of continuous carnivalesque inversion.[7]

Victor Hughes's arrival, however, signals the beginning of a second cycle. His first visit takes place on *Sábado de Gloria,* the Saturday before Easter Sunday, also called Resurrection Saturday in the Catholic tradition. Indeed, his arrival represents in more than one way the resurrection of the authority (Sofia is outraged by the ease with which Victor takes on the role of the *pater familias*) that the father's death had symbolically cancelled, the end of a period of perfect freedom and unlimited possibilities. Carpentier's first characterization of Victor gives him a certain timeless, mythical quality that prefigures both Esteban's perception of the revolutionary event as frozen in time, or suspended outside of time, and Carpentier's archetypal representation of the revolutionary process as a recurrence of cycles. Victor is "a man without age" who takes over the space of innocence opened up by the father's death and who, simultaneously, reinscribes it in the outside world, forcing the return of the three orphans to history. Under his direction, free play becomes representation and fantasy yields to historical imagination as he and the three young people play and replay the roles of great historical figures in a succession of charades that concludes with the "great massacre" wherein kings, priests, ladies, and captains are symbolically destroyed.

The archetypal projection of Carpentier's narration of these events is clear in the mythical characterization of Victor, but the specific relationship of these cycles to the revolutionary processes that follow is made even clearer by the quotation of the title of one of Francisco de Goya's *Caprichos* at the beginning of part 4. The title "Siempre sucede" (It always happens) signals the transformation of the particular into the general, identifying the private incidents in the Cuban mansion with the collective processes of the historical events that follow, and these with Revolution itself. The symbolic death of authority, followed by carnivalesque inversion and the limitless possibilities of innocence recovered through unlimited freedom, is soon succeeded by these new forms of authority and by the creation of a new order disposed and controlled by these new forms. Creativity turns into role playing, innocence into manipulation, dreams into symbolic destruction, and the playful charades staged by Victor and the orphans become the historical drama of the French Revolution.

The death of the father opens up a mythical replay of the struggle between freedom and authority, between innocence and betrayal, and this replay metaphorically anticipates Carpentier's representation of the French Revolution. The arrival of Victor Hughes signals the return of authority and the end of innocence. Within the novel the loss of innocence unfolds through a series of personal betrayals that prefigure Carpentier's representation of the Revolution as it developed in France and as its ideals were assimilated by Latin America.[8]

To the young and dazzled Esteban the revolution is first a natural process of inevitable creation. His perception is close to Sofía's when, in her observation of nature, she marvels at the ceaseless destruction of existing organisms—jellyfish, sea anemones—in the endless process of creation.

Yet while everything seems joyful, singular, unpredictable, charming, or admirable, the fabulous spectacle of the revolution gradually undermines Esteban's sense of concrete reality: "More and more one felt submerged in a gigantic allegory of the Revolution, indeed, in a metaphor of Revolution—a revolution being actually carried out somewhere else, supported by hidden pillars, developed in secret deliberations, invisible to those who wanted to know everything" (p. 97). Paradoxically, the closer Esteban gets to the events of the Revolution—Paris, Spain, the Caribbean—the more removed he feels from it, and his increasing alienation illuminates his growing inability to reconcile the concrete events of the Revolution with Victor's revolutionary rhetoric and with his own revolutionary ideals and dreams. Like Fabrizio del Dongo, who fails to see the battle of Waterloo from the very place where it is occurring, Esteban will fail to verify in Paris his heroic preconceptions about the nature of the revolutionary process; the meaning of the events and of his own involvement in the Revolution will increasingly elude him. His active participation will neither confirm his dreams nor dispel his doubts nor answer his questions; instead, it will undermine his former convictions, forcing the transition from a heroic mode to a skeptical one. Fabrizio gives way to Mosca, Stendhal to Milan Kundera, transcendental visions to the unbearable lightness of being.

Throughout the narration of Esteban's experience, the novel articulates a severe critique of the French Revolution. The revolutionary process is defined as an endless succession of betrayals; its dynamics are identified with the ups and downs of characters trapped in an endless series of power struggles, while those same power struggles appear to provide the only movement within the revolutionary process itself. Along with them, disillusionment, violence, corruption, and degradation of revolutionary ideals are the immediate yield of the revolution in this novel: the revolutionary becomes a tyrant, the freedom fighter turns into a new oppressor, the incorruptible is corrupted or murdered. Power is once again taken away from the deprived, free blacks are hunted down and returned to their former masters, innocent people are jailed or executed. Like Victor, the merchant may become a hero, the hero a politician, the politician a pirate, the pirate a merchant, in a constant permutation of roles dictated by the contingencies of the struggle for power. And the game of permutation hides the lack of true revolutionary change. The illusion of movement it creates brings neither progress nor revolutionary transformation. Rather, it results from a succession of analogous cycles in which names change but functions remain the same. The concept of progress disappears, and so does the concept of history as linear time gives way to the recurrent repetitions of mythical time. The outcome of each cycle—either death or repetition—implicitly cancels the existence of revolutionary change, while the displacement of historical time by mythical time seems to project the French Revolution beyond its specific historical context, implicitly equating its dynamics with the dynamics of revolution itself.

Within the novel, the revolutionary process begins in France and then travels to the New World. But this spatial movement, which could suggest the very concept of historical progress that cyclic repetition overturns, is offset by the symbolic equivalence of the beginning and the end of the cycle. The revolutionary action that began in a prison, the Bastille, concludes in the prison camps of Cayenne, where the former heroes of the Revolution live a lingering death of sickness and exile. The prisoners of Cayenne are different from those of the Bastille, but the identification of the beginning and end of the revolutionary cycle with the image of the prison has two immediate effects. First, it implicitly cancels any form of revolutionary change or progression; in a process that claims to be a fight for freedom, a movement toward liberation, the only movement is from prison to prison. Secondly, within the context of this equivalence, the French Revolution is demythified. Its development ceases to exemplify the struggle of light against darkness, reason against ignorance, justice against injustice; instead it becomes simply a shift from one form of oppression to another.

Besides using the Bastille and Cayenne to expose the futility of the French Revolution, Carpentier demythifies the Revolution further by challenging one of the most influential ways of defining the historical relationship between Europe and Latin America: the theory of dependency. Insofar as it represents the movement of French revolutionary ideas and processes to the New World, the novel seems to endorse the concept of Latin America as the child of Europe. But in two ways the novel explicitly rejects this model of interaction between "civilized" Europe and the "barbaric" Third World. First, Esteban's summary of his experience of the French Revolution reverses the key terms of the theory. Secondly, the novel assigns an originating role to Latin American revolutions. Reversing the direction of movement postulated by the theory of dependency, it presents Latin American black uprisings as a model for the French Revolution rather than the other way around. Sieger—the Swiss revolutionary sent to Cayenne during the Terror—says that all the French Revolution has done for blacks in Latin America is to legalize a much older political phenomenon: the "Gran Cimarronada" (the Great Escape).[9]

Esteban rejects the French revolution because of a personal experience that forces him to particularize abstract ideals and revolutionary principles, verifying them against his direct involvement in concrete historical reality. Carpentier's critique, however, moves the other way. Passing beyond the specifics of the French Revolution and Latin American history, it scrutinizes more general principles that would account not just for the dynamics of the French revolution but of other modern revolutions as well. Some stylistic features of Carpentier's writing—e.g., his use of capitalization—indicate precisely this. As he seeks to explain some of the great movements of modern Western history, he reminds us that his critique reaches beyond the specifics of its historical context.

If the French Revolution was, as Esteban claims, a failure, what explains a failure of such magnitude? If it was mythified in the historical accounts, why was it mythified and what is the key to its deconstruction? How does Carpentier evaluate the Enlightenment and the Revolution and how does he express his evaluation in *El siglo de las luces*?

Part of the answer can be found in Esteban's first and last vision of the Revolution: the *Explosion in a Cathedral*, the painting by the anonymous Neapolitan master.[10] Initially an emblem of Esteban's early fascination with revolutionary upheaval, the painting hangs in the palace of Arcos, in Madrid, long after his disillusionment with the French Revolution. It symbolizes that disillusionment by its opposed sides: the perfect order of majestic columns on one side, destruction and chaos on the other. Timelessly freezing the confrontation of permanence and change, harmony and turmoil, the painting represents for Esteban the illusion of rational order at the very site of its destruction.

But Esteban's final reading of the Revolution is not the only reading of it in the text, nor is his favorite symbolic representation of revolution the only painting in the novel. In fact, eight of the parts of the novel are introduced by titles of works from Francisco de Goya's *Los desastres de la guerra* (The disasters of war), a series of drawings that devastatingly represent Napoleon's invasion of Spain.

Their presence in the text is neither arbitrary nor decorative. They introduce sections that signal a major development within the narrative, and they are always closely related to the events narrated in these sections. In fact, used in this fashion, Goya's *Desastres* recover within the novel their original emblematic quality. *Siempre sucede* (It always happens), for instance, announces the symbolic end of the initial period of revolutionary freedom that follows the father's death and the beginning of the new forms of authority represented by Victor Hughes: forms of authority that will eventually lead to the corruption of revolutionary ideals and to the betrayal of the Revolution itself through new forms of oppression. *Sanos y enfermos* (Healthy and sick), on the other hand, introduces the section that narrates the beginning of revolutionary purges, the triumph of the

Jacobins and the ensuing Terror. *Se aprovechan* (They take advantage) initiates the ironic development of the revolutionary hero, Victor Hughes, who turns from merchant to revolutionary to pirate and back to merchant in a circular development that accomplishes much the same as the prison-prison movement of the revolutionary process, dispelling any illusion of change and implicitly replacing political ideals by economic interests.

Illuminating as it is, however, introducing sections is not the only function of the headings within the novel. In their simultaneous reference to the text of the novel and to Goya's *Desastres*, they constitute an emblematic text that unequivocally ties Carpentier's critique of the Revolution to Goya's critique of the Napoleonic invasion. They link two complementary perceptions of the French Revolution, expanding the events of the novel and identifying them with Napoleon's violent suppression of Spain's fight for freedom. The headings delocalize both events and critique. By linking his own representation to Goya's drawings, Carpentier implicitly equates the events in the novel to those represented by Goya, thus identifying a struggle for liberation (the French Revolution) with a war of oppression (Napoleon's attempt to impose French rule over Spain). At the same time the emblematic function of the eight titles that Carpentier borrows from the *Desastres* modifies the nature and the scope of his own critical representation. Deployed in tandem, Goya's and Carpentier's critiques become more than a critique of the French Revolution, a critique of a certain kind of historical process (note the use of the generalizing *los, la* in Goya). By using Goya's captions emblematically, Carpentier inscribes his narrative in a hermeneutic structure that illuminates its meaning, expands its scope, and clarifies the critique, as the focus subtly shifts from the French Revolution to modern revolutionary processes, and from modern historical processes to the development of Western thought within them.

Within this context, the question to be asked is not what went wrong with the French Revolution but, rather, what is wrong with a civilization that repeatedly forsakes its own revolutionary goals—freedom, equality, brotherhood—for what one of Goya's contemporaries called, referring to the French Revolution, "the brotherhood of the scaffold, the equality of the grave, the freedom of death." [11]

Between 1797 and 1799, Francisco de Goya produced three different versions of a drawing from the series *Sueños*, a drawing that he originally planned to use as the cover for his series *Los caprichos*. Though similar in many ways, these three versions show some fundamental differences.

The first version (1797, repr. *Goya*, p. 112) shows the painter asleep on his drawing desk. The space above and around him appears to be roughly divided in half. At left, enlightenment and creativity are represented by the movement of light, faces, and creatures of artistic inspiration: inspiration that results in the etching plate at the artist's feet. At right, the powers of darkness are represented by night and by the bats, owls, and other night creatures lurking behind him. At the feet of the artist the lynx watches, holding in the fixity of its stare the key to the enigma of the composition.

In the second version (also 1797, repr. *Goya*, p. 113), the composition has been considerably simplified. The left section of the drawing still shows an area of bright light, but no concrete representations of creation or movement remain. The space allotted to darkness has grown considerably and is dominated by a huge spread-winged bat threatening to engulf the artist, who is sleeping at a desk that has been made to look like an uninscribed pedestal. The lynx watches, motionless, holding in its bright stare the promise of revelation.

In the third version, the etched one published in 1799 as plate 43 of the *Caprichos* (repr. *Goya*, p. 116), the artist sleeps reclining on the pedestal while darkness and the creatures of the night appear to have taken over the entire space that surrounds him: a space from which all trace of light, life, or creation has disappeared. The pedestal is engraved with a caption that reads: *El sueño de la razón produce monstrous.* The lynx, a symbol of perfect vision, looks on, his bright stare turned toward us and away from the darkness around him.

The caption is impossible to translate into English with certainty or accuracy because of a central ambiguity in the word *sueño*. The Spanish language does not distinguish between *sleep* and *dream*; the word *sueño* refers to both. Nevertheless, most interpretations of the drawing made in Goya's own time take *sueño* as *sleep,* and favor, with minor differences, the same reading: The sleep of reason allows the powers of darkness and irrationality to take over man and his creations.[12]

But there is another possible reading based on the other meaning of *sueño* as *dream*. The fact that the drawing was initially composed for a series entitled *Sueños,* which used the concept in the sense of vision or revelation much as Quevedo had in the seventeenth century, suggests that, far from being farfetched, this interpretation would be consistent with the intended function of the series (to portray reality through a series of dreamlike visions).[13] It would also be consistent with Goya's own contradictory relationship to the philosophy of the Enlightenment; to quote one of his critics, he was "as eager to point out the pitfalls of reason as to show the monsters that would spring out of its sleep" (Garcia, 102; my translation). The ambiguity of *sueño* is a crucial one here because it challenges the interpretation that would be favored in the eighteenth and early nineteenth century, when the philosophy of the Enlightenment was still the dominant one. The depiction of the monsters that would surface in the sleep of reason also becomes a warning against another possible set of monsters: those that would grow out of the *dream* of pure reason, out of the search for the utopian order of a reason that would obliterate all realities threatening its purity, harmony, and control. If the sleep of reason (first drawing) unleashes a proliferation of anarchic creative impulses that need to be ordered by rational processes, the dream of reason leaves nothing behind but the empty darkness of death, a void populated by the dark shadows that threaten to engulf the artist himself, sucking him into nothingness.

It is precisely this second reading of Goya's *Sueño de la razón* that ties the artist's critique of Enlightenment rationalism to Carpentier's critique of revolution in *El siglo de las luces*. Goya's warning against the dream of reason finds its equivalent in a symbol that appears to be at the very center of Carpentier's representation of the age of Englightenment: the guillotine. That this is not just one more symbol among others in Carpentier's symbol-ridden language, but a very privileged one, is made clear in a number of ways. In fact the novel itself opens with a whole section on the guillotine, the only italicized section in the whole book.

Tonight I have seen the machine rise again. It stood at the prow like an open door against a sky that was already bringing the scent of the land over an Ocean so quiet and so master of its rhythm that the ship, gently carried over the water, seemed to lull itself to sleep, suspended between a yesterday and a tomorrow that seemed to travel with us. . . .

But the doorless frame stood at the prow, a bare frame, with that square, that inverted pediment, that black triangle, its cold and slanted steel hanging from the top. There was the structure, bare and stark, presiding again over the dream of humankind, like a presence—or a warning—that concerned us all. We had thought we had left it behind, in the stern, far away in the cold winds of April. And, all of a sudden, there it was again, leading the way, similar, in the necessary precision of its parallel sides, in its implacable geometry, to a gigantic instrument of navigation. (Carpentier, p. 7)

To Esteban the guillotine is the machine that perfectly represents the transformation of revolutionary ideals into a dehumanized, never-ending game of exclusions. But this section unfolds—as the italics indicate—at a level of consciousness different from Esteban's. The central point of the symbol is its perfect geometry—square, inverted pediment, dark triangle—and the very progression of the images signals immediately the development of Carpentier's specific critical vision of instrumentalized reason. The *square*, a neutral geometric figure, leads to a *pediment* whose inversion suggests the limitations and failure of the architectural nature of the revolutionary project, concluding with a black triangle that shares in the geometrical quality of the square and yet adds a quality of darkness that directly opposes the very notion of the Enlightenment. But the convergence of perfect geometry and revolution at the very core of the symbol evokes another convergence of perfect reason and revolutionary geometry: the revolution of Descartes's formulations in the seventeenth century and the development of Cartesian thought.

The influence of Descartes on the development of the Enlightenment was indeed a major one. Envisioning a system of logically necessary truths— like geometry—that would allow us to discover, through analytical reason, the truth about the world, Cartesian rationalism played a major role in developing the philosophical principles of enlightened humanism and the political ideals that would eventually lead to the French Revolution. But in Carpentier's novel the geometrical order of Cartesian rationalism is represented by an instrument of death (or, rather, a "machine" of death, alluding to Descartes's mechanical conception of the universe). The geometrical perfection of the guillotine may fascinate narrator and reader alike, partly a door open to the stars and partly an instrument of navigation it stands leading the way into history from the prow of the ship. As an instrument of navigation it leads, through its symbolically inverted pediment, to the political intolerance of the Jacobins and the destructiveness of the Terror (hence Esteban's hope that it would have been left behind). As a door, on the other hand, it leads not to freedom or the light promised by the stars it happens to frame, but only to death and the darkness of nothingness.

As a central symbol, the guillotine binds together Esteban's personal critique of the French Revolution and a philosophical critique that moves beyond politics to focus on one of the major developments of modern Western thought: the formulation of Descartes' revolutionary geometry and of Cartesian rationalism. But the guillotine also prefigures Goya's and Carpentier's warning about the dream of reason, introducing the skeptical literary representation of the French Revolution that will be articulated through the dynamics of Goya's *Desastres* and Esteban's participation in revolutionary events. The final scope of Carpentier's critique becomes increasingly clear. Esteban's personal rejection of the French Revolution, the skepticism that shapes the literary representation of its historical process, and the inevitable corruption of its ideals in the development of concrete political realities turn into an indictment of instrumentalized reason and a challenge to some of the most central philosophical principles of modern Western thought.[14]

The last section of *El siglo de las luces* is introduced by the title of one of Goya's *Desastres: Así sucedió* (That is how it happened). Against a black background divided in half by a wooden banister, this drawing shows the crouching figure of a priest bruised and beaten up while, on the other side of the banister, two French soldiers hurry away with the church's treasure and sacred ornaments. It is a typical scene of looting. Dramatizing a widespread complaint about the behavior of French troops at the time, it stresses three major elements: violence, desecration, and greed.[15] The section introduced by Goya's title, on the other hand, narrates Carlos' efforts to unravel the mystery surrounding the disappearance of Esteban and Sofia. They disappeared in Madrid on 2 May 1808, the day the Spanish uprising against Napoleonic domination began.

For all his questioning and probing, however, Carlos will never discover the truth he searches for, the key that might explain why, how, or when Esteban and Sofia vanished. The valet, the lacemaker, the neighbors, and the maids will come up with fragmented and contradictory accounts of their life-styles, their customs, and their actions on the day of their disappearance. The only incontestable fact is their absence. Around that void, the accounts of the witnesses weave an intricate web of partial or contradictory legends, memories, interpretations:

Out of hearsay passed on in stores and working places; out of gossip heard at a nearby tavern where brandy kindled many memories; out of the accounts of people of diverse origin, background and social class, a history began to take shape; a narrative full of gaps and broken sequences, which, like an old chronicle, grew out of a mass of disjointed fragments. (p. 352)

But this chronicle, which essentially tries to cover a void, this reconstructed, fragmented, contradictory narrative that has emptiness and uncertainty at its very center, completely contradicts the Goyan caption used as a heading for this section. The section introduced by *Así sucedió* demonstrates that written history is always a construct built around an unsolvable mystery, that we cannot and will never really know what really happened, just as Carlos will never know what happened to Sofia and Esteban.

What, then, is the status of the history of the French Revolution? Where is its truth? In the history books? In Esteban's direct experience? In Goya's critique? In Carpentier's literary representation?

Carpentier's text provides an answer to these questions. In the novel, the critique of the Enlightenment develops gradually through the dynamic interplay of Esteban's experience, Goya's drawings, and Carpentier's representation of Enlightenment dialectics. The conclusion is far from ambiguous. Like the etching entitled *Así sucedió,* the text shapes a vision of the French Revolution that links it to desecration, greed, and violence. Thus, it implicitly challenges Esteban's perception, which is symbolized by the idealist vision of *Explosion in a Cathedral,* with its remaining illusion of order and purpose, with its grandiose stage, noble columns, heroic struggle of light against darkness, and tradition against change. Against this illusory vision the text articulates a very different perception: that of Goya's *Desastres,* a dark representation of degradation, petty interests, and sordid violence. And the progression from Esteban's painting to Goya's drawings seems to duplicate the movement from Goya's first drawings of *El sueño de la razón*—centered on the heroic struggle of the artist caught between light and darkness—to the last, from which all light has disappeared.

The novel is unambiguous in its critique of the French Revolution and of the enlightened reason that nurtured it. But is this, then, the answer, the final explanation? Do we readers hold now the truth that Esteban, Sofía, and Carlos failed to discover?

The answer to this question is equally unambiguous, for, by ironically equating Goya's heading *Así sucedió* with the central uncertainty of the section it introduces, Carpentier implicitly challenges the absolute truth of his own representation, opening to question the very meaning of a text that sows the seeds of its own radical critique.

NOTES

1. Alejo Carpentier, *El siglo de las Luces* (Barcelona: Seix y Barral, 1962), 254. This and all further translations from the novel are my own.

2. José Luis Romero, ed., *El Pensamiento Político de la Emancipación* (Caracas: Biblioteca Ayacucho, 1985), xiii; my translation. The statement comes from the *Declaración de los Derechos del Hombre y el Ciudadano,* first proclaimed in Venezuela in 1793 and first published there in 1797.

3. In *El siglo de las luces,* Carpentier refers repeatedly to a historical event that illuminates the inevitability of that betrayal: the Haitian Revolution led by Toussaint, Dessaliers, and Christophe. This revolutionary development was inspired by the same universalist appeal to the Rights of Man that inspired the French revolutionary process, the same ideals that the white enlightened population of Spanish colonies would support and use in their struggle for independence. However, Carpentier speaks of "The Great Fear" that seized the same white population when the events of Haiti became known. For the enlightened ruling classes of a colonial society founded on slavery, such as in the Caribbean, the contradiction between allegiance to the principles and original goals of the French Revolution and the ruling classes' need for self-preservation was an insoluble one. Historically

it was resolved by turning revolutionary ideals into rhetorical devices that helped legitimize a transfer of power within mostly unchanged social structures, leaving, among other things, the institution of slavery untouched.

4. The perception of France as the model of European thought and culture would often, during the nineteenth century, lead local oligarchies and rising political groups to identify with Europe, "purifying" their own societies by further marginalizing or removing altogether all those populations—like blacks and Indians— that could not easily be reconciled with the terms of the model or be integrated into their own new self-image as modern countries.

5. The title of the English translation, *Explosion in The Cathedral*, is quite misleading. The painting to which the English title refers symbolizes only Esteban's partial understanding of the revolutionary processes set off by the philosophy of the Enlightenment. The Spanish title, on the other hand, signifies Carpentier's much broader perception of these processes.

6. See Roberto González Echevarría: "Socrates Among the Weeds" in *Voices From Under*, ed. W. Luis (Westport, Conn.: Greenwood Press, 1984), 35–53.

7. For an interesting discussion of the carnivalesque in the Enlightenment and, more specifically, in Francisco de Goya's art, see Theresa Lorenzo de Márquez, "Carnival Traditions in Goya's Iconic Language" in *Goya and the Spirit of Enlightenment* (Boston: Museum of Fine Arts, 1989), lxxxv–xciv—hereafter cited as *Goya*.

8. Esteban will, once cured, betray the sacred family world he shared with Sofia, leaving it for the mysteries of the harbor section of Havana. Victor will betray Sofia's hospitality in Havana and Esteban's friendship in France. Sofia will betray first Victor's love by marrying Jorge, and then her own dying husband by carefully planning her "escape" to Cayenne.

9. "All the French Revolution did in America," says Sieger, "was to legalize a Great Escape that has not stopped since the sixteenth century. Blacks did not wait for you to set themselves free innumerable times." Sieger then proceeds accurately and eruditely to list the most important black uprisings that took place on this continent since the conquest. (*El siglo de las luces*, 237). By characterizing the French Revolution as a simple process of legalizing earlier black revolutions, Carpentier reveals a simple fact: a specific event in the Third World is often not recorded anywhere else unless or until it can be linked to some process occurring in a developed country; and when the Third World event is finally acknowledged and recorded, it often appears as a reflection of that process—in violation of the actual chronology. Carpentier's novel shows, accurately, that the black struggle for equality and freedom in America took place long before the French Revolution, rather than mimicking or following it.

10. Now in the Fitzwilliam Museum, Cambridge (England), the painting is reproduced in Echevarría, "Socrates," (opposite p. 49). The photograph shows a composition neatly split into two sides. At left, two perfect parallel rows of Corinthian columns stand in timeless majesty; at right, two parallel lines of architectural elements—the first one of columns, the second one more like an altar or a pulpit— freeze at the moment of explosion.

11. F. Blanco García, *La Literatura in el siglo XIX* (Madrid, 1891), 121— hereafter cited as García. My translation.

12. For examples of what Goya's contemporaries wrote about the caption, see *Goya*, 116.

13. The caption handwritten by Goya in the second version of the drawing reads: "El autor soñando: Su intento solo es desterrar bulgaridades perjudiciales y perpetuar con esta obra de caprichos el testimonio sólido de la verdad" ["The author dreaming: His only purpose is to banish harmful ideas commonly believed, and with the work of *Caprichos* to perpetuate the solid testimony of Truth"]. *Goya*, 114.

14. Carpentier's critique of instrumentalized reason shows the limitations of the philosophy of the Enlightenment. His focus on Cartesian reason allows him to reveal the dangers of eighteenth-century belief in the existence of pure reason. In fact, as Carpentier shows by choosing the guillotine to symbolize pure reason, what turns its geometrical perfection and flawless formal rigor into an instrument of death is its ability to preserve and transmit the illusion of its own necessity and purity even from within a process of political instrumentalization. Carpentier's novel, however, does not stop there. His radical critique opens up a space for alternatives. Such is the function of another central symbol in the novel: Socrates' sculptured head standing in the middle of Remigio's patch of medicinal plants. Although at first sight this may seem an image of decay or chaos (Greek philosophy among the weeds!), the juxtaposition of Socrates' thought and Remigio's esoteric wisdom suggests new and more productive forms of knowledge to be found in the merging of African and Western traditions.

15. Published accounts of the brutality of the French army in Spain did two things. On the one hand, they expressed general outrage at the cruelty and savagery of the invaders; on the other hand, they helped the clergy to mobilize the people in a holy war against the French that would protect traditional church interests and privileges. For a more detailed discussion and for additional bibliographical information see *Goya*, 202–203.

Notes on Contributors

STEVEN BLAKEMORE, Associate Professor of English at Palm Beach Atlantic College, is the author of *Burke and the Fall of Language: The French Revolution as Linguistic Event* (1988), and editor of *Burke and the French Revolution: Bicentennial Essays* (1991).

CAROL BLUM, Professor of French, State University of New York at Stony Brook, is the author of *Diderot: The Virtue of a Philosopher* (1974), and *Rousseau and the Republic of Virtue: The Language of Politics in the French Revolution* (1986).

VÈVÈ A. CLARK, Associate Professor of African and Caribbean Literature at the University of California, Berkeley, coedited *The Legend of Maya Deren* (1985) and has published numerous articles on African-American and Caribbean theater, the Francophone novel, and African-American dance.

MARK CUMMING, Associate Professor of English at Memorial University of Newfoundland, is the author of *A Disimprisoned Epic: Form and Vision in Carlyle's French Revolution* (1988).

JAMES CUNO, Elizabeth and John Moors Cabot Director of the Harvard University Art Museums, is coauthor of *Politics and Polemics: French Caricature and the French Revolution, 1789–1799* (1988).

LIONEL GOSSMAN, Professor of French at Princeton University, has published various studies of historical writing. His books include *Augustin Thierry and Liberal Historiography* (1976), *The Empire Unpossess'd: an Essay on Gibbon's Decline and Fall* (1981), and *Between History and Literature* (1990).

MADELYN GUTWIRTH is Professor of French and Women's Studies at West Chester University. Her books include *Madame de Staël, Novelist—The Emergence of the Artist as Woman* (1978) and *The Twilight of the Goddesses*, forthcoming.

JAMES A. W. HEFFERNAN, Professor of English at Dartmouth College, is the author of *Wordsworth's Theory of Poetry: The Transforming Imagination* (1969), and *The Re-Creation of Landscape: A Study of Wordsworth, Coleridge, Constable, and Turner* (1985).

MARIE-HÉLÈNE HUET, William R. Kenan Professor of Romance Languages at Amherst College, has published several books on French literature. Her recent work includes *Rehearsing the Revolution: The Staging of Marat's Death, 1793–97* (1982).

DONNA M. HUNTER, Assistant Professor of Art History at the University of California, Santa Cruz, holds a doctorate from Harvard, where she wrote her dissertation on the portraiture of Jacques-Louis David.

WILLIAM KEACH, Professor of English at Brown University, is the author of *Elizabethan Erotic Narratives* (1977) and *Shelley's Style* (1984).

BEATRIZ PASTOR, Rosenwald Professor of Spanish and Portuguese at Dartmouth College, has published numerous essays and two books on Latin American literature, including *El Discurso Narrativo de la Conquista*, a prize-winning study of the literature provoked by the Spanish conquest of South America.

ANN RIGNEY teaches Literary Theory at the University of Utrecht and is the author of *The Rhetoric of Historical Representation: Three Nineteenth-Century Narratives of the French Revolution* (1990).

SUSANNE ZANTOP, Associate Professor of German and Comparative Literature at Dartmouth College, has published a book on history and literature, *Zeitbilder: Geschichte und Literatur bei Heinrich Heine und Mariano Jose de Larra* (1988), and edited *Paintings on the Move: Heinrich Heine and the Visual Arts* (1989). Her most recent publication is an anthology of translations titled *Bitter Healing: German Women Writers from 1700 to 1830* (1990).

Index

UNIVERSITY PRESS OF NEW ENGLAND publishes books under its own imprint and is the publisher for Brandeis University Press, Brown University Press, Clark University Press, University of Connecticut, Dartmouth College, Middlebury College Press, University of New Hampshire, University of Rhode Island, Tufts University, University of Vermont, and Wesleyan University Press.

Library of Congress Cataloging-in-Publication Data

Representing the French Revolution : literature, historiography, and art / edited by James A. W. Heffernan.
   p.   cm.
   Includes index.
   ISBN 0-87451-565-3. — ISBN 0-87451-586-6 (pbk.)
   1. France—History—Revolution, 1789-1799—Historiography. 2. France—History—Revolution, 1789-1799—Literature and the revolution. 3. France—History—Revolution, 1789-1799—Art and the revolution. 4. France—History—Revolution, 1789-1799—Foreign public opinion, British. 5. Public opinion—Great Britain. I. Heffernan, James A. W.
DC147.8.R37   1992
944.04—dc20   ∞   91-50816